Essays in Honor of William N. Kinnard, Jr

RESEARCH ISSUES IN REAL ESTATE

Sponsored by the
AMERICAN REAL ESTATE SOCIETY

Volume I
APPRAISAL, MARKET ANALYSIS, AND PUBLIC POLICY IN REAL ESTATE
edited by: James R. DeLisle and J. Sa-Aadu

Volume II
ALTERNATIVE IDEAS IN REAL ESTATE INVESTMENT
edited by: Arthur L. Schwartz, Jr and Stephen D. Kapplin

Volume III
MEGATRENDS IN RETAIL REAL ESTATE
edited by: John D. Benjamin

Volume IV
SENIORS HOUSING
edited by: Michael A. Anikeef and Glenn R. Mueller

Volume V
ETHICS IN REAL ESTATE
edited by: Stephen E. Roulac

Volume VI
ESSAYS IN HONOR OF JAMES A. GRAASKAMP: TEN YEARS AFTER
edited by: James R. DeLisle and Elaine M. Worzala

Volume VII
REAL ESTATE EDUCATION THROUGHOUT THE WORLD: PAST, PRESENT AND FUTURE
edited by: Karl-Werner Schulte

Volume VIII
REAL ESTATE VALUATION THEORY
edited by: Ko Wang and Marvin L. Wolverton

Essays in Honor of William N. Kinnard, Jr

Edited by
C.F. Sirmans and Elaine M. Worzala

SPRINGER SCIENCE+BUSINESS MEDIA, LLC

ISBN 978-1-4613-4734-7 ISBN 978-1-4419-8953-6 (eBook)
DOI 10.1007/978-1-4419-8953-6

Essays in honor of William N. Kinnard, Jr./edited by C.F. Sirmans, Elaine M. Worzala.
p. cm.—(Research issues in real estate ; v. 9)
Includes bibliographical references and index.

1.Real estate business. 2. Real property. 3. Kinnard, William N. 4. Real estate business—United States—Biography. I. Kinnard, William N. II Sirmans, C.F. III. Worzala, Elaine M. IV. Series.

HD1375.E838 2003
333.33—dc21 2003056449

2003 PRESIDENT'S COUNCIL

Appraisal Institute
CoStar Group
Fannie Mae Foundation
Institutional Real Estate, Inc.
LaSalle Investment Management
Legg Mason
Lend Lease Real Estate Investments
PricewaterhouseCoopers
Prudential Real Estate Investors
RREEF
Zicklin College of Business at Baruch College

REGENTS

Cornerstone Real Estate Advisors Inc.
International Council of Shopping Centers (ICSC)
National Association of Real Estate Investment Trusts (NAREIT)

SPONSORS

Bailard, Biehl & Kaiser
BRE Properties
CIGNA Investments
Counselors of Real Estate (CRE)
Dearborn Real Estate Education
The Dorchester Group
Freddie Mac
GIC Real Estate Pte Ltd
Heitman Capital Management Corporation
ING Real Estate Investment
Kennedy Wilson
Mortgage Banker's Association
National Association of Industrial and Office Properties (NAIOP)
National Association of REALTORS® (NAR)
National Investment Center for the Seniors Housing and Care Industries (NIC)
National Multi Housing Council (NMHC)
Real Estate Center at Texas A&M University
Real Estate Institute–University of San Diego
Research Institute for Housing America
Society of Industrial and Office REALTORS® (SIOR)
SSR Realty Advisors
Steven L. Newman Real Estate Institute
Thompson Learning
Torto Wheaton Research
UBS Realty Investors
Urban Land Institute (ULI)

2003 ARES INFORMATION

ENDOWED DOCTORAL SPONSORSHIPS

Glenn R. and Jan H. Mueller
Theron R. and Susan L. Nelson
James R. and Anais B. Webb

2003 FELLOWS

Joseph D. Albert
James Madison University

Randy I. Anderson
Baruch College

Michael A. Anikeeff
Johns Hopkins University

John S. Baen
University of North Texas

John D. Benjamin
American University

Donald H. Bleich
California State University–Northridge

Amy Bogdon
Fannie Mae Foundation

Waldo L. Born
Eastern Illinois University

Nicholas Buss
PNC Bank

Todd A. Canter
LaSalle Investment Management

James Carr
Fannie Mae Foundation

Lijian Chen
Lend Lease Real Estate Investments

Ping Cheng
Salisbury State University

Marvin F. Christensen
RREEF

Glenn E. Crellin
Washington State University

Charles G. Dannis
Crosson Dannis

Karen G. Davidson
Davidson & Associates

James R. DeLisle
Georgia State University

Gene Dilmore
Realty Researchers

Geoffrey Dohrmann
Institutional Real Estate Inc.

John T. Emery
University of Texas–Pan American

Donald R. Epley
Washington State University

Robert A. Ernst
International Real Estate

Jack P. Friedman
Jack P. Friedman & Associates

S. Michael Giliberto
J. P. Morgan Investment Management

John L. Glascock
George Washington University

Paul R. Goebel
Texas Tech University

Richard B. Gold
Consultant

William C. Goolsby
University of Arkansas–Little Rock

Jacques Gordon
LaSalle Investment Management

D. Wylie Greig
RREEF

Karl L. Guntermann
Arizona State University

Otis Hackett
Otis E. Hackett & Associates

Jun Han
John Hancock Real Estate Investments Group

William N. Kinnard, Jr.

BIOGRAPHY OF WILLIAM N. KINNARD, Jr.

William N. Kinnard Jr, PhD, MAI, SRA, was the president of the Real Estate Consulting Group of Connecticut and professor emeritus at the University of Connecticut. He published many ground-breaking articles. He had a very diverse field of research interests during his more than 40 years in the real estate profession including: real estate valuation, real estate market and feasibility analysis, environmental/contamination issues, business enterprise value/tax assessment issues, expert witnessing and real estate education.

Bill retired from University of Connecticut in 1981 after 26 years. In addition to teaching, he published numerous articles in academic and professional journals, as well as authoring or co-authoring several major texts on property valuation and appraisal. Some of the awards Dr Kinnard received are the Alfred Reinman Award from SREA, the George Bloom Award from AREUEA, and the James Graaskamp Award from ARES. Two awards were named after him, the annual award for outstanding contributions to appraisal education given by the Appraisal Institute, and the William N. Kinnard, Jr Scholarship in the School of Business Administration at University of Connecticut. Family and friends fondly remember Bill as a man with a wonderful sense of humor, a caring and thoughtful man who loved life and lived it to the fullest. He enjoyed good food and wine, sports, music, the theater, reading, crossword puzzles, travel, and the company of family and friends.

ABOUT THE EDITORS

C.F. SIRMANS

C.F. Sirmans is the Director of the Center for Real Estate and Urban Economic Studies and Professor of Real Estate and Finance at the University of Connecticut.

Professor Sirmans is currently serving as editor of *The Journal of Real Estate Finance and Economics* and is past editor of the *Journal of Real Estate Literature* and *Real Estate Economics*. He has published numerous articles in academic journals, including, *The Quarterly Journal of Economics, Journal of Finance, Journal of Financial Economics, Review of Economics and Statistics, Journal of Law and Economics, Journal of Legal Studies, Economic Inquiry, Journal of Money, Credit and Banking, National Tax Journal, Land Economics, Journal of Financial and Quantitative Analysis, Journal of Regional Science, Journal of Urban Economics, Real Estate Economics, Journal of Real Estate Research,* and *Regional Science and Urban Economics*. He has also published extensively in professional journals, such as, *Real Estate Finance, The Appraisal Journal, Property Tax Journal, Real Estate Issues, Real Estate Review,* and *The Journal of Portfolio Management*. He is the author of several textbooks, including *Fundamentals of Real Estate Investment* (Third edition, Prentice-Hall), *Real Estate Investment Decision Making* (Prentice-Hall), *Tax Planning for Real Estate Investors* (Third edition, Prentice-Hall), and *Real Estate Finance* (Second edition, McGraw-Hill). Professor Sirmans has received numerous teaching awards, and is a fellow of the Homer Hoyt Institute and a past fellow of the Urban Land Institute.

Professor Sirmans has lectured extensively in continuing education and professional development programs for such organizations as The Mortgage Bankers Association of America, The International Council of Shopping Centers, The American Institute of Real Estate Appraisers and The International Association of Assessing Officers. He has served as a consultant to numerous US federal and state government agencies, professional organizations, and private business firms, including the Pension Real Estate Association, Federal National Mortgage Association, and National Council of Real Estate Investment Fiduciaries. Dr Sirmans has held teaching positions at Louisiana State University, University of Georgia, and the University of Illinois. He received his Ph.D. in Real Estate and Urban Development from the University of Georgia in 1976.

DR ELAINE WORZALA, RESEARCH DIRECTOR AND PROFESSOR OF REAL ESTATE

Dr Worzala joined the Real Estate Institute at the University of San Diego as the Research Director after 10 years of teaching and research at Colorado State University. During 1996 she also served as a visiting professor at the Real Estate Center of the University of Connecticut. This is where she first encountered Dr Kinnard as they began two research projects while she was there, one on lenders' willingness to invest in contaminated property and the other focused on the existence of client pressure within the appraisal industry. She has taught a wide range of real estate courses, including real estate principles, real estate valuation, real estate finance and investments, and a graduate level real estate investments case course.

Dr Worzala has a strong interest in commercial real estate valuation which is how she first met Bill Kinnard, although she was first introduced to his work while studying under the late James A. Graaskamp at the University of Wisconsin-Madison from 1982 until his death in 1988. She holds a Ph.D. in Real Estate and Urban Land Economics (1992) and an M.S. in Real Estate Appraisal and Investment Analysis (1984). About half of her Ph.D. candidacy was spent under the direction of Jim Graaskamp. Dr Worzala assisted in the compilation of Jim Graaskamp's papers, which resulted in *The Graaskamp Collection*, a CD ROM set. She also was the Associate Editor for *Essays in Honor of James A. Graaskamp: Ten Years Later*, a compilation of essays that have been written to examine Graaskamp's impact not only on real estate education but more importantly upon the real estate profession as a whole.

An active member of several academic associations, Dr Worzala presently sits on the Board of Directors of the American Real Estate Society and is the 2002 President of the International Real Estate Society. With over 40 refereed academic publications, Dr Worzala has published in many of the mainstream real estate journals including the *Journal of Real Estate Research, Urban Studies, Real Estate Finance, The Journal of Real Estate Portfolio Management, The Appraisal Journal,* and *The Journal of Property Valuation and Investment.* Her research interests lie primarily in institutional real estate investment and valuation. Additionally, many of her studies take on an international perspective as she works to open up the real estate markets. Her practical experience includes being a commercial real estate appraiser for one of the Nation's largest pension fund advisory firms from 1986–89, which has led to her continued strong interest in the valuation area.

CONTENTS

LIST OF CONTRIBUTORS

S. Alan Aycock
Morehouse College, Atlanta, Ga.

Herman G. Berkman
Past President of the American Real Estate and Urban Economics Association.

Gail Beron
The Beron Company,
7008 Bridge Way,
W. Bloomfield, MI 48322-3527.

William A. Blake
Director, Acquisitions,
UBS Realty Investors, LLC,
Hartford, Connecticut.

Sandy Bond
Faculty of Architecture, Property, Planning & Fine Arts,
University of Auckland,
Private Bag 92019,
Auckland, New Zealand.

Paul A. Champagne
Vice President,
CIGNA Real Estate.

John M. Clapp
University of Connecticut,
Department of Finance,
2100 Hillside Road,
Storrs, CT 06269-1041.

Peter F. Colwell
Department of Finance,
University of Illinois,
1407 W. Gregory Dr,
Urbana, IL 61801.

Jeffrey D. Fisher
Director, Center for Real Estate Studies,
School of Business,
Indiana University,
Bloomington, IN.

Nick French
Acacia Senior Lecturer,
Jonathan Edwards Consulting, Fellow in Corporate Real Estate,
The Department of Real Estate & Planning,
The School of Business,
The University of Reading,
Whiteknights, Reading,
Berkshire, England, RG6 6AW.

Mary Beth Geckler, Deceased

Carmelo Giaccotto
University of Connecticut,
Department of Finance,
2100 Hillside Road,
Storrs, CT 06269-1041.

Mark Goldman
Goldman Realty Corporation.

Edward F. Heberger
Executive Vice President,
CB Richard Ellis.

Thomas O. Jackson
Real Property Analytics, Inc.,
4805 Spearman Drive,
College Station, TX 77845-4412.
Land Economics and Real Estate Program,
Department of Finance,
310F Wehner Building, Mail Stop 4218,
Mays Business School,
Texas A&M University,
College Station, TX 77843-4218.

Austin J. Jaffe
The Smeal College of Business Administration,
The Pennsylvania State University,
University Park, PA 16802.

Keith B. Johnson
Professor Emeritus,
University of Connecticut.

Jeff Kinnard
Hartford, CT.

John R. Knight
University of the Pacific,
Stockton, CA.

Paul Lagassey

Margarita M. Lenk
Colorado State University

Kenneth M. Lusht
The Smeal College of Business Administration,
The Pennsylvania State University,
University Park, PA 16802.

Stephen D. Messner
Professor Emeritus,
University of Connecticut.

Mike E. Miles
Guggenheim Real Estate

Bill Mundy
President, Mundy & Associates,
Seattle, Washington.

Hugh O. Nourse
Past President of the American Real Estate and Urban Economics Association.

Judith Bartell Paesani
Former assistant director,
Center of Real Estate and Urban Studies,
University of Connecticut.

Elliot B. Pollack
Pullman & Comley, LLC.

Frederick Richard
CB Richard Ellis.

Greg Richo

Dan Swango
Appraisal Institute,
Tucson, AZ, USA.

Bruce R. Weber, MAI
Integra Realty Resources.

John C. Weicher
Past President of the American Real Estate and Urban Economics Association.

Elaine M. Worzala
Real Estate Institute
University of San Diego

FOREWORD

The Appraisal Institute (AI) and the RICS (Royal Institute of Chartered Surveyors) Foundation are very pleased to be able to sponsor this volume commemorating the life and accomplishments of William N. Kinnard, Jr. Bill was one of the major figures in real estate research and practice of the 20th century. He was a man, as much respected as a scholar in the pages of learned journals, as he was an expert witness in a court of law. All those who had met him and who had experienced at first hand his dynamism, warmth and enthusiasm mourned his passing. Whether young or old, he had a kindly and encouraging word for all. Across the world, his contributions were widely recognized and acknowledged.

His contribution to a greater understanding of valuation in all its forms was immense. It is rare for a single person to develop and take forward new lines of inquiry and new ways of thinking, but William Kinnard achieved both of these. Both in his work on the valuation of contaminated land and on his insights into the impact of behavior on valuation in practice, he was one of the leading thinkers. His deep understanding of the day to day work of a valuer meant that his work was both relevant and topical, in addition to rigorous.

The chapters presented in this volume address many of the issues with which Bill was passionately concerned. We hope that they will act as a lasting tribute to his person and great works. In addition, we would like to thank all those who contributed to this special ARES Monograph, in memory of a special man.

He will be missed. We will not see his like again soon.

Alan E. Hummel
Appraisal Institute

Stephen Brown
RICS Foundation

INTRODUCTION

C.F. SIRMANS AND ELAINE WORZALA

In 2001, the real estate profession lost Dr William N. Kinnard, Jr, a major contributor to the advancement of real estate, both as an academic discipline and professional practice. This monograph, sponsored by the Appraisal Institute, the RICS Foundation and the American Real Estate Society (with additional support by the Homer Hoyt Advanced Studies Institute and the Real Estate Counseling Group of America), is in honor of Bill's accomplishments and highlights his impact on the real estate profession. The book includes three sections: original articles written in honor of Bill on areas that he found important, reprinted publications of Bill's that cover his research themes over his 40 year career, and testimonials written by colleagues, family and friends that provide some personal reflections and evidence of the active role Bill played as an academic, practitioner, mentor, and friend to so many in the real estate profession.

The first section of the book contains seven original essays. We have arranged them in order to coincide with Bill's (chronological) professional career. Two chapters focus on the theory of valuation. The first, by Ken Lusht and Austin Jaffe, takes an historical viewpoint of value and its role in academia and society. Nick French discusses the practical nature of defining market value and argues that much of the debate can be credited to Bill's early work, which clearly spells out that most probable use and most probable price are the more important areas on which to focus. To coin a phrase often cited by Bill, "It is value of what and value to whom" that are important criteria to establish when trying to estimate the value of a property.

The chapter by John Clapp and Carmelo Gioccatto focuses on two additional aspects of the real estate discipline that were near and dear to Bill's heart—market analysis and statistics. Bill was a pioneer in encouraging appraisers to do complete and thorough market analysis and in his work he often employed cutting edge, statistical models to understand real estate markets.

The fourth chapter is the only manuscript that includes Bill as one of the co-authors. This chapter, written with Peter Colwell and Gail Beron, focuses on the appraisal process, a major theme in Bill's work. Specifically, they critique the cost approach and provide insights on how to deal with the elusive but important aspect—functional obsolescence. This chapter is very characteristic of Bill's work where he takes an issue and helps the practitioner work through ways to solve the problem.

The next two chapters focus on the work Bill was doing during the latter part of his career where he built an international reputation as an expert witness, particularly in the area of environmental contamination. As illustrated in his CV, Bill "retired" from the University of Connecticut in 1981. He formed the Real Estate counseling Group of Connecticut where he did appraisal and feasibility work, primarily as an expert witness in court cases. The first chapter by Tom Jackson reviews the work Bill published in the environmental area, while the chapter by Alan Aycock highlights Bill's contributions to the role of expert witnesses.

In the 1990s, Kinnard began to explore international real estate issues with colleagues from the United Kingdom, Australia, and New Zealand. In the spring of 2001, Bill had planned a traveling celebration for his 75th birthday using real estate conference venues as his road map. He had plans to attend the International AREUEA Conference in Cancun, on to the IRES First World Congress in Alaska and finally to London for the RICS Cutting Edge Conference in time to celebrate his birthday on September 12, 2001. The chapter by Sandy Bond was originally presented as part of a set of panels Bill was in the process of organizing. For the AREUEA International Conference, Bill organized a session entitled *"Valuation Issues that Perplex and Vex Practitioners and Theorists in Selected Countries,"* illustrating his continuing commitment to both research and practice.

Since his death on April 6, 2001, panels in his honor have been organized at the International AREUEA meetings in Cancun, Mexico, the IRES World Congress in Girdwood, Alaska, the ARES meetings in Santa Barbara, and the ERES meetings in Glasgow, Scotland. In 2003, a session in Bill's honor at the ARES meeting in Monterey will focus on the manuscripts in this book as well as a discussion of Bill's most influential papers. With the help of over 40 colleagues we selected the "The Best of Bill," which are the reprints found in the second section of this monograph. This section begins with a manuscript written by Austin Jaffe and Ken Lusht highlighting one of Bill's books, *Income Property Valuation.* This book is one of his most influential publications and is frequently cited in the testimonials as groundbreaking work in the valuation area. These eleven articles, written by Bill with various co-authors, represent only a portion of his contributions to real estate theory and practice.

The final section of the monograph contains personal reflections by colleagues, family and friends of Bill. These testimonials provide clear evidence that Bill was an excellent teacher and real estate professional. He truly cared about his students and colleagues and worked hard to move the real estate profession forward.

And, of course, Bill helped the two of us tremendously. We are honored to be the editors of this monograph. We owe a lot to Bill. At various stages of our careers, he helped us in many different ways and was always there to provide advice, guidance, and humor. As some of his colleagues put it, Bill was a mentor to many and we are grateful to have had the opportunity to work with and learn from his vast knowledge about real estate and life in general. We hope that this collection of original essays, reprints, and testimonials will allow others to also benefit from Bill's influence.

We thank Fran Jaffe, Debbie Philips, and Mari Hardick for their assistance in putting this monograph together. In addition, we thank the individuals listed below for their contribution toward this volume. The sheer volume of help we received pays tribute to this man that helped so many—a true scholar, mentor, and friend. Thanks Bill; we miss you!!

Alastair Adair; Alan Aycock; Stephen Brown; Sandy Bond; John Clapp; Peter Colwell; Marsha Courchane; Mike Crean; Neil Crosby; Gene Dilmore; John Dorchester; Mohammad Faishal; Jeff Fisher; Nick French; Mary Beth Geckler; Terry Grissom; Emilio Haddad; Stanley Hamilton; Ned Heberger; Thomas Jackson; Austin Jaffe; Michael Jayne; Olga Kaganova; Jeff Kinnard; John Knight; Max Kummerow; David Ling; Ken Lusht; Norm Miller; Bryan MacGregor; Richard Marchitelli; Matt Meyers; Graeme Newell; Ron Racster; Mike Robbins; Robert Simons; Stacy Sirmans; Nikolai Trifonov; Joe Vella; Jim Webb; Marvin Wolverton.

Part I. Original Essays

1. The History of Value Theory: The Early Years

AUSTIN J. JAFFE AND KENNETH M. LUSHT*

> It is commonplace of economics that exchange is necessary only in so far as production has passed beyond the self-sufficing basis and has become specialized.... The fact of exchange raises the problem of valuation.
>
> E. WHITTAKER (1940)

> Value is a price. This price reflects the capacity of an economic good to command other goods in exchange.
>
> WILLIAM N. KINNARD, JR. (1971)

This chapter is submitted to this volume to honor our friend and colleague, Bill Kinnard. Fittingly, the research that led to the chapter was funded by the American Institute of Real Estate Appraisers (now the Appraisal Institute). Bill was an influential member of both the Institute and the Society of Real Estate Appraisers, and he worked tirelessly to forge links between those associations and higher education.

Bill wrote courses, seminars, and texts. He served on editorial boards and on education committees. He encouraged professional association funding of research such as this. He and his colleagues at Connecticut: Byrl Boyce and Steve Messner, were pioneers in the establishment of academic real estate. All of us in AREUEA and ARES today owe a great debt to his early leadership.

*The authors wish to thank C.F. Sirmans and an anonymous referee for their comments. Any errors are attributed to the authors, of course.

We have one regret. Our research was originally intended to produce a book, for which Bill had graciously agreed to write the Preface. We did not finish in time for that to happen, and that is our loss. A second (forthcoming) paper traces appraisal thought through the modern era, an era in which Bill is a prominent figure.

We hope with this chapter and the next, that we have done justice to his memory.

INTRODUCTION

The lofty place of value theory has only a few competitors in the entire body of economics literature. This is due to the fact that the notion of what gives value to objects is central to the impetus for exchange, production, investment, and the measurement of well-being. Indeed, value theory is fundamental to the capitalist structure and provides a sticky thorn in the Marxist system. The history of value theory in economics is a fascinating adventure which has captured the energies of scores of economic historians and almost without exception, occupies a major place in every general economic history.[1]

The real estate valuation literature has its own set of economic historical surveys on the topic of value theory in economic thought. There are several well-cited sources which generally provide a consensus on the fundamental development of the meaning of value in economic history.[2] It is, in fact, a bit surprising that such unanimity exists, given the vastness of the literature and the period over which the development has occurred. This result suggests that either real estate historians have been extremely careful when examining the ancients or that the correct path and interpretation had already been laid out by others. Perhaps there is some truth to both possibilities.

Previous Work

There have also been several doctoral dissertations on value.[3] These range from disciplines such as philosophy and economic history to accounting, finance, and of course,

[1]The reader is encouraged to review the surveys cited below as evidence in support of this claim.

[2]The major studies in chronological form include Thurston H. Ross, History of Value Theory, *The Appraisal Journal* 6 (April 1938); Arthur M. Weimer, History of Value Theory for the Appraiser, *The Appraisal Journal* 21 (January 1953), reprinted in American Institute of Real Estate Appraisers, in *Appraisal Thought: A 50-Year Beginning* American Institute of Real Estate Appraiser, Chicago, 1982, pp. 164–178; Paul F. Wendt, *Real Estate Appraisal—A Critical Analysis of Theory and Practice* Henry Holt and Company, New York, 1956; Halbert C. Smith, Carl J. Tschappat, and Ronald L. Racster, *Real Estate and Urban Development* Richard D. Irwin, Inc., Homewood, Ill., 1967, First edition only; J.B. Featherston, Historical Influences on Development of the Theory of Value, *The Appraisal Journal* 43 (April 1975); and James H. Boykin, Real Property Appraisal in the American Colonial Era, *The Appraisal Journal* 44 (July 1976).

[3]Since 1938, several dissertations have dealt with the concept and meaning of value. See Nathaniel Wollman, The Development and Use of the Market Concept in Value Analysis (unpublished Ph.D. dissertation, Princeton University, 1940); Stephen W. Rousseas, An Inquiry Into the Logical and Empirical Foundations of the Subjective Theory of Value (unpublished Ph.D. dissertation, Columbia University, 1954); Irving D. Shapiro, An Economic Basis for Real Estate Development (unpublished Ph.D. dissertation, Columbia University, 1961); David G. Edens, Economic Aspects of Eminent Domain (unpublished Ph.D. dissertation, University of Virginia, 1962); Norman E. Dittrich, Accounting Implications of the Relative Objectivity of the Appraisal Process (unpublished Ph.D. dissertation, The Ohio State University, 1966); David P. Weiner, The Feasibility of Obtaining an Objective Measure of the Current Value of Land and

real estate. The subject of value is so broad that it is virtually impossible to harness the entire scope of all of the literature on the topic, despite our best efforts.

Economic historians have developed their own literature on the subject of value. This is perhaps the most voluminous set of papers and books of all; not only does value theory retain a major role in the history of economic thought, but entire volumes are devoted to the history of value theory in economic thought.[4] Consider, for example, a study entitled "The Theory of Value Before Adam Smith" by Hannah Robie Sewall, which was published by the American Economic Association in 1901.[5] It is more than 125 pages in length and is sufficiently comprehensive to include the period of the ancient Greeks and Romans to the publication of Adam Smith's *The Wealth of Nations* in 1776. While most economists acknowledge predecessors to the classical economists such as Adam Smith, David Ricardo, and Thomas Malthus on the subject of the theory of value, the formal development of value theory is generally said to begin in the late 18th and early 19th centuries.

This chapter does not claim to include everything that has ever been written about the development and history of the concept of value, given the magnitude of the literature on the topic. Rather, it is intended to provide a comprehensive and detailed survey of value theory and its development with special reference to how the economic notions of value affect the appraiser's notion of market value. It is hoped that this survey demonstrates that despite the criticism of the appraiser's "three approaches to value" paradigm, this valuation perspective is firmly steeped in economic tradition and thought.[6] In addition, this survey suggests that the modern general concepts and

(*continued*)
Buildings for Disclosure in Published Financial Statements (unpublished Ph.D. dissertation, University of Michigan, 1972); A.K. Zawati, The Reliability of Appraisal Methods in Determining Current Asset Value (unpublished Ph.D. dissertation, Louisiana State University, 1977); James H. Burton, The Evolution of the Income Approach in Real Estate Valuation Literature: 1662–1969 (unpublished Ph.D. dissertation, Georgia State University, 1978); Terry V. Grissom, Analysis of the Appraisal Process as Applied to Land Corridors (unpublished Ph.D. dissertation, University of Wisconsin-Madison, 1981); James R. DeLisle, Toward a Formal Statement of Residential Real Estate Appraisal Theory: A Behavioral Approach (unpublished Ph.D. dissertation, University of Wisconsin-Madison, 1982); and William H. Walker, Sales Price, A Surrogate for Market Value of Single Family Residences (unpublished Ph.D. dissertation, Louisiana State University, 1982).

[4]For example, see Herbert J. Davenport, *Value and Distribution*. The University of Chicago Press, Chicago, 1908; Correa Moylan Walsh, *The Four Kinds of Economic Value*. Harvard University Press, Cambridge, Mass, 1926; Charles W. MacFarlane, *Value and Distribution*. Privately printed, K.S. MacFarlane, n.d.; John Laird, *The Idea of Value*. Cambridge University Press, Cambridge, 1929; Rudolf Kaulla, *Theory of Just Price*, translated from the German 1936 version by Robert O. Hogg. George Allen and Unwin Ltd., London, 1940; Maurice Dobb, *Theories of Value and Distribution Since Adam Smith*. Cambridge University Press, Cambridge, 1973; Jeffrey T. Young, *Classical Theories of Value: From Smith to Sraffa*. Westview Press, Boulder, Colo, 1978; Lynn Mainwaring, *Value and Distribution in Capitalist Economies*. Cambridge University Press, London, 1984; and others.

[5]See Hannah Robie Sewall, The Theory of Value Before Adam Smith. *American Economic Association*, 1901 Third Series, No. 3 (August), pp. 633–766.

[6]In Kinnard's *Income Property Valuation*, there is support and criticism for the traditional three approach framework and despite it's orientation toward income property, the cost and market data approaches are represented. See William N. Kinnard, Jr. *Income Property Valuation*. D. C. Heath & Co., Lexington, MA, 1971.

problems in valuation are not fundamentally different from those which have plagued thinkers and philosophers since the beginning of civilization.

Overview of the Chapter

We survey the economic literature with passing reference to philosophers and other writers as contributions were made to the theory of value literature on a chronological basis. This approach permits the reader to appreciate the long process of the growth and maturation of thinking in the area of value theory. In particular, while notions of both the labor theory of value and the marginal utility approach to value are exhibited in early economic thought, it was not until the classical economists debated the cost theory over nearly a century of writing and correspondence that the issues were relatively settled. At that point, the Austrian marginalist school took over and revolutionized thinking about the meaning of value. However, it was not until the beginning of the present century that any type of reconciliation was developed with the work of Alfred Marshall, Irving Fisher, and others.

We proceed as follows. First, a review of the initial ideas about value in writings of ancient Greece and Rome is provided. There is also a discussion of the idea of a "just price" at this time; an idea which is greatly developed throughout the Early Christian and Late Medieval periods and ultimately has found its way into the early appraisal literature. Next, a survey is presented of thinking about value by economists and others in the pre-Adam Smith era. This period covers more than 200 years and provides insight into later formal theoretical developments by well-known economists. In fact, several of the important ideas which are fundamental to the theory of value are directly taken from the writings of Mercantilists, Physiocrats, and their critics.

The development of the labor and the cost theories of value are generally associated with Adam Smith, David Ricardo, Samuel Bailey, J.B. Say, Nassau Senior, Thomas Malthus, John Stuart Mill, and Karl Marx. Each of these major figures' contributions are developed in this chapter. In particular, it is shown that despite the predominance of the theory, conceptual difficulties with several of the basic notions eventually led to a new movement and a more robust treatment of the concept of value.

This movement was called the Marginal Utility school and began as a challenge to the classical value theory about 1870 with works by Jevons, Menger, and to some extent, Leon Walras. Later, the ideas were expanded upon by Wieser, Böhm-Bawerk, and others. It should also be pointed out that it is generally agreed that the seeds of utility had been planted considerably earlier than the late 19th century by relatively obscure economists including Rossi, Galiani, Cournot, Lloyd, Duprit, and others.

With the widespread impact of Marshall's textbook and the development of mathematical models of economic behavior by Edgeworth, Fisher, and Pareto from 1890 to 1910, a reconciliation of the Classical and Marginalist Schools of economics began, especially on the issue of value theory. Marshall was perhaps most influential in this regard and has given rise to a blending of value concepts and the development of value in neo-classical and other modern schools of economics.

The survey concludes with the rise of neo-classical economics at the beginning of the 20th century. Bill Kinnard's academic foundation stems from the Marginalist traditions.[7] Yet, Bill would have been the first to appreciate the debt of gratitude owed by the valuation community to the ancients.

SURVEY OF VALUATION THINKING

There is no doubt that the subject of value and its application to land and buildings, can trace its roots back to antiquity.

The Ancients

Value was a useful concept in Biblical times.[8] However, most critical studies have concluded that value as an ethical and philosophical construct began in Greece.

The Greeks did not concern themselves much with the concept of value but were more interested in ethics and "what kind of actions constituted noble lives, rather than to know the ultimate relations of all actions."[9] The Greeks believed that the price ought to correspond to quality, even if it did not always do so. For example, Plato regarded value as an inherent attribute in a commodity.[10]

> ... when a man undertakes a work, the law gives him the same advice which was given to the seller, that he should not attempt to raise the price, but simply ask for the value; this the law enjoins also on the contractor; for the craftsman assuredly knows the value of his work.[11]

Aristotle

Credit is generally given to Aristotle as being the first to distinguish between "value in use" and "value in exchange." This distinction forms one of the major cornerstones of modern value theory and is often cited in the modern literature.[12] It is, in fact, a recurring theme in the appraisal literature, including a special emphasis by Kinnard. Aristotle's famous analogy dealt with the use and value of shoes.

> For example, a shoe is used for wear, and is used for exchange; both are uses of the shoe .... The same may be said of all possessions ...[13]

[7]See, for example, Kinnard, *op. cit.*, p. 60.

[8]See Featherston, *op. cit.*, p. 167.

[9]See Sewall, *op. cit.*, p. 639.

[10]See Edmund Whittaker, *A History of Economic Ideas*. Longmans, Green and Co, New York, 1940, p. 407.

[11]Plato, *Laws*, Book XI, Chapter 921, quoted in Sewall, *op. cit.*, p. 639.

[12]See Kinnard, *op. cit.*, pp.11–15.

[13]Quoted from The Works of Aristotle, *Politica*, Volume 10, 1257a, as noted in Whittaker, *op. cit.*, p. 407. See also the following passage:

> Aristotle distinguished between the utility of an article when put to its intended use, as of a shoe being worn, and its utility in procuring for its owner something else in exchange for it. In modern times Locke applied the same distinction to value, and called the one "intrinsic value" and the other "marketable value." Before him, Petty made another division, to the effect that things should be valued by "land and labor," land

However, the main thrust of the Greek writings dealt with what "should be" rather than what "was." This ethical perspective did not produce a theory of value. What did result was the precedence to the concept of a "just price" which was so fundamental in the Middle Ages. In the modern appraisal literature, the "should be" versus "is" debate emerges as the normative versus positive perspective in the appraisal function.

The ancients frowned on trade and according to one source, relied primarily on agriculture for subsistence.[14] However, another source notes that Aristotle implied that the idea of value should be expressed "by the proportion in which things exchange for each other and therefore the notion of value becomes a part of the subject of justice."[15] This attempt to compare utilities from exchange must be regarded as a forerunner of Aquinas' "just price" theory.[16]

Roman Law

The establishment of the Twelve Tables, a set of governing documents, which date back to the 5th century BC, provided a set of fundamental laws but left the determination of prices to the "mercy of personal caprice; not even the most extravagant prices were checked by the legislator."[17] Value in Roman society was determined by the justness of the people.

The Romans had no theory of value beyond a general conception of a degree of esteem (*estimatio*), or of an equivalence between two things (*pretium*) expressed by the amount of the price (also *pretium*). They recognized that value bore some relation to desire. Cicero, speaking of the great price of bronze statutes, said: "The only limit to the valuation of such things is the desire which anyone has for them, for it is difficult to set bounds to the price unless you first set bounds to the wish." But in the main they held that the value of goods commonly exchanged did not depend upon desire but upon what they could sell for, *i.e.*, the price ...[18]

In about 186 BC, the Romans passed a law to protect minors against fraud by specifying a requirement that prices had to be considered "just." With this legislation, the impact was felt for several generations.

The idea of the just price (*justum pretium*) thus became a *legal concept*, destined to retain practical significance during the centuries to come.[19]

(*continued*)
standing for its material purpose, and labor for cost. Later, Turgot made another division into "valeur estimative" and "valeur echangeable." ... Meanwhile, other economists were using the term "value" in one or another of these senses, or in more than one .... Thus Quesnay and Adam Smith followed Locke ... making the division into "value in use" and "value in exchange" ...

See Walsh, *op. cit.*, p. 4.

[14]See Weimer, *op. cit.*, p. 167.

[15]Sewall, *op. cit.*, p. 640.

[16]See Whittaker, *op. cit.*, p. 407.

[17]See Kualla, *op. cit.*, p. 23.

[18]See Sewall, *op. cit.*, pp. 642–643.

[19]See Kaulla, *op. cit.*, p. 31.

While the development of Roman law is extensive in many areas, it is surprising that so little attention is paid beyond what has been described about the concept of value.[20] One study describes the requirements for prices on land contracts and the specifications needed to fulfill the various stipulations.[21] But essentially, the relationship between price and value is left vague and undefined. For example, it was thought that a sale did not take place if goods were bartered because there was no "price" paid as part of the exchange.[22]

While the Romans were not as concerned about ethical considerations as were the Greeks, the question often to be resolved in the courts was whether the price was a fair one. For the judge, this was a difficult matter in the absence of a theory of value.

> The judge was ... required in forming an estimate of value in use, to place himself in the position of the normal, average person. This was an idea with which the Roman jurists, trained in the Stoic philosophy were thoroughly familiar, for the Stoics had never tired of describing, in the greatest detail, the wise, ideal man whose every thought and action was right. And since the estimate of value in use was to be based on the views of the normal person, the estimate of value in exchange ... must be normally applicable. It was the value thus determined that constituted the *ustum pretium* as conceived in the legislation ...[23]

We are reminded of the modern market value definitions, which are couched in language suggesting typical investors and markets in equilibrium.

Value in the Declining Roman Empire

In the later period of the Roman Empire, changes in the notion of value emerged. For example, two laws were passed by Diocletian, which indicates movement during the period.[24] First, it was specified that "the seller of an object for which it was subsequently found that less than one-half the just price had been paid was given the right to cancel the sale" or the purchaser was permitted to pay the additional amount. A second law established death penalties for persons charging prices in excess of fixed price schedules. This led to compulsory "just prices" and represented an attempt "to guarantee the producing classes selling prices which would enable them to make ends meet."[25] The theory of value under Diocletian was that prices are just if recognized by the State.

[20]For example, see Max Kaser, *Roman Private Law*, Third edition, Translated by Rolf Dannenbring. University of South Africa, Pretoria, 1980; Alan Rodger, *Owners and Neighbours in Roman Law*. Clarendon Press, Oxford, 1972; M.I. Finley (ed.) *Studies in Roman Property*. Cambridge University Press, London, 1976, and others for detailed studies of the legal environment of ancient Rome and historical studies of Roman legislation. Little attention was paid to value or related concepts.

[21]See John Crook, Classical Roman Law and the Sale of Land, in Finley, *ibid.*, pp. 71–83.

[22]See Sewall, *op. cit.*, p. 643.

[23]See Sewall, *op. cit.*, pp. 31–32.

[24]*Ibid.*, p. 32.

[25]*Ibid.*, pp. 33–34.

Value in the Middle Ages

Most of the historical reviews of value leaped to the Middle Ages after a few, cursory references to the ancients. Indeed, a careful search reveals that little development seems to have occurred after the fall of the Roman Empire. The invasions of the barbarian hordes ended the commercial life of the ancient world. More importantly for the purposes of this study, these changes led to a decline of market structures and the reliance upon self-sufficiency and, thus, a more primitive economy lacking economic exchange and valuation. Given the reduced emphasis on exchange, there was little need for money and valuation. Value theory did not progress for centuries.

The Revival of Exchange

At about the year 1000, the money economy began to develop in Europe once again. Exchange developed slowly over the next three centuries and with it, the necessity for valuation. As the economy grew, opportunities developed for producers to specialize and thus, buying and selling became increasingly important throughout the European economy. It was during this time that foreign merchants and traders were influential in modifying the meaning of the concept of value.

Early Christian Era

The industrial revival of the 11th century forced Church thinkers to deal with economic matters.

> The ecclesiastical jurists ... found the problem of value forcing itself upon their attention. In dealing with economic subjects they were not actuated by a desire to build up a science; their object was rather to establish rules for the guidance of human conduct. They were not seeking to explain phenomena, but to apply certain principles to existing social conditions, in order that human conduct might follow the course which seemed to them to be laid out for it by divine command.[26]

The process of buying or selling involved great spiritual danger, according to the Church, since the accumulation of wealth came to be regarded as sin. It is not surprising that the notion of a "just price" was created as a necessity and that special requirements were placed on the parties to inform each other of known qualities or defects.[27]

Late Medieval Period

In the later centuries of the Dark Ages (12th and 13th centuries), Aristotle's work began to be translated and taught. His influence on Church scholars is known to have influenced their doctrine. The most important writing was by Thomas Aquinas in the *Summa Theologica*. The contribution to value theory by the Church scholars and Aquinas, in particular, are nearly universally cited.[28]

[26]See Sewall, *op. cit.*, p. 649.

[27]One study reported that Lactantius required that the buyer inform the seller of any good quality of the articles and the latter should reveal any defects in the commodities. See Whittaker, *op. cit.*, p. 409.

[28]See Weimer, *op. cit.*, p. 167; Featherston, *op. cit.*, p. 168; E.A.J. Johnson, *Predecessors of Adam Smith* (1937), reprinted by New York: Augustus M. Kelley, 1960, p. 304; Kaulla, *op. cit.*, pp. 35–38; Whittaker, *op. cit.*, pp. 410–411; and Sewall, *op. cit.*, pp. 651–662.

The central problem for the scholars of the Middle Ages was justice in exchange. This natural concept was the determination of the just price, or the "price corresponding to the true value of the object."[29] Note that this approach was considerably different from the Stoic values of the ancients. The teachings of Christianity held contempt for earthly treasures while the Stoics taught it was wise to obtain riches. Stoicism also taught that commercial contracts should not be interfered with while Christianity held that if private contracts were created which were contrary to the supreme principle of austerity, the Church could and should void the contract.[30]

Aquinas recognized that both the utility of an article and the quantity offered for sale affected the value and the price of the article. This price was unjust only if there was fraud on either side of the transaction. It was furthered by Albertus Magnus who stated that two commodities were of equal value and their exchange prices were just if "their production represented equal amounts of labour and expense."[31] Note the connection to the Cost Approach in modern appraisal writing. If so, the value was determined by both of these factors. Thomas Aquinas "adopted" this concept "almost word for word" and as a result, this idea carried forward having "been expounded by the two leading authorities, remained supreme throughout the Scholastic period."[32]

It is important to note that Christian doctrine linked labor with the just price.

> [The teachings] placed labour in a position of honour, [such that] renumeration should be proportionate to labour. Justice ... demanded the observance of a definite proportion between labor applied and remuneration paid.[33]

While the development of the labor theory of value in economics was still centuries away, the groundwork was set in the Church doctrine as well as in ancient times in the writings of Aristotle. Further, while the notion of just price was prevalent, it could not be determined with any degree of precision. Clearly, the lack of a theory of value precluded a precise measure of worth. Even Aquinas acknowledged this limitation when he said "the just price of things is not fixed with mathematical precision, but depends on a kind of estimate."[34]

In effect, the practical result of the doctrine of just price was the regulation of prices by civil authorities. This also occurred at a time when foreign trade was booming and merchants from the trade routes were regularly appearing throughout Europe. Over time, there came to be a recognition of utility as a part of value as well as labor. But, as a general statement of the era, Aquinas' medieval theory of value is adequately captured in the following passage.

> ... value can, does and should increase in relation to the amount of labor which has been expended in the improvement of commodities.[35]

[29]See Kaulla, *op. cit.*, p. 35.
[30]*Ibid.*
[31]*Ibid.*, pp. 37–38.
[32]*Ibid.*, p. 38.
[33]*Ibid.*, p. 39.
[34]Thomas Aquinas, *Summa Theologia*, Q 77, Article 1, as quoted in Whittaker, *op. cit.*, p. 411.
[35]*Ibid.*, as quoted in Johnson, *op. cit.*, p. 304.

Changes in Church Doctrine

By the end of the 13th century, some other changes in Church teachings were occurring. Bernardin of Siena and Antonius, the Archbishop of Florence, modified the rigid requirements of time and place.

> [They] justified prices that allowed for risks and the utilities of something inherent in the commodity passed away and, in its stead, appeared a value that was more flexible and more in accordance with modern thought.[36]

The "modern thought" would be a long time in developing. However, the next period would bring great advances as society moved away from feudalism to what became known as "mercantilism." It is not surprising that various notions of value were quite rampant during the prosperous centuries ahead.

VALUE IN ECONOMICS

The late 18th and early 19th centuries involved fundamental changes in the nature of the economic system and the growth of civilization.

> The old trappings of feudalism were gradually discarded and new, strong states arose. The metaphysical concept of a "natural" economy and the Scholastic teachings were discarded. The church and state controversy abated with each recognizing its own sphere of influence and enjoying supremacy therein. No longer were efforts made to stop trade and commerce on moral and religious grounds; on the contrary, the highest premium was paid on economic activity, for the rewards of trade and commerce provided the sinews of national greatness. A body of economic thought known as mercantilism was developed in association with the emergence of the modern state and the changing economic practices.[37]

Mercantilism meant changes in economic policy by nations, especially regarding foreign trade and the protection of domestic industries. It should also be pointed out that the term "mercantilism" is a general, descriptive term of an era in European economic history rather than a specific social, political, or economic system.

Unlike the previous era, this period is fertile for an examination of value concepts. Although the existing histories of value theory in the appraisal literature tend to note the importance of this period in very brief treatments, generally with attention paid to the Mercantilists and the Physiocrats,[38] reviewers have generally neglected some of the specific and important contributions. The writers of the era led to the development of formal value theory in the 18th and 19th centuries.

Several of the leading writers on the topic of value during the 16th, 17th, and early 18th centuries are briefly described below.

[36]See Whittaker, *op. cit.*, p. 412.

[37]See John F. Bell, *A History of Economic Thought*. The Ronald Press Co., New York, 1953, p. 77.

[38]For example, see Featherston, *op. cit.*, pp. 168–170; and Weimer, *op. cit.*, pp. 167–169.

John Hales

A "self-acquired philosopher" and a humanist, John Hales wrote a book entitled *A Discourse of the Common Weal of this Realm of England* (1581). In this book, he developed some basic notions implicit in later value theory. For example, he observed that scarcity was a basic notion in the value of crops.

> ... whan god sendeth dearthe of corne, or of other thinges, Theare is nether Emperour nor kinge can healpe it.[39]

Note also the reliance upon trade in the following Hales' quote and the relationship of value to scarcity.

> ... yt is the varietie and plentie therof that maketh the price thereof base or higher.[40]

Hales represents one of the earliest post-Middle Ages writers to treat economic value. While there is no theory developed on the subject, these passages provide clues of the things to come.

Gerard de Malynes

This writer was one of the first to oppose free trade, a notion which became a major foundation of the Mercantilist era. His book, *Conseuetudo, vel, Lex Marcatoria*, was written in 1622 and argued that society was being tricked by the "exchangers" and that the nature of life was under threat. On the topic of value, he argued that value had little to do with trade of goods; it was the greed and craftiness of merchants that led to increased prices.

> It was an error to "suppose that bills of exchange derive their value" in the same manner as commodities; indeed, it is the abuse of exchange that has produced the "rising and falling in price," according to plenty and scarcity of money.[41]

His work began a dispute among the Mercantilists and in particular sparked a pamphlet by Edward Misselden in the following year.

Edward Misselden

This writer was a member of the Merchant Adventurers, a trade group of cloth merchants who lobbied for change in the cartel rules affecting the export of cloth.

[39]John Hales, *A Discourse of the Common Weal of this Realm of England*. 1581, p. 6, as quoted by Johnson, *op. cit.*, p. 29.

[40]See Hales, *ibid.*, p. 71, as quoted in Johnson, *ibid.*, p. 30.

[41]See Johnson, *ibid.*, p. 52.

His book was entitled *The Circle of Commerce* (1623) and appeared as a pro-trade response to Malynes. The book was written as a propaganda piece for the Merchant Adventurers and like Thomas Mun, who followed him, Misselden's background was as a full-time lifelong merchant. Unlike Mun, however, Misselden's reputation rested more on "notoriety than admiration."[42]

According to Misselden, there were only two types of transactions: those which were "personall" [sic] or exchanges of goods or money "between man and man" and those which were "provinciall" [sic] or exchanges of goods or money between kingdoms. He argued that the market for foreign trade sets prices of goods in the same manner as does any other market.

> There is a quality of commodities, a "goodness" which "directeth the price" but this quality, although constantly operative, does not actually determine the price. The actual price may be "greater or less" than what is individually this intrinsic "goodness;" it varies with the "use of the thing" and with the "judgment of the buyer and the seller."[43]

But it was not until 1664 with the publication of Thomas Mun's treatise that a more careful view of the importance of foreign trade was presented.

Thomas Mun

This merchant turned writer was recognized as one of the most influential voices in the Mercantilist era. His book, *England's Treasure by Forraign Trade, or, the Balance of Our Forraign Trade is The Rule of Our Treasure* was written during the same time as Malynes and Misselden wrote their works, but it did not appear until his son, Sir John Mun, published it in 1664. Mun was quite well-known during his lifetime as director of the East India Company. His son proclaimed that he was "famous among Merchants, and well known to most men of business."[44] Adam Smith claimed that Mun's influence extended to both financial and commercial policy in England to such an extent that Mun's views became the fundamental economic policy in England and other European states.[45]

There are two important points about his work. First, he developed a "theory of national opulence" based on equating wealth with money. He argued that by encouraging foreign trade, nations could accumulate treasures. Second, while Mun did not develop a theory of value per se, he clearly regarded the opportunity to trade as influential in affecting national well-being since trade increased the values of domestic commodities.

[42] *Ibid.*, p. 73.

[43] See Edward Misselden, *A Circle of Commerce*, London, 1623, p. 97, as quoted in Johnson, *op. cit.*, p. 67.

[44] See Johnson, *ibid.*, p. 73.

[45] See Bell, *op. cit.*, p. 86.

One source claims, with documented evidence, that Adam Smith's *The Wealth of Nations* was "unconsciously patterned" after Mun's *England's Treasure by Forraign Trade* in terms of design.[46] This is powerful testimony of the impact of Mun's work.

Sir William Petty

This gentleman is frequently cited as one of the early economic writers on value and unlike those cited previously, Petty is generally noted as an economist. He was, in fact, perhaps the first "political economist" (albeit a crude one), although he was more interested in statistics than theories of value.[47] Petty did develop a theory of value, however, in effect, it was a labor theory of value variant merged with a surplus theory of rent.[48]

"Let another man, go travel into a Country where is Silver, there Dig it, Define it, Bring it to the same place where the other man planted his Corn," subtract from his product the miner's subsistence, and "the Silver of the one, must be esteemed of equal value with the Corn of the other," and the ratio between the respective quantities will be the price of the corn.[49]

Clearly, labor constituted a major element in Petty's theory of value. The other important element was the contribution of the land.[50] Petty is best known for his emphasis on statistical measurement in deriving wealth from land and labor. However, he foreshadowed the classical school of economics with notions of exchange value, natural value and what came to be known as the "labor theory of value." Petty may be thus regarded as the first economist in the history of value theory.

To sum up Petty's theory of value, we may say that he conceived the ultimate source of value, as of wealth, to be land and labor. By value he meant wealth measured. Hence the natural value of a commodity would be the result of the quantity of land labor required to produce it. But its value in the market, its extrinsic value, might vary from the natural value according to the relation of supply to demand.[51]

It is interesting to note that the first economist in value theory is the one who foreshadowed the distinction between the cost to produce and market value in modern appraisal theory.

[46]See Johnson, *op. cit.*, p. 335.
[47]See Bell, *op. cit.*, p. 89.
[48]An extensive study of Petty's work was provided by C.H. Hull, *The Economic Writings of Sir William Petty*, 2 Volumes. Cambridge University Press, Cambridge, 1899.
[49]See William Petty, as quoted in Johnson, *op. cit.*, p. 102.
[50]Note Petty's language on this point.

... all things ought to be valued by two natural Denominations which is Land and Labour.

See *ibid.*, p. 103.
[51]See Sewall, *op. cit.*, p. 711.

Nicholas Barbon

In 1690, Nicholas Barbon published a pamphlet entitled *A Discourse of Trade*. In this work, he advanced the notion that utility was more important than labor in determining value. As such, he is regarded as a predecessor of utility theory by more than two centuries.[52] He argued that value was not intrinsic to the good but was dependent upon the nature of human wants.

> The Value of all Wares arise from their Use; Things of no use have no Value, as the *English Phrase* is, *They are good for nothing*.... The Price of Wares is the present Value; and ariseth by computing the occasions or use for them, with the Quantity to serve that occasion ... so that Plenty, in respect of the Occasion, makes things cheap; and Scarcity dear.[53]

This anti-Mercantilist doctrine branded Barbon as heretic to the given doctrine. However, with Dudley North, Sir William Petty, Roger Coke and others, he was not alone.[54]

Consider the modern flavor of these passages by Barbon and the relevance to the appraiser.

> There are two ways by which the value of things are a little guessed at; by the price of the merchant, and the price of the artificer: the price that the merchant sets upon his wares, is by reckoning prime cost, charges and interest. The price of the artificer, is by reckoning the cost of the materials, with the time of working them; the price of time is according to the value of the art, and the skill of the artist.... Interest is the rule that the merchant trades by; and time, the artificer, by which they cast up profit, and loss ...[55]

> The market is the best judge of Value.[56]

> Things are just worth so much, as they can be sold for ...[57]

Barbon contended that the market value of goods was determined by the "competition of subjective valuations." Such valuations were expressions of the worth of the objects and of the esteem with which individuals and society held these objects. This idea was far ahead of its time in the history of value theory doctrine. Barbon's reputation as an economist has been suggested to have been downgraded because of his insistence that the value of coins were dependent upon the government stamp placed

[52]See Whittaker, *op. cit.*

[53]Nicholas Barbon, *A Discourse of Trade*. London, 1690. Reprinted and edited by J.H. Hollander, Baltimore, Johns Hopkins University Press, 1905, pp. 13, 15. The quote is also cited in a slightly different form in Whittaker, *op. cit.*

[54]See Philip W. Buck, *The Politics of Mercantilism*. Henry Holt and Co., New York, 1947, p. 68.

[55]As quoted in Sewall, *op. cit.*, p. 697.

[56]As quoted in Buck, *op. cit.*, p. 67.

[57]As quoted in Sewall, *op. cit.*, p. 698.

upon them.[58] But his ideas were influential on the writing of John Locke, who credited Barbon with affecting his thinking on the concept of value.

John Locke

As an important philosopher, John Locke is rarely heralded for economic work and he will not be so in this study either. However, he is said to have had "great profoundity and breadth in his [understanding of] general economic concepts.[59] In two pamphlets, he showed the impact of Barbon and others who argued against the Mercantilist doctrine. In *A Tract against the High Rate of Usurie* (1691), he insisted that "intrinsic value is not natural but is only the opinion of men consenting to it."[60] In *Some Considerations of the Lowering of Interest and Measuring the Value of Money* (1691), he noted that "the vent [*i.e.*, sale] of a thing depends upon its necessity or usefulness."[61]

Locke was led to review the causes of value in his work on interest and money. Later, in 1726, he rejected the traditional notion of intrinsic value.

> ... the intrinsick [sic] natural worth of anything, consists in its fitness to supply the necessities, or serve the conveniences of human life; and the more necessary it is to our being, or the more it contributes to our well being, the greater is its worth ... [However], the marketable value of any assigned quantities of two, or more commodities, are ... equal, when they will exchange one for another .... [T]here is no such intrinsic natural settled value in any thing, as to make any assigned quantity of it, constantly worth any assigned quantity of another.[62]

It is unfortunate that most of the legacy of John Locke lies in the philosophical impact he has had in the concept of the role of government rather than in the nature of value. His influence on the founding fathers regarding the origin of property cannot be overstated. Clearly, many of his ideas remain fresh today for economists as well as appraisers.

John Law

This minor, economic writer is remembered for a 1705 pamphlet entitled *Money and Trade Consider'd; with a Proposal for Supplying the Nation with Money*. In it, he produced the original comparison between the value of water and the value of diamonds.

> Goods have a Value from the Uses they are appl'd to; and their Value is Greater or Lessor ... as from the greater or lesser Quantity of them in proportion to their Demand for them. *Example.* Water is of great use, yet of little Value; because the Quantity of Water is much greater than the

[58]This was attributed to J.R. McCulloch, an economist generally regarded as Ricardo's major disciple. See Sewall, *op. cit.*, p. 698.

[59]See Bell, *op. cit.*, p. 89.

[60]As quoted in *ibid.*, p. 89. It is interesting that Bell points out that Locke's motivation in 1691 was to argue that lowering interest rates was a means of increasing national prosperity. See *ibid.*, p. 89f.

[61]From *The Works of John Locke*, Volume 5, pp. 30–31, as quoted in Whittaker, p. 415.

[62]See John Locke, *Civil Government Works*, Volume 2, p. 160 (1726), and *The Works of John Locke*, Volume 2, pp. 21–22, as quoted in Sewall, *op. cit.*, pp. 699–700.

Demand for it. Diamonds are of little use, yet of great Value, because the Demand for Diamonds is much greater, than the Quantity of them. Goods of the same kind differ in Value, from any difference in their Quality.[63]

In 1950, in an article on the development of the utility theory, George Stigler noted that Adam Smith, by making this story famous in *The Wealth of Nations*, caused problems for generations of readers. Stigler claimed that the story was rivaled only by its ambiguity and neglect of the notion of marginal utility compared to its fame.[64]

Richard Cantillon

A French writer, Cantillon was interested in national wealth, exchange and foreign trade. Cantillon's book, *Essai sur la nature du commerce en general* (1730) probably had little effect on economic policy in France. He is credited, though, with several original ideas and is regarded as one of the forerunners of the Physiocrats and he helped to lay the foundation for the Classical School.[65] He adopted the "intrinsic value" notion as related to the cost of production.

Price or intrinsic value [of a thing is] the measure of the quantity of land and of labour entering into its production, having regard to the fertility or produce of the Land and to the quality of the Labour.[66]

However, Cantillon believed that market values could differ from this cost of production value.

... it often happens that many things which have actually this intrinsic value are not sold in the Market according to that value: that will depend on the Humours and Fancies of men and on their consumption. If a gentleman cuts Canals and Terraces in his Garden, their intrinsic value will be proportionate to the Land and Labour; but the Price in reality will not always follow this proportion. If he offers to sell the Garden possibly no one will give him half the expense he has incurred. It is also possible that if several persons desire it he may be given double the intrinsic value ...[67]

Like Petty, this early writer distinguished between value as a function of the cost to produce and value as measured in the marketplace, a distinction which was to be confused throughout the classical school period.

Charles King

At about the same time in England, Charles King, "The Propagandist" was writing political columns in *The British Merchant*, a twice-weekly protectionist publication.[68]

[63]See John Law, *Money and Trade Consider'd; with a Proposal for Supplyinq the Nation with Money*, Glasgow, 1705, as quoted by Whittaker, *op. cit.*, p. 416.

[64]See George J. Stigler, The Development of Utility Theory, *Journal of Political Economy*, 1950, 58: 308.

[65]See Whittaker, *op. cit.*, p. 418.

[66]See Richard Cantillon, *Essai sur la nature du commerce en general.* 1730, p. 29, as quoted in *ibid.*, pp. 417–418.

[67]Cantillon, *op. cit.*, as quoted in *ibid.*, p. 418.

[68]See Johnson, *op. cit.*, p. 155.

One critic called King's writings "the most unimpeachable exposition of mercantilist thought" because the message throughout the series of articles was that protectionism was a "fundamental creed."[69] In an article written in 1721, King argued that "the new Value that is superadded" to the initial value of raw materials stems from protectionist legislation. As a result, this type of thinking gave further impetus to the importance of costs in determining value, even if his basic approach was subsequently rejected.

Francois Quesnay

The founder of the Physiocrats, Francois Quesnay was the court physician to Madame de Pompadour and Louis XV. Physiocrats believed themselves to be the first economists and they developed a system based on a concept of natural order and that the laws of nature could be used in conjunction with the laws of God.[70] The development of the Physiocrats occurred after a period of heavy spending by Louis XIV. Farmers had been overtaxed and the world was experiencing a declining stock of wealth under Mercantilism. Quesnay has been credited with the concept of natural law and the basis for the theory and famous motto of "laissez faire, laissez passer," although there is some question about the origin of the term.[71]

The economic contributions of the Physiocrats relate to the role of land in producing wealth and the relationship of trade to prosperity. Regarding the former, their ideas relate closely to those of Cantillon.

> The fundamental economic postulate of the physiocrats was that the cultivation of the soil is the sole source of new wealth, and alone gives a net income. Thus they differed from Locke and Petty, who derived wealth not only through the agency of agricultural labor but also through that of industrial labor ... [Cantillon and the Physiocrats] regarded money as wealth only in the sense in which other commodities are wealth, *i.e.*, by being useful to man ...[72]

With respect to foreign trade, the Physiocrats, as a reaction to the Mercantilists, rejected any restrictions on industry and urged that a single tax be placed on the net income derived from land.

On concepts of value, Quesnay distinguished between value in exchange and value in use as had Locke and others before him,

> The savages of Louisiana ... enjoyed a quantity of goods, such as water, wood, game, fruits of the earth, etc., which were not wealth because they had no exchange value. But since some branches of commerce have been established among them ... a part of these goods have acquired an exchange value and have become wealth.[73]

[69]Attributed to Lipson in *Economic History of England*, Volume 3, pp. 89–90.

[70]Brief reviews of the Physiocrats are provided in nearly every history and survey. See Featherston, *op. cit.*, pp. 169–170; Weimer, *op. cit.*, pp. 168–169; Bell, *op. cit.*, pp. 121–144; and others.

[71]See Bell, *op. cit.*, p. 127 and especially, p. 127f.

[72]See Sewall, *op. cit.*, p. 718.

[73]Francois Quesnay, *Notes sur Les Maximes*, as quoted in Sweall, *op. cit.*, pp. 723–724.

Therefore, according to Quesnay, it was the creation of exchange value that translates products from the land into wealth and this was the concept of value which most concerned the Physiocrats. Furthermore, Quesnay developed separate notions about prices and the determination of value. To the Physiocrats, value was the cost related by the exchange of products.

To the orthodox physiocrat, value was cost made manifest in a rate of exchange predetermined by the condition of things, *i.e.*, by the actual production compared with the necessary consumption. Hence the statement that in exchange equal value is given for equal value, as often reiterated by them, was a mere truism, for if the cost determined the rate of exchange, things would exchange in proportion to costs. The doctrine was not a new one .... The canonists believed that whenever prices were just, equal value was exchanged for equal value .... The orthodox physiocrats disregarded temporary variations in value. They kept in view only normal exchange value determined by cost .... They saw that all things which are used by man come originally from the earth, that is, are "gifts of nature." ... Those "gifts of nature" which have value are wealth, because value is the social expression of that usefulness which furnishes the motive for industry ...[74]

Other Physiocrats

These converts to the Physiocrat school included Mirabeau the Elder, Pierre Samuel du Pont de Nemours, Ferdinando Galiani, and A. Robert Jacques Turgot. Each is important in his own right and is discussed elsewhere in detail.[75] Mirabeau's writings were mostly concerned with taxes. Du Pont de Nemours popularized the Physiocrats' general principles. Galiani developed preliminary notions of utility and is regarded as a major forerunner in this area (and is discussed again later in this chapter). Finally, Turgot is the most well-known of the Physiocrats, especially in the area of value theory.

Turgot's value theory corresponded to utility as well as Galiani's. He questioned whether values could be measured.

But [the value of an individual object] ... will not be susceptible of measurement, and the thing which has worth will not be rated ...[76]

However, when objects could be exchanged, the price was regarded as equal to its value. Thus, value was not inherent in the goods but was reflected as a quantitative market ratio, according to Turgot.

One critic has concluded that although Quesnay, Turgot, and the Physiocrats were concerned with value, their writings do not constitute a value theory.[77] They were

[74]Sewall, *ibid.*, pp. 727–728.

[75]*Ibid.*; and Bell, *op. cit.*

[76]See Sewall, *op. cit.*, p. 735.

[77]For a complete discussion of the Physiocrats, see Bell, *op. cit.*, pp. 121–144. Another source notes that while the idea of utility and value is found in Turgot, the notion of marginal utility was left for Walras and Jevons. See Whittaker, *op. cit.*, pp. 416–417. See also Dobb, *op. cit.*, pp. 39–40 for a discussion of the Physiocrats.

more concerned with rents and the role of natural resources in society. Their importance rests as predecessors of later thought rather than are designers of carefully crafted economic systems.

Sir James Steuart

The final early economic writer is an extremely interesting one. One historian has called Steuart the "most enlightened forerunner" of the Classical School[78] despite the fact that his place in economic history is generally delegated to footnotes or as afterthoughts. His economic treatise, *An Inquiry into the Principles of Political Economy*, was published in 1767, 9 years ahead of Adam Smith's *The Wealth of Nations*. This fellow Scot has elements of Petty's role of agricultural surplus, Hume's experimental method, Petty's notion of political authority, and other adaptations.[79] Adam Smith is known to have written a letter about Steuart's book before the publication of *The Wealth of Nations*, and one observer believes that the failure of Smith to recognize it, led to the rapid decline of the book throughout the economics profession.[80]

Steuart has been called a "moderate mercantilist" and his book is not a system of economic analysis but rather a series of essays. He considered cost as an element in the determination of value, but he also considered demand. Intrinsic value was determined by cost, but the market determined whether the price paid is too high or too low, dependent on the level of competition in the market.

> Exchange of commodities is facilitated by merchants, who relieve both consumers and producers of the trouble of transportation and also adjust wants to wants.[81]

This was similar to the work of Locke, Law, and in some respects, Adam Smith in the very near future.

The State of Value Theory Before 1776

The initial ideas about the concept and measurement of value took a very long time to nurture. Most of the early concepts of value were reinvented time after time because it was so difficult to evaluate these ideas without any formal doctrine and methodological grounding. However, it is fair to say that the period before 1776 is filled with ideas and notions about the meaning of value.

One study concluded that two main results can be obtained by examining the evolution of the early literature on value.[82] First, the concept of exchange value developed over a long period of time. Second, the idea that value was a subjective notion has its seeds in the early periods. Exchange value depended upon an economy with money and trade; institutions which did not always exist. Subjective value relates

[78]Sigmund Feilbogen, James Steuart und Adam Smith, in *Zeitschrift fur die gesamle Stuartswissenschaft*, 45 Tubingen, 1889, pp. 218–260.

[79]See Johnson, *op. cit.*, p. 209.

[80]Cited in John Rae, *Life of Adam Smith* (London, 1895), p. 253, as quoted in Johnson, *ibid.*

[81]As quoted in Johnson, *ibid.*, p. 220.

[82]See Sewall, *op. cit.*, pp. 754–762.

directly to utility and to paraphrase Barbon, if the mind changes, things lose their value. But in the end, the classical school took on the task of developing a theory of value. Nevertheless, this school only reached a limited amount of success with such an incredibly difficult topic, despite attracting the attention of the major thinkers in economics over several decades.

THE LABOR THEORY OF VALUE

The classical economists did not band together in response to the existing doctrine as had the Physiocrats in response to the Mercantilists. Instead, the leading economists in England and in one instance, France, set out to formalize economic thought into a distinct set of components. These economists included Adam Smith, Thomas Malthus, David Ricardo, James Mill, and J.B. Say. Their disciples included Nassau Senior, John Stuart Mill, and John E. Cairnes, with an influence virtually unchallenged for about 100 years.

While the classical economists were interested in a wide range of topics, value theory played a key role in the description of their economic models. Indeed, it is the value theory laid out by Adam Smith which became to be known as the "labor theory of value," employing as has been shown, several elements of earlier thinkers and writers.

Some General Comments

According to the classical economists, this school of thought sought to develop a theory of value because they wished "to explain why goods exchange at particular ratios, why some are relatively expensive and others cheap."[83] The classical economic paradigm divided the total product of a producer into three shares: wages of labor, the profits of capital, and the rent of land. (Subsequently, during the 20th century, the payment to managers was added as a fourth payment.) However, costs of production also included the "real" costs, involving human sacrifice and pain. This "real" cost element would be important since labor was the factor upon which the classical school would base its theory of value.

While even Adam Smith recognized that changes in preferences could lead to rising or falling prices, the classical school's approach was to look only at long-run results. The issue of short- versus long-run was not really addressed by the classical school, but it has clearly proven to be relevant for the theory of value.

> It should be noted, as all modern economists have recognized, that the cost explanation of value applies only in a long-run view, over time sufficient to adjust production to demand.[84]

It was not until Marshall's 1890 textbook that the relationship between long-run equilibrium and short-run adjustments was made clear.

[83] See Frank H. Knight, *On the History and Method of Economics*. University of Chicago Press, Chicago, 1956, p. 11.

[84] *Ibid.*, p. 13.

> But in the longer run, production itself responds to price and price to supply, so that the long run or normal equilibrium "price is that at which the amount consumers will take is equal to the amount which producers find it profitable to produce."[85]

In the world of 1776, the theory of value was a long-run concept and short-run adjustments were of limited interest in developing the theory. We see that the modern appraisal concept that the Cost Approach is reliable only in markets near equilibrium can be traced to Adam Smith.

An Overview of the Important Economists

In the next section, we briefly highlight the contributions of the most influential economists on value theory: Adam Smith, David Ricardo, Thomas Malthus, John Stuart Mill, and Karl Marx. In addition, we examine several of their contemporary critics as well.

Adam Smith

Few economists are as well-cited as Adam Smith; indeed, an entire series of biographies exist on his work.[86] Of course, a figure as important as Adam Smith is evaluated in every economic history as well.

Regarding the theory of value, Smith's famous book, *An Inquiry into the Nature and Causes of The Wealth of Nations* (1776) set out an elaborate value theory as an alternative to the Mercantilists. To Smith, the Mercantilists were guilty of several fallacies since they identified wealth with money. The problem was that the labor spent on the commodity was argued to be the true measure of worth.

> Labour alone, therefore, never varying in its own value, is alone the ultimate and real standard by which the value of all commodities can at all times be estimated and compared.[87]

Note how the concept changes very little from the first edition to the eleventh edition of *The Wealth of Nations*, published in 1811.

> Labour, therefore, it appears evidently, is the only universal, as well as the only accurate measure of value, or the only standard of which we can compare the values of different commodities at all times and at all places.[88]

At another place in the book, Smith relates price to cost.

[85]This quote is credited to Alfred Marshall, *Principles of Economics* (1890), as quoted in Knight, *ibid.*, p. 20.

[86]The most well-known are John Rae, *Life of Adam Smith* (London, 1895); Ougald Stewart, *Biographical Memoirs of Adam Smith, L.L.D* (Dublin, 1795); R.B. Haldane, *Life of Adam Smith* (London, 1887); James Bonar, *A Catalogue of the Library of Adam Smith* (London, 1932); and W.R. Scott, *Adam Smith as Student and Professor* (Glasgow, 1937).

[87]Adam Smith, *An Inquiry into the Nature and Causes of The Wealth of Nations* (London, 1776), p. 37, as quoted by Knight, *op. cit.*, p. 48.

[88]See Adam Smith, *An Inquiry into the Nature and Causes of the Wealth of Nations*, Eleventh edition. Peter B. Gleason and Co., Hartforn, CT. 1811, p. 25.

The real price of everything, what everything really costs to the man who wants to acquire it, is the toil and trouble of acquiring it.[89]

However, it has been suggested that Smith believed that the labor theory of value would be useful only, in his words, "to that early and rude state of society" where individuals were forced to labor for their own subsistence. Subsequently, individuals would be free to engage in trade. The important question was what value would be placed on the commodities in the market. To Smith, the answer followed directly.

... the rate at which commodities would exchange for one another would be in proportion to the total amount of labour used in producing them.[90]

Labour, therefore, is the real measure of the exchangeable volume of all commodities.[91]

Smith also was aware of the historical differences between "exchangeable value" and what he termed "natural value." One historian illustrated this point with the following passage.

When the owner of a commodity A exchanges it for a commodity B, Adam Smith said that to this man the "exchangeable value," or simply the "value," of A is B, but the "price" of B is A. Here, to the other party, the "value" of 6 is A, and the "price" of A is 8, so that, in such an exchange, "value" and "price" are practically the same thing viewed from opposite sides. Not so, when a commodity is supposed to be exchanged for labor.... When A is given for a day's labor, and a day's labor is given for A, Adam Smith now said that the "real exchangeable value," or simply the "real value" of A to its owner is the day's labor he obtains for it, while the "real price" of the day's labor is A; but to the laborer the "real price" of A is the same day's labor he has given to obtain it, and the "real value" of the day's labor would be A... This obviously is not exchange-value, since no reference is made to any exchange.[92]

The notion of natural value based upon the labor cost became a cornerstone of Adam Smith's theory of value. For Smith, the natural price was "the central price, to which the prices of all commodities" continued to move towards.[93]

This notion of a natural price may be regarded as the summing up of factor costs. Sraffa, a famous Adam Smith biographer, termed this theory of price, the "adding-up theory."[94] Smith's natural values became the standard of comparison or norm to which other prices could be compared, for example, the market price's an interesting application.

[89]See *ibid.*, Book 1, p. 56, as quoted in Harlan Linneus McCracken, *Value Theory and Business Cycles*. Falcon Press, Inc., Binghamton, NY, 1933.

[90]As quoted in Lynn Mainwaring, *Value and Distribution in Capitalist Economies*. Cambridge University Press, London, 1984, p. 15.

[91]Smith, Eleventh edition, *op. cit.*, p. 21.

[92] See Walsh, *op. cit.*, p. 5.

[93]See Vernard Foley, *The Social Physics of Adam Smith*. Purdue University Press, Lafayette, Ind., 1976, p. 166.

[94]See Dobb, *op. cit.*, p. 46. Sraffa is also discussed in Young *op. cit.*, pp. 101–107.

... the actual price at which any commodity is commonly sold is called its market price. It may either be above, or below, or exactly the same with its natural price.[95]

Thus, to Smith, the market price was determined by the particular supply and demand conditions at any given time and place. In the long run, this price would "gravitate" towards the "natural" level. Note in the words of a well-known historian that this notion gives rise to the modern idea of a long-run equilibrium value.

When it came to more precise definitions of this natural value and its determination, Adam Smith had remarkably little to say beyond the statement that this was the equilibrium price that competition would in due course yield through the operations of supply and demand—toward which "the prices of all commodities are continually gravitating."[96]

Finally, there are several well-known analogies which appeared in *The Wealth of Nations*. Two of the more famous are (1) the deer and beaver fable and (2) the so-called "paradox of value" between diamonds and water, (the latter of which was mentioned earlier since it first appeared in John Law's writings at the beginning of the 18th century). The deer and beaver example demonstrates Smith's belief in a cost of production theory of value, specifically, labor expended to produce the commodity.

if it usually cost twice the labour to kill a beaver which it does to kill a deer, one beaver should naturally exchange for, or be worth two deer.[97]

As is shown below, this fable was criticized by Ricardo in his theory of value.

Regarding the water and diamonds paradox, Smith argued that water had a low exchange value but was dear while diamonds had limited usefulness but commanded high prices. Smith sought to demonstrate that the term value means different things depending on use.

The word value ... has different meanings, and sometimes expresses the utility of some particular object, and sometimes the power of purchasing other goods which the possessor of that object conveys. The one may be called "value in use," the other, "value in exchange." The things which have the greatest value in use have frequently little or no value in exchange; and on the contrary, those which have the greatest value in exchange have frequently little or no value in use. Nothing is more useful than water: but it will purchase scarce anything; scarce anything can be had in exchange for it. A diamond, on the contrary, has scarce any value in use; but a very great quantity of other goods may frequently be had in exchange for it.[98]

Adam Smith had read Aristotle as well.

[95]See Smith, Eleventh edition, *op. cit.*

[96]See Dobb, *op. cit.*, p. 44.

[97]Taken from Smith in *ibid.*, pp. 77–78. This story is also quoted in Daniel M. Hausman, *Capital, Profits and Prices*. Columbia University Press, New York, 1981, p. 16.

[98]See Smith, Eleventh edition, *op. cit.*, p. 20.

It has previously been pointed out that in Stigler's critique of utility theory, he found Smith's famous analogy wanting. He stated that "Smith's statement that value in use could be less than value in exchange was clearly a moral judgment, not shared by the possessors of diamonds."[99] Stigler concluded that the water and diamonds story deserves to be forgotten rather than criticized in terms of its neglect of utilitarian characteristics of value.

In general, the labor theory of value according to Adam Smith, was fundamentally a physical cost theory of value, and as pointed out elsewhere, the physical cost was measured in labor time.[100] This notion made it plausible for subsequent readers to believe that exchange values were proportional to physical costs, despite the fact that clearly this might not be true. Consider the conclusion of one well-known reviewer of Smith's theory of value.

> This idea of an exchange of commodities and labor ... which underlies Adam Smith's conception of value, is a tremendous blunder, and has been a far-reaching cause of error ever since his day. It is utterly improper, being only metaphorical, since no such exchange is made in reality .... Labor itself is not a commodity .... A very mischievous misuse of words is it to speak of laborers "selling" their labor. It gives then the impression that all they have to do is perform for a certain time certain operations called labor, and thereby they are fulfilling their side of the contract and need not concern themselves about the thing they are really giving in return for their pay—the thing produced.[101]

It was left for David Ricardo and Thomas Malthus to develop further the classical economics approach. In the area of value theory, Ricardo devoted a considerable amount of effort to this book.

David Ricardo

Economic historians have penned a considerable volume of pages about Ricardo as well as Adam Smith. His book, *On the Principles of Economy and Taxation*, published in 1817, was extremely influential. The scope of his inquiry extended to theories of rent, foreign exchange, wage determination, and to other areas. As a major figure in the history of economic thought, there is an abundance of material about his interesting personal life as well as his contributions to economics.

In Ricardo's *Principles* book, the theory of value was the longest chapter and began where Adam Smith began: the difference between value in use and value in exchange. However, soon he found fault with Smith's labor theory of value because he argued that utility mattered in determining the value of commodities.

In particular, Ricardo recognized that sometimes the amount of labor expended could purchase more or less goods but "it is their value which varies, not that of the labour which produces them."[102] In concluding, Ricardo differed from Smith and

[99]See Stigler, *op. cit.*, p. 309.

[100]See Hausman, *op. cit.*, p. 17.

[101]See Walsh, *op. cit.*, p. 7.

[102]David Ricardo, *On the Principles of Economy and Taxation* (London, 1817), as quoted in Bell, *op. cit.*, p. 223.

helped to refine the labor theory of value into a labor-based theory, where labor was not fixed in proportion to value.

... it is the comparative quantity of commodities which labour will produce, that determines their present or past relative value, and not the comparative quantities of commodities, which are given to the Tabourer in exchange for his labour ...[103]

Ricardo did not reject Smith's labor theory of value; he believed it was a good approximation to the determination of value.

In estimating ... the causes of the variations in the value of commodities, although it would be wrong wholly to omit the consideration of the effect produced by the rise or fall of labour, it would be equally incorrect to attach much importance to it; and consequently ... though I shall occasionally refer to this cause of variation I shall consider all the great variations which take place in the relative value of commodities to be produced by the greater or less quantity of labour which may be acquired from time to time to produce them.[104]

But he argued that value was determined by "labour bestowed and in proportion to labor embodied" instead of the natural price due to labor cost.[105] This refinement was sufficient to ensure Ricardo's place in the development of the theory of value. However, some critics have concluded that the Ricardian theory of value is little more than a refined cost-value doctrine, which, as earlier, neglected the proper treatment of exchange value.[106]

There are several interesting issues in Ricardo's theory of value. For example, Ricardo was quite concerned about the measurement of value. He claimed that there were two requisites for a standard of measurement: (1) the commodity which was chosen should require the same quantity of labor for its production and (2) the commodity chosen should be such that the prices of other commodities would remain constant to changes in the distribution of the commodity.[107] As a result, unlike earlier economists, Ricardo rejected gold or any other commodity as a suitable numeraire since there would never be "a perfect measure of value of all things."[108] In conclusion, he questioned whether valuation would ever proceed farther than a relation to the labor cost of production.

It must be confessed that there is no such thing in nature as a perfect measure of value, and that all that is left to the Political Economist is to admit that the great cause of the variation of commodities is the greater or less quantity of labour that may be necessary to produce them.[109]

[103]Ricardo, *op. cit.*, p. 11, as quoted in Bell, *ibid.*, p. 223.

[104]Ricardo, *op. cit.*, pp. 36–37, as quoted in Giovanni A. Caravale and Domenico A. Tosato, *Ricardo and the Theory of Value Distribution and Growth*. Routledge and Kegan Paul, London. 1980, pp. 54–55.

[105]See McCracken, *op. cit.*, p. 8.

[106]See Walsh, *op. cit.*, p. 8.

[107]Caravale and Tosato, *op. cit.*, p. 55.

[108]*Ibid.*, p. 56.

[109]Taken from David Ricardo, *Absolute Value and Exchange Value*. London. 1823, p. 404, as quoted in *ibid.*, p. 57.

It has already been noted that Ricardo did not agree with Smith's "beaver and deere" illustration. Specifically, Ricardo claimed that the prices of the slain animals "would be in proportion to the actual labour bestowed, both in the formation of capital [a weapon] and on the destruction of the animals."[110] Thus, there would be no forced mechanism that would equate the value of the animals. Ricardo also disagreed with the labor theory on the issue of wages. If wages were to rise, the labor theory of Smith presumed that prices would rise as the value of the products would henceforth be greater. Ricardo claimed that another result might obtain: a reduction in profits and if so, the traditional labor theory must be lacking.[111]

Finally, it is often pointed out that Ricardo's theory of value differs from Adam Smith's by fitting together a theory of rent with the labor theory to get a theory of profits. This is sometimes related through the story of the production of corn.

> The exchangeable value of all commodities rises as the difficulty of their production increases. If then new difficulties occur in the production of corn, from more labour being necessary, whilst no more labour is required to produce gold, silver, linen, etc., the exchangeable value of corn will necessarily rise, as compared with those things ... It has been thought that the price of corn regulates the prices of all other things. This appears to me to be a mistake. If the price of corn is affected by the rise or fall of the precious metals themselves, then indeed will the price of commodities be also affected, but they vary because the value of money varies not because the value of corn is altered ...[112]

What Ricardo tried to argue (despite his obscure language) was that Smith's argument that corn prices determined other prices was wrong; corn prices were determined by the amount of wages and other production costs. Clearly, the appraisal notion that land value is a residual follows Smith, not Ricardo.

Reaction to Ricardo. The Ricardian refinements on value brought considerable attention to value theory, including disciples like McCulloch and critics like Bailey and Torrens. It is apparent, however, that the value theory of Ricardo was "a cardinal feature of [his] system of economics."[113] Torrens claimed that by 1831, "all the great principles of Ricardo's work have been successively abandoned, and that his Theories of Value, Rent and Profits were now generally acknowledged to have been erroneous."[114] Samuel Bailey attacked Ricardo's notion of absolute value.

> Value denotes ... nothing positive or intrinsic, but merely the relation in which two objects stand to each other as exchangeable commodities ... it denotes a relation between two objects.[115]

In the 20th century, Ricardo's theory of value continued to have influence. For example, Vladimir Dmitriev, the first Russian mathematical economist, is considered

[110]See Dobb, *op. cit.*, p. 78.
[111]*Ibid.*, p. 79.
[112]As quoted in *ibid.*, p. 75.
[113]See Whittaker, *op. cit.*, p. 422.
[114]See Dobb, *op. cit.*, p. 96.
[115]See *ibid.*, p. 99.

a Ricardian with respect to the theory of value.[116] Both Stigler and Samuelson have had harsh words for the Ricardian theory of value. For example, Samuelson argued that the phenomenon of rent itself is sufficient to refute the labor theory of value.[117] Stigler rejected the notion of Ricardo's cost of production theory of value since utility is for all practical purposes rejected as a determining factor.[118]

But renewed interest in Ricardo's value theory continues. A disciple named Sraffa reconstructed the theory in 1960. He rejected the neo-classical notion of supply and demand as determinants of values and replaced it with the idea that natural prices of production form the basis of value.[119]

Thomas Malthus

This writer was more interested in population control than value. His book, *Essay on the Principle of Population* published in 1798 led him into economics since land was an important factor of production to feed the poor. In 1823, Malthus published a pamphlet entitled *The Measure of Value* and by 1836 with his *Principles of Political Economy*, Malthus had laid claim to economics as his domain and a theory of value was developed, based on the work of Smith's and Ricardo's doctrine.

In *Principles*, Malthus identified three types of value. First, there was value in use, where the intrinsic utility of an object was important. Second, the nominal value or price in exchange which was found in the marketplace existed. Third, the intrinsic value or price in exchange which, according to Malthus deriving "purchasing power from the intrinsic causes also prevailed."[120] Malthus was clearly part of the labor theory of value school but differed from Adam Smith in explaining value.

The price which fulfills these conditions (cost of labor, capital, rent on land) is precisely what Adam Smith calls the natural price; and when a commodity is sold at this price, he says it is sold for precisely what it is worth. But I think he has used the term worth in an unusual and improper sense. Commodities are continually said to be worth more than they have cost, ordinary profits included ...[121]

[116]See V.K. Dmitriev, *Economic Essays on Value, Competition and Utility*, translated by D. Fry and edited with an introduction by O.M. Nuti. Cambridge University Press, London. 1974, p. 19. Note the following quote by Omitriev on the relationship between price and cost.

The simplest formula expressing the relationship between price and production cost is

Price $\geq$ production costs. (1)

The formula is not a result of a scientific analysis of the phenomena of economic life, but a simple statement of the self-evident fact that production cannot continue (at least for any appreciable length of time) if the price of the product does not cover the costs incurred.

See Dmitriev, *op. cit.*, p. 39.

[117]As cited by Hausman, *op. cit.*, p. 18f.

[118]See Stigler, *op. cit.*, p. 312.

[119]For a discussion of Sraffa, see Caravale and Tosato, *op. cit.*, See also Young, *op. cit.*, p. 3.

[120]See Thomas R. Malthus, *Principles of Political Economy*. London. 1836, Reprinted, New York: Augustus M. Kelley, Inc., Second edition, 1951, p. 60.

[121]*Ibid.*, p. 77.

Malthus was a firm believer in the labor theory ("the great instrument of production is labour"), but note the difference between Malthus's fish analogy and Smith's deer and beaver example.

... if ten mackerel were, on an average, obtained by the same quantity of labour as two soals, it would be necessary, in order to continue the supply of both in the market, that the value of a soal should be five times as great is the power of purchasing similar commodities as the value of a mackerel; because if it were less, none would apply themselves to the catching of soals.... Now supposing that the skill and power of the labourers were so to increase, that in the same time and with the same personal exertions, they could obtain three soals and fifteen mackerel, it is obvious that the relative value of soals to mackerel would remain the same, but they could both have essentially altered their value compared with all those commodities which still required the same quantity of labour to produce the same supply of them.[122]

Thus, to Malthus the value of the commodities was determined by the labor and profit potential but more importantly, the exchange value was not solely a function of the labor cost. He made this clear in *The Measure of Value*.

Of the two main elements of value, labour and profits, the former ... is much the largest and most powerful ... [However], it cannot be said with anything like an approximation towards correctness that the labour worked up in commodities is the measure of their exchangeable value.[123]

However, if "the quantity of labor a commodity could command constituted a satisfactory measure of that commodity's value" as Malthus argued, it was left for Bailey and others to point out the Malthus, like Smith, confused exchange value with value as cost.

On the choice of a standard for measurement, Malthus differed from Smith again in arguing that labor cost could not be the standard.

Now [Smith's] definition makes the value of a commodity to depend as much upon the causes affecting all others which may be exchanged for it, as upon those which may affect itself; and of value so understood, it is perfectly clear that there can be no standard, since there is no one object which can at all times purchase or exchange for a uniform quantity of all others.[124]

For Malthus, the labor cost of production was an insufficient proxy as a measure of value since the purchasing power of labor expended was never constant. The market determined value, not the cost of production.

The worth of a commodity, in the place where it is estimated, is its market price, not its natural price. It is its intrinsic value in exchange, determined by the state of the supply compared with the demand at the time, and not its ordinary cost.[125]

[122]See Thomas R. Malthus, *The Measure of Value*. London 1823, Reprinted by Kelley and Millman, New York, 1957, p. 5.

[123]*Ibid.*, pp. 5, 13.

[124]See Malthus, *Principles, op. cit.*, pp. vii–ix.

[125]*Ibid.*, p. 78.

It would be misleading to conclude that Malthus's writings were in agreement with Ricardo's work. Malthus felt that Ricardo's theory returned to the idea that exchange value was based on costs. In fact Malthus provided an alternative path, which was picked up later by the Austrian school, by emphasizing the demand side of the market in determining value. The demand side required that major attention be paid to the utility of an object or the so-called "subjective value." While Smith and Ricardo emphasized costs, Malthus looked toward demand. However, Malthus is generally regarded as a Ricardian by critics, although differences remain between their ideas.[126]

John Stuart Mill

There is no doubt that John Stuart Mill was one of the great thinkers of all times. Much has been made of his writings in logic, government, sociology, and economics. However, it should be noted that most economic historians do not claim that Mill's contributions to economics involved much original thinking or new doctrine. His book, *Principles of Political Economy* (published in 1847), was *the* textbook for half a century.[127] However, Mill's infamous quote about value has tended to place him a bit below the other writers on the topic.

> Happily there is nothing in the laws of Nature which remains for the present or any future work to clear up; the theory of the subject is complete.[128]

The critics of Mill's theory have been long and persevering, expecting great achievements where none were to be found. He is generally placed as a member of the cost of production theory combined with a residual theory of the distribution of rent from land. He "adds up" the cost components in the theory of Adam Smith and as such resembles the work of Alfred Marshal and previously to David Ricardo.[129] Schumpeter called the line of thought on the cost theory of value "Smith-Mills-Marshall."[130] Another critic stated that Mill's value theory was no more than arguing that the price established in the market will be the price where supply equals demand.[131] This, of course, is hardly a theory of value, but more of a tautology. To Mill, there was only one value: exchange value, although later, he wrote of "cost value" and of "scarcity value."[132]

Mill's work was vulgarized in France by Bastiat and his followers as a "harmonic interpretation of the classical cost doctrines."[133] A recent economic historian noted that Mill's reputation had as rapid a rise as a fall.

[126]See McCracken, *op. cit.*, p. 14. See also Robert M. Rauner, *Samuel Bailey and the Classical Theory of Value*. Harvard University Press, Cambridge, Mass, 1961, p. 21.

[127]See Bell, *op. cit.*, p. 276.

[128]As quoted in Dobb, *op. cit.*, p. 129; and frequently elsewhere.

[129]*Ibid.*

[130]*Ibid.*

[131]See Omitriev, *op. cit.*, p. 183.

[132]See Walsh, *op. cit.*, p. 12.

[133]See Carl G. Uhr, *Economic Doctrines of Knut Wicksell*. University of California Press, Berkeley, CA, 1960, p. 17.

No one in the history of economics was more celebrated, even sometime after his death ... and no one has faded more completely.[134]

Critics of Ricardo and Malthus

In 1825, Samuel Bailey published *A Critical Dissertation on the Nature, Measures, and Causes of Value: Chiefly in Reference to the Writings of Mr. Ricardo and His Followers.* At the time, the economic community regarded Ricardo's work as orthodoxy. Bailey's book reexamined the Ricardian notion of value and found it wanting. In particular, Bailey asserted that all value was relative and the idea of absolute value had no meaning.

The value of A is expressed by the quantity of B for which it will exchange, and the value of B is in the same way expressed by the quantity of A. Hence the value of A may be termed the power which it possesses or confers of purchasing B, or commanding B in exchange.[135]

As such, Bailey is generally recognized as an early predecessor of the utility theory school.

Bailey argued that value was conceptual rather than physical. He believed that valuation meant the fixing of the quantifiable relation between objects. What the classical school failed to understand, he argued, was that the cost told little about exchange value and exchange value was what determined the worth of commodities. Consider Bailey's definition:

Value ... appears to mean the esteem in which any object is held. It denotes, strictly speaking, an effect produced on the mind ...[136]

Bailey recognized that concepts of value were slippery and the classical school kept changing value concepts. One of Bailey's historians notes that Bailey was very adept at pointing out inconsistencies between many members of the cost theory approach.

Like Adam Smith, Malthus contended that the value of labor remained constant. But if, as again with Adam Smith, he had already declared that value meant exchange value, or power of purchasing, then he was evidently wrong. It was a logical impossibility, said Bailey, that labour should at times receive a greater or smaller quantity in exchange for its services, while postulating at the same time that its value did not change.[137]

It is not surprising that the established economics profession dismissed Bailey's book out of hand. The *Westminster Review* in January 1826 reviewed it and declared there was "much ado about nothing."[138] J.R. McCulloch, the leading follower of Ricardo, declared in his bibliographical work, *The Literature of Political Economy* in 1845, that

[134]Eduard Heimann, *History of Economic Doctrines* Oxford University Press, New York, *op. cit.*, p. 119, as quoted in Bell, *op. cit.*, p. 276.

[135]See Rauner, *op. cit.*, pp. 5–6.

[136]As quoted in *ibid.*, p. 4.

[137]*Ibid.*, p. 20.

[138]*Ibid.*, p. 1.

"Bailey does not appear to have properly appreciated the Ricardian theory of value or to have succeeded in any degree in shaking its foundations."[139] In fact, however, one study showed that McCulloch's *The Principles of Political Economy* (1842) used parts of Bailey's doctrine, despite this criticism.[140]

But the criticism stuck and with it, the postponement of long, overdue recognition. Robert Torrens brought the book to the attention of the London Political Economics Club where it was read and discussed. John Stuart Mill is said to have included it on his student's reading list with only James Mill's *Elements* and Ricardo's *Principles* ahead of it.[141] Seligman called Bailey one of the "neglected British economists in 1903 and he began a rediscovery of his work.[142] In 1954, Schumpete judged that Bailey's book said "virtually all that was required" on the "fundamentals" of value theory, that it was among the "masterpieces" of economics, and that the author should have a "place in or near front rank in the history of scientific economics."[143]

Finally, an economic dictionary in 1863 argued that Bailey showed "with complete success" the error in the value theories of Ricardo, Malthus, and others. He proved that value was an "external relation" not an "internal quality" of objects and that "two objects should be brought into comparison" before value can be determined.

> Value denotes consequently nothing positive or intrinsic, but merely the relation in which two objects stand to each other as exchangeable commodities.[144]

To Bailey, and subsequent economists, value did not exist beyond man's mind. Value was a relative concept of esteem and not a measure of labor cost. A cursory review indicates that some of the appraisal literature follows Bailey's ideas directly.

The other critics of the classical theory of value included Robert Torrens and Nassau Senior. Torrens' book *Essay on the Production of Wealth* in 1821 denied the existence of any value except relative value.[145] Ricardo is said to have tried to refute this notion by claiming that every value was a mere relative value. The notion of "natural value" was said to be "something more" than exchange value.[146]

Nassau Senior's book, *Outline of Political Economy* in 1836 placed Senior as a disciple of the work of J.B. Say and others who treated value as dependent on utility. According to one biographer, Senior demolished the labor and real cost theories of value. In fact, this writer claims that Ricardo switched camps in the third edition of

[139] *Ibid.*

[140] On p. 6, McCulloch writes "the value of a commodity may be considered in a double point of view ... Value, considered in the first point of view, may be denominated exchangeable or relative value. Value, considered in the second point of view, may be denominated real value ..." This paradigm is the same as Bailey's explicit reference to the double meaning of value. See Rauner, *ibid.*, p. 103.

[141] *Ibid.*, p. 1.

[142] Edwin R.A. Seligman, On Some Neglected British Economists. *Economic Journal*, 1903, 13: 352–355.

[143] Joseph Schumpeter, *History of Economic Analysis*. New York. 1954, p. 486.

[144] As quoted in Rauner, *op. cit.*, pp. 6, 140.

[145] *Ibid.*, p. 58.

[146] *Ibid.*, p. 59.

his *Principles*.[147] Senior developed a relative utility theory of value since "utility denotes no intrinsic quality in the things which we call useful; it merely expresses their relations to the pains and pleasures of mankind."[148]

Although Torrens and Senior's writings were received coldly by their contemporaries, they led to the development of new value theories. The labor and cost of production theories were under severe reexamination and by the 1870s, there was little future for Ricardian value theory. But, one final writer was interested in this theory of value for a different purpose. His name was Karl Marx.

Karl Marx

The philosophical importance of Marx's writings is beyond the scope of this survey. However, Marx brought a special perspective to the theory of value literature. As a point of fact, he is often classified as a Ricardian, who made no distinction made between rent and profits.[149]

To Marx, labor was not a source of wealth but a source of capitalist exploitation.

> Labour is not the source of all wealth. Nature is just as much the source of use value ... as labor .... Man's labor only becomes a source of use values, and hence also of wealth if his relation to nature, the primary source of all instruments and objects of labor, is one of ownership from the start.[150]

For Marx, the theory of value was not a theory about exchange but a theory about the relations between classes in a capitalist society. However, he believed that the labor theory of value was fundamental to the capitalist system. In the later writings of Marxist economists, this point was made explicit.

> The key to unlocking the inner nature of capitalism is the labor theory of value ... This [is the] view, that value theory is the theory of capitalistic society. Placing value theory at the center of the analysis of capitalism is not common to all those who consider themselves Marxists .... However a growing group of writers recognizes the central role of value theory in the analysis of capitalism.[151]

It is well-known that Fredrich Engels modified Marx's thoughts in developing a more robust theory of value. Marx's theory of surplus value has been analyzed at length and dismissed at length as wel1.[152] In fact, an 1895 note on Marx's surplus value concludes that "for all useful purposes, the entire surplus value theory is virtually

[147]Marian Bowley, *Nassau Senior and Classical Economics*. George Allen and Unwin, Ltd., London, 1937, p. 105.

[148]As quoted in Bowley, *ibid.*, p. 95. This is also noted in Dobb, *op. cit.*, p. 107.

[149]Nicholas Kaldor, Alternative Theories of Distribution, in *Essays in Value and Distribution*. The Free Press, Glencoe, III., 1960, p. 215.

[150]Karl Marx, *The First International and After*. Vintage Books, New York, 1974, p. 341, as quoted in John Weeks, *Capital and Exploitation*. Princeton University Press, Princeton, NJ, 1981, p. 53.

[151]See Weeks, *ibid.*, pp. 4–6.

[152]For example, one critic states that the theory of surplus-value "enjoys the distinction of being assumed away more than any other economist." See Dobb, *op. cit.*, p. 141. Böhm-Bawerk claimed the downfall of

avowed to be meaningless lumber."[153] But it was Engel who provided a clearer notion of the theory of value.

> ... exchange occurs because of the production of a technologically available surplus and specialization that is prompted by producers achieving quality or most advantages based on access to raw materials or individual abilities; the magnitude of value is determined by the knowledge or perception by the exchanging parties of the labor time required in production; and this knowledge is obtained from direct observation. Further, this system of exchange is based upon each independent producer possessing the right to the fuel product of his labour.[154]

Even Engels acknowledged that the law of value had been ruled by exchanges in the history of the world. However, he claimed that the theory of value was interwoven with the exploitation of labor.

As a final word on Marx, it has been noted that Marx admitted that the exchange prices were related to the "prices of production" under capitalism. This observation about value was sufficient for Böhm-Bawerk to claim that this was the "great contradiction of Marxism" and that Marx's theory, or Engel's revision of it, had little to say.[155]

THE MARGINALIST CHALLENGE

In the latter portion of the 19th century, the history of economic thought broadened in an important direction: the theory of demand.

Beyond the Classical School

In many ways, the classical school of economists had developed the primary notions of value. All of the elements of value theory were discussed (with the exception of marginal analysis of utility). As argued earlier, it has taken a very long time to sort out the issues. However, it is fair to say that the legacy is rich with ideas and to this day, remains contemporary in thought.

The real estate appraisal literature owes much to the classical school. Not only does the cost approach stem from their ideas, the distinction between types of values can easily be traced to their writings. Also, the lofty place in which value theory has been placed has secured the operational aspects of valuation in an important place in capitalist society.

(*Continued*)
Marx's system in 1996 and declared there to be no future for the theory. Marshall claimed Marx misunderstood Ricardo. Edgeworth said "the importance of Marx's theories" were "wholly emotional." See F.Y. Edgeworth, *Papers Relating to Political Economy*. London, Macmillan, 1925, Volume 3, p. 275. Keynes called Marx a "luminary of the dim underworld of heretics." See Dobb, *op. cit.*, p. 142. Samuelson referred to Marx as a "minor Post-Ricardian." See Paul Samuelson, Wages and Interest: Marxian Economic Models. *American Economic Review*, 1957, 47 (December): 911. Mises said that "Marxism is against logic, against Science and against the activity of thought itself." Ludwig von Mises, *Socialism*. London, Jonathan Capl, 1936, p. 17. It should also be noted that Schumpeter called Marx "Ricardo's only great follower." See Schumpeter, *op. cit.*, p. 384.

[153]See Note, Marx's Theory of Surplus-Value. *Journal of Political Economy*, 3 (December 1894–September 1895): 219.

[154]See Weeks, *op. cit.*, pp. 17–18.

[155]See Dobb, *op. cit.*, p. 158.

As noted earlier, during the 19th century, the notions about the cost of production theories of value were under fire. The seeds of thought had been planted in several places that the notion that utility would be an important factor in determining values. It was left to the so-called "Austrian school," namely, the writings of Jevons and Menger to develop the new theory around 1870. This became known as the "marginal utility" school of economics or simply as the "marginalist revolution."

Predecessors of the Marginal Utility School

While it is true that Smith, Ricardo, Malthus, and others recognized utility as a characteristic of all goods, for the most part, utility did not impact their theories of value. One reason was that they only recognized *total* rather than *marginal* utility. However, there were some writers during the 18th and early 19th centuries who led the way for the development of marginal utility economics in the later part of the 19th century.

F. Galiani

This Italian economist was one of the first thinkers to develop a theory of value based on utility. In 1750, Galiani wrote a book differentiating between exchange value and use value on the basis of marginal utilities.[156] This theory went virtually unnoticed but had been mentioned in the work of Senior and Rossi. The latter wrote that "utility [was] the basis of exchange (market) value," in his 1843 book.[157] Galiani himself asked what determined the importance of a thing to an individual? He concluded that the primary factor was the "primary utility" of the thing (i.e., the importance placed on the object for the individual). Therefore, value was a subjective valuation placed on things by the parties to the exchange.

> ... the exchange value is determined by the subjective value of a thing to an individual; this is determined in its turn by two factors: (1) the importance of the need which the thing is capable of satisfying, and (2) the extent to which the need is satisfied.[158]

Galiani recognized that the concept of value in exchange was a relative rather than an absolute term:

> I understand that others say that a pound of bread is more useful than a pound of gold. My answer is: this is a disgraceful play of words, deriving from the lack of realization that more useful and less useful are relative notions, and that they are measured according to different conditions of individuals.[159]

[156]See Dmitriev, *op. cit.*, p. 189.

[157]See M.P. Rossi, *Cours d'economiqie politique*. Paris, 1843, 3 Volumes.

[158]As quoted in Dmitriev, *op. cit.*, p. 188.

[159]Quoted in *ibid.*

Regarding the paradox of value issue which would soon be taken up by Adam Smith, Galiani made the following comment:

> If then somebody wonders how is it that all the most useful things have a low value, while the less useful ones have great or exorbitant value, he will have to realize that this world is so well constructed with marvelous providence for our own good, that utility in general does not correspond to scarcity: indeed the greater the primary utility of a thing, the greater its abundance is, hence its value cannot be great.[160]

Other Predecessors

There were also others with early notions of utility and value. These names include Lloyd (1833), Senior (1836), Dupuit (1844), Gossen (1854), Jennings (1855), and Hearn (1864).[161] Some others were also credited with some early writing about utility. Barbon was amongst the earliest in 1690 as indicated earlier in this survey. Cournot noted that the price of a commodity "is fixed by the law of demand whether or not there is competition."[162] Mill was incorrect when he claimed that "the price of products may fall when production costs decrease."[163] J.B. Say concluded that use value, not labor cost, was the basis of value theory.[164]

In general, there was a good bit of preliminary thought given to utility during the era of the classical school. As a result, it is incorrect to suggest that the Austrian School "discovered" the demand side of the market with respect to value. In fact, the new contribution was not its discovery but the development of the theory, especially in mathematical terms, so as to better identify and test the basic premises of the theory of value.

The Marginal Utility Theory of Value

By the late 19th century, the leading concepts of value were split between use value, cost value, and exchange value. The Marginalists led by Jevons' *Theory of Political Economy* in 1870, Menger's *Grundsatze der Volkswirtschaftslehre* in 1871, and Leon Walras' *Elements d'economie politique* in 1874, rejected cost value as a useful value concept. This was actually an attack on Ricardo's notion that value existed in relation to cost. These books were followed by Wieser's books, *The Origin and Leading Principles of Economic Value* in 1884 and *Natural Value* in 1889 and Böhm-Bawerk's essay entitled "Grundzuge der Theories des wirtschaftlichen Guterwertes" in 1886 and in his books, *The Positive Theory of Capital* in 1889, and *Capital and Interest* in 1890. Marshall had joined this movement by 1879 in *Economics of Industry* and with Edgeworth's *Math*

[160] As quoted in *ibid.*

[161] These early contributors to the marginal utility theory are listed and discussed in several sources including Dmitriev, *ibid.*, p. 192; Stigler, *op. cit.*, pp. 314–317; Bell, *op. cit.*, pp. 399–418; and others.

[162] A. Cournot, Recherches sur les *Principles mathematiques de la Theorie des richesses.* Paris, 1838, as quoted in Dmitriev, *op. cit.*, p. 192.

[163] As quoted in *ibid.*

[164] As noted in Uhr, *op. cit.*, p. 17.

Psychics in 1881, the Austrian School as a movement had gathered enough steam such that Marshall's influential *Principles of Economics* (1890) contained a detailed survey of the marginal utility school.[165]

According to Stigler, the marginalists found three deficiencies with the Ricardian theory of value. These were: (1) that a special theory was needed for commodities with fixed supplies, (2) large labor costs would not cause high values on a commodity if the demand in the future was not forecasted correctly, and (3) labor was heterogeneous in supply and thus, labor could only be compared in terms of its output.[166] In Stigler's view, the disciples of Wieser and Böhm-Bawerk failed to advance the new theory and often confused it in their popularizations of it.

William Jevons

The conceptual breakthrough credited to Jevons was that he identified a mechanism for quantifying Adam Smith's use value. Specifically, he singled out "the final degree of utility" as the determinant of value. This notion was called "marginal utility" and required that all previous units be valued by the contribution of the last unit.

> I never attempted to estimate the whole pleasure gained by purchasing a commodity; the theory merely expresses that, when a man has purchased enough, he derives an equal pleasure from the possession of a small quantity more or from the money price of it.[167]

Jevons based his theory on a unit, which was not measurable. He claimed that "there is no unit of labour for suffering or enjoyment."[168] He also claimed that utility has no inherent qualities and could not be associated with a commodity in any physical proportion. Finally, he and others claimed that value was solely determined by the utility as well as, the disutility associated with the commodity.[169] As a result, the cost of production was irrelevant to the exchange value of any commodity.

Friedrich von Wieser

Following the subjective analysis of Carl Menger, Wieser went further in relating utility to exchange value.

> The price of an article never completely expresses the exchange-value it has for its owner. This depends, further upon the "personal equation" of money to him ... The "personal equation" of

[165]See Alfred Marshall, *Principles of Economics*. London, Macmillon and Co, Ltd 1890. This should not suggest that Marshall was a marginalist. As argued below, Marshall is generally regarded as the founder of the Neo-classical School of Economics, which combined notions of marginal utility and price theory with classical economic beliefs and theories.

[166]See Stigler, *op. cit.*, p. 320.

[167]William Jevons, *Theory of Political Economy*. London, Macmillon and Co, Ltd 1871, p. 20, as quoted in Dobb, *op. cit.*, p. 183.

[168]As quoted in Stigler, *op. cit.*, p. 373.

[169]See John A. Sinden and Albert C. Worrell, *Unpriced Values—Decisions without Market Prices*. John Wiley and Sons, New York, 1979, p. 57.

money is indisposable in every economy, in order that we may weigh against each other goods estimated according to their exchange value ... Every separate act of exchange depends upon it.[170]

Wieser claimed that the value of goods rested with the intensity of wants and with the notion of diminishing marginal utility, that any want can be satisfied.[171] Following Wieser, Böhm-Bawerk defined value "as the importance which a good or complex of goods possess with respect to the well-being of a subject."[172] In the end, value was determined by the amount of its marginal utility, which is subjectively determined by each individual.

Other Marginalists

Subsequently, other economists contributed to the marginalist theory. In 1893, Wicksell provided an "interpretation and critical appraisal" of value and found the theory incomplete as an explanation of market value.[173] He provided economics with the method of comparative statics and demonstrated that commodities sometimes are interrelated such that joint supply and demand problems can exist. But essentially, Wicksell was a part of the marginalist's movement.

Obviously, objects have a value for us only in virtue of their *utility*, that is to say, because of the enjoyment and satisfaction which they give us or—and this is fundamentally the same—because of the pain and discomfort from which they free us;[174]

Others have also had a considerable amount to say about the marginalist revolution. For example, the Russian economist, Dmitriev offered the following interesting jab.

[Marginal utility theory] is a subject in which everything is confused .... Most often authors completely avoid any precise definitions, and content themselves with general meaningless phrases.[175]

Clearly, this economist's perspective differs from most others. Irving Fisher claimed that utility was made synonymous with pleasure and that this definition might lead to conceptual problems.[176] Fisher's solution was to define a precise, mathematical, and marginalist definition of value:

The name utility-value of a commodity may be given to the product of the quantity of that commodity by its marginal utility or $x \star (dU/dx)$.[177]

[170]Friedrich von Wieser, *Natural Value* (1889), W. Smart (ed.), 1956 edition, pp. 45–50, as quoted in Dobb, *op. cit.*, p. 171.

[171]For a more complete discussion, see Bell, *op. cit.*, pp. 419–453.

[172]As quoted in *ibid.*, p. 442.

[173]See Uhr, *op. cit.*, p. 32.

[174]See Knut Wicksell, *Value, Capital and Rent* (1893) Translated by S.H. Frowein. Rinehart and Co., Inc., New York, 1954, p. 33.

[175]See Dmitriev, *op. cit.*, p. 182.

[176]See Irving Fisher, *Mathematical Investigations in the Theory of Value and Prices.* Yale University Press, New Haven, Conn, 1892, reprinted, 1925, p. 11.

[177]*Ibid.*, p. 19.

Finally, we come to Alfred Marshall, who attempted to reconcile Jevons with the classical school. His success led to the formation of the neo-classical school of economics.

Alfred Marshall and the 20th Century

Marshall noted that in Ricardo's *Principles*, Ricardo agreed that utility was "absolutely essential" in the determination of "normal value" although it could not be used in its measurement.[178] Marshall has also been regarded as a Ricardian in that he claimed that Ricardo tried to distinguish between total and marginal utility long before the Austrian school was conceived. At the same time, however, Marshall was sympathetic to Jevons' argument that utility is essential in the theory of value.

> Repeated reflection and inquiry has led me to the somewhat novel opinion that value depends entirely upon utility.[179]

Thus, Marshall was fond of noting that Jevons' claim that "labour is found often to determine value, but only in an indirect manner ..."[180] as an attempt to bring the two schools together. Consider the following passage from Marshall's book on this point.

> Perhaps Jevons' antagonism to Ricardo and Mill would have been less if he had not himself fallen into the habit of speaking of relations which really exist only between demand price and value as though they held between utility and value; and if he had emphasized as Cournot had done, that fundamental symmetry of the general relations in which demand and supply stand to value, which coexists with striking differences in the details of those relations.[181]

In a sentence, Marshall's contribution as leader of the new, neo-classical school was to integrate the marginalist revolution into a general theory of demand and supply. The neo-classical school could now reevaluate the theory of production with a modern theory of demand. As a result, neo-classical economics has virtually settled on a fundamental theory of value with both cost and utility components.

CONCLUSIONS

What conclusions can be drawn from this survey of the history of economic thought on the concept of value? What does history tell us for real property appraisal theory and practice? What are the links between modern real estate appraisal theory and the history of value?

First, the survey provides evidence that, without question, value theory in economics retains a central place in the development of economics as a science. Second, this survey as well as most economic histories on the topic demonstrate that the development of the concept of value has taken a very long time to unfold. The gems have been costly to obtain in that an exorbitant amount of writing has occurred on this single

[178] See Marshall, *op. cit.*, p. 814.
[179] Jevons, *op. cit.*, as quoted in Marshall, *ibid.*, p. 817.
[180] See Marshall, *ibid.*, p. 817.
[181] *Ibid.*

Table 1-1 Chronology of the Leading Contributors to the History of Value Theory

Period/Contributor	Date of major work
THE ANCIENTS	
The twelve tables	ca. 450 BCE
Plato	360 BCE
Aristotle	350 BCE
THE DARK AGES AND EARLY MIDDLE AGES	
(No developments)	2nd–10th centuries
EARLY MEDIEVAL ERA	
Doctrine of "Just Price"	11th–12th centuries
LATE MEDIEVAL PERIOD	
Thomas Aquinas	1261
THE MERCANTILISTS	
John Hales	1581
Gerard de Malynes	1622
Edward Misselden	1623
Thomas Mun	1664
EARLY POLITICAL ECONOMISTS	
Sir William Petty	1682
Nicholas Barbon	1690
John Locke	1691
John Law	1705
Richard Cantillon	1730
Charles King	1721
THE PHYSIOCRATS	
Francois Quesnay	1758
A. Robert Jacques Turgot	1766
THE CLASSICAL SCHOOL	
Sir James Steuart	1767
Adam Smith	1776
David Ricardo	1817
Thomas Malthus	1836
John Stuart Mill	1847
Karl Marx	1867
CRITICS OF THE CLASSICAL SCHOOL	
Samuel Bailey	1825
Robert Torrens	1821
Nassau Senior	1836
THE MARGINALIST SCHOOL	
Ferdinando Galiani	1750
William Jevons	1870
Carl Menger	1871
Leon Walras	1874
Friedrich von Wieser	1884
Eugen von Böhm-Bawerk	1889
Knut Wicksell	1893
THE NEO-CLASSICAL SCHOOL	
Francis Edgeworth	1881
Alfred Marshall	1890

topic alone. Third, it is apparent that the history of economic thought is filled with suggestions that economists themselves grew weary of attempting to settle the difficult conceptual and practical issues of value. Fourth, the thrust of much of the inquiry has occurred in two areas: the labor and cost of production theories and the demand-oriented utility theories. Finally, it appears as if the best minds in economics have settled many of the issues dealing with the concept of value; despite the fact that some remain for future debate.

Regarding the theory and practice of appraisal, the good news is that the underlying economic bases of the standard and revised methodologies are solid. It is clear that the three approach methodology did not casually develop. It is equally clear that appraisal methodology captures several elements of the value theory debate. The bad news is that the debate has produced some answers, which in the authors' view, do not seem to be currently implemented in real estate appraisal practice.

There are several links between real estate appraisal and economic theory. A poor understanding of economics can lead to unfounded conclusions regarding the practice of valuation. Theories are only useful if they can be tested and verified or tested and rejected. In the practice of real estate appraisal, some ideas seem to hold despite the theoretical and in some cases, empirical evidence, that such beliefs cannot be justified. With the development of new measurement tools, appraisers have increasing opportunities for better valuation results. A good understanding of economic theory about the meaning of value may be requisite to better valuations in the future.

Table 1-1 provides a time-line of the leading thinkers on the history of value up to the beginning of the 20th century. This table illustrates the lengthy journey these ideas have followed. Given this body of knowledge, the stage was set for the development of valuation theory throughout most of the 20th century. It was left to writers such as Bill Kinard to build upon the giants of the past and extend valuation thinking into modern times.

REFERENCES

Aqinas, Thomas, *Summa Theologia*, Q 77, Article 1.

Aristotle, *Politica*, Volume 10, 1257a.

Barbon, Nicholas, *A Discourse of Trade*. London, 1690. Reprinted and edited by J.H. Hollander. Johns Hopkins University Press, Baltimore. 1905.

Bell, John F., *A History of Economic Thought*. The Ronald Press Co., New York. 1953.

Bonar, James, *A Catalogue of the Library of Adam Smith*. London. 1932.

Bowley, Marian, *Nassau Senior and Classical Economics*. George Allen and Unwin, Ltd., London. 1937.

Boykin, James H., Real Property Appraisal in the American Colonial Era. *The Appraisal Journal*, 1976, 44 (July).

Buck, Philip W., *The Politics of Mercantilism*. Henry Holt and Co., New York. 1947.

Burton, James H., The Evolution of the Income Approach in Real Estate Valuation Literature: 1662–1969. Ph.D. dissertation, Georgia State University, 1978 (Unpublished).

Cantillon, Richard, *Essai sur la nature du commerce en general*. Henry Higgs.

Caravale, Giovanni A. and Tosato, Domenico A., *Ricardo and the Theory of Value Distribution and Growth*. Routledge and Kegan Paul, London. 1980.

Cournot, A., *Recherches sur les Principles mathematiques de la Theorie des richesses*. Paris. Nachette 1838.

Davenport, Herbert J., *Value and Distribution*. The University of Chicago Press, Chicago. 1908.

DeLisle, James R., Toward a Formal Statement of Residential Real Estate Appraisal Theory: A Behavioral Approach. Ph.D. dissertation, University of Wisconsin-Madison, 1982 (Unpublished).

Dittrich, Norman E. Accounting Implications of the Relative Objectivity of the Appraisal Process. Ph.D. dissertation, The Ohio State University, 1966 (Unpublished).
Dmitriev, V.K., *Economic Essays on Value, Competition and Utility*. Translated by D. Fry and edited with an introduction by O.M. Nuti. Cambridge University Press, London. 1974.
Dobb, Maurice, *Theories of Value and Distribution Since Adam Smith*. Cambridge University Press, Cambridge. 1973.
Edens, David G. Economic Aspects of Eminent Domain. Ph.D. dissertation, University of Virginia, 1962 (Unpublished).
Edgeworth, F.Y., *Papers Relating to Political Economy*, Volume 3. London. Macmillan 1925.
Featherston, J.B., Historical Influences on Development of the Theory of Value. *The Appraisal Journal*. 1975, 43 (April).
Feilbogen, Sigmund, Steuart, James, and Smith, Adam, in the *Zeitschrift fur die gesamle Stuartswissenschaft*, 45 Tubingen, 1889.
Finley, M.I. (ed.), *Studies in Roman Property*. Cambridge University Press, London. 1976.
Fisher, Irving, *Mathematical Investigations in the Theory of Value and Price*. Yale University Press, New Haven, Conn. 1892, reprinted, 1925.
Foley, Vernard, *The Social Physics of Adam Smith*. Purdue University Press, Lafayette, Ind. 1976.
Grissom, Terry V., Analysis of the Appraisal Process as Applied to Land Corridors. Ph.D. dissertation, University of Wisconsin-Madison, 1981 (Unpublished).
Haldane, R.B., *Life of Adam Smith*. London. Scott 1887.
Hales, John, *A Discourse of the Common Weal of this Realm of England*. 1581.
Hausman, Daniel M., *Capital, Profits and Prices*. Columbia University Press, New York. 1981.
Heimann, Eduard, *History of Economic Doctrines*. Oxford University Press. New York.
Hull, C.H., *The Economic Writings of Sir William Petty*, 2 Volumes. Cambridge University Press, Cambridge. 1899.
Jevons, William, *Theory of Political Economy*. London. Macmillon and Co, Ltd 1870.
Johnson, E. A. J., *Predecessors of Adam Smith*. 1937. Reprinted by Augustus M. Kelley, 1960.
Kaldor, Nicholas, Alternative Theories of Distribution, in *Essays in Value and Distribution*. The Free Press, Glencoe, Ill. 1960.
Kaser, Max, *Roman Private Law*, Third edition. Translated by Rolf Dannenbring. University of South Africa, Pretoria. 1980.
Kaulla, Rudolf, *Theory of Just Price*. Translated from the German 1936 version by Robert O. Hogg. George Allen and Unwin Ltd., London. 1940.
Kinnard, William N., *Income Property Valuation*. D. C. Heath & Co., Lexington, MA. 1971.
Knight, Frank H., *On the History and Method of Economics*. University of Chicago Press, Chicago. 1956.
Laird, John, *The Idea of Value*. Cambridge University Press, Cambridge. 1929.
Law, John, *Money and Trade Consider'd; with a Proposal for Supplyinq the Nation with Money*. Glasgow. 1705.
Lipson (attributed), in *Economic History of England*, Volume 3.
Locke, John, *Civil Government Works*, Volume 2.
——, *The Works of John Locke*, Volume 2.
MacFarlane, Charles W., *Value and Distribution*. Privately printed, K.S. MacFarlane, n.d..
Mainwaring, Lynn, *Value and Distribution in Capitalist Economies*. Cambridge University Press, London. 1984.
Malthus, Thomas R., *Principles of Political Economy*. London. 1836. Reprinted by Augustus M. Kelley, Inc., [Second edition], 1951.
——, *The Measure of Value*. London, 1823. Reprinted by Kelley and Millman, New York. 1957.
Marshall, Alfred, *Principles of Economics*. London. 1890.
Marx, Karl, Marx's Theory of Surplus-Value. *Journal of Political Economy* 3 (December 1894–September 1895), p. 219.
——, *The First International and After*. Vintage Books, New York. 1974.
McCracken, Harlan Linneus, *Value Theory and Business Cycles*. Falcon Press, Inc., Binghamton, NY. 1933.
Misselden, Edward, *A Circle of Commerce*. London, John Dawson 1623.
Plato, *Laws*, Book XI, Chapter 921.
Quesnay, Francois, *Notes sur Les Maximes*.
Rae, John, *Life of Adam Smith*. London. 1895.
Rauner, Robert M., *Samuel Bailey and the Classical Theory of Value*. Harvard University Press, Cambridge, MA. 1961.
Ricardo, David, *Absolute Value and Exchange Value*. London. Murray 1823.
——, *On the Principles of Economy and Taxation*. London, John Murray, Albamarte-Street 1817.

Rodger, Alan, *Owners and Neighbours in Roman Law*. Clarendon Press, Oxford. 1972.
Ross, Thurston H., History of Value Theory. *The Appraisal Journal*. 1938, 6 (April).
Rossi, M.P., *Cours d'economiqie politique*, 3 Volumes, Paris. 1843.
Rousseas, Stephen W., An Inquiry Into the Logical and Empirical Foundations of the Subjective Theory of Value. Ph.D. dissertation, Columbia University, 1954 (Unpublished).
Samuelson, Paul, Wages and Interest: Marxian Economic Models. *American Economic Review*. 1957, 47 (December), p. 911.
Schumpeter, Joseph, *History of Economic Analysis*. New York. 1954.
Scott, W. R., *Adam Smith as Student and Professor*. Glasgow. Oxford University Press, Glasgow University.
Seligman, Edwin R. A., On Some Neglected British Economists. *Economic Journal*. 1903, 13: 352–355.
Sewall, Hannah Robie, The Theory of Value Before Adam Smith. *American Economic Association*. Third Series, No. 3, August 1901, pp. 633–766.
Shapiro, Irving D., An Economic Basis for Real Estate Development. Ph.D. dissertation, Columbia University, 1961 (Unpublished).
Sinden, John A. and Worrell, Albert C., *Unpriced Values—Decisions without Market Prices*. John Wiley and Sons, New York. 1979.
Smith, Adam, *An Inquiry into the Nature and Causes of the Wealth of Nations*. Eleventh edition, Peter B. Gleason and Co., Hartforn, CT. 1811, p. 25.
Smith, Halbert C., Tschappat, Carl J., and Racster, Ronald L., *Real Estate and Urban Development*. Richard D. Irwin, Inc., Homewood, III. 1967.
Stewart, Ougald, *Biographical Memoirs of Adam Smith, L.L.D.* Dublin. 1795.
Stigler, George J., The Development of Utility Theory. *Journal of Political Economy*. 1950, 58: 308.
Uhr, Carl G., *Economic Doctrines of Knut Wicksell*. University of California Press, Berkeley, CA. 1960.
von Mises, Ludwig, *Socialism*. London. Jonathan Capl, 1936.
von Wieser, Friedrich, *Natural Value*. 1889, edition W. Smart. 1956 edition.
Walker, William H., Sales Price, A Surrogate for Market Value of Single Family Residences. Ph.D. dissertation, Louisiana State University, 1982 (Unpublished).
Walsh, Correa Moylan, *The Four Kinds of Economic Value*. Harvard University Press, Cambridge, MA.. 1926.
Weeks, John, Capital and Exploitation. Princeton University Press, Princeton, NJ. 1981, p. 53.
Weimer, Arthur M., History of Value Theory for the Appraiser. *The Appraisal Journal*. 1953, 21 (January), reprinted in American Institute of Real Estate Appraisers, in *Appraisal Thought: A 50-Year Beginning*. American Institute of Real Estate Appraiser, Chicago. 1982, pp. 164–178.
Weiner, David P., The Feasibility of Obtaining an Objective Measure of the Current Value of Land and Buildings for Disclosure in Published Financial Statements. Ph.D. dissertation, University of Michigan, 1972 (Unpublished).
Wendt, Paul F., *Real Estate Appraisal—A Critical Analysis of Theory and Practice*. Henry Holt and Company, New York. 1956.
Whittaker, Edmund, *A History of Economic Ideas*. Longmans, Green and Co., New York. 1940.
Wicksell, Knut, *Value, Capital and Rent*. 1893. Translated by S.H. Frowein. Rinehart and Co., Inc., New York. 1954.
Wollman, Nathaniel, The Development and Use of the Market Concept in Value Analysis. Ph.D. dissertation, Princeton University, 1940 (Unpublished).
Young, Jeffrey T., *Classical Theories of Value: From Smith to Sraffa*. Boulder, CO. Westview Press, 1978.
Zawati, A.K., The Reliability of Appraisal Methods in Determining Current Asset Value. Ph.D. dissertation, Louisiana State University, 1977 (Unpublished).

2. A Question of Value: A Discussion of Definitions and the Property Pricing Process

NICK FRENCH

Abstract

Appraisal is often said to be "an art not a science" but this relates to the techniques employed to calculate value not to the underlying concept itself. Appraisal practice has documented different bases of value or definitions of value both internationally and nationally. This paper discusses these definitions and suggests that there is a common thread that ties the definitions together.

In Life ... no new thing has ever arisen, or can arise
D. H. LAWRENCE (1936)

INTRODUCTION

Appraisal practice in America has historically been driven by the single discipline of finance. Real Estate Appraisal was seen as a subset of finance and treated accordingly, with definitive and rigid mathematical models being applied. However, a number of commentators recognized that Real Estate was distinct from other forms of investment, in as much as it was influenced by other factors such as legal interests, physical constraints, zoning restrictions, and the like. As such, they began to advocate that the role of Aprasial was much more interdisciplinary and that a new holistic approach should be adopted. This became known as the "New School of Appraisal Thought."

There were three principal proponents of the "New School of Appraisal Thought," Ely, Ratcliff, and Graaskamp (e.g., 1977) all from the University of Wisconsin. Whilst their work stemmed from the 1930s and resulted in seminal books such as *Urban Land Economics* (Ratcliff 1949), much of their work on definitions was by article[1] and was not published in a comprehensive form until the 1970s.

[1]Interestingly, prior to the 1960s there was not an academic tradition in Real Estate for the publication of articles; work was published on an ad hoc basis as working papers and professional briefings. Books were therefore the principal form for the dissemination of academic work.

It was against this background that William Kinnard published his seminal work, *Income Property Valuation* (1971) and in his preface he notes his work builds upon many others before him including Ratcliff and Graaskamp.

In this chapter, the value definitions of Kinnard and Ratcliff are discussed in context of the UK experience and the definitions adopted as professional standards in the 1990s (RICS 1996). Until 1994, the United Kingdom definition (of Open Market Value) was different to that used in the United States, however, there is now an internationally accepted definition of Market Value,[2] which is endorsed by both the Royal Institution of Chartered Surveyors (RICS) in the United Kingdom and the Appraisal Institute in the United States. This chapter therefore concentrates upon that definition (see on). However, it should be remembered that there is nothing new in appraisal theory; we are simply finding new words to express concepts that have been expressed in many different ways by many different people. We are not redefining the language of appraisal; we are drawing upon the experiences of others to help the profession understand the service that it offers.

PRINCIPAL CONCEPTS OF VALUE

Kinnard (1971) stated

> Value is a price. It is a price that would tend to prevail under specified market conditions as a result of the interaction of the forces of supply and demand. This price reflects the capacity of an economic good to command other goods in exchange. This is the basis for Value in Exchange. Value is also the present worth of future benefits anticipated or forecast to be receivable from the ownership of an asset. This is the basis for Value in Use. Rights in real estate represent ownership of an asset. Their Value in Use is measured in appraisal analysis by Investment Value. In the perfect market of economic theory, informed and rational buyers would pay no more, and informed and rational sellers would accept no less, than the present worth of the anticipated future benefits from ownership of an asset (discounted at market-determined rates). Thus, all transactions would take place at prices that reflected Value in Use, and represented Value in Exchange. Value in Use would equal Value in Exchange, and Price would be synonymous with Value.

This analysis corresponds to the view of Ratcliff (1949). Ratcliff recognized that there were different, interrelated, definitions of value. The principal three capital value figures that he identified as impacting upon real estate decisions were:

V_t: Price at which property is sold
V_p: Market value
Vs: Subjective value to owner

These also correspond directly to the definitions (or bases) of appraisal adopted by the RICS in the RICS Manual of Valuation and Appraisal (1996) [commonly

[2]The definition of "Market Value" was proffered and agreed by the International Valuation Standards Committee (IVSC) in March 1994 and has been universally adopted as the principal definition in the 35 member countries of the IVSC.

known as The Red Book], which contains definitions of *Valuation* and *Calculation of Worth*.

One of the enduring problems for the appraisal profession is that in many definitions (Ratcliff and Kinnard included), the word "value" is often used to describe distinct, albeit related, concepts. In this chapter, the following convention from the RICS is adopted:

Price (V_t)	is the actual observable exchange price in the open market
Market Value (V_p)	is an estimation of the price that would be achieved if were the property to be sold in the market, and
Worth (V_s)	is a specific investor's (or occupies) perception of the capital sum that he/she would be prepared to pay (or accept) for the stream of benefits that he/she expects to be produced by the property

In the language of economics Worth (V_s) can be considered as value in use, whereas Price (V_t) or Market Value (V_p) can be considered as value in exchange. The term value in use is also recognized in the International Valuation Standards (2000, p. 106), which states it is "the value a specific property has for a specific use to specific user and is, therefore, non-market related." It is also a term that is adopted by the accounting profession.[3] Confusingly, the International Valuation Standards (2000, p. 106), then lists "Worth" as a separate definition as specifically relating to investment property; it also calls this "Investment Value." It states it is "the value of property to a particular investor, or a class of investors, for identified investment objectives ... it should not be confused with the Market Value of an investment property."

This distinction between the worth to an individual "user" and a "particular investor" is unhelpful and unnecessary; both are concepts of worth and should be included in one definition. In the United Kingdom, the RICS has recognized that instead of clarifying matter, a proliferation of definitions actually confuses both the valuer and the user of the appraisal. As a result, the latest edition of the Red Book has decreased the number of definitions from 14 to 10.

APPRAISAL AND CALCULATION OF WORTH

However, as illustrated above, there are actually only three concepts of "value" these are market value, price, and worth. Although each of these can be related to a potential owner-occupier or user, it is easier to restrict the analysis to investment property. A rational investor will make the decision to buy an asset if the price in the market is equal to or below his/her assessment of the present worth of the future cash flow (rent and reversionary sales price), that is, likely (or predicted) to be produced by that asset. Conversely, all other things being equal, a decision to sell will be triggered at a point

[3] International Accounting Standard 36 (p. 102) "Value in Use is the present value of estimated future cash flows expected to arise from the continuing use of an asset and from its disposal at the end of its useful life."

where the price in the market is equal to or greater than the owner's calculation of worth. Thus, in the property market, what is often called "an appraisal" is the best estimate of the trading price of the building and "calculation of worth" is the individual assessment of worth to a potential purchaser.

Pricing Models—Appraisal

Appraisal is the process of determining market value. An estimation of the price of exchange in the market place. There is one internationally accepted definition of Market Value (IVSC 2001, TEGoVA 2000, and RICS 1996).[4]

Kinnard (1971, p. 11) stated, "If Market Value is to be estimated, it is a forecast of a transaction price that would most probably occur provided specified market conditions are met. If Investment Value (Worth) is to be estimated, it is a forecast of what a rational investor/decision-maker would pay for the right to receive the benefits of ownership under specified investment decision criteria." This corresponds to the accepted TEGoVA/RICS/IVSC definition of Market Value.

> *Market Value* is the estimated amount for which an asset should exchange on the date of valuation between a willing buyer and a willing seller in an arm's length transaction after proper marketing wherein the parties had each acted knowledgeably, prudently, and without compulsion (RICS, 1996 Practice Statement 4).

It is important that the link between "price" and "value" is fully appreciated, the latter is an estimate of the former. This can be illustrated by incorporating minor amendments into the above definition so that it reads as "price" [changes in bold].

> ***Price*** is the amount for which an asset exchanges on the date of **sale** between a willing buyer and a willing seller in an arm's length transaction after proper marketing wherein the parties had **have** each acted knowledgeably, prudently and without compulsion.

MARKET PRICE

The purpose of any method of appraisal is therefore to estimate the price at which it is expected that a property asset might change hands in the free market. It should be remembered that transactions do not occur at the point where most players in the market would assess its worth; the transaction occurs at the highest point. An appraisal is therefore endeavoring to determine the "highest" price at which the property will be sold.

This can be illustrated by reference to the market bids (by tender) for an asset. Assume that "The Asset" is placed on the market and that there are 52 players in the market. Each player assesses the "worth" of that item to himself or herself, some of them believe

[4]The European Group of Valuers' Associations (TEGoVA) has published a comparative study of the European Valuation Standards 2000 and International Valuation Standards 2001 on their Web site, www.tegova.org

Table 2-1 Market Pricing—Number of Bids at Each $ Level

	$0	$2	$4	$6	$8	$10	$12	$14	$16	$18	$20
Number of bids	1	2	4	6	8	10	8	6	4	2	1

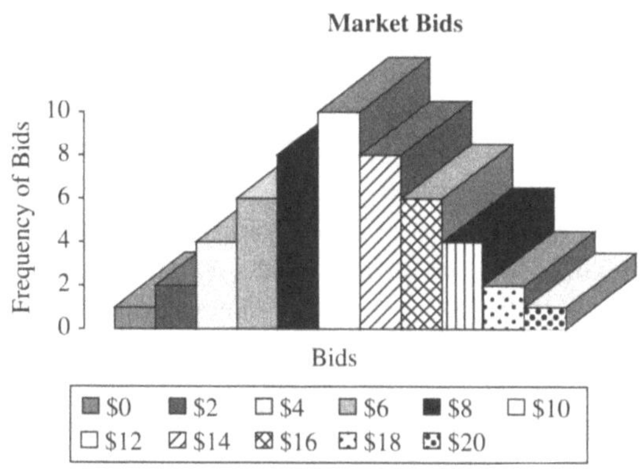

Figure 2-1. Distribution of Bids (worths) in the Market.

the asset to be exactly what they require and are willing to bid a high figure; others do not want the asset at all and will either bid zero or a low bid. Table 2-1 illustrates a potential pattern of bids. A number of players bid low figures, most bid $10 but one person bids $20. Each of the bids represents an individual's "calculation of worth," but a sale will occur NOT where the majority of the bids are concentrated but at the highest point. In a free market, the transaction will always occur at the highest figure. This represents the "calculation of worth" for the person who has the most bullish view of the asset/market. He/she is willing to pay $20 because they believe that the asset is worth that amount to them. The fact that other players do not share that view will not affect the sale price on that particular day. Their views, however, may influence our thinking on the appraisal of the asset at a later date (in this example, tomorrow).

In Table 2-1, it can be seen that one person did not "like" the asset at all and bid $0. Most people assessed its worth at $10 and the highest frequency of bids happened at that point. However, the price is determined (i.e., the exchange will actually happen) at the highest figure of $20.[5] Graphically, the market has performed as a normal or bell distribution and the sale is determined at the furthest point on the x-axis (see Figure 2-1).

[5]The "price" of $20 will only be achieved if the bids are not influenced by the bids of others. It assumes that the bids are "sealed" and that they do not have the information on the other bids. If they have full information about other bids (say at an auction) then the player who would be willing to pay $20 would only have to pay slightly more than $18 to outbid the next highest bid.

The person who has bid $20 obviously has the most optimistic view of that performance of that asset in the future. Only with hindsight will we be able to determine if their "view of the world" is correct or not. If, over time, the asset provides returns (or utility) in excess of a present value of $20, then the purchaser will have bought a good investment. If, however, it produces returns below the present value of $20, then it will have been a poor investment based upon the criteria that the purchaser has set himself or herself.

THE APPRAISAL PROCESS

A valuation model should reflect how the buyers in that market would assess the worth of the asset and identify what is likely to be the highest and best bid. It is that highest bid that will determine the market value of that property, not the consensus view.

Thus, if we look at our previous example, lets assume that that sale occurred yesterday and that the same asset, which sold at $20, is now placed back on the market today. We are then asked to "value" or "appraise" the asset. In other words, we are being asked to estimate the market value (price) of the asset.

Lets us also assume that we have no other information except what was observed in the market yesterday. The best "comparable" would be the actual sale price of $20. However, it could be argued that if ALL players in the market think and act as they did yesterday, then the highest bid will be at the $18 level. The purchaser yesterday is now the seller and thus their $20 bid must be discounted in today's market. It might therefore be reasonable to think that one of the two bidders yesterday at $18 might bid that number today.

However, that assumes that everything has stayed the same. The problem with markets is that they rarely stay the same. The asset might be the same, the players might be the same, but the way in which those players think changes with new market information. The big difference between yesterday and today is that a sale occurred at $20. Prior to the sale, the individual bids were based on a view isolated from an actual sale. Now that sale has occurred, it is possible that some of the players in the market will re-assess their calculation of worth taking into account this new information. In other words, their bids might be influenced upwards now that they have seen that the "price" in the market was $20. They may now bid up to, or beyond that figure. In other words, markets are eco-systems. They feed on themselves.

The task of the appraiser is therefore very difficult. They are attempting to identify not only the best bidder in the market today, but the level of their bid. This cannot be an exact science and as a result, until the sale actually occurs, it must be remembered that the appraisal is a "best estimate" of what that price might be when the sale is completed.

In deference to the difficulty of this task, many appraisers might choose to be conservative and simply state the under bid of the previous day[6] but in doing so they are abdicating their responsibility. They are being employed to give a professional expert

[6]This obviously assumes that the appraiser has verifiable access to the underbid information of the previous sale; this is not always the case and often the appraiser relies upon hearsay or conjecture to assess the bid level of previous sales.

opinion and that includes an interpretation of the market at the point of the appraisal. Just because it is difficult to assess the market, does not mean that the appraiser should ignore it and give an historic view of the underbid. If, the appraiser honestly believes that the market conditions are such that the best bid today would be $18, then that is a valid and appropriate appraisal. Similarly, if they believe that the sale yesterday would have influenced people in a positive manner and they believe that a $22 value is achievable today, then that is also a valid and appropriate appraisal. Likewise, if they believe the figure would remain at $20.

In other words, as the Market Value can only be an estimate, then a range of possible figures would occur. This would suggest that, contrary to the normal practice of providing a single figure, an appraisal would actually be a range of possible figures at a single point of time. In our example, we might say the upper limit of the range is $22 and the lower limit $18, but the most probable figure will be $20.

When preparing an appraisal, the appraiser is seeking to estimate market price; the price at which the property might be expected to transact on the basis of the given assumptions. In reaching his/her judgement, uncertainty will arise in the valuer's/appraiser's mind, either due to the difficulty of assessing the market itself or in assessing how the market would price the particularities of the subject property. The appraisal is actually a range based on probability.

The appraiser is instructed to view the transaction through the eyes of a hypothetical buyer. The appraiser must consider all possible buyers in the market in order to identify the "best" price likely to be forthcoming. In performing this task, the appraiser will be uncertain about the current availability of buyers, their current attitude to price, and how the players in the market would assess the attractiveness of the particular property as an investment. In order to produce the appraisal, the appraiser must weigh all the variables, using his or her skill and experience, and decide upon the most probable conclusion.

There are great difficulties in identifying accuracy in property appraisal. From the perspective of the Courts, judges commonly refer to the "correct figure." However, this is misleading. They actually are referring to a figure somewhere within a range that a number of competent appraisers would have reached. They will have no idea whether such a figure would, if tested by an actual sale at that point in time, would have proved "correct" or "accurate." (e.g., see Crosby 2000.)

For the purposes of this chapter we are seeking to identify the substance and the characteristics of the uncertainty that lies in the appraiser's mind as he or she attempts to assess the hypothetical purchaser's view of the variables involved. This is of interest because the appraiser is expert in the field and we are talking of his or her view of the variables that are driving, or will drive, price. In many circumstances this would be an insight of great value to clients. At present clients make decisions upon a single figure provided bay the appraiser, yet the client has no idea of how "certain" the appraiser is that this or her figure is "correct." It would be helpful to a client if the valuer was able to provide some measure of reliability to accompany the valuation figure (see French 1997).

In this chapter, therefore, we are trying to identify uncertainty in the appraiser's mind when he or she is attempting to determine their estimate of market price. Indeed;

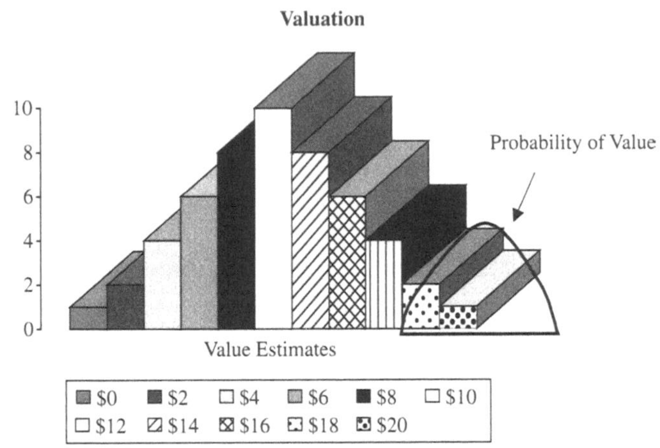

Figure 2-2. Market Appraisal in Relation to Previous Bids.

Ratcliff refers to Market Value as the probable selling price of the property. Figure 2-2 is an illustration of a "normal" distribution of the market. The horizontal axis represents the possible spread of "bids" in the market based on the appraiser's knowledge of current market players and conditions. The vertical axis is an estimate of the frequency of any individual figure.

However, the appraiser is concerned with assessing the "best" price. As with Figure 2-1, the transaction will happen at the high end of the graph. However, the appraiser will not know exactly where. There is, therefore, a second normal distribution at the top end of the graph that represents the appraiser's range of possible values (see Mallinson and French 2000).

Drawing on the work of Ratcliff, Kinnard (1971, p. 13) stated

> Market Value is a rather rigidly defined concept. Frequently, not all of its conditions can be strictly met. Yet single-figure value estimates are widely sought and required by buyers, sellers, lenders, taxing authorities, and courts to serve as a basis for significant decisions about interests in realty. One alternative way of looking at such a figure is to consider it a forecast of Most Probable Selling Price (MPSP). This is the price at which a transaction is most likely to occur under actually existing market conditions and actually prevailing levels of information on the part of buyers and sellers. MPSP is somewhat less rigid and idealistic a concept than Market Value.... When Most Probable Selling Price is estimated, the use pattern in terms of which value is estimated (or selling price is forecast) should be Most Probable Use rather than Highest and Best Use.

This can be shown in Figure 2-3, which is a representation of the value distribution at the top end of the graph illustrated in Figure 2-2. As before, the horizontal axis represents the possible spread of "bids" in the market at the transaction end of the market. This again will be based on the appraiser's knowledge of current market players

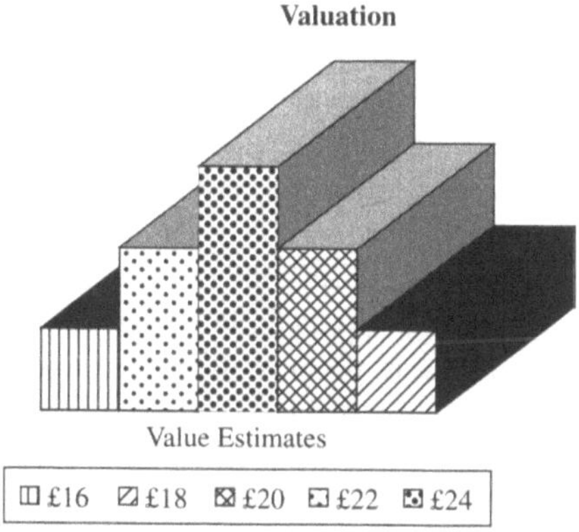

Figure 2-3. Most Probable Selling Price.

and conditions. The vertical axis is the probability of any individual figure with the total line amounting to 100%.

Thus the curve represents a 100% probability of the value lying between $16 and $24, with the highest probability of an individual paying $20. As drawn, the curve also shows that the probability of the value lying above or below $20 is equally distributed either side. However, this relationship may be skewed in certain market conditions based on the data available to the valuer/appraiser. The better the information the tighter the distribution and the smaller the range. If date is limited and poor the valuer will be less certain of the value estimate and thereby have a wider distribution of probable value. The graph is a representation of the "uncertainty" in the appraisal. Unfortunately, convention and to make their life easy, lenders, dictate that the valuer must provide a single figure. In this example, most appraisers would probably opt for $20. As previously discussed, lenders and other users of appraisals, generally fail to appreciate that it could be beneficial to their decision making process if they had a sense for how good the data is, that is, underlying the valuation and how accurate the appraisal will be as an estimate of price.

Ratcliff (1979) stated, "This recognition of the uncertainties in market value is to demonstrate the need for an explicit expression of this dimension of price prediction," yet 25 years later, across the Atlantic, the RICS was still seeking a method by which to address the subject. In the 1990s, the RICS published a report that looked at the way in which appraisals were being undertaken in the United Kingdom and how the profession could address the problems that arose from the property crash of the late 1980s. This report, the Mallinson Report (1994), made 43 recommendations on how to improve the service that appraisers provide to their clients. One of those recommendations (no. 34) was "Common professional standards and methods should be developed for measuring and expressing valuation uncertainty." This is the only recommendation that has yet to be adopted by the RICS (see French 1996).

CONCLUSION

From the analysis above, it can be seen that the way in which the results of the appraisal process are currently presented, as a single figure appraisal, does not lend itself to requiring the appraiser to provide a commentary or explanation of their appraisal. If the appraiser is truly an expert, then understanding the full extent of his or her considerations may be very important to a client who intends to act on the appraisal.

In this chapter, we have discussed "normal uncertainty" in appraisal. The production of most appraisals, and all property appraisals, is a process which involves managing probabilities. The appraiser's task is to produce the most probable price. In determining market price, the model adopted should mirror the thought process of the investors/players in the market. The information available should be used and analyzed in the same way as it would be by other players in the market. The Market Value (or price) should be determined by the thought process of the player in the market with the most bullish (optimistic) view of the future.

As Kinnard stated (1971, p. 12), "market value can be regarded as the price that a willing buyer would pay, and a willing seller would accept, with each acting rationally on the basis of available market information, under no undue pressure or constraint, with no fraud or collusion present. It represents value in exchange for interests in Real Estate."

It is perplexing as to why there is so much discussion on the definition of Market Value (as related to Real Estate) when we have such a clear exposition from over 30 years ago, which not only stands the test of time, but also applies internationally.

REFERENCES

Crosby, N., Valuation Accuracy, Variation and Bias in the Context of Standards and Expectations. *Journal of Property Valuation and Investment*, 2000, 18(2): 130–161.
French, N., Market Information Management for Better Valuations: Concepts and Definitions of Price and Worth. *Journal of Property Valuation and Investment*, 1997, 15(5): 403–411.
Graaskamp, J.A. *The Appraisal of 25 N. Pinckney: A Demonstration Case for Contemporary Appraisal Methods*, James A. Graaskamp. (1977). Landmark Research Inc, Madison.
IVSC, *International Valuation Standards*. International Valuation Standards Committee, London. 2001.
Kinnard, William N., New Thinking in Appraisal Theory. *The Real Estate Appraiser*, 1966: 2–13.
Kinnard, W. N., *Income Property Valuation*. Heath Lexington Books, Lexington. 1971.
IVSC, *International Valuation Standards*, International Valuation Standards Committee, London. 2000.
Mallinson Report, *Commercial Property Valuations*. Royal Institution of Chartered Surveyors. 1994.
Mallinson, M. and French, N., Uncertainty in Property Valuation: The Nature and Relevance of Uncertainty and How it Might be Measured and Reported. *Journal of Property Investment & Finance*, 2000, 18(1): 13–32.
Ratcliff, R., *Urban Land Economics*. McGraw Hill, New York. 1949.
——, *Valuation for Real Estate Decisions*. Democrat Press, Santa Cruz. 1972.
——, *Readings on Appraisal and its Foundation Economics*. Landmark Research, Madison. 1979.
RICS, *RICS Appraisal and Valuation Manual*. Royal Institution of Chartered Surveyors, London. 1996.
TEGoVA (The European Group of Valuer Associations) *European Valuation Standards* (2nd Edition), Estates Gazette, London. 2000.

3. Dealing with Measurement Error in Real Estate Market Analysis: An Application to the Assessed Value Price Index Method

JOHN M. CLAPP AND CARMELO GIACCOTTO

Abstract

Applied researchers are aware that errors in measurement for one of the explanatory variables can reduce or eliminate the accuracy of conclusions from the research. In real estate market analysis, this issue is prominent in two areas: (1) the evaluation of the accuracy of property tax assessments and (2) The assessed value method for house price index construction. This chapter proposes practical methods for dealing with measurement error as applied to these two areas.

Econometricians often focus on inferences about parameters of variables measured without error. However, even one variable measured with error introduces bias and inconsistency to the estimates of interest. In this study, we point out that auxiliary regressions can be combined with other readily available information to diagnose the extent of any "smearing" from variables measured with error. We propose several strategies to obtain bounds on the bias and report an application where even in the presence of badly measured variables the extent of bias is relatively small.

INTRODUCTION

Many areas of real estate market analysis must deal with the problem of measurement error in one or more of the explanatory variables. Two of these—monitoring property tax assessors and producing house price indices using the assessed value method of Clapp and Giaccotto (1991)—will be addressed in this chapter.

It is well known that the property tax assessor measures property values with error. Evaluation of the extent of this error, and evaluation of whether the error is regressive, neutral or progressive, is a matter of considerable interest to tax payers and to state officials who are charged with monitoring local tax assessors.[1] This chapter proposes simple, practical methods for dealing with measurement error when evaluating the regressivity or progressivity of property tax assessment.

The assessed valued price index method has been used in several papers, including Ling and Gatzlaff (1994), Jud (1999), and Clapp and Giaccotto (1991). In this method, the log

[1] William N. Kinnard, Jr., worked with assessed values in many areas of his practice. He often testified about the accuracy of the assessor's opinion of value. In anything he did, he always paid meticulous attention to the accuracy of his statements. Thus, he would have been very receptive to the methods proposed in this chapter.

of sales price is regressed on the log of assessed value and on time dummy variables: the log price index is the coefficients on the time dummy variables. But, measurement error in assessed value may cause bias in the estimates of the house price index.

The econometrics textbooks offer only two solutions to the error in variables problem. The first involves a priori information on the value of the parameter involved in measurement error. The second involves instrumental variables: that is, variables that are highly correlated with the true variable and uncorrelated with the measurement error. The problem for applied research is that the researcher is unlikely to have precise a priori information, although some range may be available as discussed below.

Most applied econometricians are aware of the need to use instrumental variables to identify the parameter on a single mismeasured variable (e.g., Shilling 1993). When many variables are measured with error, the results of Klepper and Leamer (1984) have been used to bound the coefficients of interest.

Relatively little attention has been paid to inferences, in the presence of at least one mismeasured variable, about the coefficients of variables measured *without* error, despite excellent theory provided by Chow (1957, 1983), Rao (1973), Garber and Klepper (1980), Fuller (1987), and by Erickson (1993), among others.[2] This research concludes that the estimated coefficients on the correctly measured variables are inconsistent. The inconsistency is proportional to the bias in the coefficients on variables measured with error.

This chapter proposes some practical solutions to the problem. Most importantly, we point out something that has been overlooked in econometric textbooks: a set of "auxiliary regressions" can be used to evaluate the extent of measurement error. These regressions involved the variables measured with error regressed on those that are not prone to error. They are simple, easy to do, and can reveal a lot of information about the direction and extent of the problem with measurement error.

The theory in this area could be applied to a broad class of issues such as inferences based on dummy variables for the introduction of a hazardous waste facility or spatial variables for proximity to a source of noise pollution. Similarly, the rapidly developing literature on hedonic price indices (Goetzmann and Spiegel 1995; Hill, Knight, and Sirmans 1997) uses well-measured time dummy variables along with poorly-measured variables for house and neighborhood characteristics; nuisance parameters are associated with the latter set of variables. Also, tests of asset pricing models rely on well-measured rates of return on individual assets or portfolios but a mismeasured market index as a proxy for the return on the true market portfolio. Our model can evaluate the amount of smearing from the mismeasured variables to the parameters of interest.

[2]For example, Greene (1993) concludes that "badly measured variables contaminates all of the least squares estimates" (p. 284) in unknown directions. A more elaborate analysis in Judge et al. (1985, pp. 706–709) reaches the same conclusion. Chow (1983) derives the auxiliary regressions, but fails to note their value to practitioners. Amemiya (1985), Davidson and MacKinnon (1993), Kennedy (1992), and Geraci (1990) omit discussion of the coefficients on the well measured variables.

The Theory of Measurement Error section of this chapter develops theory for the use of simple auxiliary regressions in which each variable measured with error is regressed on *all correctly measured* explanatory variables. We illustrate the theory by fitting Fairfax County, Virginia, data to an hedonic price index model (see section Application to House Price Indices), and examine the potential bias introduced by measurement error in one or two variables (see section Empirical Results). Our conclusions are presented in Conclusions section.

THE THEORY OF MEASUREMENT ERROR

A typical regression model is:

$$y_i = x_i^{*\prime} a + z_i' \beta + \nu_i \tag{1}$$

where y_i is the observed dependent variable for the ith observation, x_i^* is a $K \times 1$ vector of true but unobserved explanatory variables, z_i is an $H \times 1$ vector of correctly measured variables, α and β are, respectively, $K \times 1$ and $H \times 1$ vectors of coefficients to be estimated, and ν_i is an i.i.d. disturbance term uncorrelated with x_i^* and z_i. The observed x_i variables are:

$$x_i = x_i^* + u_i \tag{2}$$

where u_i is a $K \times 1$ vector of measurement errors that are independent of x_i^* and ν_i. The regression model, stated in terms of observed demeaned variables is:

$$y = X\alpha + Z\beta + (\nu - U\alpha) \tag{3}$$

where matrices with N observations are given by uppercase letters, vectors by lower case. Let $\hat{\alpha}$ and $\hat{\beta}$ be the ordinary least squares estimators of α and β. It is well known that both estimators are inconsistent. Define:

$$\Sigma_{ZZ} = \text{plim}\left(\frac{Z'Z}{N}\right), \quad \Sigma_{XX} = \text{plim}\left(\frac{X'X}{N}\right), \quad \Sigma_{UU} = \text{plim}\left(\frac{U'U}{N}\right), \quad \text{and} \quad \Sigma_{XZ} = \text{plim}\left(\frac{X'Z}{N}\right)$$

Then, the limit of the inverse of the partitioned matrix $(X\ Z)'(X\ Z)$ together with the probability limit of $(X\ Z)'(\nu - U\alpha)$ implies that:[3]

$$\text{plim}(\hat{\alpha} - \alpha) = -(\Sigma_{XX} - \Sigma_{XZ}\Sigma_{ZZ}^{-1}\Sigma_{XZ}')^{-1}\Sigma_{UU}\alpha \tag{4}$$

Thus, $\hat{\alpha}$ does not converge to α, and the direction of bias is not easy to discern, except when only one variable is measured with error. In this case, $\hat{\alpha}$ is attenuated (shrunk towards zero).

[3]It is assumed that all of these limits exist, and all inverses are nonsingular. Equations (4) and (5) follow from standard results on matrix inverses: for example, see Amemiya (1985, p. 460).

Bias of the Coefficients of Variables Measured without Error

For the variables measured without error we have:

$$\text{plim}(\hat{\beta} - \beta) = \Sigma_{ZZ}^{-1} \Sigma'_{XZ} \, \text{plim}(\alpha - \hat{\alpha}) \tag{5}$$

But $\Sigma_{ZZ}^{-1} \Sigma'_{XZ}$ is a matrix of coefficients from the "auxiliary" regressions of X on Z. Specifically, we define the kth auxiliary regression as follows:

$$x_k = Zb_k + \varepsilon_k, \quad k = 1, 2, \ldots, K \tag{6}$$

The estimated coefficient vector $\hat{b}_k = (Z' \, Z)^{-1} \, Z' x_k$ is unbiased for the $H \times 1$ vector b_k even though x_k measures x_k^* with error. Next, define the $H \times K$ matrix of coefficients, $B \neq [\hat{b}_{hk}]$, where $\hat{b}_{hk}$ is the hth element of $\hat{b}_k$, and observe that B equals $\Sigma_{ZZ}^{-1} \Sigma'_{XZ}$.

Now we can rewrite the bias in Equation (5) for the hth element of $\hat{\beta}$ as a weighted average of the kth row of B and the bias in $\hat{\alpha}$:

$$\text{plim}(\hat{\beta}_h - \beta_h) = \sum_{k=1}^{K} \hat{b}_{hk} \, \text{plim}(\alpha_k - \hat{\alpha}_k) \tag{7}$$

The bad news from Equations (5) or (7) is that even the coefficients of variables measured without error are affected by the large sample bias in $\hat{\alpha}$. But, there is also a good news story from Equation (7); if the badly-measured variables are uncorrelated with the correctly measured variables, then the bias of $\hat{\beta}_h$ will vanish in large samples. Alternatively, one may obtain offsetting $(\alpha_k - \hat{\alpha}_k)$ biases in Equation (7) forcing the sum towards zero. Finally, if the estimated coefficients in the auxiliary regressions are statistically different from zero, then it may be possible to obtain bounds on the β coefficients. We investigate this point in the next section.

Significant Auxiliary Regressions Coefficients

There are several strategies available for using the information contained in the coefficients from the auxiliary regression; all strategies use Equation (7). If reasonable bounds can be placed on the bias in the estimated α coefficients, then a bound can be placed on the bias in the estimated β coefficients. The auxiliary regression coefficients may show that large bias in $\hat{\alpha}$ has relatively little effect on $\hat{\beta}$.

Strategies for estimating the amount of bias in the coefficients on the variables measured *with error* (α coefficients) can be summarized as follows:

1. Use theory to obtain reasonable values for the α coefficients.
2. An upper bound on the percentage bias can be obtained from a priori information; presumably the researcher would not have used the X variable unless it were believed that some information is being added. As a reasonable rule of thumb, we suggest plus or minus 50% bias as an upper bound; that is, $\hat{\alpha}_{\max} = 1.5\alpha$ and

$\hat{\alpha}_{min} = 0.5\alpha$; thus, $[0.5\alpha, 1.5\alpha]$ contains the estimated parameter.[4] Then, it can be shown that the bias $\alpha - \hat{\alpha}$ lies between $-0.34\hat{\alpha}_{max}$ and $\hat{\alpha}_{min}$.

3. Gini bounds for the true alpha may be used when only one variable is measured with error. These bounds are $\hat{\alpha}$ and $1/\hat{\gamma}$, where $\hat{\gamma}$ is the coefficient on Y from the regression of X on Y and Z.[5]
4. Use an instrumental variables (IV) technique to estimate the coefficients. See Kennedy (1992) for a summary of these techniques and Shilling (1993) for an application to the measurement of risk in the FRC/NCREIF returns on real estate investments. Since instrumental variables are usually imperfect, IV is not a complete solution to the problem. But, IV regressions can indicate the direction of the bias in $\hat{\alpha}$.

APPLICATION TO HOUSE PRICE INDICES

The literature on house price indices provides one example where auxiliary regressions, Equation (6), are helpful. In this literature, interest focuses on the dates of sale and sales prices of single-family properties; both numbers are checked carefully by tax assessors who use this information to establish fair market values. In price index estimation, the dates of sale are used to form time dummy variables, further mitigating errors in variables.[6]

Errors in variables (and its cousin, omitted variables) creep into price index estimations because of heterogeneous location and property characteristics. But, the coefficients on the variables designed to control for heterogeneity are nuisance parameters. Thus, the main interest in the price index literature focuses on the coefficients of the well-measured time dummies. The purpose of this section is to develop estimation forms and data for the price index example.

The Hedonic and Assessed Value Models

The hedonic price index model is estimated with the following equation:

$$\ln S = f(\ln H, D1, D2, \ldots, DT) \tag{8}$$

where

S = the sales price of the property at time t (time and property subscripts suppressed), $t = 1, 2, \ldots, T$;

H = a vector of property and locational characteristics at time t;

[4]Garber and Klepper (1980) point out that the direction of bias in any α coefficient is difficult to determine when two or more variables are measured with error.

[5]Erickson (1993) proposes use of a priori information to set Gini-like bounds when the two error terms in Equations (1) and (2) are not independent.

[6]The day of sale is discarded and the month of sale must fall within the range of 1–12. Quarterly price indices further reduce any measurement error.

Dt = time dummies, each equal to 1 if the sale took place in period t, otherwise 0;
ln = natural logarithm.

Two important characteristics of this hedonic model are: (1) the implicit price of each locational and housing characteristic is held constant throughout the sample period; and (2) the regression coefficient on the time dummy, Dt, represents a logarithmic price trend, namely the log of the ratio of the market value (for any given H) at time t to market value at time 0.

Structural characteristics are typically measured with few variables such as square footage, number of baths, number of bedrooms, and number of fireplaces. The importance of controlling for the physical characteristics will become obvious, when it is noted that the taste for bathrooms and fireplaces has changed dramatically over the past 10 to 20 years. Measurement error enters because the quality of the house is usually unmeasured. For example, the kitchen may have been renovated or there may be a recreation room in the basement that is omitted from the analysis. Also, one of the key characteristics, square footage, is not available in all data sets.

The assessed value model substitutes the tax assessors' estimate of value at one point in time ($t = 0$) for the vector of structural and locational characteristics. Since there is some error in the assessment process, assessed value has been represented in the literature as:

$$\ln A = a + g \ln V + f \tag{9}$$

where A stands for assessed value; a is a constant intercept; V = true market value (most probable sales price); and f represents a random measurement error. If the parameter g has a value of unity, then the tax assessor treats high and low valued properties uniformly.

Since the vector ln H weighted by implicit market prices at time zero (the date of tax assessment) represents market value, V, Equations (8) and (9) can be solved and expressed as a linear regression equation:

$$\ln S = (1/g)\ln A + c_1 D1 + c_2 D2 + \cdots + c_T DT - f/g + e \tag{10}$$

The constant term is omitted from the regression to avoid perfect collinearity with the Dt terms. The "assessed value" approach to estimating price indices uses Equation (10) as the estimating equation; errors-in-variables enter in the usual way through the $-f/g$ term (see Clapp (1990) for more details).[7]

The Data

The database for our study comes from the County Assessors' Office of Fairfax, Virginia. We used about 49,300 transactions of single-family properties that sold from

[7]Note that assessed value is a cross section at one point in time; it may be viewed as controlling for cross-sectional differences in house size and location.

the first quarter of 1975 to the first quarter of 1992. These are all of the transactions with complete data. In particular, all transactions had data within acceptable ranges for sales price and date of sale.

We controlled for heterogeneous property and locational characteristics with: lot area, total rooms, bathrooms, fire places, age of the structure, and assessed value as of 1992. We used a geographical information system (GIS) to match the street address of the transactions with Census tract boundaries; a 1990 Census tract number was assigned to each transaction. This was done in order to test for omitted locational variables.

EMPIRICAL RESULTS

One Variable Measured with Error

Table 3-1 gives the results for a single variable measured with error. Biannual time dummies were used to reduce the number of price index coefficients that must be viewed.

The assessed value model has good explanatory power. The coefficient on log of assessed value (LNAV) can be compared to its theoretical value of 1.0.[8] The errors-in-variables model says that the coefficient (0.906) is biased downward. Thus, it is reasonable to conclude that the true value of the parameter is close to its theoretical value of 1. Confidence in the model is increased by plausible movements in the log price index (the coefficients on the time dummies).

The auxiliary regression with LNAV as the dependent variable has a small R^2, but the coefficients on the time dummy variables are statistically significant. These coefficients range from a maximum of 0.059 in 1977–78 to a minimum of -0.03 in 1987–88. Therefore, the range of bias can be bracketed using these two time periods.

Theory indicates that the downward bias in the coefficient on assessed value is about 0.10. Equation (7) brackets the bias in the coefficients on the time dummies between 0.00588 ($= 0.0588 \times 0.1$) and -0.00305 ($= -0.030491 \times 0.1$). These biases are approximately $\pm 1\%$ of the value of the estimated price index. If one were not confident in predictions from theory, a 50% downward bias would give a value of 0.91 for $\alpha - \hat{\alpha}$; bias in the price index coefficients would be between $+8\%$ (for 1977–78) and -12% (for 1987–88).

The Gini bounds for these data are 0.906 (the coefficient on LNAV, Table 3.1) and 1.013 (the inverse of 0.9877, the coefficient on log of sales price (LNSP) estimated from the regression of LNAV on LNSP and time dummies). The maximum bias estimated from these bounds is approximately $\pm 1\%$ for the same reasons explained in the previous paragraph. Likewise, the methods proposed by Erickson (1993), who assumes an interdependency between the error terms in Equations (1) and (2), do not broaden the Gini bounds substantially.

[8]If the property tax assessor is neutral, then the coefficient is 1.0; see the discussion of Equation (9).

Table 3-1 Price Index Models and Auxiliary Regressions

Equation	AV price index (3.3)		Hedonic index (3.1)		Auxiliary Regression (2.6)						Wald IV (3.1)	
Dependent variable	LNSP		LNSP		LNAV		LROOMCNT		LAGEOLD		LNSP	
Independent variables	Est.	*t*-Value	Est.	*t*-Value	Est.	*t*-Value	Est.	*t*-Value	Est.	*t*-Value	Est.	*t*-Value
D7576	−0.816	−303.8	−2.290	−172.5	0.055	6.321	−1.196	−175.7	−0.230	−4.3	−2.309	−177.0
D7778	−0.657	−324.0	−2.116	−163.7	0.059	9.000	−1.203	−185.4	−0.163	−3.2	−2.136	−168.2
D7980	−0.434	−212.3	−1.891	−147.3	0.057	8.723	−1.194	−184.9	−0.057	−1.1	−1.911	−151.5
D8182	−0.285	−120.7	−1.730	−133.8	0.036	4.721	−1.193	−182.3	0.043	0.8	−1.750	−137.6
D8384	−0.211	−132.8	−1.657	−131.5	0.018	3.468	−1.202	−193.1	0.015	0.3	−1.678	−135.5
D8586	−0.045	−35.8	−1.490	−119.8	−0.019	−4.732	−1.208	−199.5	0.075	1.6	−1.511	−123.8
D8788	0.229	201.9	−1.207	−98.5	−0.030	−8.349	−1.197	−201.6	0.118	2.5	−1.228	−102.1
D8990	0.398	325.4	−1.023	−83.5	−0.015	−3.920	−1.192	−200.0	0.309	6.6	−1.044	−86.7
D9192	0.341	181.2	−1.058	−83.9	−0.010	−1.672	−1.200	−192.0			−1.080	−87.1
LNAV	0.906	648.0										
LROOMCNT			0.502	72.7							0.483	70.0
LFPLS			0.322	109.9			−0.012	−6.4	0.718	49.2	0.321	110.7
LLAND			0.122	106.2			0.094	157.1	0.199	42.5	0.124	109.9
LBATH			0.307	67.5			0.358	155.4	−1.980	−110.4	0.332	77.0
LAGE			−0.036	−48.5			−0.004	−8.1	−0.260	−73.2	−0.037	−56.1
LAGEOLD			−0.039	−44.5								
Adj. R^2	0.943		0.8323		0.0067		0.533		0.3042		0.8319	
N-Obs	49,277		49,277		49,277		49,277		49,277		49,277	

Notes: LNSP, Log of sales price; LNAV, Log of assessed value; LROOMCNT, Log of number of rooms; LAGEOLD, Log of building age if greater than 20, otherwise 0; LAGE, Log of building age if 20 or less, otherwise 0; LFPLS, Log of number of fireplaces; LLAND, Log of square footage of the lot; LBATH, Log of number of bathrooms; D7576–D9192 are 1 if the transaction took place within the 2-year-period, otherwise zero. The Wald IV regression has −1, 0, +1 instruments for LROOMCNT and LAGE where the latter is not truncated after 20 years. All dependent variables have zero means.

Two Variables Measured with Error

Estimation of the hedonic model, Equation (8), introduces two sources of measurement error. This occurs despite the fact that all physical characteristics are measured accurately through periodic inspections. But, the total number of rooms is just a proxy for the correct variable, interior square footage. In fact, some hedonic models add number of rooms to square footage in order to evaluate the way in which the square footage is subdivided. Thus, total rooms, with its rather limited variation, is a poor measure of interior space.

Secondly, age is not well measured for older properties because the year built is reported by the current property owners. We introduce two age variables, one for properties built within the last 20 years and the other for properties built more than 20 years ago; the latter, LAGEOLD, is measured with error.

The auxiliary regression with log of building age (LAGEOLD) as a dependent variable reveals coefficients that range from -0.23 to $+0.31$. The estimated parameter on LAGEOLD in the hedonic price index equation is -0.039; no theory is available to determine whether this coefficient is biased upward or downward. However, if the estimated parameters is within $\pm 50\%$ of the true parameter then the amount of bias in the estimated price index can be bracketed at between -0.0259 and $+0.0090$. These percentage biases are 1% or less. Therefore, we conclude that no significant bias exist in the estimated price index because of the LAGEOLD variable.

The auxiliary regression for log of room count (LROOMCNT) revealed strongly significant coefficients. However, all the coefficients have about the same value, -1.20. Using Equation (7), we conclude that the amount of bias introduced by measurement error does not change over time; interest in the price index usually centers on changes rather than levels.

If one were interested in the level of the price index, errors in measurement of LROOMCNT would introduce very substantial bias; Equation (7) indicates that the amount of bias from this source could range from about -10% (for a 50% upward bias in the α coefficient) to $+26\%$ (for a 50% downward bias).

An instrumental variables approach suggested by Wald can be used to get more information about the amount and direction of bias when auxiliary coefficients are large and significant. The Wald IV approach is attractive to applied researchers because it requires no additional information; the variable measured with error is ranked and the instrumental variables is -1 for observations in the lower third, 0 for the middle third, and $+1$ for the upper third. Of course, an endogenous instrumental variable does not produce consistent estimators of the α coefficients. But, it does reduce the effects of measurement error (see Kennedy 1992, chapter 9). Thus, the Wald IV approach suggests bounds on the direction and extent of bias in the $\hat{\alpha}$ coefficients.

The Wald IV regression indicates that the coefficient on room count is biased *upward* by about 0.02 so that the quantity $\alpha - \hat{\alpha} = -0.02$. Equation (7) gives a bias of about $+0.024$, or 1–2% in the price index coefficients. Thus, even if one were to assume that the actual $\hat{\alpha}$ bias were greater than 0.02 by a factor of 2 or 3, the estimators of interest would contain small bias.

CONCLUSIONS

Auxiliary regressions can be used to diagnose the effects of variables measured with error on the estimated coefficients of correctly measured variables. In this chapter we have proposed a number of strategies for determining whether bias is present and for bounding the magnitude of bias. In the case of price index estimates for Fairfax, Virginia, the auxiliary regressions show little or no "smearing" of the measurement error when one variable is measured with error. Furthermore, Equation (7) may provide useful information on the direction and magnitude of bias in the coefficients on correctly measured variables in the presence of two or more poorly measured variables. Our data illustrate the use of Wald's instrumental variables approach to estimate the bias when a poorly-measured variable is strongly correlated with the well-measured variables.

REFERENCES

Amemiya, T., *Advanced Econometrics*. Harvard University Press, Cambridge, MA. 1985.

Atkinson, S.E. and Crocker, T.D., Econometric Health Production Functions: Relative Bias from Omitted Variables and Measurement Error. *Journal of Environmental Economics and Management*, 1992, 22: 12–24.

Chow, G.C., *Econometrics*. McGraw-Hill Book Company, New York. 1983.

——, *Demand for Automobiles in the United States*: A Study in Consumer Durables (North Holland Publishing Company, Amsterdam, 1957).

Clapp, J.M., A New Test for Equitable Real Estate Tax Assessment. *Journal of Real Estate Finance and Economics*, 1990, 3: 233–249.

Clapp, J.M. and Giaccotto, C., Estimating Price Trends for Residential Property: A Comparison of Repeat Sales and Assessed Value Methods. *Journal of the American Statistical Association*, 1991, 87: 300–306.

Davidson, R. and MacKinnon, J.G., *Estimation and Inference in Econometrics*. Oxford University Press, New York. 1993.

Dhrymes, P.J., *Introductory Econometrics*. Springer Verlag, New York. 1978.

Erickson, T., Restricting Regression Slopes in the Errors-in-Variables Model by Bounding the Error Correlation. *Econometrica*, 1993, 61(4): 959–969.

Fuller, W., *Measurement Error Models*. Wiley, New York. 1987.

Garber, S. and Klepper, S., Extending the Classical Normal Errors-in-Variables Model. *Econometrica*, 1980, 48(6).

Geraci, V. J., Errors in Variables, in *The New Palgrave Econometrics*, John Eatwell, Murray Milgate, and Peter Newman (eds.). W.W. Norton & Co., New York. 1990.

Goetzmann, W.N. and Spiegel, M., Non-Temporal Components of Residential Real Estate Appreciation. *Review of Economics and Statistics*, 1995, 77(1): 199–206.

Greene, W.H., *Econometric Analysis*, Second edition. Macmillan Publishing Company, New York. 1993.

Hill, C., Knight, J.R., and Sirmans, C.F., Estimating Capital Asset Price Indexes. *Review of Economics and Statistics*, 1997, 78(2): 226–233.

Jud, D., Price, Indexes for Commercial and Office Properties: An Application of the Assessed Value Method. *Journal of Real Estate Portfolio Management*, 1999, 5: 71–82.

Judge, G.G., Griffiths, W.E., Hill, R.C., Lutkepohl, H., and Lee, T., *The Theory and Practice of Econometrics*, Second edition. John Wiley and Sons, New York. 1985.

Kennedy, P. *A Guide to Econometrics*, Third edition. MIT Press. 1992.

Klepper, S. and Leamer, E., Consistent Sets of Estimates for Regressions with Errors in all Variables. *Econometrica*, 1984, 52(1), January.

Ling, D. and Getzlaff, D., Measuring Changes in Local House Prices: An Empirical Investigation of Alternative Methodologies. *Journal of Urban Economics*, 1994, 35: 300–306.

Rao, P., Some Notes on the Errors-in-Variables Model. *The American Statistician*, 1973, 27: 217–218.

Shilling, J., Measurement Errors in FRC/NCREIF Returns on Real Estate. *Southern Economic Journal*, 1993, 60(1): 210–219.

4. The Cost Approach and Functional Obsolescence

PETER F. COLWELL, WILLIAM N. KINNARD, JR., AND GAIL BERON*

Abstract

The cost approach in appraisal utilizes the concept of functional obsolescence as one of three components of depreciation. The theory of functional obsolescence is developed from notions about how present value and the cost-new vary across different levels of an attribute of a building as well as how the costs to cure functional obsolescence vary with changes in the attribute. The implications for appraisal practice are derived from the theory. A number of formulations of the cost approach are found that look different but are essentially identical. Reproduction cost estimates are discovered to be irrelevant, but replacement cost estimates are not. The theory justifies the use of a traditional replacement cost approach when dealing with functional obsolescence.

INTRODUCTION

Appraisers frequently use the cost approach to estimate the value of buildings. Unfortunately, theoretical justifications for the cost approach have not been available. As a consequence, specifications for estimating items as fundamental as functional obsolescence have been, at least, controversial. The purpose of this chapter is to utilize a theoretical analysis of functional obsolescence in developing some first principles of the cost approach. The theory that provides the structure for this chapter was first developed by Colwell (1991) and tested in Colwell and Ramsland (JREFE, 2003). This application of the theory allows the analyst to understand important components of the cost approach and to distinguish between reproduction cost and replacement cost methods. More importantly, this theory allows the analyst to focus on the role of functional obsolescence to the exclusion of the other two components of depreciation, physical deterioration, and locational obsolescence (also called external or economic obsolescence).

The discoveries in this chapter are both expected and unexpected. It is discovered that the traditional replacement cost approach is correct. This is not surprising. The most surprising discovery is that the magnitude of reproduction cost in a correct reproduction cost approach is totally irrelevant. That is, any magnitude of reproduction cost will provide the same market value estimate as any other estimate. To anticipate the

*The authors are grateful to Roger E. Cannaday, Joseph W. Trefzger, and an anonymous referee for providing many thoughtful comments.

reason for this result, we will show that reproduction cost enters the correct measure of functional obsolescence. So subracting functional obsolescence from reproduction cost causes these two terms to cancel out.

The chapter is organized into four additional sections. The next section Elements of the theory describes the elements of the theory, whereas the following section, A Theory of Functional Obsolescence develops the theory to the point where the various measures of interest can be found. The fourth section Cost Approaches of the chapter derives the reproduction and replacement cost approaches. The fifth and final section describes the conclusions that can be drawn from the analysis.

ELEMENTS OF THE THEORY

The theory in this chapter focuses on one type of depreciation: functional obsolescence. The theory's simplicity is partly due to holding physical deterioration and locational obsolescence constant at zero. Issues of physical deterioration are very significant; however, they do not pose difficult analytical questions. Issues of locational obsolescence as they affect building value have been previously explored in Colwell and Trefzger (1993). Thus, depreciation will consist only of functional obsolescence in this chapter.

Also for the sake of simplicity, we consider buildings with only one attribute, A, that varies across buildings. That is, all other attributes are held constant. One can conceive of A as being any number of things: the length of interior partitions, the number of bath fixtures, or the ratio of window area to floor area, or another similar attribute.

Present Value

The analysis is limited to income properties and proceeds without reference to utility. Instead, present value (PV) will be substituted. While it is understood that appraisal doctrine often refers to utility, these references are made outside of the context of the economics of utility functions and consumer choice. It is simpler to break with appraisal doctrine and just use monetized magnitudes like the present value of income than it would be to properly introduce utility. In addition, the use of present values is an appropriate choice if the decision-maker's problem is to maximize profit rather than to maximize satisfaction or utility.

Buildings come in all magnitudes of attribute A. Even when there is some optimal amount of the attribute A or some optimal range of As, the analyst will find all sorts of As, including As that are outside the range of optimality and therefore exhibit functional obsolescence. There are two explanations for this observation. First, buildings often have relatively long lives, so they may have been developed in another era when the prices, rents, costs, and technology were markedly different. Thus, the optimal A or As could have been markedly different from what today's standards would dictate. Second, developers may make mistakes regarding the A of the building they develop. Thus, even some new buildings may embody varying degrees of functional obsolescence.

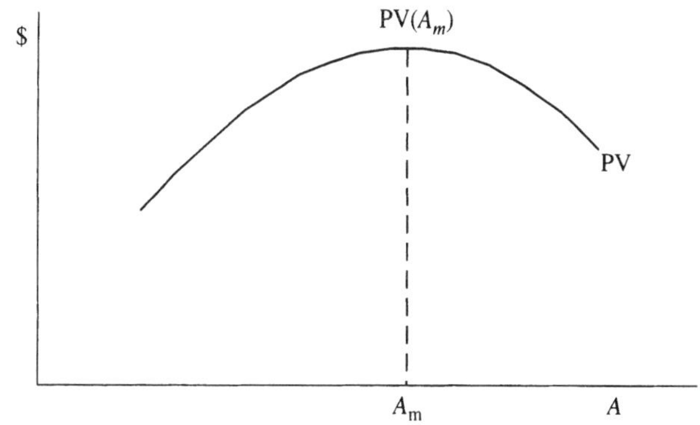

Figure 4-1. Present Value and Attribute Magnitude.

The PV of a building probably increases as A increases, and then decreases after the attribute A has reached some critical point. The PV must actually decrease if functional obsolescence due to an excess (i.e., also called a superadequacy, Boyce (p. 114)) can ever be curable. If an excess merely did not contribute to value, as indicated by Derbes (1998, p. 132), then the PV curve would be horizontal in the range of excess. In this case, there could never be value added by curing the excess (i.e., expending real resources to reduce the degree of the excess). In addition, if an excess merely did not contribute to value, then there would not be any reason to take the excess into consideration in a cost approach. The first-increasing-and-then-decreasing PV curve is illustrated in Figure 4-1 where A_m, measured horizontally, is the critical point for the magnitude of attribute A, and PV(A_m) is the PV associated with that point. For example, windows are nice because they admit natural light and may provide for a pleasant view. More windows increase the present value of the building to a point. Beyond that point the infiltration and low R-values of fenestration overwhelm the good features, and the present value declines. It is important, however, not to give this critical point too much importance. The critical point does not suggest the optimal magnitude of attribute A for the building, because this figure shows only the benefits of additional window area. Consideration of the cost-new will cause the decision-maker to systematically choose a magnitude below the critical point.

Cost-New

We assume that the cost-new of producing A has a straight line relationship with the attribute A. Alternatives to the straight line assumption could be considered as long as the cost curve is less concave than the PV curve. Figure 4-2 shows the cost-new as C. The positive intercept on the vertical axis represents the cost of the attributes that are held constant in this analysis. The positive slope of the cost-new line is the marginal cost of attribute A. It should be recognized that cost is defined as economic cost and includes normal profit (i.e., just enough profit to keep the entrepreneur in the activity of producing such buildings).

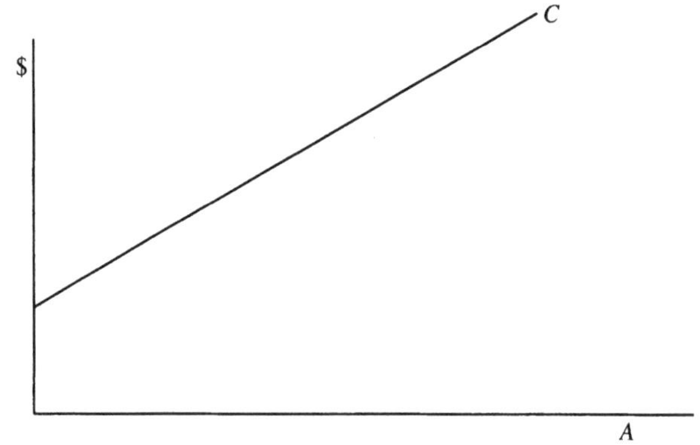

Figure 4-2. Cost-New and Attribute Magnitude.

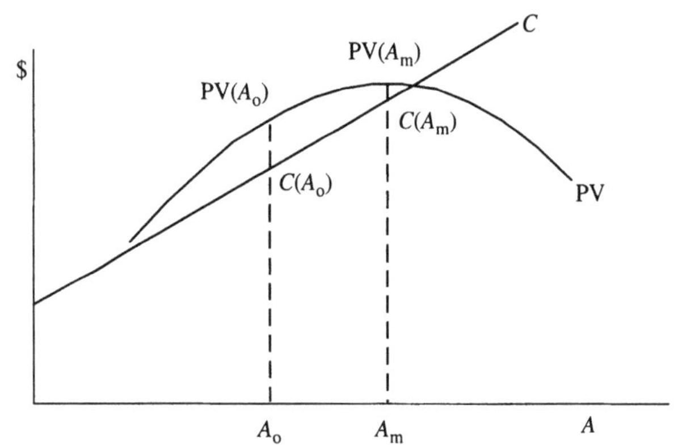

Figure 4-3. Net Present Value and Market Out of Equilibrium.

Net Present Value

Plotting the PV curve and the cost-new line together allows the analyst to visualize net present value (NPV) and the optimal magnitude of attribute A. Figure 4-3 illustrates a situation in which the PV curve is intersected by the cost function. The gap between the PV function and the cost function is NPV. Where the PV curve is above the cost line, there is positive NPV. Where the PV curve is below the cost line, there is negative NPV. The rational developer will want to maximize the NPV of A at A_o. Note that as in the earlier figures the attribute A is measured along the horizontal axis. One particular magnitude of the variable A is A_o. This is the magnitude of A, that is, associated with the maximum difference between the PV curve and the cost-new line measured vertically (i.e., it is associated with the maximum NPV). The maximum NPV is PV(A_o) − $C(A_o)$ [this should be read as the PV of A_o minus the cost-new of A_o].

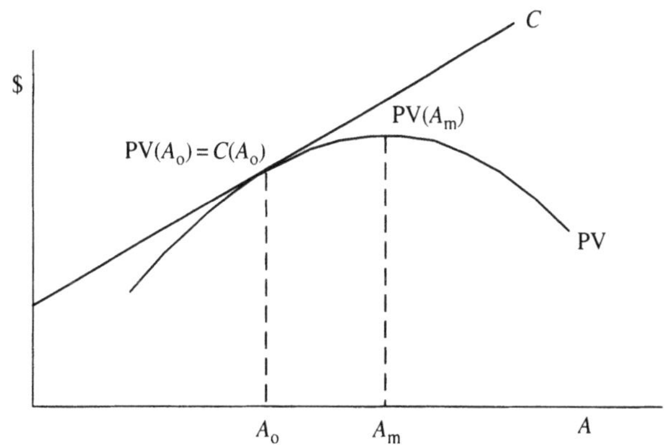

Figure 4-4. Market in Equilibrium.

Compare this magnitude to the dramatically smaller *NPV* at the critical point, PV(A_m) − $C(A_m)$. So the optimal amount of attribute A is A_o.[1] One can see that the optimal A is less than the critical point discussed earlier, at which PV is maximized (i.e., $A_o < A_m$). To emphasize the issue, NPV is *not* maximized for the building configuration that maximizes PV. To reinvigorate the windows metaphor, the developer should install fewer windows if additional windows add an increment to cost than if additional windows are costless.

The situation shown in Figure 4-3 is not an equilibrium in a competitive market.[2] If there were positive NPV projects, then developers would enter that market and drive these excess returns away. That is, the prediction of excess returns is a self-*defeating* prophesy. The entry of developers into the market increases the total amount of product available and drives down rents. In turn, the PV curve would be driven downward until it is just tangent to the cost line. This equilibrium situation is illustrated in Figure 4-4. In this equilibrium, the production of buildings with optimal A is associated with zero NPV. That is, $PV(A_o) - C(A_o) = 0$ in competitive equilibrium.

A THEORY OF FUNCTIONAL OBSOLESCENCE

As indicated earlier, there are a variety of magnitudes of attribute A that will actually coexist in the market. These nonoptimal As exist because of changes in the market environment, and/or because of developer error. The central question is, "What are these non-optimal (i.e., functionally obsolescent) buildings worth?" In the remainder of this chapter, we answer that question.

[1]The optimal magnitude of attribute A is found where the slopes of PV(A) and $C(A)$ are equal. That is, where marginal PV, PV′(A), equals marginal cost, $C'(A)$ (these represent the slopes of the curves shown in the figure). Marginal PV is the extra PV from one extra unit of A and the marginal cost is the extra cost from one extra unit of A.

[2]The term equilibrium means no tendency to change unless the market is hit by a change in some outside or exogenous factor such as a technological or regulatory change.

We use the concepts of reproduction cost and replacement cost throughout the remainder of this chapter. By "reproduction cost" we mean the cost-new of the building with the existing quantity of the attribute. By "replacement cost" we mean the cost-new of the building with the optimal quantity of the attribute. Note first that because we are abstracting from physical deterioration and locational obsolescence, value equals reproduction cost for new buildings if there is no functional obsolescence (i.e., if the existing attribute is optimal), while value is never equal to reproduction cost for functionally obsolete buildings. Second, for functionally obsolete buildings, value is hardly ever equal to replacement cost.[3] For buildings with functional obsolescence due to a deficiency, value is never equal to replacement cost, yet for buildings with functional obsolescence due to an excess, value also is *generally* not equal to replacement cost, even in the absence of physical deterioration and locational obsolescence. One special, but unlikely, exception is illustrated later.

Curable Functional Obsolescence

There may be a portion of functional obsolescence, that is, curable. Here, functional obsolescence occurs in a single attribute of a building. Therefore, the cure of functional obsolescence is at the margin. That is, we do not contemplate replacing the entire structure. A casual way to define curable obsolescence is the obsolescence, that is, profitable to remediate. A precise definition is that curable obsolescence is the obsolescence for which the incremental PV exceeds the incremental cost to cure. In the parlance of microeconomics, this is the range where marginal benefits exceed marginal cost. Boyce (p. 114) defines curable functional obsolescence as existing "when the demonstrable value added from completing the cure or correction equals or exceeds the cost to cure." However, to maximize the gain from the cure it is necessary to stop short of the level specified by Boyce. Instead, curable functional obsolescence ends, when the value added by a small increment to the cure no longer equals or exceeds the cost of that increment.

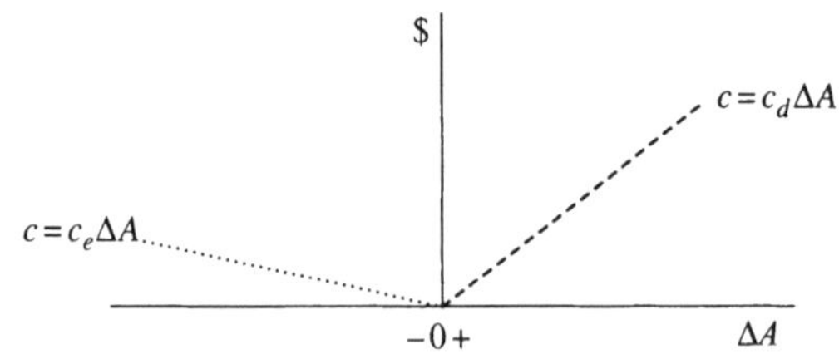

Figure 4-5. Cost-to-Cure.

[3]Of course, under our assumption of no physical deterioration or locational obsolescence, value is equal to replacement cost for buildings without functional obsolescence. In the context of our model, a building without functional obsolescence has A_o of attribute A. Looking ahead, see Figure 4-6. The magnitude of the attribute, that is, curable is $A_s - A_c$, and the magnitude, that is, incurable is $A_c - A_o$.

In order to proceed with the analysis, it is necessary to develop the cost to cure. The cost to cure a deficiency is ordinarily higher than the cost to cure an equally severe excess. While this is not necessarily the case, it is the case, that is, illustrated in Figure 4-5 by *c*. Initially, our focus will be on the cost to cure an excess (i.e., the part of Figure 4-5 to the left of the origin).

The cost to cure an excess is illustrated as being proportional to the amount of excess to be cured (i.e., costs increase at a constant rate with the amount to be cured). Similarly, the cost to cure a deficiency is illustrated as being proportional to the amount of deficiency to be cured. The reason that these costs are not modeled as increasing at an increasing rate with the amount to be cured is that doing so creates a "cost of adjustment" model. This is a model in which cures are protracted, with each period experiencing a smaller cure than the period preceeding it as the optimum building configuration is approached. Thus, the level of complication would be much greater if we were to allow for a "cost of adjustment" model. We gain simplicity in terms of having all adjustment (i.e., the cure) occuring at once by the assumption of proportional costs.

Market Value

Market value of curable functionally obsolete buildings is dependent on the cost to cure. Figure 4-4 can be combined with the cost of curing an excess from Figure 4-5 by placing the origin from Figure 4-5 on a PV point in Figure 4-4 that reflects the PV of a subject property with A_s, an excess of the attribute A. The result of combining these figures is shown in Figure 4-6. It is maximally profitable to cure the excess at the point where the gap between the PV curve and the cost to cure line is maximized (i.e., at A_c, the amount of the attribute after an optimal cure). This gap between the PV curve and the cost to cure line (i.e., between the dots in Figure 4-6) is the NPV associated with the cure. A seller of this building prior to its being cured will attempt to extract this excess return (i.e., positive NPV) via a higher sales price. On the other side of the market, buyers will compete for the positive NPV by increasing

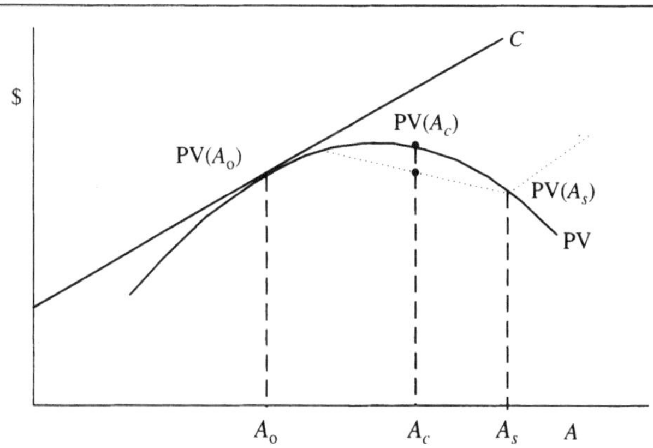

Figure 4-6. Curing an Excess.

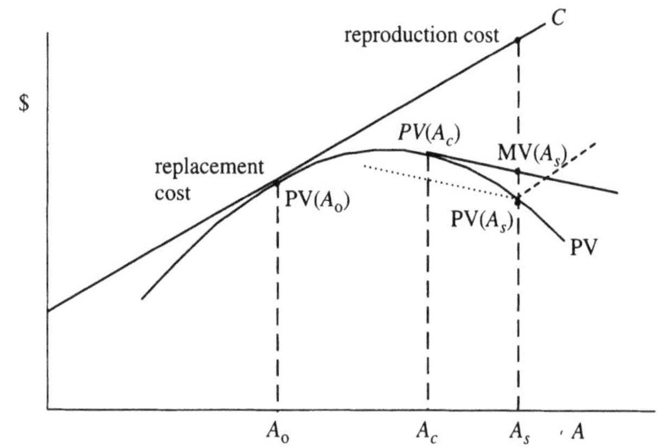

Figure 4-7. Market Value.

their bids until NPV is driven to zero. Thus, in equilibrium the value of the obsolete building must be the sum of the *PV* associated with maintaining the current configuration and the NPV due to the cure. As a result, there is no pure economic profit or excess return associated with buying the functionally obsolete, but partially curable, building and undertaking the cure.

Figure 4-7 shows another way to visualize the market value of the subject property with A_s of the attribute A. Note that the gap between the dots in Figure 4-7 is equal to the gap between the dots in Figure 4-6. The gap in Figure 4-7 is the vertical distance between the pre-cure PV and the straight line, that is, tangent to the PV curve having a slope equal to the marginal cost of curing an excess. This measure of market value can be generalized for all buildings with curable functional obsolescence associated with an excess of an attribute. That is, the market value is equal to the sum of the pre-cure PV plus the NPV of the optimal cure. Graphically, the straight line that is tangent to the PV curve and has a slope equal to the marginal cost to cure an excess is the market value function for all buildings with curable excesses.

The cost to cure is equal to the difference between the market value of the subject building and the PV of the cured building as follows:

$$c_e(A_c - A_s) = \mathrm{PV}(A_c) - \mathrm{MV}(A_s) \tag{1}$$

where c_e = the marginal cost to cure an excess which is negative as shown in Figure 4-5, thus the product of the negative marginal cost to cure and the decline in the attribute associated with the cure yields the positive cost to cure on the left side of Equation (1),

$\mathrm{MV}(A_s)$ = the market value of the subject building,
$\mathrm{PV}(A_c)$ = the PV of the cured building, and
$(A_c - A_s)$ is negative so that the left side of Equation (1) is positive.

The NPV of the cure is the post-cure PV minus the pre-cure PV minus the cost-to-cure. Substituting from Equation (1), then the NPV of the cure is as follows:

$$\mathrm{NPV}(\mathrm{cure}) = \mathrm{PV}(A_c) - \mathrm{PV}(A_s) - (\mathrm{PV}(A_c) - \mathrm{MV}(A_s)) \tag{2}$$

Simplifying yields

$$\mathrm{NPV}(\mathrm{cure}) = \mathrm{MV}(A_s) - \mathrm{PV}(A_s) \tag{3}$$

Solving for market value yields status quo PV plus the NPV of the cure,

$$\mathrm{MV}(A_s) = \mathrm{PV}(A_s) + \mathrm{NPV}(\mathrm{cure}) \tag{4}$$

which we believe to be true. Thus, Equation (1) is consistent with our beliefs about market processes. This result provides a formal proof that market value of functionally obsolete buildings is found along the tangent line as shown in Figure 4-7.

By substituting the NPV of a cure from Equation (2) and the cost of the cure from Equation (1) into Equation (4) and simplifying, we create an equation for market value that may be operational,

$$\mathrm{MV}(A_s) = \mathrm{PV}(A_c) - c_e(A_c - A_s) \tag{5}$$

Unfortunately, Equation (5) does not have the appearance of a cost approach, because it does not include either reproduction cost or replacement cost, C_s or C_o.

COST APPROACHES

The Replacement Cost Approach

Now, we can consider interpretations of the ordinary processes of the cost approach. Figure 4-8 shows one subject building, with A_s of A and $A_s - A_c$ of curable functional obsolescence. Let us begin with replacement cost, $C(A_o)$, and proceed with a traditional cost approach. Next, we subtract the incurable functional obsolescence and the cost-to-cure the curable functional obsolescence. The amount of the incurable functional obsolescence is the PV of the replacement building minus the PV of the cured building. The cost-to-cure is simply the marginal cost to cure multiplied by the difference between the cured attribute and the subject's current level of the attribute. The result is the market value by the replacement cost approach, if we assume that there is no physical deterioration or locational obsolescence.

This traditional replacement cost approach is developed symbolically as follows:

$$\mathrm{MV}(A_s) = C(A_o) - (\mathrm{PV}(A_o) - \mathrm{PV}(A_c)) - c_e(A_c - A_s) \tag{6}$$

where $C(A_o)$ = replacement cost, and $\mathrm{PV}(A_o) - \mathrm{PV}(A_c)$ = the incurable functional obsolescence.

Due to the fact that $C(A_o) = \mathrm{PV}(A_o)$ in equilibrium, it can be shown that Equation (6) is identical to Equation (5). That is, we have shown that the traditional approach to

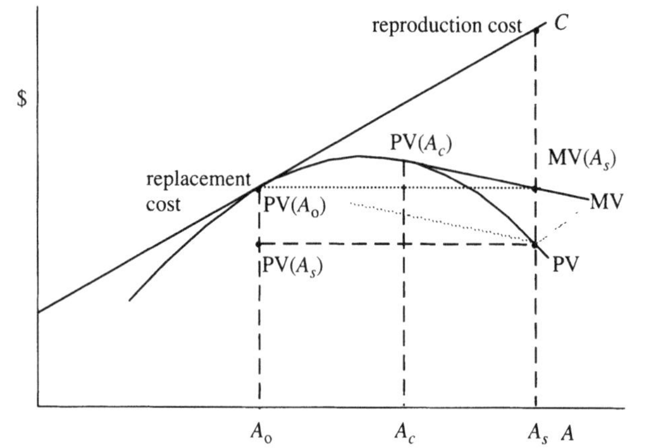

Figure 4-8. Cost Approach with an Excess.

functional obsolescence is correct in the sense that it can be derived from the theory. We can achieve a similar result with a graphical approach (see Figure 4-8). Start with $C(A_0)$, which equals PV(A_0). Then subtract (PV(A_0) − PV(A_c)), which is the same thing as adding (PV(A_c) − PV(A_0)), to obtain PV(A_c). Then by subtracting $c_e(A_c - A_s)$ from PV(A_c), we obtain MV(A_s). Thus, the graphical result also comports perfectly with the traditional replacement cost approach.

There are other equivalent ways to structure the replacement cost approach. Each of these begins with the replacement cost, $C(A_0)$. Suppose that we account for the fact that the PV of the subject may be different from that of the replacement building. We do so by adding the difference in the PV. That is, we add the PV of the subject, minus the PV of the replacement, to the replacement cost. The next step is to add the PV of the cure. This is the PV of A_c minus the PV of A_s. If there is no curable functional obsolescence, omit the previous and the next step. This next step is to subtract the cost of the cure. Symbolically, the entire computation is expressed as follows:

$$\mathrm{MV}(A_s) = C(A_0) + (\mathrm{PV}(A_s) - \mathrm{PV}(A_0)) + (\mathrm{PV}(A_c) - \mathrm{PV}(A_s)) - c_e\,(A_c - A_s) \qquad (7)$$

where PV(A_s) − PV(A_0) = the difference in the PVs for a status quo subject and for the replacement building, and PV(A_c) − PV(A_s) = the incremental PV of the cure.

To repeat, this approach indicates that market value is equal to replacement cost plus the difference between the PV of the subject building and the replacement building, plus the NPV of the cure. Since the two PV(A_s) terms have opposite signs and therefore cancel out, Equation (7) is identical to Equation (6), demonstrating that there is really nothing different about these two versions of the replacement cost approach. It is possible to find still other alternative but equivalent formulations.

There are other ways to represent these two versions of the replacement cost approach. For the first version, the traditional version,

Replacement cost
− the incurable functional obsolescence
− cost-to-cure the curable functional obsolescence
= Market value.

For the second version of the replacement cost approach,

Replacement cost
+ the difference in PV between the subject and the replacement
+ the difference in PV between the cured property and the subject
− cost-to-cure the curable functional obsolescence
= Market value.

The Reproduction Cost Approach

One traditional version of the reproduction cost approach is to subtract the functional obsolescence from the reproduction cost. That is,

$$\mathrm{MV}(A_s) = C(A_s) - F \tag{8}$$

according to a traditional version of the reproduction cost approach, where physical deterioration and locational obsolescence are nonexistent, F = total functional obsolescence, and $C(A_s)$ = reproduction cost.

If we were to follow the approach suggested by Laronge (2000), we could set the market value by the replacement cost approach (e.g., Equation (6)) equal to this statement of the market value by the reproduction cost approach and solve for functional obsolescence. Setting the two approaches to be equal to each other yields

$$C(A_o) - (\mathrm{PV}(A_o) - \mathrm{PV}(A_c)) - c_e(A_c - A_s) = C(A_s) - F \tag{9}$$

Solving for total functional obsolescence yields

$$F = C(A_s) - C(A_o) + (\mathrm{PV}(A_o) - \mathrm{PV}(A_c)) + c_e(A_c - A_s) \tag{10}$$

Equation (10) indicates that functional obsolescence almost equals the magnitude that Laronge derived. The difference is the extra middle term that Laronge omitted from his equation but included in his text (Laronge 2000, p. 329), incurable functional obsolescence. Equation (10) can be further simplified, because replacement cost equals the PV of the replacement property in equilibrium (i.e., $C(A_o) = \mathrm{PV}(A_o)$). Therefore,

$$F = C(A_s) - \mathrm{PV}(A_c) + c_e(A_c - A_s) \tag{11}$$

Thus, total functional obsolescence equals replacement cost minus the PV of the cured property plus the cost-to-cure the curable functional obsolescence. Substituting Equation (11) into Equation (8) yields a traditional reproduction cost approach,

$$\mathrm{MV}(A_s) = C(A_s) - (C(A_s) - \mathrm{PV}(A_c) + c_e(A_c - A_s)) \tag{12}$$

Equation (12) comports perfectly with the graphical analysis. While it is clear that reproduction cost cancels out in Equation (12), resulting in Equation (5), it is unlikely that a valuation approach could be considered a cost approach if there were no cost-new component in it. Thus, we are stuck with a cost approach in which cost-new is irrelevant. That is, it is irrelevant what magnitude is used for reproduction cost-new in Equation (12), because it enters twice with opposite signs.

There are other ways to approach a reproduction cost method. We can begin with reproduction cost as before, but we must include another step, the subtraction of the cost differential between the reproduction and replacement cost. Note that this term is utilized in Equation (10). $(C(A_s) - C(A_o))$ = reproduction cost minus replacement cost, called "superadequate construction" by Derbes (1998).

We can substitute reproduction cost minus "superadequate construction" for replacement cost in Equation (7) in order to develop a cost approach that begins with reproduction cost as shown in Equation (13). That is, $C(A_o) = C(A_s) - (C(A_s) - C(A_o))$, so substituting into Equation (7) yields

$$\begin{aligned} MV(A_s) = C(A_s) - (C(A_s) - C(A_o)) + (PV(A_s) - PV(A_o)) \\ + (PV(A_c) - PV(A_s)) - c_e(A_c - A_s) \end{aligned} \quad 13)$$

Two of the middle terms in Equation (13), $+ (PV(A_s) - PV(A_o)) + (PV(A_c) - PV(A_s))$ can be simplified to be $- (PV(A_o) - PV(A_c))$ which is incurable obsolescence, or "baseline obsolescence" according to Derbes (1998).

Equation (13), just like Equation (12), reveals that the use of reproduction cost adds nothing substantive to the cost approach but requires additional information. This requirement is trivial, however, because it does not matter whether the information is correct or incorrect. That is, Equation (13) simplifies into Equation (7), a replacement cost approach, because the two reproduction cost terms in Equation (13) cancel each other out. Although this conclusion follows from the algebra, it cannot be said to follow appraisal tradition. Derbes has written that "reproduction cost of the existing facility is the only reasonable and logical starting point in the cost approach" (Derbes, circa 1990). He suggests that beginning with reproduction cost provides some discipline in that the analyst must consider the improvements actually being appraised and then reveal the reasons for any diminution in value from that standard. While Derbes' view reflects a traditional approach, the algebra reveals that the analyst obtains the same market value estimate regardless of the magnitude of reproduction cost used. This result strongly suggests that a dependence on reproduction cost as a starting point is not mathematically useful.

When Value Equals Replacement Cost

There are circumstances under which a building with functional obsolescence will have a value equal to the replacement cost of the building. First, there must be an excess, since market value is always less than replacement cost with a deficiency. Second, it requires an excess of a very special magnitude. Figure 4-9 illustrates this situation. Note that for A_s of the attribute the building's market value, $MV(A_s)$, is equal to the replacement cost. The reason is that the difference in the PVs of the replacement property and

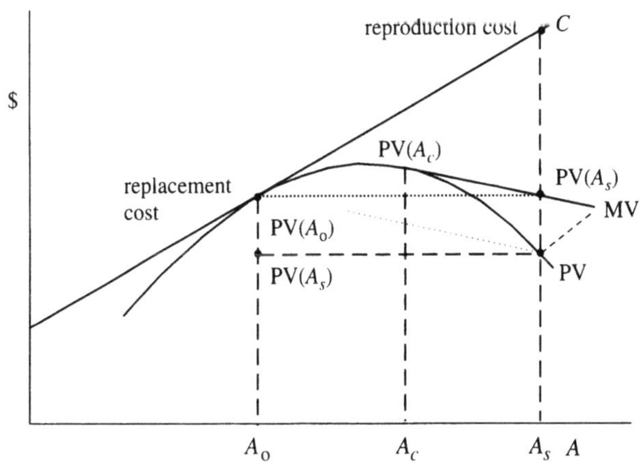

Figure 4-9. Value Equals Replacement Cost.

the subject is exactly equal to the NPV of the cure. This circumstance exists for one and only one attribute magnitude. So, while it is possible for a functionally obsolete building's value to equal replacement cost, it is also highly unlikely.

Deficiencies

At this point in the analysis, we have considered functional obsolescence due to an excess, but we have ignored functional obsolescence due to a deficiency. Deficiencies are addressed in this section. The bottom line is that the analysis is the same for a deficiency as it was for an excess. In fact, all the market value equations are as applicable for a deficiency as for an excess with the following change: the marginal cost of the cure for a deficiency must be substituted for the marginal cost of the cure for an excess.

There are some details that distinguish the excess case from the deficiency case. For example, reproduction cost is less than replacement cost with a deficiency, whereas it is more with an excess. Nevertheless the market value equations work as well with one as with the other, even though the signs on certain terms may change.

The graphical analysis is very similar with a deficiency and an excess. The primary difference is the use of a different segment of the cost-to-cure relationship. Figure 4-10 illustrates a subject property with functional obsolescence due to a deficiency, represented by quantity A_s of attribute A. The replacement building's PV and cost-new are the same as for the excess, but only because we have created a situation in which there is but one optimal new building configuration, A_0. If we had generated an optimal *range* for new buildings, the replacement configurations would be different for the excess and the deficiency.[4] The configuration of the cured property does differ in this model with respect to whether one considers an excess or a deficiency. For the deficiency, the cured property

[4] An optimal range can be the result of different cost structures and technology of developer/contractors resulting in various intersecting C lines. Alternatively, varying uses of the building would give rise to various PV curves.

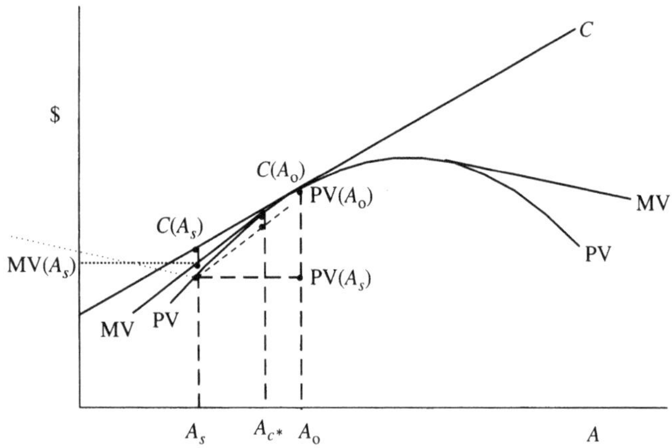

Figure 4-10. Cost Approach with a Deficiency.

has quantity $A_{c\star}$ of attribute A. If the marginal cost-to-cure with a deficiency should happen to be equal to the marginal cost new, then the cured property is configured just like an optimal new property. This could never be the case for a building with an excess. That is, there are no reasonable circumstances in which a building with an excess can be cured so as to produce the same configuration as an optimal new building. The case illustrated in Figure 4-10 is one in which the cured property has a smaller magnitude for attribute A than that of the replacement property. This is, due to the marginal cost-new being less than the marginal cost-to-cure a deficiency. Stallings has previously identified the situation in which the value added from a cure can exceed the reproduction cost-new of adding the same feature (Stallings, 28–29). Stallings suggests that this phenomenon may be attributed to some component beyond the cure item itself. We find that the phenomenon identified by Stallings will be the case when the marginal cost-new is less than the marginal cost-to-cure. This should be the typical circumstance.

The market value of a building that suffers from a curable deficiency is found on a line (see Figure 4-10) having a slope equal to the marginal cost of the cure, which is also tangent to the PV curve at $PV(A_{c\star})$. The market value of the subject building is found along this line; let us call it $MV(A_s)$. This magnitude is above the PV of the subject property, $PV(A_s)$, by an amount equal to the incremental NPV of the cure. This incremental NPV is also shown above $A_{c\star}$ as the gap between the $PV(A_{c\star})$ and the cost to cure line that was borrowed from Figure 4-6 and inserted into Figure 4-10, running through the $PV(A_s)$ point.

Just as with the excess, market value for the deficiency case can be computed as follows:

Replacement cost
− incurable functional obsolescence
− cost-to-cure the curable functional obsolescence
= Market value

CONCLUSIONS

The PV must rise, and then fall, as a building attribute increases if there is the possibility of both functional obsolescence due to an excess and functional obsolescence due to a deficiency associated with that attribute. This shape of the function creates a maximum PV. However, the magnitude of the attribute associated with this maximum is larger than the optimal magnitude. The optimal magnitude for attribute A maximizes *net* present value. In equilibrium, the maximum NPV is equal to zero.

Functionally obsolete buildings may be curable to some extent. Excesses can never be fully curable. Deficiencies are fully curable only if the marginal cost to cure equals the marginal cost-new. If, as one would suspect, the marginal cost-to-cure is greater than the marginal cost-new, then deficiencies also are only, at most, partially curable. There is no possibility for a building with a deficiency in an attribute to be cured to the same configuration as a building with an excess of that attribute. The value of a functionally obsolete building will reflect the PV of the building in its obsolete configuration plus the NPV of any possible cure. Approaches to valuation that include cost-new measures require us to go beyond this simple statement of value.

Regardless of whether there is a deficiency or an excess, the cost approach to the value of a building with functional obsolescence can proceed as follows:

Replacement cost
− incurable functional obsolescence
− cost-to-cure the curable functional obsolescence
= Market value

There are two differences between dealing with an excess and a deficiency. One difference is that the second term, minus incurable functional obsolescence, will be zero or negative with a deficiency. It can be positive, zero, or negative with an excess. The second difference is that the marginal cost to cure is different for an excess than for a deficiency. All other versions of the cost approach as it deals with functional obsolescence can be reduced to this basic, traditional, and correct version.

There are some surprising results from this analysis. Foremost among these is that the estimation of reproduction cost is mathematically irrelevant, since it cancels out. We can avoid it entirely by just starting the cost approach with replacement cost. At the same time, an expression for the total amount of functional obsolescence is presented that utilizes the reproduction cost:

Reproduction cost
− present value of the cured property
+ cost-to-cure the curable functional obsolescence
= functional obsolescence.

Another surprising result is that a building with functional obsolescence due to an excess (but not due to a deficiency) may have a market value equal to replacement cost, but this outcome is quite unlikely.

REFERENCES

Boyce, B., Real Estate Appraisal Terminology, SREA, Cambridge, 1975.

Colwell, P.F., Functional Obsolescence and an Extension of Hedonic Theory. *Journal of Real Estate Finance and Economics*, 1991, 4: 49–58.

Colwell, P.F. and Trefzger, J.W., Allocation, Externalities and Building Value. *Journal of Real Estate Finance and Economics*, 1993, 7: 53–69.

Colwell, P.F. and Ramsland, M., Coping with Technological Change: The Case of Retail. *Journal of Real Estate Finance and Economics*, 2003, 1: 47–63.

Derbes, M.J., Jr., Under the Microscope: The Cost Approach, manuscript, circa 1990.

——, Accrued Depreciation Redefined and Reordered. *Appraisal Journal*, 1998, 66: 131–144.

Laronge, J.A., Solving the Functional Obsolescence Calculation Question. *Appraisal Journal*, 2000, 69: 327–339.

Stallings, R.L., Functional Obsolescence: Chapter 4, *Depreciation Analysis*. SREA, 1984, pp. 1–37.

5. The Contributions of William N. Kinnard, Jr to the Field of Contaminated Property Valuation

THOMAS O. JACKSON

Abstract

This chapter addresses some of the many significant contributions of Dr. Bill Kinnard, MAI, SRA (1926–2001) to the field of contaminated property valuation. This field has continued to evolve theoretically and empirically due in no small measure to the professional and academic contributions of Bill Kinnard. These contributions are evident in Kinnard's published research and writings as well as his impact on practitioners and researchers in the field who have been, and continue to be influenced by him. This chapter profiles Kinnard's contributions in the areas of valuation methodology, market perceptions research, and research on the impacts of contamination upon real estate prices and values. In his work, Kinnard considered and attempted to reconcile research on price impacts with findings on market perceptions to better understand and quantify the impacts of environmental contamination on property value.

INTRODUCTION

This chapter is organized in three parts. In the first part, Kinnard's contributions in the general area of methods and techniques are profiled. This section discusses some of his pioneering work in developing methodological framework for valuing contaminated property and estimating the impact of contamination on property values. The second section reviews Kinnard's research on the perceptions of market participants with respect to environmental risk. Key market participants in this regard are lenders and investors. In addition, this section compares Kinnard's findings with respect to recent research findings on this topic. The third section provides an overview of some of Kinnard's empirical research on the effect of contamination on real estate prices and values. For comparison, this section will also discuss some recent empirical research on the price effects of contamination. Continued interest in the field of contaminated property valuation, as pioneered by Kinnard and others, is evidenced by the large body of research published in several professional and academic journals (Jackson 2001a).

METHODS AND TECHNIQUES FOR VALUING CONTAMINATED PROPERTY

Kinnard's early thinking on contaminated property valuation methods is represented in a short article in the now discontinued *Environmental Watch* publication by the Appraisal Institute (Kinnard 1989). Therein, Kinnard cautions appraisers about the complexity of assignments involving the measurement of stigma impacts on property value, but notes that "appraisers are trained to identify and measure market behavior." Further, it is this market behavior and perceptions of hazards that produce the "stigma effect," according to Kinnard. In analyzing the effect of proximity to hazardous sites. Within the context of appraisal methodology, Kinnard maintains that analyzing proximity effects is akin to "identifying, measuring and then applying a location adjustment" (Kinnard 1989).

There are five elements in the analysis recommended by Kinnard (1989): (1) sales price comparisons, using inflation adjusted sales price unit measures; (2) sales volume analysis, since as Kinnard asserts it is "much more common for sales volume rather than sales price to decline" in response to environmental contamination, (3) days on market, or the potential lengthening of the turnover period for impacted properties; (4) comparative price trends between the potentially impacted area and more distant "control" areas; and (5) an analysis of the distance and strength of potential proximity impacts through some form of regression analysis. In the latter analysis, Kinnard recommends that any distance related impacts should be studied over time, as an "interactive time–distance relationship."

In 1991, the Appraisal Institute sponsored a symposium entitled "Measuring the Effects of Hazardous Materials on Real Estate Values: Techniques and Applications." The event was organized by Bill Kinnard and he contributed his research and thinking to the symposium and its published proceedings (Kinnard 1992). Through this forum, Kinnard (1992) stated that there are three main measures of market value loss due to contamination: (1) *cost to correct*, or the cost to remediate a site, which he notes is primarily a task for trained professionals (environmental engineers) who can detect contamination and develop a corrective action plan in compliance with appropriate regulatory standards; (2) *reduced marketability*, reflecting a decrease in demand and downward shift in the demand curve for a particular category of properties; and (3) *reduced net operating income (NOI)*, since rental and occupancy levels can decrease and operating expenses can increase in response to contamination. Kinnard also notes that increased risk translates into increased discount rates and capitalization rates that in combination with reduced NOI result in reduced property value. Arguably, decreased occupancies are a form of reduced marketability and increases in perceived risk, albeit by another category of market participants, the tenants. Increased operating expenses could also be related to the cost to correct element insofar as they reflect remediation costs. Interestingly, in this period of research, approximately 10 years ago, Kinnard observes that "lending institutions completely avoid contaminated properties and those suspected of being contaminated" (Kinnard 1992, p. 3). Kinnard and others later found this situation to have changed, as will be discussed in the section on market perceptions, below.

With respect to specific methods for "measuring reduced property values," Kinnard (1992) suggests: paired sales or sale–resale analysis; valuation by analogy (similar to today's case studies analysis (Jackson and Bell 2002); study of "distance zones" from the contamination source; and comparison of trends (with control areas). Kinnard recommends that when sufficient data are available, regression analysis should be performed, in linear or log-linear format. Kinnard also discusses the use of survey research techniques, but cautions that proper controls should be employed to avoid misapplication and misinterpretation. Kinnard discourages what he refers to as "a judgment model in the abstract," based on assumptions and the logical reasoning of the "expert." Kinnard strongly recommends empirical models based on "bona fide market data." Lastly, Kinnard underscores the importance of "perceptions of risk and uncertainty" as the driving forces in explaining and predicting market reactions to contamination and its effect on property value.

More recently, Kinnard and Worzala (1999) surveyed appraisers to determine which methods were being used in practice to value contaminated properties. They note that the literature on contaminated property valuation, and especially the early literature, primarily emphasized income capitalization, with adjustments to discount and capitalization rates, as the preferred method to value contaminated properties. In this approach, Kinnard and Worzala point out that the rates are adjusted upwards to account for the perception of increased risk due to contamination, as also reflected in reduced loan amounts, higher interest rates, and higher required equity rates of return. One of the reasons they attribute to this early reliance on income capitalization techniques was the lack of market transactions involving contaminated properties. More recently, they found that United States and Canadian appraisers are using sales comparison analysis (80%) nearly as frequently as income techniques (79%). There were 86 usable responses to the survey, for a response rate of 43%. Within the income capitalization approach, the most frequently selected adjustments were to increase the capitalization rate (70%), increase the discount rate (67%), and reduce income (60%). More respondents preferred direct capitalization (72%) than discounted cash flow analysis (64%).

In summary, over the past 10 years Kinnard has espoused and monitored the changing methods and techniques for valuing contaminated property. In his work in this area, Kinnard has established a framework that links environmental contamination to decreased demand attributable to increased perceptions of risk by market participants. The measurement of the most elusive of these effects, environmental stigma, is to be accomplished with "bona fide" market data, using variations of traditional valuation techniques as well as more sophisticated statistical analyses, when data is of sufficient quality and quantity. Two primary analyses are discussed: "proximity analysis," using multiple regression analysis to ascertain the impacts of distance on price and value; and "comparative analysis," using a control area that matches the subject, or impacted, area. In a subsequent section of this chapter, Kinnard's empirical research and findings using these techniques are reviewed.

MARKET PERCEPTIONS OF ENVIRONMENTAL RISK

In the view of Kinnard and others, the perceptions of relevant and key market participants underlie the impacts of contamination on property value. As the market perceives increased risk and uncertainty due to a property's environmental condition, the value of the property tends to decline. For commercial and industrial properties, this effect is manifested in environmental risk premiums in capitalization and discount rates. For residential properties, lower sales prices are due to perceived uncertainties about potential health effects and other factors. As Kinnard's research shows, the perceptions of key market participants vary with the type of contamination and its conveyance, such as soil or groundwater.

Worzala and Kinnard (1997) observe that although financing for a contaminated property was "virtually impossible" to obtain in the 1980s, mortgage lenders' perceptions of risk with respect to certain types of contamination have changed over time, and as a result loans on contaminated properties are obtainable. Reporting on a 1996 survey of 145 lenders and investors, Worzala and Kinnard found significant variation in the perceptions of environmental risk due to the type of contamination. Their survey addressed the locale (conveyance) of contamination, type of contamination for source site properties and the effect on lender and investor risk perceptions for properties near various types of contamination. Of the three possible contamination conveyance types/locales—groundwater, soil, and building, investors and lenders were most willing to lend or invest on a property with building contamination and least willing to lend or invest on properties with groundwater contamination. Soil contamination was perceived as only slightly less risky than groundwater contamination, with 11.3% willing to lend or invest.

Comparing different types of contamination, Worzala and Kinnard found that lenders and investors were most willing to lend or invest in properties known to be contaminated with asbestos (26.5% answering "yes" or "probably") and underground storage tanks (28.7%). They were least likely to invest/lend (highest perceived risk) on properties with volatile chemicals (5.2%) and toxic chemicals (4.3%). The finding about asbestos is consistent with the finding on building contamination, as this type of contamination is considered somewhat benign by the market. The general order of these perceived risks were similar for investors and lenders. Worzala and Kinnard assess these same risks for properties "alleged" to be contaminated rather than properties "known" to be contaminated. Similar perceptions of environmental risk are found.

Lastly, they gauge the willingness of their respondents to lend or invest on properties within 300 feet of a variety of potential environmental disamenities. Least perceived risk, and greatest willingness to lend and invest, was found for proximity to such potential environmental issues as high traffic streets (55.7% willing to lend or invest) and natural gas lines (24.3% willing to lend or invest). Greatest perceived lending and investment risk was found for proximity to radioactive materials sites and for land contaminated by radioactive materials (0.0% willing to lend or invest). As with the other findings of the Worzala and Kinnard survey, these results show the wide range of perceptions held by real estate lenders and investors with respect to environmental contamination related issues.

Subsequently, the results of 1996 Kinnard and Worzala surveys of US investors and lenders were compared to survey from lenders and investors in New Zealand (Bond et al. 1998). Bond obtained responses from 21 New Zealand lenders and 48 investors using similar questions to that of the Kinnard and Worzala surveys. Bond's survey responses indicated that lenders and investors in New Zealand had less experience with contaminated properties. In the United States, Kinnard and Worzala found that 85% of lenders and 75% of investors had invested or lent on a contaminated property, while in New Zealand Bond found only 45% of lenders and 39% of investors had a similar level of experience with these properties. On the other hand, with respect to perceived environmental risk, the comparative results indicated that more (84%) of the New Zealand lender respondents, would lend on a property with "known" contamination than in the United States (51%). Bond's survey also found that more New Zealand investors (73%) would invest on a property "known" to be contaminated than would those in the United States, where Kinnard and Worzala found 53% of their investor respondents willing to do so. These results suggest that the less experienced New Zealand market participants are nonetheless not deterred from making loans and investing in contaminated properties to the same extent as their counterparts in the United States. Lastly, the New Zealand lenders and investors perceive radioactive materials as the highest risk, with asbestos and underground storage tanks as having the least perceived risk. These findings parallel those from the Kinnard and Worzala (1997) surveys of US lenders and investors, as previously discussed.

For comparison, Jackson (2001b) provides a recent survey of lenders on some of these issues. In 1999, Jackson conducted a national survey of a representative sample of 453 lenders, obtaining 238 usable responses. The survey primarily addressed the perceptions of environmental risk, as manifested by willingness to lend, for source site contaminated commercial and industrial properties before, during, and after remediation. This is most similar to the questions from the Kinnard and Worzala survey on willingness to lend on properties "known" to be contaminated, although they did not differentiate by stage of remediation. Overall, as noted, Kinnard and Worzala found that 51% of their US lender respondents would loan on such properties. The results of Jackson's survey indicated that before cleanup, only 1.3% of lenders perceive a normal level of lending risk and would provide a loan at typical rates and terms. During cleanup, and with cleanup proceeding under an approved plan, 6.4% of US lenders would provide a loan at normal typical rates and terms, and another 54.2% would provide a loan but with some adjustments to those rates and terms or other loan conditions. After cleanup to applicable regulatory standards, Jackson found that 65.3% of US lenders would provide a loan with no adjustments and another 30.5% would provide a loan with some adjustments to their credit underwriting.

The importance of this line of research and thinking to the field of contaminated property valuation lies in its focus on market perceptions as important determinants of the pricing and value of impacted properties. Kinnard was one of the first to recognize that market perceptions of environmental risk, and the inherent uncertainties of remediating such sites, were a key to understanding the effect of contamination on market behavior, and ultimately the price and value of contaminated properties. Indeed, comparing perceptual research with findings on price and value effects, as discussed in the next section, was an important contribution of Kinnard to the field and to real property valuation, generally.

PRICE AND VALUE EFFECTS OF ENVIRONMENTAL CONTAMINATION

The studies in this section profile Kinnard's empirical research on the effects of environmental contamination on the price and value of real property. As explained, the market's perceptions of environmental risk due to contamination and hazards is hypothesized to underlie these price and value effects. Three of Kinnard's empirical studies of price effects, published from 1991 to 1996, are summarized below, together with a 2001 study of impacts on value by Jackson (2002). In all of these studies, sophisticated statistical modeling is used to test the effects of contamination, if any, on price and value.

Kinnard and Geckler (1991) report on their study of impacts due to proximity to three Superfund sites in New Jersey in the 1980s. The contamination constituents at issue were radon and gamma radiation. As noted, radioactive contamination elicited the most negative reactions from the lenders and investors in the survey research. The study design for analyzing potential impacts on single-family residential properties in the towns surrounding the three sites included a "before and after" analysis, comparing sales occurring before the announcement of the Superfund status of the sites and those occurring after the announcement to test the hypothesis that the announcement adversely influenced market behavior and ultimately sales prices and values. The results of the before and after analysis presented some evidence of a "possible negative impact" on price appreciation, but were not conclusive.

Another set of analyses focused on "proximity impacts" by testing price differences due to the distance of the sales properties from the Superfund sites. A multiple regression based hedonic pricing model was developed with price per square foot dependent and living area, house age, lot size, number of garage stalls, and locations within one of seven distance zones as predictor variables. The furthest distance zone was the baseline, or reference, category. This zone could also be viewed as the "control area." The results showed negative area coefficients, indicating lower prices, for residential properties in only one of the three towns surrounding the Superfund sites, and these coefficients were not statistically significant. Residential real estate prices in proximity to the other two sites showed no adverse impacts. Thus, none of the coefficients corresponding to distance zones close to the sites were significant and negative. Kinnard and Geckler note that in the one town for which the results were less conclusive, the Superfund site had not been remediated, and adverse publicity about the radioactive contamination persisted much longer than in the other two towns.

Continuing with this same theme and approach, Kinnard et al. (1991) analyzed the effects of the announcement of an airborne release of radioactive material in a rural residential area in the Midwest. The authors note that there had been substantial publicity about the incident and that many local real estate professionals indicated "widespread expectations of declining market prices." There was some disagreement among these individuals as to the permanence of the expected effects on prices, though. Local taxing districts reacted as well. One local assessment authority granted an across-the-board reduction of 20% on all residential properties within two miles of the source site.

The study design was similar to the New Jersey study, with an analysis of proximity impacts using a series of concentric rings outward from the release site using a multiple regression format. The outer most ring served as the baseline, or control, category and the direction and statistical significance of price differences relative to this baseline were analyzed for any potential impacts. In addition, a variable reflecting the straight-line linear distance to the site was analyzed, as were time related variables corresponding to sales occurring before and after the announcement of the release. The results indicated that despite the publicity and the expectations of local market participants, there was no discernable impact on prices that could be attributed to the announcement of the release. The indicator variable for sales in the after period was not significant as was the linear distance variable. Likewise, there was no discernable pattern to the concentric ring indicators. The authors conclude that there was "no significant, measurable, marketwide negative effect" due to announced release. Interestingly, Kinnard and his co-authors again present evidence showing a discrepancy between expectations and stated perceptions relative to observed sales price effects.

Market perceptions and price impacts are also addressed in a study by Kinnard, Geckler, and DeLottie (1996). In the context of ad valorem assessments, the authors observe that in some jurisdictions assessors have reduced values based on fear or "stigma," without analyzing actual transactions and sales. The authors' refer to stigma as an "adverse opinion about, or reputation of, a submarket area that leads to diminished property values relative to otherwise similar submarket areas without the stigma" (Kinnard, Geckler, and DeLottie 1996, p. 35). Further, they note that some of these reductions are granted on a temporary basis, while in other cases the reductions are indefinite. The authors assert that stigma can and should only be measured through a "market record of sales and prices, reflecting buyer and seller beliefs and attitudes" (Kinnard, Geckler, and DeLottie 1996, p. 35).

To illustrate their points regarding the measurement of adverse price impacts and to inform ad valorem assessment practices, the authors discuss their study of an area within one mile of an abandoned smelter Superfund site with soil contaminated by arsenic and lead. There had been considerable publicity about the site and the Superfund listing. Their study identified a control area beyond the allegedly impacted area for purposes of comparing sales prices and the volume or frequency of sales for single-family residential properties. Four proximity zones closer to the former smelter site were analyzed for any effects on prices as well as sales volumes over a 17 year period that included years before and after the Superfund designation relative to the control area.

The results of the study indicated that sales volumes declined following the publicity about the site and contamination, but these declines were temporary and were followed by a rapid recovery. There was also a modest decline in average sales price per square foot, ranging from 1.8% to 4.2%, in the closest proximity zones for periods of 1 year or less. However, Kinnard, Geckler, and DeLottie conclude that in general sales prices and volumes throughout the four zones comprising the class area "paralleled those for the control area" (Kinnard, Geckler, and DeLottie 1996, p. 39). Only temporary impacts of short duration following intense publicity were found. The researchers observe that the class area made a "full recovery" thereafter. They also conclude that the extent of the adverse publicity and expected market declines were not borne out in the sales data, and caution other researchers against over reliance on opinion surveys of affected homeowners to predict price and value impacts.

Again for comparison, Jackson (2002) provides a recent study of the price impacts of contamination that evaluates impacts before and after remediation. As previously discussed, Jackson had also conducted surveys of lenders as to their willingness to lend on contaminated properties before, during, and after remediation. The findings from the survey research indicated that nearly all of the lenders would be deterred from providing a loan on a contaminated property before remediation had begun, with a greater percentage willing to lend once remediation had commenced. These two periods, before and after cleanup, were combined into a "before" period in Jackson's sales price analysis. The survey research also indicated that 95.8% of US lenders would be willing to loan on a previously contaminated property that had been remediated to applicable regulatory standards.

The results of analyzing 140 sales of industrial properties in the Southern California area from 1995 to 1999 essentially paralleled the survey research findings. In the period prior to completion of required remediation, there was a statistically significant reduction in sales price of approximately 30% relative to similar but uncontaminated properties. In the period after cleanup, though, sales prices of remediated properties were not significantly different from the uncontaminated comparables. As with the other studies discussed herein, a multiple regression analysis was used to statistically control for price differences due to non-environmental variables. The consistency of Jackson's survey research and sales price analysis findings contrasts with some of Kinnard's observations. A possible explanation is that the markets and market participants for industrial and commercial properties are different than for single-family residential properties. Also, Jackson's results were obtained from more recent sales data, perhaps reflecting improving market knowledge over time. Industrial and commercial lenders with substantial experience dealing with environmental issues would have a much different perspective than homeowners and homebuyers. Perhaps their knowledge and experience results in greater consistency between their perceptions and actions. This is a topic for further research.

Lastly, it should be noted that the findings of temporary effects of stigma are not universal. There are other researchers who have concluded that these effects can be long-term. One of these is Reichert (1999), who studied the price impacts of single-family residential properties in proximity to a Superfund landfill site in Ohio over time. Using a concentric ring proximity analysis, Reichert analyzed impacts on price during an "initial" period, from 1988 to 1994 and an "expanded" period, from 1988 to 1994, and found that reductions in price in rings closets to the landfill were relatively constant, with reductions of approximately 14% in the closest ring relative to prices in a control area away from the landfill. However, Reichert notes that "a successful remediation effort that removes the site from the EPA Superfund list could have a significant positive impact on the surrounding housing market" (Reichert 1999, p. 127). The site studied by Reichert had not yet undergone remediation, although surrounding properties had been hooked up to a central water system in an effort to reduce potential health impacts.

CONCLUSIONS

Kinnard has been a catalyst for research in the field of contaminated property valuation and the impacts of contamination on market value and market perceptions. His insight and perspective on appraisal and valuation methods, the markets' perceptions of environmental risk and the effects on real estate prices and values have served this field of inquiry well and have been a guide to researchers who continue to grapple with these ideas. The somewhat surprising findings showing a lack of residential property impacts in the face of adverse publicity and stated market expectations are pioneering and point out the need for additional research. Kinnard's early work in setting forth appropriate valuation methods has greatly aided practitioners in the field. These contributions will continue to be reflected in future research and in the way in which practitioners deal with these complex issues.

REFERENCES

Bond, S.G., Kinnard, W.N. Jr., Worzala, E.M., and Kapplin, S.D., Market Participants' Reactions Toward Contaminated Property in New Zealand and the USA. *Journal of Property Valuation and Investment*, 1998, 16(3): 251–271.

Jackson, T.O., The Effects of Environmental Contamination on Real Estate: A Literature Review. *Journal of Real Estate Literature*, 2001a, 9(2): 93–116.

——, Environmental Risk Perceptions of Commercial and Industrial Real Estate Lenders. *Journal of Real Estate Research*, 2001b, 22(3): 271–288.

——, Environmental Contamination and Industrial Real Estate Prices. *Journal of Real Estate Research*, 2002, 23(1/2): 179–199. *Winner of the Industrial Real Estate Manuscript Prize Presented at the American Real Estate 2001 Annual Meeting.*

Jackson, T.O. and Bell, R., The Analysis of Environmental Case Studies. *The Appraisal Journal*, 2002, 70(1): 86–95.

Kinnard, W.N., Jr., Analyzing the Stigma Effect of Proximity to a Hazardous Materials Site. *Environmental Watch*, 1989, December: 4–7.

——, Measuring the Effects of Contamination on Property Values: The Focus of the Symposium in the Context of Current Knowledge, in *Measuring the Effects of Hazardous Materials on Real Estate Values: Techniques and Applications*. Appraisal Institute, Chicago, IL. 1992.

Kinnard, W.N., Jr. and Geckler, M.B., The Effects of Residential Real Estate Prices from Proximity to Properties Contaminated with Radioactive Materials. *Real Estate Issues*, 1991, 16: Fall/Winter.

Kinnard, W.N., Jr., and Worzala, E.M., How North American Appraisers Value Contaminated Property and Associated Stigma. *The Appraisal Journal*, 1999, 67(3): 269–278.

Kinnard, W.N., Jr., Geckler, M.B., and DeLottie, J.W., The Effect of Varying Levels of Negative Publicity on Single-Family Property Values: A Case Study of Soil Contamination. *Assessment Journal*, 1996, 3(5): 35–44.

Kinnard, W.N., Jr., Mitchell, P.S., Beron, G.L., and Webb, J.R., Market Reactions to an Announced Release of Radioactive Materials: The Impact on Assessable Value. *Property Tax Journal*, 1991, 10(3): 283–297. *Winner of the 1992 Bernard L. Bernard Award for Best Article on Assessment Administration.*

Reichert, A., The Persistence of Contamination Effects: A Superfund Site Revisited. *The Appraisal Journal*, 1999, 67(2): 126–135.

Worzala, E.M. and Kinnard, W.N., Jr., Investor and Lender Reactions to Alternative Sources of Contamination. *Real Estate Issues*, 1997, August: 42–47.

6. Expert Witness Testimony and the Use of Environmental Contamination Research in Eminent Domain Cases

S. ALAN AYCOCK

Abstract

This chapter will discuss the basic aspects of expert witness testimony in eminent domain cases, and the use in court of prior academic research in the areas of environmental contamination. William Kinnard was active as an expert witness in a variety of real estate litigation, but his seminal work in valuation losses due to environmental issues has been invaluable in presenting property damage considerations in court. This chapter will also explore the impact of recent court decisions regarding expert witness testimony.

INTRODUCTION

William Kinnard enjoyed an illustrious career as an educator, researcher, and expert witness. His research in environmental contamination, and how the contamination affects property values, has been critical in assessing damages in eminent domain cases. This chapter will review the use of expert testimony in eminent domain cases, the literature on environmental contamination and valuation, and discuss how such research can be appropriately entered into trial testimony. This chapter will also discuss the valuation of consequential damages to the remaining property.

Valuation in eminent domain cases can be complex, and often involves considerations of value beyond the scope of a normal loan appraisal. The expert witness in these cases must be able both to recognize potential damage to the property and to assess the amount of compensation due to the owner. For example, a road widening in front of a shopping center may take only a minimal amount of property, but have a dire effect on the visibility and access to the center (Rabianski and Vernor 1993). An electric power line may present perceptions of health risks to neighboring property owners, hence diminishing property value (Kung and Seagle 1992; Delaney and Timmons 1992; MvEvoy 1994; Kinnard and Worzala 1999; Kinnard and Dickey 2000). Roddewig (1999a) found that diminution of value due to fears of environmental stigma may occur as a result of additional site investigation costs, remediation and monitoring costs, potential marketing issues in leasing or selling the property, and possible problems in obtaining finance. The expert witness considers all such issues when determining compensation to the property owner.

THE VALUATION PROCESS IN EMINENT DOMAIN CASES

Eminent domain is the legal right of a political entity or other party authorized by statute to acquire private property for public use. The actual legal process to obtain the property is called condemnation. The most common condemnors are state transportation departments for road improvements, public utility companies, local governments for parks and facilities, railroads, petroleum pipelines, and special purpose entities such as cable television companies, and fiber optic networks. The condemning authority may take all or a portion of the property; taking a portion may result in damages, also known as consequential damages or severance, to the remainder. A property owner has several procedural safeguards in a condemnation proceeding (Hinkle 1991):

- The condemnor must establish that there is a legitimate public need for the property.
- The property owner must have a judicial hearing, may request a jury trial on compensation, may be represented by counsel, and may dispute either the need for the taking or the compensation offered.
- The owner must be paid just compensation both for the property taken and for the consequential damages, if any, to the remaining property.

Shilling (1995) noted that compensation may include:

- loss of business profits,
- moving costs and costs of obtaining replacement facilities,
- and the adverse impact caused by the use of the condemned property, such as having a sewer plant next door.

The typical valuation process in an eminent domain case involves determining the value of the actual property, or property rights, being condemned, any consequential damages to the remainder, and any other business losses caused by the condemnation action. The format used by many states is:

1. Determine the value of the entire property prior to the taking.
2. Determine the value of the actual property or property rights, such as easements, actually being taken.
3. Calculate the consequential benefits, if any, to the remainder.
4. Calculate the consequential damages, if any, to the remainder. The general rule is that consequential benefits are offset against consequential damages in determining the net cost/benefit to the remainder.
5. Determine the value of the entire property remaining after the taking.

Both parties employ expert witnesses to testify on these value issues. Condemnors rarely, if ever, admit to the existence of consequential damages. This is particularly true if the condemnor is an electric utility company or similar enterprise where there is controversy over the extent, or even the existence, of compensable damages. The expert witness for the property owner must be prepared to enter the debate armed with the quality research on the value impact of such environmental contamination exemplified by the writings of Bill Kinnard.

LITERATURE REVIEW—ENVIRONMENTAL ISSUES AND VALUATION

Frequently, eminent domain cases involve only a partial taking, leaving a remainder that may itself be damaged by the nature of the use of the taking. Electric power lines are an example. William Kinnard and others extensively studied the impact on property values when environmental contamination was involved; Kinnard published or presented dozens of articles on the subject.

Kinnard was perhaps the first academic researcher to study the relationship of power lines and property values (1967). Kinnard and Dickey (1995, 2000) studied the impact of electrical power lines on property value, segregating their research in value impacts from proximity/visibility of power poles and value impacts from fear of electromagnetic fields ("EMF"). The authors noted that property values can be negatively affected in three ways: a decrease in sales volume, an increase in the marketing time or time on market, and by a decrease in sales price. This chapter also reviewed other recent studies on the effect of EMF and high-voltage transmission lines ("HVTL"), and serves as an excellent review of the research for the nascent expert witness. The authors found that diminution of property values was directly related to proximity of the property to the power line; the closer the property, the greater the loss in value. Losses ranged from 5.0% to 6.5% in value. Kinnard and Geckler (1997) studied the price effect caused by an unobstructed view of a HVTL, finding some diminution of value. The authors also noted that any difference in effect between proximity and visibility was difficult to distinguish; with proximity came visibility. Des Rosiers (2002) studied the price impact of both visibility and proximity of HVTL, using data from the sale of 507 houses in Canada that had either a direct frontal view of a pylon, a partial view, or were screened. Des Rosiers found that a direct view of a pylon could reduce prices up to 10%; when the line was also in close proximity—50 feet—the loss in value was 15–20%. The author also found that negative price adjustments tended to decrease as the distance from the HVTL increased. Kinnard and Dickey (2000) also cite a similar study in 1998 in southwest Virginia, conducted by the Real Estate Counseling Group of Connecticut (a Kinnard affiliate), which found similar results, including that the amount of line voltage itself made little difference in the price impact. Colwell (1990) also studied the issue of proximity to HVTL and property values, finding that land prices were negatively affected by proximity to HVTL, but that the price effect declined both as distance from the HVTL increased and as elapsed time from date of purchase increased.

The fear of EMF and the perception of loss of property value has been widely studied. Delaney and Timmons (1992) conducted a survey of appraisers who had valued properties adjacent to HVTL, which indicated a loss in property values of 7.77–15.5%. Kung and Seagle (1992) surveyed homeowners, separating the respondents into two groups—those who knew of the health risks attributed to EMF, and those who did not. Their survey noted that respondents who were informed of the potential health risks of EMF attributed a loss in property values due to the proximity of EMF. Bryant and Epley (1998) studied the fear of EMF, which they termed "cancerphobia," by reviewing the relevant court cases and analyzing the various appraisal and statistical methods used in those cases, which generally were eminent domain cases. The authors observed three basic rules used by different courts: (1) no compensation for fear of EMF, or (2) compensation for fear was reasonable, or (3) fear is reasonable but reasonableness may be irrelevant—the only issue is the impact on market value. The authors reviewed a number of court cases (to be discussed later in this chapter) and found that courts in general had been supportive of the fear concept in relation to the diminution of property values. The authors argued that expert witnesses hired to calculate consequential damages in condemnation cases involving EMF had to be knowledgeable of the court precedents, research methodology, and statistical analysis used to support the findings in these cases. Kinnard and Dickey (2000) offered a cautionary note on the "fear" research, arguing that the researchers had misread court decisions and had relied too heavily on surveys to the exclusion of more market-driven data.

Kinnard and Worzala (1999) conducted a survey of appraisers to determine what methodology was employed in valuing contaminated property. The respondents were primarily Member Appraisal Institute (MAI)—designated appraisers with experience appraising such properties. The survey showed that most respondents valued property in the hypothetical "before" and "after" state involving the contamination, and most often used the market data approach to value the property. The majority surveyed felt that no one technique was universally applicable when valuing contaminated properties; instead, a variety of approaches was acceptable based on the unique aspects of the individual situation. Most of the respondents relied on professional engineers to assess the cost of remediation. Roddewig (1999a) developed a classification process for appraisers to use in valuing contaminated property, which relied on specific case study analysis. The appraiser would review a case where the property is similar to the actual property being appraised; then, assess damages based on the intensity of the contamination, the time and cost of remediation, future monitoring requirement, the availability of financing, and any other claims on the property.

Other techniques to assess the loss of value due to contamination were proposed by Mitchell (2000) and Bell (1998). Mitchell developed a statistical model to measure loss of value due to lessened marketability, rentability, and remaining stigma of the property. The statistical model was termed "expected discounted value," and utilizes expected value probabilities combined with discounted cash flow adjusted for reductions due to lessened marketability and remaining stigma after cleanup. Mitchell argues that the technique and model are highly relevant to the expert witness in property litigation, since they utilize market data with proven statistical technique. Bell suggested that the various issues with contaminated properties, including other items like airport noise or remnants from a natural disaster, be defined as "detrimental conditions," and classified into ten categories. Bell asserts that each category of detrimental conditions needs to be assessed separately based on their unique characteristics, using market data whenever possible. Once classified, typical techniques such as paired-sales or discounted cash flow analysis could be employed. Bell charted typical loss in value based on these classifications, which ranged from remediation/repair costs, to residual stigma, and lessened marketability.

Further research on environmental issues and valuation can be found in three articles by Jackson (2000, 2001, 2002) that break new ground by analyzing commercial income properties. Jackson found that capitalization rates were affected negatively by detrimental environmental conditions. The 2001 article is a complete literature review and is required reading for an expert witness in this area. Hoyt and Aalberts (2002) wrote on the legal and valuation issues when damage occurs due to toxic mold, an area of growing litigation concern. Simons (1999) studied the impact on adjacent home prices of a petroleum pipeline rupture, finding that much like HVTL, the stigma due to the pipeline rupture affected nearby properties in much the same manner. Simon found a loss in property values from 3.5% to 6%, and like HVTL, the loss was related to the proximity of the property to the pipeline.

LEGAL ISSUES AND THE EXPERT WITNESS

This section will outline some of the legal issues and case law that are important to the expert witness in an eminent domain case, particularly such cases that involve environmental issues. In the *Daubert* case (1993), the US Supreme Court reinterpreted the role and the qualifications of expert witnesses, establishing the following criteria (Hoyt and Aalberts 1997):

1. The theory invoked has or can be tested.
2. The theory has been subject to peer review and publication.
3. For any scientific technique employed, there is a known error rate the Court should consider.
4. The technique in question is generally accepted.
5. The expert witness testimony must "rest on a reliable foundation and be relevant to the task at hand."

Hoyt and Aalberts (1996, 1997) studied the role of the real estate expert witness after *Daubert*. They describe the need for the expert witness to have the proper expertise, professional designations and licensure. Black, Ayala, and Saffran-Brinks (1994) wrote a detailed analysis of the new standards imposed by *Daubert*, creating a more expansive checklist to evaluate expert witnesses and scientific testimony based upon the four guiding principles of the Supreme Court. The authors stress that scientific testimony needs to be precise, with a well-grounded hypothesis that has been exposed to rigorous examination and testing. Such hypotheses and methods must have logical consistency, be consistent with accepted theories, have been exposed to peer review in the publication process, and be accepted or adopted by others in the scientific community. Dorchester (2000) expands on this line of reasoning by showing that courts in general prefer value testimony based on market data. He argues that market concepts/analysis promulgated by the expert witness must be carefully tailored to the unique situation at hand, rather than rely on broad market trends. This property-specific market analysis and the determination of value must rely on techniques that accurately reflect proven methods of assessing market value.

Rule 702 of the Federal Rules of Evidence was amended in December, 2000 to reflect *Daubert* and to provide guidance both to litigants and to the courts on the reliability of expert witness testimony (Scully and Dirkes 2001). The rule reads as follows:

> If scientific, technical, or other specialized knowledge will assist the trier of fact to understand the evidence or to determine the fact in issue, a witness qualified by knowledge, skill, training, experience, or education may testify thereto in the form of an opinion or otherwise, if (1) the testimony is based on sufficient facts or data, (2) the testimony is the product of reliable facts or data, and (3) the witness has applied the principles and methods reliably to the facts of the case.

Roddewig (1999b) further explores these issues of standards and scientific reliability in the post-*Daubert* world of expert testimony. While he first argues the theory, techniques, professional standards, and peer review process of the Appraisal Institute meet the scientific standards imposed by *Daubert*, he admits that these existing standards may not be fully sufficient in cases involving environmental contamination. He points out that:

1. The valuation of contaminated property is still in its infancy and techniques are still under development.
2. Many appraisers have no training or expertise in this area, the work is specialized, and thus the "scientific community" referenced by the Court is still quite small.
3. The Appraisal Institute must provide more guidance, training, and standards in this specific area.

The author also notes that the use of opinion surveys prepared by expert witnesses to support damage claims in these cases is a questionable technique and one that is often thrown out by the courts. This questioning of surveys as appropriate valuation tools is supported by Kinnard and Dickey (2000). Kinnard (2001), in his final publication, supports the call for a new paradigm of appraisal theory and methods, arguing that "... the fundamental theoretical structure on which (appraisal) practice is based is outmoded, excessively abstract ... and not generally descriptive of market behavior."

IMPORTANT EMINENT DOMAIN LEGAL CASES ON ENVIRONMENTAL CONTAMINATION

There are numerous eminent domain state court cases concerning valuation and environmental concerns, and voluminous writings on these cases. An exhaustive case review is outside of the scope of this chapter, instead the focus will be on the major cases frequently cited in valuation literature, such as Bryant and Epley (1998), Kinnard and Dickey (2000), Hoyt and Aalberts (1996). Table 6-1 summarizes the major court cases.

Table 6-1 Major Court Cases on Valuation and Environmental Contamination

Case—citation	Issue	Ruling
1. Hicks vs. United States (1959)—US Supreme Court	Fear of power lines as a component of compensation.	The Court found that fear of power lines was reasonable, and compensable, holding "The apprehension of injuries to persons or property by the presence of power lines on the property is founded on practical experience and may be taken into consideration in so far as the lines and towers affect market value of the land." This case was decided before the controversy on EMF as carcinogenic began.
2. T.V.A. vs. Easement and Right of Way (US 6th Circuit Court of Appeals)	Fear of injury from power lines as cause for consequential damages to remaining property.	The Court held that fear of injury from power lines was cause for consequential damages, and awarded damages equal to 50% of the value of the remaining land.
3. Florida Power and Light Co. vs. Jennings (Florida Supreme Court)	Reasonableness of public fear as a component of valuation by an expert witness.	The Florida Supreme Court ruled, "... the reasonableness of the fear is either assumed or considered irrelevant ... any factor, including public fear, which impacts the value of the land taken ... may be considered to explain the basis of an expert's valuation opinion."
4. San Diego Gas and Electric Co. vs. Daley (California Court of Appeals)	Whether or not fear of power lines affected market value of property.	The Court ruled that the predominate issue was not whether EMF were in fact a health hazard, but whether fear of power lines impacted the market value of the land.
5. Willsey vs. Kansas City Power and Light Company (Kansas Court of Appeals)	Whether the source of a loss in property value affected the compensable amount.	The ruling stated that, "... any loss in property value proven should be compensable," regardless of the source of the loss, and that the reasonableness of fear was not a matter of law but a matter of fact in each case.
6. Criscuola vs. Power Authority of the State of New York (New York Court of Appeals)	Can property owners seek specific damages based on the public perception of risk from EMF.	The Court affirmed that specific damages could be sought based on the public perception of risk from EMF.

Kinnard and Dickey (2000) reviewed several additional cases dealing primarily with EMF and power companies, noting that while case law had affirmed the "fear" issue as legitimate cause for damages, in very few cases were consequential damages actually awarded to property owners. The US Supreme Court has not specifically dealt with the perception of fear from contamination in any appellate cases.

Table 6-2 Legal Cases on Techniques/Methods of Expert Witnesses

Case	Issue	Ruling
1. Joy vs. Bell Helicopter Textron Inc. (US Court of Appeals)	Location of comparable sales relative to the subject property; estimation of future appreciation.	The expert testimony was thrown out by the court because it was based on, "... speculation and guesswork." The witness used house appreciation statistics from Washington, D.C. to value unimproved land in the Virgin Islands.
2. United States vs. 14.28 Acres of Land (US District Court)	Were compensable damages due based on the possibility of future flooding.	This condemnation case involved construction of a levee on a river. The expert witness opined that since there was a possibility of future flooding, a 50% reduction in land value was warranted. The river had not flooded in the past, and no evidence was introduced to justify claims that it might flood in the future. The testimony was thrown out as speculative and without scientific basis.
3. Newport Limited vs. Sears, Roebuck and Company (US District Court)	Use of statistical techniques to estimate business lost profits.	The expert witness used a regression analysis model to estimate lost profits from an industrial park development. The court found that regression analysis was a proven, acceptable scientific technique and hence admissible as evidence. The court also commented that the actual assumptions employed in the regression were subject to the same scientific scrutiny, and the witness must also show that the assumptions were valid and reasonable.

There are several cases that deal with the scientific techniques and methods of expert witnesses in real estate litigation (Hoyt and Aalberts 1997), all of which invoke *Daubert* concerns for use of proven scientific techniques and market data. Table 6-2 summarizes these cases.

The overall conclusion from these and other cases is that the testimony from an expert witness must have scientific validity, based on existing facts in the specific case at hand, and utilize proven and acceptable professional practices.

ENTERING ACADEMIC ENVIRONMENTAL RESEARCH INTO EVIDENCE DURING A COURT PROCEEDING

In an eminent domain proceeding, which may take the form of an arbitration/special master hearing, a bench trial, or a jury trial, the expert witness may face the hurdle of "hearsay" testimony. There are many exceptions to the hearsay rule, and expert witnesses are generally given some latitude. Most of the common actions of an appraiser—confirming sales, for example—fall under the category of hearsay, but are generally admissible. Case law in this matter will vary by state, but quoting academic research performed by others is often challenged by the condemnor's attorney on the grounds of hearsay. The author has testified extensively in eminent domain cases, and has found several methods for entering the research findings into evidence.

1. Generalized comments in court about what the "literature" says on a topic, such as "... the literature shows that EMF reduce property values" are very likely to be challenged by the opposing attorney. You are better to say "... my own research into EMF shows ...;" if challenged, be prepared to quote specific articles.
2. Enter all the articles in full into evidence as defendant exhibits, then via visual exhibits or oral testimony, present the summarized findings of the research and how it relates to the case at hand. Entering the entire article does expose it to detailed review by opposing counsel, but the generally short time frame of a trial in condemnation cases may somewhat negate this. However, the expert witness should be prepared in these instances for a vigorous cross examination where the prior research in question may be quoted out of context by the opposing counsel (Kinnard 1993).
3. Take one research study that closely aligns with the eminent domain case being tried, and show precisely how the prior study supports your findings in this case.
4. Publishing your own study that cites other published research on the valuation impact of environmental issues, even if not specifically relevant to the case at hand, or on eminent domain valuation, will serve both to make you a more credible witness and afford you latitude in entering other research into testimony.
5. Be prepared to explain how your valuation methodology in the present case is based on generally accepted appraisal theory and practice, consistent with the prior research, reflects market conditions, and properly applies any statistical or measurement technique. Expert witnesses in condemnation cases should expect to be thoroughly challenged if they find any consequential or severance damages to the remainder property (Rabianski and Carn 1992), hence, they must be prepared to show how their testimony complies with the Supreme Court guidelines in *Daubert* (1993), and with Rule 702 of the Federal Rules of Evidence. Black, Ayala, and Saffran-Banks (1994) expand on *Daubert* and provide a detailed interpretation of acceptable scientific methodology. Kinnard (1993) further explained and defined the role of the expert witness in real estate litigation. Kinnard advised that the expert witness be "hyperprepared" on the facts in the case, and stressed that the expert witness, to be credible, cannot be seen as an advocate for the client or the attorney.

CONCLUSION

As evidenced by the many citations throughout this chapter on expert testimony, appraisal theory, and valuing environmental contamination, William Kinnard had an extraordinary impact on real estate theory and appraisal practice. This chapter was designed both to highlight his many intellectual contributions and to assist the expert witness in eminent domain litigation on valuing environmentally damaged property and on understanding the related legal issues. Basic legal and procedural issues in eminent domain cases were also examined, including the impact on consequential damages of environmental contamination. This chapter was also designed to assist the expert witness in utilizing and entering into trial testimony the academic research of others, particularly on environmental contamination. The author has utilized Kinnard's environmental research frequently in court testimony, and had the pleasure of meeting him, and thanking him, at his last American Real Estate Society meeting in April, 2000.

REFERENCES

Bell, R., The Impact of Detrimental Conditions on Property Value. *The Appraisal Journal*, 1998, 66(4): 380–391.

Black, B., Ayala, F., and Saffran-Banks, C., Science and the Law in the Wake of Daubert: A New Search for Scientific Knowledge. *Texas Law Review*, 1994, 72(4): 715–802.

Bryant, J. and Epley, D., Cancerphobia: Electromagnetic Fields and Their Impact on Residential Loan Values. *Journal of Real Estate Research*, 1998, 15(1/2): 115–129.

Colwell, P., Power Lines and Land Value. *Journal of Real Estate Research*, 1990, 5(1): 117–127.

Delaney, C. and Timmons, D., High Voltage Power Lines: Do They Affect Residential Property Value? *Journal of Real Estate Research*, 1992, 7(3): 315–329.

Des Rosiers, F., Power Lines, Visual Encumbrance, and House Values—A Microspatial Approach to Impact Measurement. *Journal of Real Estate Research*, 2002, 23(3): 275–301.

Dorchester, J., The Federal Rules of Evidence and *Daubert*: Evaluating Real Property Valuation Witnesses. *The Appraisal Journal*, 2000, 7(3): 290–302.

Hinkle, D., *Practical Real Estate Law*. West Publishing Company, New York. 1991.

Hoyt, R. and Aalberts, R., The New World of Real Estate Expert Testimony. *Real Estate Finance*, 1996, 2(2): 38–44.

——, New Requirements for the Appraisal Expert Witness. *The Appraisal Journal*, 1997, 10(4): 342–349.

——, Appraisers and Toxic Mold. *Working Paper*, The American Real Estate Society Annual Conference, 2002.

Jackson, T., Environmental Risk Perceptions of Lenders and Investors in Commercial and Industrial Real Estate. *Working Paper*, The American Real Estate Society Annual Conference, 2000.

——, The Effects of Environmental Contamination on Real Estate: A Literature Review. *Journal of Real Estate Literature*, 2001, 9(2): 91–116.

——, The Effects of Environmental Contamination on Commercial Real Estate prices and Income Capitalization Rates. *Working Paper*, The American Real Estate Society Annual Conference, 2002.

Kinnard, W., Tower Lines and Residential Property Values. *The Appraisal Journal*, 1967, 35(2): 141–152.

——, The Counselor as Expert Witness: Hazards, Pitfalls, and Defenses. *Real Estate Issues*, 1993, 61(3): 1–5.

——, New Thinking in Appraisal Theory. *The Appraisal Journal*, 2001, 69(3): 235–243.

Kinnard, W. and Dickey, S., A Primer on Proximity Impact Research: Residential Property Values Near High—Voltage Transmission Lines. *Real Estate Issues*, 1995, 20(2): 23–30.

——, High Voltage Transmission Lines and Residential Property Values: New Findings about Unobstructed Views and Tower Construction. *Working Paper*, American Real Estate Society conference, April, 2000.

Kinnard, W. and Geckler, M., HVTL Proximity, Fear of EMF, and Residential Property Values: Research Results from the USA, Canada, and New Zealand. *Working Paper*, presented at International Association of Assessing Officers, Toronto, Canada, 1997.

Kinnard, W. and Worzala, E., How North American Appraisers Value Contaminated Property and Associated Stigma. *The Appraisal Journal*, 1999, 67(3): 269–279.

Kung, H. and Seagle, C., Impact of Power Transmission Lines on Property Values: A Case Study. *The Appraisal Journal*, 1992, 60(3): 413–422.

McEvoy, S., Double-edged Sword of Damocles: Utility Companies' Liability for Diminution of Property Values due to Electromagnetic Fields. *Real Estate Law Journal*, 1994, 23(2): 109–123.

Mitchell, P., Estimating Economic Damages to Real Property due to Loss of Marketability, Rentability, and Stigma. *The Appraisal Journal*, 2000, 68(2): 162–170.

Rabianski, J. and Carn, N., Cross Examination: How to Protect Yourself and the Appraisal Report. *The Appraisal Journal*, 1992, 60(4): 472–481.

Rabianski, J. and Vernor, J., *Shopping Center Appraisal and Analysis*. The Appraisal Institute, 1993.

Roddewig, R., Classifying the Level of Risk and Stigma Affecting Contaminated Property. *The Appraisal Journal*, 1999a, 67(1): 98–102.

——, Junk Science, Environmental Stigma, Market Surveys, and Proper Appraisal Methodology: Recent Lessons from the Litigation Trenches. *The Appraisal Journal*, 1999b, 67(4): 447–453.
Scully, D. and Dirkes, M., Daubert Now Becomes the Rule in the Rules. *Defense Counsel Journal*, 2001, 4(4): 248–250.
Shilling, J., Real Estate, Thirteenth Edition. South-Western Publishing, 1995. Memphis, TN USA.
Simons, R., The Effect of Pipeline Ruptures on Noncontaminated Residential Easement-holding Property in Fairfax County. *The Appraisal Journal*, 1999, 67(3): 255–263.

Legal Cases

Criscuola vs. Power Authority of the State of New York, 188 A.D. 951; 81 N.Y. 2nd 79 (1993).
Daubert vs. Merrill Dow, 125 L. Ed. 2nd 469 (1993).
Florida Power & Light Company vs. Jennings, 518 So. 2d. 895 (1987).
Hicks vs. United States, 266 F.2d. 515 (1959).
Joy vs. Bell Helicopter Textron, Inc., 999 F. 2nd, 549 (D.C. Circuit, 1993).
Newport Limited vs. Sears, Roebuck and Company, 86-2319, LEXIS 7652 (E.D. La. May 31, 1995).
San Diego Gas & Electric Company vs. Daley, 205 Cal. App. 3d., 1334 (1998).
T.V.A. vs. Easement and Right of Way, 405 F.2d, 305 (6th Cir., 1968).
U.S. vs. 14.38 Acres of Land, 884 F. Supp. (N.D. Miss., 1995).
Willsey vs. Kansas City Power, 631 P. 2d., Kan. App. (1981).

7. Challenges Confronting Property Valuation Practitioners in Australasia

SANDY BOND*

Abstract

Valuation is becoming a global profession particularly with the recognition of various designations internationally. The issues facing valuers in one country are impacting on valuation professionals in other countries. This chapter provides an Australasian perspective of the issues confronting valuers in that region.

The findings indicate that many of the issues are interconnected. There are enormous pressures for valuers to produce more work but in less time and to meet increasingly complex and stringent standards of professional practice. This is in addition to competition for valuation work from related professions, both nationally and internationally. Fee reductions to compete for work have become the norm. Further, a failure to keep abreast of industry changes has led to falling standards of valuation practice with an associated increase in the number of claims made on professional indemnity insurance funds. Insurance companies are no longer prepared to underwrite valuers' professional indemnity (PI) cover. The chapter concludes with suggestions for dealing with the challenges outlined herein.

INTRODUCTION

As a valuation proponent and avid researcher of valuation issues Kinnard (Bill) was acutely aware of the rising number of issues facing valuers globally. This was a primary motivation for him to call together a panel of international valuation experts to

*I would like to thank the following valuers and property academicians who provided their perceptions and views of the valuation issues facing the Australasian profession: Gwendoline Daly, Colliers Jardine, NZPI Wellington Branch Committee member and Fellow of NZPI. E-mail: gwendoline_daly@cj-group.com; Robert Fraser, sole practitioner and former lecturer, Property Department, Curtin University of Technology, Western Australia. E-mail: bobfraser@primus.com.au; Iain Gribble, partner in Mahoney Gardner Churton Ltd., and member of the Professional Practice Standards Committee NZPI, fellow of NZPI. E-mail: mgc@clear.net.nz; Rob Kooymans, Program Director, Property Programs, School of International Business, University of South Australia. E-mail: rob.kooymans@unisa.edu.au; Dr David Parker, Property Portfolio Manager, Suncorp Metway, Board member of the Pacific Rim Real Estate Society, E-mail: david.parker@suncorpmetway.com.au; and Jeff Spencer, Jeff Spencer & Associates, Fellow of the API, 1994 National Chairman of the API Committee that prepared the valuation standard for the Assessment of contaminated sites in Australia. E-mail: jaspence@q-net.net.au.

In memory of William N. Kinnard, Jr. 1926–2001. Beloved friend, colleague, mentor, dissertation examiner (2000), co-author, job & fellowship referee.

present their findings of the issues facing valuers in their region at the AREUEA meeting in Cancun, Mexico in May 2000. The main aim of this panel was for the regional representatives to share the challenges their valuers are grappling with and to help raise the level of awareness amongst valuers that the issues faced are shared globally and that, they need to be addressed in this way, that is, globally.

The author of this chapter was the Australasian representative invited to participate on the panel. It was with great regret to hear of Bill's death just weeks before the conference but the panellists decided that Bill would have wanted the panel to continue. This chapter is a result of that presentation. The chapter begins with a background of the valuation professions in New Zealand and Australia, and outlines the moves that have been made to globalize the profession. A discussion of the various issues valuers in Australasia are facing and how some of them are being addressed follows. For the issues that remain unaddressed, such as falling standards and declining fees, solutions are suggested to help resolve them. The final section provides a summary and conclusion. A primary aim of this chapter is to inform valuers from other countries about the Australasian experience so they can learn from it and avoid similar issues as well as to garner ideas on how to address those currently faced.

BACKGROUND

Valuation is an evolving profession in Australasia, having existed for less than a century. This section provides an overview of the current state of the professional bodies that govern valuation in both New Zealand and Australia and how these are becoming more closely linked.

New Zealand

The New Zealand Property Institute (NZPI) was launched in 2000 following the overwhelming support for a new organisation by members of the New Zealand

Institute of Valuers (NZIV), the Institute of Plant & Machinery Valuers (IPMV), and the Property & Land Economy Institute of New Zealand (PLEINZ). The new institute has a membership of some 3000 key property professionals who provide services in a number of property related areas. These include: property management, property consultancy, property development, property valuation, facilities management, plant and machinery valuation, financial analysis, real estate sales and leasing, project management, and others. The Institute has 17 branches across provincial and metropolitan New Zealand, a number of overseas members, and is affiliated to a number of other international property organizations, the World Association of Valuation Organizations (WAVO), including the Royal Institute of Chartered Surveyors (RICS), The Pacific Rim Real Estate Society (PRRES), and others.

The NZPI Registration Board provides registration in the following streams: Property Consultancy; Property Management; Facilities Management, and Plant and Machinery Valuation. Members who are Registered Valuers are administered by the Valuers Registration Board (VRB). The VRB's role is to ensure a minimum standard of entry for valuers becoming recognized by registration. Further, the VRB is responsible for keeping an up-to-date register of all registered valuers, and the issuing of Annual Practising Certificates. To obtain Registration applicants must be at least 23 years old, completed an approved tertiary degree and have not less than 3 years practical experience in New Zealand within the 10 years immediately preceding applying for registration.

Australia

The Australian Institute of Valuers and Land Economists (AIVLE) was repositioned in 1998 in response to the changing needs of, and influences on, the property profession. It was renamed *The Australian Property Institute (API).*

The API is a national body with over 7500 members who are experts professionally involved in the valuation, administration and use of land, property, and plant and machinery. The Institute has eight divisions including the National Office that are generally determined by the state boundaries of Australia. Membership entry to the API is based upon tertiary educations standards, accompanied by recognized practical experience, similar to the requirements of the NZPI.

Closer Links: The Trans-Tasman Mutual Recognition Act 1997 and the 2001 Memorandum of Understanding

The Trans-Tasman Mutual Recognition (TTMR) Act between New Zealand and Australia came into effect on May 1, 1998. Its objective is to reduce regulatory barriers to the movement of goods and services between New Zealand and Australia. For valuers, it means that if a person is registered to practise as a valuer in New Zealand, then they will be entitled to practise an equivalent occupation in an Australian jurisdiction (and vice versa).

This arrangement has a similar outcome to reciprocity agreements being instigated by various valuation bodies around the world. For example, the NZPI has reciprocity agreements with similar bodies in Singapore, Canada, and Malaysia. These agreements aim to bring the profession closer, allowing valuers to practice globally.

A Memorandum of Understanding (MOU) between the NZPI and API was signed in 2001. The aim of this was to establish a closer working relationship in order to develop a cross border common membership for each Institute's members in recognition of each other's equivalent occupation status and to give effect to the TTMR Act 1997. The two bodies aim to put in place mirror rules of each Institute, establish and publish a common Professional Practice Manual, and develop and introduce a common set of valuation standards, etc.

ISSUES AND CHALLENGES FACING PROPERTY VALUERS IN AUSTRALASIA

With professional valuation bodies forming closer links internationally the issues facing valuers in one country are impacting on valuers in other countries. The current issues facing Australasian valuers outlined below, include: globalization of services, legislative issues, rising costs of obtaining professional indemnity insurance, declining levels of fees, and uncertainties of how to value public sector infrastructure assets.

A Global Profession: RICS

The Royal Institution of Chartered Surveyors (RICS) is an international organization with some 108,000 members working in over 120 countries (Armstrong 2000). The importance of establishing a truly global profession was identified as a key part of the "status agenda" in the *Harris report* of 1998. According to the RICS Chief Executive Louis Armstrong: "From July 2001, the Institute will become more recognizably international with the advent of a governing council made up of representatives from all world regions. The governing council will make policy for the whole profession," (Armstrong 2000, p. 12). Globalization of business has become a reality and the Internet is forcing the pace of change. The overall mission of the RICS is "to elevate the status of the RICS qualifications worldwide..." Key strategic objectives are to:

- Increase the profession's influence and business potential worldwide
- Promote the qualification
- Attract top quality entrants, qualifying indigenously
- Create a global brand.

Priority areas for the next 3 years are Europe, United States, Australasia, and China. The RICS was established in Australia with an office in Sydney in December 1999. However, the inaugural meeting of WAVO was held in Kuala Lumpur, Malaysia on 12 October 2002. Current member organisations include: the American Society of Appraisal (ASA); American Institute (AI); Australian Property Institute (API); Appraisal Institute of Canada (AIC); International Valuation Standards Committee (IVSC): Singapore Institute of Surveyors and Valuers (SISV); NZPI, and RICS. The objectives of WAVO include:

1. Supporting the consistent application of valuation standards and methodologies
2. Encouraging standard terminology and worldwide transparency

3. Improving educational and training opportunities
4. Providing a quality assured WAVO accreditation to member organizations
5. Working in parallel with IVSC.

Undoubtedly, all members conscious of the need to strengthen their profession and have a more global focus will view the benefits of an international organization more favorably. However, some Australasian members remain parochial and resistant to change in the face of the challenges of internationalization and doing business in the global economy. Sole practitioners are particularly at risk of not managing to keep pace with change and compete at an international level. Concern has been expressed that the larger firms will get larger and that the sole practitioners will not be able to compete and will be forced out of business. It is true that the pace of change threatens the livelihood of many valuers and only those that can meet the challenges will survive.

Legislative Challenges

This section outlines recent legislative changes that are impacting on the valuation profession. In particular, it discusses structural changes to the profession, the opening up of the market for conducting rating valuations (previously restricted to government-employed valuers) and how to account for new taxation laws affecting property transactions.

New Zealand—The Valuers Act of 1948, Deregulation and Rating Legislation

The Valuers Act of 1948 is the piece of legislation that gives formal statutory recognition to valuers. Further, it provided for the establishment of the Valuers Registration Board, the body responsible for registering valuers. However, many of the references made in the Act relate to the old NZIV and now, with the merger of NZIV with PLEINZ and IPMV, the future of this Act is questioned. A significant amount of debate has ensued over the relevance of the Act in light of the new Institute and in particular, the question of deregulation of the profession. The options currently suggested to deal with the issue include:

- Status quo: "If it ain't broke why fix it?"
- Amended status quo: correcting defects and changing references to NZPI and NZIV.
- State Registration (New Minimalist Act): protects the public and professional recognition of valuers.
- Land Information New Zealand (LINZ) proposal: repeal the Act and replace it with mandatory disclosure and banning regime. This would require all valuers to provide potential clients certain information:
    - Qualifications obtained.
    - Level of experience.

- ○ Membership to a professional body.
- ○ Level of indemnity insurance held.

If no disclosure is provided, exposure to the implications of the Fair Trading Act would result.

- Self-governance (deregulation): total control of own future.

From a survey of membership opinions the status quo and amended status quo options seem to be those preferred. No final decision has yet been reached over the option to be adopted.

A major change to the tradition of rating valuations in New Zealand occurred in 1998. *The Rating Valuations Act 1998* repealed the *Valuation of Land Act 1951* and amended the *Rating Powers Act 1988*. Under the previous legislation all properties in New Zealand had to be valued for rating purposes by a quasi-government body: Valuation New Zealand (VNZ, previously named The Valuation Department). The new Acts formalized the corporatization of VNZ and provided for the appointment of a Valuer-General within LINZ and for the creation of a crown-owned company (Quotable Value New Zealand). The new Act also provided for contestability of valuations. Now all territorial authorities can choose who provides their valuations that they use for rating purposes. Quotable Value New Zealand will have to compete with other valuation service providers. The only requirement is that the valuation services provided must be carried out under the authority of a registered valuer.

This change has not only made the market for territorial valuations more competitive but also more contentious in terms of uniformity despite regulation by the Valuer-General. Standardization of valuation methods and access to a central database are no longer possible when the rating valuation work and associated databases are spread between various organizations. The quality and maintenance of those databases is left to the discretion of each independent valuation provider. This brings into question the quality and fairness of the valuations for rating purposes where a level "playing field" is paramount.

Australian taxation valuations are still undertaken by the equivalent of the New Zealand Valuation Department, The Valuer General's Office (VGO). It will be interesting to see if similar privatization and free-market moves that have occurred in New Zealand are replicated in Australia.

Australia—Goods and Services Tax

A New Tax System (Goods and Services Tax) Act 1999 became effective in Australia on July 1, 2000. The introduction of GST follows similar moves in New Zealand (1987) and Canada (1991). The Howard Government instigated a major reform of the taxation system reducing personal income taxation and introducing the Goods and Services Tax (GST). This has given rise to a number of questions from valuers over the application of GST to property transactions and its impact on business-owners.

An example of the uncertainty that exists over GST liability relates to commercial property and whether it is a going concern or not. A commercial property sold as a "Going Concern" is GST-free. For a commercial property to be sold as a "Going Concern" the following must apply:

- the purchaser must be registered or required to be registered for GST,
- the sale of the property is for consideration, and
- the vendor and the purchaser must agree in writing that the supply is of a going concern.

In addition:

- the vendor must supply to the purchaser all of the things necessary for the continued operation of the enterprise, and
- the vendor must carry on, or will carry on, the enterprise until the day of transfer of the property.

However, at present there is no defined level of occupancy of leased commercial premises included in the definition of "Going Concern." The sale of a commercial property with an income stream may be viewed as a going concern and the vendor is responsible for remitting GST to the Australian Tax Office (ATO). For the vendor to recoup the GST from the purchaser, the sale contract must state the method of disposal utilized and include a clause requiring the purchaser to pay the GST to the vendor. Purchasers of commercial property do not have to be registered for GST to acquire property. They may, however, be required to be registered in order to claim an input tax credit.[2]

Another issue arises over whether or not landlords can recoup GST payable on building expenses regardless of whether or not a lease is explicit on the payment of GST. As can be seen from the above examples the treatment of GST is not straightforward. Clarification from the ATO is necessary where interpretation of the Act is unclear.

To help address these issues the API established a national GST Committee headed by KPMG Tax Partner Peter Poulos and other leading practitioners from the property profession to review the GST legislation and provide advice to members. The API has since released a series of advice notes for its members on GST and Real Property.[3] The package provides practical guidance to the property profession in applying GST to construction contracts, leases and a number of other relevant topics and goes some way to help clarify what should be considered when applying the GST.[4]

[2]Purchasers of services will be entitled to GST input tax credits on inputs (goods and services) that they purchase in the course of their business. That is, if they purchase inputs solely for business purposes, they will be entitled to a GST credit for the full amount of the GST paid on the input (1/11th of the price).

[3]See http://www.propertyinstitute.com.au/resources/tax/apialerts.htm.

[4]Of note is the effect GST has had on the property market. For example, in 2000/1 there was a severe post-GST slump in the residential market. The construction of new dwellings reduced by 33% (Goodman, 2002).

Professional Indemnity Insurance Challenges

Associated with the above challenges is the growing concern over the availability and cost of PI insurance to cover the greater risks involved in providing valuation services. External factors, such as the collapse of insurance company HIH Australia in March 2001 and the insurance events of September 11th in New York have had damaging effects on insurance markets globally.

There are currently *no* Australian insurance companies prepared to underwrite PI insurance for valuers and only one international insurer (Lloyds of London)[5] that is willing to do so. Further, the premiums have escalated sharply. Apparently, Australian valuers have claimed 350% of the premium-pool for the last several years due to huge court settlements making a hefty contribution to these claims. Australian courts have set precedents that allow for higher awards to litigants than is common in some other jurisdictions. The highest settlement awarded to date has been for $3.5AU million in 1999 (Kooymans 2001). Premiums for certified practicing valuers (CPVs) are between $4000AU and $12,000AU per annum for an average of $1 million in cover having increased by around 100% p.a. in the last 3 years.[6] Excesses (also referred to as deductibles, i.e., the amount of a claim the insured is liable for) have increased 10-fold in the last 12 months. This is an enormous expense when CPVs fees average only a few hundred dollars and their incomes are often quite modest by professional standards, (API 2002).

Spencer (2001), a sole practitioner in Perth, Western Australia, points out that many major clients require a continuing PI cover before they will enter a valuation contract. Valuers are understandably concerned about what will happen with those clients in the event that PI cover is unavailable.

> Senior members of the API appear to be speculating that many valuation practices, if not all, may not be able to afford to arrange PI cover next year ... if this worst prognosis is correct, many practices will have to consider whether to continue without cover or do something else (Spencer 2001).

The Australian Property Institute is currently examining the problems of PI insurance within the property profession and believes the crisis in PI insurance is now an issue that state governments should examine, if they want to ensure that Australian consumers can afford the services of their professionals. The API National Council Sub-Committee on PI Insurance (formed in early 2001) surveyed members to ascertain members' experience with PI and have developed a Compulsory CPD Risk Management course for practising valuers (piloted April 2002). The aim of these initiatives is to deliver sustainable and affordable PI insurance coverage to members (API 2002).

[5]Brian King, Managing Director of Crown Insurance Group (the API's broker), managed to reach an agreement with Lloyds of London to underwrite valuers PI insurance but this was greed to at a price (i.e., substantially higher premiums).

[6]Spencer (2001) reports that a small operator, such as himself, has to pay around $5,000 per annum for a $1m coverage and $15,000 excess (i.e., the amount of money the valuer has to pay towards the cost of a claim) and that this premium has almost doubled in just 2 years.

The concept of the Compulsory CPD Risk Management course is that on completion of the course separate CPD risk management certificates will be issued. The intention is that PI insurers will require individual valuers certificates to be appended to a firms PI policy renewals each year. The course will be administered by the API national office. Topics to be covered in the Module include: best practice, better communication, better client selection, rules of conduct/code of ethics/disciplinary procedures, principles of law, professional office practice procedures, and adherence to basic valuation principles.

New Zealand valuers are facing similar problems to their Australian colleagues. There are only two PI insurance companies and costs to obtain coverage are rising. However, initiatives to deal with PI coverage availability and the rising costs of obtaining it have only recently been addressed by the NZPI. The NZPI has sent out a survey to members (October 2002) to determine members' experience of the problem and they propose to introduce a Risk Management CPD module in late 2002.

Another PI issue valuers face is the need to obtain "running cover." This need arises due to the definition of the "loss date" of a PI claim. When a claim is made against a valuer the loss date is not usually taken to be the date of valuation, as may be expected, but is most commonly the date the claim was made. Yet, valuers are not always aware of this clause in their PI policy. Thus, in the situation where a valuer has ceased practising and later a claim is made against him/her if they have not obtained "running cover" under a PI policy then they will not be covered. In New Zealand, the Statue of Limitations applies (liability is limited to 6 years) and a valuer can be sued up to six years after a valuation has been completed. As such, it is recommended that "running cover" be obtained for this period. While various options exist for obtaining "running cover" the most popular option is to apply for this annually with premiums amounting to around 85% of the premium for full PI coverage (Thomson 2002).

The Declining Level of Fees

While the costs of doing business are rising, as evidenced from the previous section, charges for professional valuation services are falling. The level of fees for valuation services has been dropping over recent years. This is partly due to the competition for valuation work from nontraditional suppliers of valuation services banks, accountants and lawyers. These related disciplines are seen by many valuers to be encroaching and poaching on their area of specialization. Further, some lending institutions no longer require a registered valuer's report before lending, basing their decision instead on the property's current rating value.

It is not uncommon for valuers in New Zealand to be charging a mere $113US for a residential valuation (and in some instances, even less). These fee levels compromise a reasonable duty of care. According to a survey of 16 valuation firms in New Zealand conducted by Waikato University in 2001 (Lawrence 2002) the average annual turnover for a firm is US$ 218,200 (US$ 70,200 per valuer) with net profit to the working owner of US$ 36,300 p.a. (compared to US$ 60,200 p.a. in the accountancy profession). This level of income is lower than 2000. Lawrence points out that to earn a salary of US$ 50,200 p.a. valuers would have to be charging $50–70/hour or US$ 196–200 per valuation, nearly double the rate of fees that is currently charged.

The message is clear that valuers are under-charging for their services especially considering their exposure to risk, costs of operation and time taken to prepare valuation reports. Some valuers are suggesting that the NZPI return to a recommended scale of fees for valuers yet set scales of fees are not permitted under the Fair Trading Act 1997.

While under fee pressure, valuers are pushed at an increasing pace in the hopes of increasing their turnover volume resulting in increased chances of making mistakes and providing lower grade work. In Australia, according to the API,

> Market practices have also seen some lenders instructing and/or encouraging valuers to deviate from robustly developed API standards... and of addressing reports to multiple instructing parties (for example up to 30 parties for some lenders) so that lenders may hawk valuations between lenders... However, the "catch 22" nature of these issues is that, in the scramble to achieve panel appointments and compete for work, members will accept unreasonable terms of appointment (API 2002, p. 3).

In connection with the above, enormous pressure is being placed on valuers by banks to provide a greater level of detail in valuations particularly for commercial lending on proposed developments. Pressure to produce work involving greater detail and exactness is also coming from landlords and tenants in rent-review valuations. In practice, an increase in valuation detail and accuracy is to be encouraged but it is posing a major challenge for valuers as clients resist paying higher fees for the time necessary to achieve the more detailed analysis.

A related issue is the use, or abuse, of the computer. While technological advancements have made valuers' tasks more efficient they also pose huge challenges to valuers to maintain high standards, especially when clients expect portfolios to also be valued in shorter time frames. The potential for error is enormous. Valuers are cutting and pasting documents incorrectly, printing out documents and sending them to clients without proof-reading them, or mistakenly sending out old drafts. All of these errors are a result of valuers trying to do too much in too little time, an indirect consequence of low fees according to Daly (2001), the design and implementation of robust and mandatory self-audit functions, including the meticulous checking of all work, would help overcome many of the potential pitfalls outlined above.

Valuing Public Sector Infrastructural Assets

Together with the increased pressure to do more for less valuers are now being asked to value non-traditional asset classes including public sector infrastructure. As a result of legislative changes[7] and the movement towards public accountability and more efficient resource management[8] local authority assets and resources are now required to

[7]Introduction of the Financial Reporting Act 1993 and The Local Government Act (No. 3) 1996.

[8]Including the inclusion of infrastructure and utilities in the Rating Valuation Roll.

be defined, valued and recorded, using specific financial reporting guidelines. The main purpose of this process is to enable authorities to make the most cost-effective use of their capital and to ensure that no asset is overlooked or under-utilized. This exercise is not unique to Australasia, other countries such as the United Kingdom and Thailand are in the process of, or have completed, the collation of such data and are examining the implementation of this policy.

The Local Govt Amendment Act 1996 classifies infrastructural assets as depreciable assets and so a valuation basis has to be established for charging depreciation. Yet, according to Kellett (2001), in 1996 most local authorities in New Zealand did not even have detailed information on the historic cost of their infrastructural assets. Independent valuers using accounting and valuation standards available at the time carried out most of the infrastructure valuations.

Results from a 1995 study of practitioners from both the United Kingdom and New Zealand showed that the procedures and methods adopted by local authorities, and the valuers they employ to account for infrastructural assets, varies widely (see Dent and Bond 1994; Bond and Dent 1996, 1998). Interestingly, the UK authorities are not required to value many of the more difficult to value asset classes, such as infrastructure and yet, the New Zealand authorities are. Given that the current legislation requires these assets to be valued in New Zealand, clear and specific guidelines are needed on the methodology to use when valuing public sector infrastructural assets. Thomson (1993) outlines the three traditional approaches to valuation and how applicable they are for this type of real estate. He finds the sales comparison approach for valuing city utilities inappropriate as these assets are rarely traded and little market evidence exists. Even where sales do exist, he feels these could not be sensibly compared due to New Zealand's small size. He considers the net income approach to also be invalid and notes that these assets are often monopolistic businesses, where the price of services are not set by market forces and thus will not reflect Net Current Worth.

The literature indicates that the replacement cost, or variation of this (e.g., the Optimized Replacement Cost Approach)[9] has being relied on where no active market exists for an asset and/or the assets are non-income generating. This is the method, that is, generally accepted within the New Zealand profession for valuing infrastructural assets. Perhaps the most difficult aspect of the replacement cost approach is in the assessment of depreciation and the economic lives of assets. Yet as the depreciation of New Zealand's local authority assets in 2000 amounted to $771.4 million[10] it is critical that valuers get this estimate right.

The most common and simplest method of assessing depreciation is by estimating the economic life of the asset and calculating the annual rate of depreciation that will reduce the value of the asset to nil by the end of its economic life. Kellett (2001) questions the

[9]Horsley (1991) lists factors that the approach accounts for that the traditional replacement cost approach ignores such as: exposure to private sector competition, obsolescence due to changes in public policy, or other confounding factors, such as industry regulation.

[10]As reported in Kellett (2001).

reasonableness of this approach, particularly for certain assets, such as a road, that are to be maintained in perpetuity whereby an estimate of economic life is non-sensible. Further, the approach to assessing depreciation, as outlined, assumes that depreciation accrues in equal annual amounts over the estimated life of a property but this may not be the case and is difficult to prove. Another element of depreciation difficult to measure is obsolescence due to its largely intangible nature and uncertainties over causes. Thus, any allowance for depreciation contains an element of judgement not capable of proof.

As depreciation charges are commonly determined by application of a depreciation rate to a valuation estimate, Kellett (2001) points out the dangers in wrongly assessing those values and the importance of getting it right: "If values are too low, depreciation charges will not be adequate to sustain the infrastructure. If values are too high we, as ratepayers, will be paying too much for the infrastructure services" (p. 36).

Some of the issues surrounding the valuation of infrastructural assets will be resolved with the introduction of new valuation standards. A New Zealand local government initiative formed a national asset management steering (NAMS) group that published guidelines for the valuation of infrastructure assets as part of The NZ Infrastructure Asset Management Manual (996). These original guidelines were revised in April 2001 (Kellett 2001). However, until these standards, together with the new standards, outlined below, become widely known, inconsistencies in valuation approaches are likely to continue.

VALUATION STANDARDS

Some of the issues outlined above relating to valuation methodology are being addressed by the introduction of comprehensive valuation standards.

In response to the huge range in both the quality of reports produced and the advice provided by valuers in Australasia, the NZPI and API Standards Boards were established to set standards for the valuation profession and contribute to international standards. The NZPI standards board currently focuses on three key areas:

1. Provide input into the development of international valuation standards through membership to The International Valuation Standards (IVS) Committee.

   The IVS Committee released IVS 2001, a substantial document that has received international recognition by valuers, standards setters and institutional users of valuation standards. This document provided the substance for the re-write of the New Zealand Valuation Standard 3. In areas other than financial reporting, globalization is also creating a demand for standardization in banking, securitization and insurance reporting. Expert groups have been established for public sector property, securitization, bank lending, and emerging markets. Reports will be received from these groups over the next year. The next edition of IVS is due out in early 2003.
2. To introduce a new financial reporting standard.

   "Valuation Standard 3—Valuations for Financial Statements" was introduced in 2002 and became effective in February 2002. Introduction of the Standard was undertaken to incorporate changes introduced by Financial Reporting Standard 3: Accounting for Property, Plant and Equipment. The key changes for valuers are that "market value existing use" has gone as the standard and has been replaced by a "fair value" basis. Secondly, depreciated replacement cost has been strengthened as an application where no direct market evidence exists.

3. The integration of the New Zealand and Australian Standards by the year 2003 so there is only one set of standards across the two economies.

   This project will be an important step in the globalization process for Australiasia. The IVS 2001 is to be adopted as the foundation of the API-NZPI Professional Practice Standards and Guidance Notes 2003. The number of Standards is to be reduced from five to three and will include:

   - PS01—Valuation Procedures
   - PS02—Valuations for Mortgage and Loan Security Purposes
   - PS03—Valuations for Financial Reporting.

   The Standards recommended are to become mandatory in New Zealand as they currently are in Australia. The Professional Practice 2003 manual is to be a combined API/NZPI publication and is likely to be presented as a CD-ROM.

SUMMARY AND CONCLUSIONS

The above discussion indicates that many of the challenges confronting the valuation profession in Australasia are interconnected. There are enormous pressures for valuers to compete for work, to produce more of it but in less time, and to meet increasingly complex and stringent standards of professional practice. The inability of some valuers to keep abreast of the dynamic and changing environment through failure to attend Continuing Professional Development (CPD) courses has led to falling standards of valuation practice and greater exposure to risk. It is not surprising that insurance companies are no longer prepared to underwrite valuers' PI coverage.

The way forward for the profession in Australasia is open to speculation but appears to be pivotal on the following moves:

- Establishment of risk reduction and risk management processes including, mandatory self-audit functions,
- Introduction and enforcement of valuation standards relating to methodology and reporting,
- Internationalization of services,
- Raising the profile of the profession, both nationally and globally, and
- Raising fees.

Until such moves are instigated the future of the valuation profession within the region remains in doubt.

REFERENCES

Armstrong, L., A Global Profession—Dream or Deliverable Goal?. *Chartered Surveyor Monthly*, 2000, October: 12.

Australian Property Institute, Professional Indemnity Insurance News, 2002, Issue 1, June Quarter.

Australian Property Institute, 'GST Page' [Online], Available: http://www.propertyinstitute.com.au/GST-Page.htm [2001, April 19].

Bond, S.G. and Dent, P. R., The Valuation of Public Sector Assets: Identifying the Appropriate Methodology, Paper presented at the Fifth Annual American Real Estate and Urban Economics Association Conference, Orlando, Florida, USA, 23–25 May, 1996.

Bond, S.G. and Dent, P., Efficient Management of Public Sector Assets. *Journal of Property Valuation and Investment*, 1998, 16(4): 369–385.

Daly, G., Colliers Jardine, NZPI Wellington Branch Committee member and Fellow of NZPI. Valuation Issues [Online]. Available E-mail: s.bond@auckland.ac.nz [2001, March, 26].

Dent, P. and Bond, S.G., Public Property Holdings: Evaluating the Asset. *Property Management*, 1994, 11(4): 314–318.

Goodman, G., Positioning for Growth and Professionalism. *National API Newsletter*, 2002, Issue 1, May, 2.

Horsley, G., Asset Valuations and Site Assessment: Knowing Where You Stand. Paper presented at the Critical Issues in Public Sector Property Conference, Wellington, September 9–10, 1991.

Hudson, N., Education manager, Asia Pacific, RICS Oceania, Sydney. RICS and NZPI, [Online]. Available E-mail: s.bond@auckland.ac.nz [2002, December, 12].

Kellett, B., Infrastructure valuations. *New Zealand Property Journal*, 2001, July, 27–36.

Kooymans, R. Program Director, Property Programs, School of International Business, University of South Australia, Challenges Facing Australian Valuers [Online]. Available E-mail: s.bond@auckland.ac.nz [2001, March, 22].

Lawrence, M., How to value your own services. Paper presented at the NZPI Manawatu Branch CPD Seminar, Palmerston North, NZ, September 11, 2002.

Parker, D., Property Portfolio Manager, Suncorp Metway. AREUEA [Online]. Available E-mail: s.bond@auckland.ac.nz [2001, March, 25].

Southwick, P., Constitution gets the once over, *National API Newsletter*, 2002, Issue 1, May, 7.

Spencer, J., Challenges Affecting Australian Valuers [Online]. Available E-mail: s.bond@auckland.ac.nz [2001, March, 24].

Thomson, G., Professional Indemnity Insurance Cover. Paper presented at the NZPI Manawatu Branch CPD Seminar, Palmerston North, NZ, September 11, 2002.

Thomson, A., City Utilities Valuations. *New Zealand Valuers' Journal*, 1993, June, 23–27.

Part II. Best of Kinnard

8. Professional Qualifications

WILLIAM N. KINNARD, JR

President, Real Estate Counseling Group of Connecticut, Inc.
P.O. Box 558
Storrs, Connecticut 06268–0558

Principal, The Real Estate Counseling Group of America, Inc.
Professor Emeritus, Finance and Real Estate, The University of Connecticut

DEGREES AND PROFESSIONAL DESIGNATIONS

B.A., Swarthmore College (Economics-Honors)
M.B.A., University of Pennsylvania, Wharton School (Finance)
Ph.D., University of Pennsylvania (Finance and Economics)

SREA	Society of Real Estate Appraisers
MAI	American Institute of Real Estate Appraisers
CRE	American Society of Real Estate Counselors
ASA	American Society of Appraisers
CMI	Institute of Property Taxation
FCA	American Institute of Corporate Asset Management
Realtor	National Association of Realtors

HONORS AND RECOGNITIONS

Beta Gamma Sigma
Pi Gamma Mu
Phi Kappa Phi

National Science Foundation, Post-Doctoral Fellow (Regional Science), 1962
Arthur A. May Award, American Institute of Real Estate Appraisers, 1968
President, American Real Estate and Urban Economics Association, 1968
Faculty Fellow, Mortgage Bankers Association of America, 1977–78
Beta Gamma Sigma Distinguished Scholar, 1979–1980
Honoree, William N. Kinnard, Jr., Scholarship, Connecticut Chapter 38, Society of Real Estate Appraisers, 1981–85
Harrison-Winder Award, Philadelphia SREA Chapter, 1982
Honorary Fellow, Homer Hoyt Institute, 1984–Present
Alfred E. Reinman Award, Society of Real Estate Appraisers, 1985
George F. Bloom Award, American Real Estate and Urban Economics Association, 1985
Honoree, William N. Kinnard, Jr. Alumni Scholarship, The University of Connecticut, 1986–Present
Honoree, William N. Kinnard, Jr. Educational Achievement Award, Society of Real Estate Appraisers, 1988–Present
Neville Allison Award, Houston SREA Chapter, 1988
Ballard Award, American Society of Real Estate Counselors, November 1991 (co-recipient)
Bernard L. Barnard Award, International Association of Assessing Officers, 1992 (co-recipient)
ARES Annual Meeting Manuscript Award, International Council of Shopping Centers, 1994 (co-recipient)
ARES James A. Graaskamp Award, March 1995
Appraisal Institute, Armstrong/Kahn Award, April 1999
Listed In:
- Who's Who in the East
- American Men of Science, III (Social Sciences)
- Leaders in American Education
- Outstanding Educators of America

CERTIFICATIONS/RECERTIFICATIONS OF PROFESSIONAL DESIGNATIONS

CRE	December 2000
ASA	September 2001
CMI	December 2000
MAI	December 2002
SREA	December 1995 (Recertification Program Discontinued 1995)

KINNARD PURBLICATIONS

Books and Manuals

The Turnover and Mortality of Manufacturing Firms in the Hartford, Connecticut, Economic Area, 1953–1958 (with Z. S. Malinowski). The University of Connecticut, Storrs, CT. 1960.
Use of External Assistance by Small Manufacturers (with Z. S. Malinowski). Center for Real Estate and Urban Economic Studies, School of Business Administration, The University of Connecticut, Storrs, CT. 1961.

Personal Factors Influencing Small Manufacturing Plant Locations (with Z.S. Malinowski). Center for Real Estate and Urban Economic Studies, The University of Connecticut, Storrs, CT. 1961.

The Impact of Dislocation from Urban Renewal Project Areas on Small Business (with Z.S. Malinowski). Small Business Management Research Report. Bureau of Business Research and Services, The University of Connecticut, Storrs, CT. 1962.

Highways as a Factor in Small Manufacturing Plant Locations (with Z.S. Malinowski), Small Business Management Research Report. Bureau of Business Research and Services, The University of Connecticut, Storrs, CT. 1962.

The Place of Small Business in Planned Industrial Districts (with Z.S. Malinowski). Center for Real Estate and Urban Economic Studies, The University of Connecticut, Storrs, CT. 1963.

How Small Manufacturers Buy (with Tamlin K. Lindsay). Center for Real Estate and Urban Economic Studies, The University of Connecticut, Storrs, CT. 1964.

Issues in Business Relocation and Property Acquisition Relating to Just Compensation. Institute of Urban Research, University of Connecticut, Storrs, CT. 1964.

Transmission Line Rights of Way and Residential Values, Connecticut Urban Research Report 7. Institute of Urban Research, The University of Connecticut, Storrs, CT. 1965.

A Guide to Appraising Apartments. Society of Real Estate Appraisers, 1965; fifth edition with E. Roger Everett, Chicago, IL. 1979.

Industrial Real Estate. Society of Industrial Realtors, 1967; third edition with S.D. Messner and B.N. Boyce, Washington, DC. 1979.

The New England Region: Problems of a Mature Economy. Papers and proceedings of a conference held at the University of Connecticut, November 18, 1967. Center for Real Estate and Urban Economic Studies, The University of Connecticut, Storrs, CT. 1968.

Housing Strategy for Southeastern Connecticut (with S.D. Messner and J.C. Thompson), two volumes, Real Estate Report No. 3. Center for Real Estate and Urban Economic Studies, The University of Connecticut, Storrs, CT. 1968.

An Educational Program for the American Right of Way Association; Requirements, Opportunities and Recommendations. Center for Real Estate and Urban Economic Studies, The University of Connecticut, Storrs, CT. 1968.

Effective Business Relocation (with S.D. Messner). D.C. Heath and Company, Lexington Books, Lexington, MA. 1970.

Principles of Income Property Appraising: Course Manual (with B.N. Boyce). Society of Real Estate Appraisers, 1970; fifth edition, with B.N. Boyce, Chicago, IL. 1988.

Income Property Valuation. D.C. Heath and Company, Lexington Books, Lexington, MA. 1971.

Special Applications of Real Estate Analysis (with S.D. Messner and B.N. Boyce) Society of Real Estate Appraisers, Chicago, IL. 1972; Second edition, 1979.

Management of an Appraisal Firm (with B.N. Boyce and S.D. Messner). Society of Real Estate Appraisers, Chicago, IL. 1972.

Employment and Industrial Development Opportunities in the Inner City (with W.R. Thompson). Center for Real Estate and Urban Economic Studies, School of Business Administration, The University of Connecticut, Storrs, CT. 1974.

Calculator Techniques for Real Estate (with H.M. Benedict and F. Herman). Realtors National Marketing Institute, Chicago, IL. 1977.

An Appraisal Report Primer for Residential Lenders and Underwriters. General Series 10. Center for Real Estate and Urban Economic Studies, The University of Connecticut, Storrs, CT. June 1978.

A Critical Analysis of Site Value Taxation (with B.N. Boyce, with special reference to property taxation in Hartford, CT). Real Estate Report No. 24. Center for Real Estate and Urban Economic Studies, The University of Connecticut, Storrs, CT. October 1978.

Residential Property Valuation (with B.N. Boyce and S.D. Messner). BWM International Consultants, Inc., Orlando, FL. November 1978. (Dutch translation copyright by Educatie Onroerend Goed, b.v., an educational subsidiary of Westland/Utrecht Hypotheekbank; Amsterdam, The Netherlands, January 1979.)

A Critical Analysis of the Property Tax (with B.N. Boyce, with special reference to property taxation in Hartford, CT). Real Estate Report No. 27. Center for Real Estate and Urban Economic Studies, The University of Connecticut, Storrs, CT. March 1979.

Appraising Real Property (with B.N. Boyce). D.C. Heath and Company, Lexington Books, Lexington, MA. 1984.

R41-b and the Appraiser. Society of Real Estate Appraisers, Chicago, IL. 1985.

The Challenge of Measuring Economic Obsolescence (with G.L. Beron). Real Estate Counseling Group of Connecticut, Inc., Storrs, CT. 1985. (Appraisal Institute edition, 1992), Seminar Manual.

R41c and the Appraiser (and Underwriter) (with G.L. Beron). Society of Real Estate Appraisers, Chicago, IL. 1986, Seminar Manual.
1984 Real Estate Valuation Colloquium: A Redefinition of Real Estate Appraisal Theory and Practices (ed). Lincoln Institute of Land Policy, Cambridge, MA. 1986.
Effects of Proximity to Marcy South Transmission Line Right of Way on Vacant Land Sales, Towns of Hamptonburgh and Wawayanda, Orange County, New York. Real Estate Counseling Group of Connecticut, Inc., Storrs, CT. May 1988.
The Effect of High-Voltage Overhead Transmission Lines on Sales Prices and Market Values of Nearby Real Estate: An Annotated Bibliography and Evaluative Analysis. Real Estate Counseling Group of Connecticut, Inc., Storrs, CT. September 1988.
Annotated Bibliography and Court Decision Review: The Impact of Proximity to Hazardous and Toxic Materials Facilities on the Market Value of Surrounding Properties (with G.L. Beron, J.B. Kinnard, and R.D. Magann). Real Estate Counseling Group of Connecticut, Inc., Storrs, CT. May 1989.
The Applicability of the Land Development Method in the Valuation of Undeveloped Acreage (with Mary Beth Geckler). Real Estate Counseling Group of Connecticut, Inc., Storrs, CT. November 1991.
Connecticut State Appraisal License Law and Administrative Regulations (with Mary Beth Geckler). Real Estate Counseling Group of Connecticut, Inc., Storrs, CT. February 1992 (revised June 1993).
Market Rentals of Anchor Department Stores Located in Canadian Regional/Superregional Shopping Centers, 1975–1990 (with Mary Beth Geckler, Jeffrey B. Kinnard and John R. Knight). Real Estate Counseling Group of Connecticut, Inc., Storrs, CT. April 1993.
Size, Sales, and Rents: Comparing Shopping Centers in Canada and the United States (with J.R. Knight, M.B. Geckler and J.B. Kinnard), *Megatrends in Retail Real Estate.* Kluwer Academic Publishers, 3, Ch. 15, Norwell, MA. 1996.

Published Articles

"Junior Mortgages and Real Estate Finance: A Case Study". *Journal of Finance*, 1956, 11(1): 42–57.
"Educating Tomorrow's Appraiser". *The Real Estate Appraiser*, 1965, 31(7): 2–11.
"New Thinking in Appraisal Theory." *The Real Estate Appraiser*, August 1966.
"The Ellwood Analysis in Valuation: A Return to Fundamentals". *The Real Estate Appraiser*, 1966, 32(5): 18–24.
"Tower Lines and Residential Property Values", *The Appraisal Journal*, 1967, 35: 269–284.
"The Approaching Crisis in Appraisal Education". *The Appraisal Journal*, 1968, 36: 166–174.
"Reducing Uncertainty in Real estate Decisions". *The Real Estate Appraiser*, 1968, 34(7): 10–16.
"The Financial Logic of Investment Property Appraising". *The Real Estate Appraiser*, 1969, 35(4): 13–21.
"Lender Participation Financing: Its Nature and Significance to Appraisers". *The Real Estate Appraiser*, 1971, 37(2): 13–19.
"Lender Participation Financing: Case Applications in Appraising Participation Properties (Part II)". *The Real Estate Appraiser*, 1971, 37(3): 11–25.
"Lender Participation Financing: Conclusion Applications of Sensitivity and Investment Analysis". *The Real Estate Appraiser*, 1971, 37(4): 33–40.
"Counseling Investor-Clients Through Mortgage-Equity Analysis." *The Appraisal Journal*, Chicago, July, 1972.
"The Challenge of Measuring Economic Obsolescence" (with G.L. Beron). *Real Estate Counseling Group of Connecticut, Inc.*, 1985.
"The First Twenty Years of AREUEA" (with H.G. Berkman, H.O. Nourse and J.C. Weicher), *AREUEA Journal*, 1988, 16(2).
"Corporate Real Estate: A Course Outline and Rationale" (with J. Dasso and J.S. Rabianski). *The Journal of Real Estate Research*, 1989, 4(3).
"Analyzing the Stigma Effect of Proximity to a Hazardous Materials Site." *Environmental Watch*, Appraisal Institute, December 1989, 11(4).
"The Impact of High Voltage Transmission Lines on Real Estate Values." *Journal of Property Tax Management*, Spring 1990, 1(4).
"The Market Impact of a Release of Radioactive Materials on Local Housing Values: An Econometric Study" (with Phillip S. Mitchell and Gail L. Beron). *Journal of Property Tax Management*, Fall 1990, pp. 38–52.
"The Business Enterprise Value Component of Operating Properties" (with Jeffrey D. Fisher). *Journal of Property Tax Management*, October 1990, 2(1): 19–27.
"The Effects on Residential Real Estate Prices from Proximity to Properties Contaminated with Radioactive Materials" (with Mary Beth Geckler). *Real Estate Issues*, Fall/Winter 1991, 16(2): 25–26.

"Market Reactions to an Announced Release of Radioactive Materials: The Impact on Assessable Value" (with Phillip S. Mitchell, Gail L. Beron and James R. Webb), *Property Tax Journal*, September 1991, 10(3): 283–297. Winner of the 1992 Bernard L. Barnard Award for the best article on Assessment Administration.

"Tools and Techniques for Measuring the Effects of Proximity to Radioactive Contamination of Soil on Single-Family Residential Sales Prices: A Case Study of Three Superfund Sites," *Appraisal Institute Symposium*, Philadelphia, PA, October 1991.

"Market-Extracted Adjustments for Size of Major Tracts of Land," *Journal of Property Tax Management*, Winter 1991.

"Measuring the Effects of Hazardous Materials Contamination on Real Estate Values: Techniques and Applications," *Technical Report*, Appraisal Institute, 1992, pp. 1–22.

"The Effects of Proximity to Sources of Pollution and Contamination on Market Value of Nearby Residential Properties and Vacant Residential Land: An Overview," *Appraisal Institute*, 1992.

"Measuring the Effects of Contamination on Property Values," *Environmental Watch*, Appraisal Institute, Winter 1992, IV(4).

"Standards for Measuring the Business Enterprise Value Component of Regional and Superregional Shopping Centers: A Retrospective Review," International Association of Assessing Officers/California Association of Assessors, *Technical Seminars*, Burbank, CA and Sacramento, CA, February 1992. [Also published by IAAO in *Proceedings*, Chicago: IAAO, 1992.]

"Market Reactions to an Announced Release of Radioactive Materials: The Impact on Assessable Value" (with Phillip S. Mitchell, Gail L. Beron and James R. Webb), *Assessment Digest*, January/February 1993, 15(1): 18–25.

"The Uniform Standards of Professional Appraisal Practice: Their Impact on Property Tax Clients and Attorneys," *Journal of Property Tax Management*, August 1993.

"Real Estate Valuation: Guide to Investment Strategies," *Appraisal Journal*, October 1993, 61(4).

"The Counselor as Expert Witness: Hazards, Pitfalls and Defenses," *Real Estate Issues*, Fall/Winter 1993, 18(2).

"Transfer of Ownership Rights via Rent Control," Chapter in *Appraisal, Market Analysis, and Public Policy in Real Estate: Essays in Honor of James A. Graaskamp*, James de Lisle and J. Sa-Aadu, Eds., American Real Estate Society, Real Estate Research Issues, 1994. 1.

"Natural Gas Pipeline Impact on Residential Property Values: An Empirical Study of Two Market Areas" (with Sue Ann Dickey and Mary Beth Geckler), *Right of Way*, June 1994, 26–32.

"Canadian Anchor Department Store Rentals: Are They Too Low, Subsidized or at Market?" (with Mary Beth Geckler), *The Canadian Appraiser*, Winter 1994. 38, Book 4.

"A Primer on Proximity Impact Research: Residential Property Values Near High-Voltage Transmission Lines" (with Sue Ann Dickey). *Real Estate Issues*, April 1995, 20, Number One.

"Retooling a Profession and Its Professionals." *Appraisal Institute Symposium*, September 1995, New Orleans, LA.

"Are Residential Property Values Affected by Proximity to Alleged Hazards to Human Health and Safety?" (with Mary Beth Geckler and John K. Geckler). *Journal of Property Tax Management*, Fall 1995.

"Capitalization Rates for Regional Shopping Centers: Anchor Department Stores vs. Mall Stores" (with Mary Beth Geckler, John K. Geckler and Jake W. DeLottie), *Real Estate Issues*, August 1996, 21(2).

"The Effect of Varying Levels of Negative Publicity on Single-Family Property Values: A Case Study of Soil Contamination" (with Mary Beth Geckler and Jake W. DeLottie). *Assessment Journal*, September/October 1996, 3(5).

"Residential Valuations and Surveys, Electromagnetic Fields: Property Value Impacts" (with Allisdair Philips and David Jeffers), *Television Education Network*, The Royal Institution of Chartered Surveyors, London, England, November/December 1996.

"Client Pressure in the Commercial Appraisal Industry: How Prevalent Is It?" (with Margarita M. Lenk and Elaine M. Worzala), *Journal of Property Valuation & Investment*, 1997, 15(3).

"The Contribution of Anchor Department Stores to Mall Value: A Comparison of Sales and Rentals per Square Foot in U.S. Superregional and Community Shopping Centers 1975–1995," (with Mary Beth Geckler and Jake W. DeLottie), *Journal of Applied Real Property Analysis*, 1997, 1(1).

"Identifying and Measuring Business Enterprise Value for Shopping Centers" (with Mary Beth Geckler). *The Real Estate Finance Journal*, Spring 1997, 12(4).

"Team Performance, Attendance and Risk for Major League Baseball Stadiums: 1970–1994" (with Mary Beth Geckler and Jake W. DeLottie). *Real Estate Issues*, April 1997, 22(1).

"Investor & Lender Reactions to Alternative Sources of Contamination" (with Elaine M. Worzala). *Real Estate Issues*, August 1997, 22(2).

"Lenders' and Investors' Attitudes and Policies Toward Property Contamination: New Zealand and America Compared" (with S. G. Bond and Elaine M. Worzala). *Australian Land Economics Review*, 1997, 3(2).

"Lenders' and Investors' Attitudes and Policies Toward Property Contamination in New Zealand" (with S.G. Bond and Elaine M. Worzala). *New Zealand Valuers' Journal*, November 1997.
"The New Noneconomics: Public Interest Value, Market Value and Economic Use" (with Bill Mundy). *The Appraisal Journal*, April 1998, LXVI(2).
"Market Participants' Reactions Toward Contaminated Property in New Zealand and the USA" (with S.G. Bond, Elaine M. Worzala and Steven D. Kapplin). *Journal of Property Valuation and Investment*, 1998, 16(3).
"How Client Pressure Affects the Appraisal of Residential Property" *The Appraisal Journal*, October 1998, Chicago, 66(4).
"Quantifying Business Enterprise Value for Malls" (with Maxwell O. Ramsland, Jr.), *The Appraisal Journal*, April 1999, LXVII(2).
"How North American Appraisers Value Contaminated Property and Associated Stigma" (with Elaine M. Worzala). *The Appraisal Journal*, July 1999.
"Estimating Market Rent for Major League Stadiums" (with Mary Beth Geckler). *Real Estate Issues*, Summer 1999, 24(2).
"The Effect of Electricity Market Deregulation on Local Property Tax Assessments and Fiscal Stability" (with Gail L. Beron). *Real Estate Issues*, Spring 2000.
"Graaskamp and Business Enterprise Value: It's in the Profit Centers (A Case Study of a Hotel)" (with Elaine M. Worzala), in *Essays in Honor of James A. Graaskamp: Ten Years After*, James R. DeLisle and Elaine M. Worzala (eds), American Real Estate Society, Research Issues in Real Estate, Volume 6, 2000.
"Intangible Assets in an Operating First-Class Downtown Hotel: A Comparison of Sources of Information in a Profit Center Approach to Valuation" (with Elaine M. Worzala and Dan L. Swango). *The Appraisal Journal*, January 2001. LXIX(1).
"The Resurgence of Nuclear Power in the U.S." (with Gail L. Beron). *Real Estate Issues*, Winter 2000/2001.
"There is REIT Value and Pension Fund Value, But Neither is Market Value (Usually)" (with Mary Beth Geckler). *Journal of Property Tax Management*, Spring 2001, 12(4).
"An International Perspective on Incorporating Risk in the Valuation of Contaminated Land" (with Sandy G. Bond, Paul J. Kennedy and Elaine M. Worzala). *The Australian Property Journal*, 2001, 36(6).
"New Thinking in Appraisal Theory." *The Appraisal Journal*, July 2001, 69(3).
"Mitigating Currency Risk for International hotel Investments: Can it be Done?" (with Richard D. Johnson, Elaine M. Worzala and Colin Lizieri). *Real Estate Finance*, Summer 2001, 18(2).
"Industrial Property Contamination: Marketability Effects and Proximity Impacts". *Professional Report*, March/April 1993.

Papers Presented at Professional Conferences and Seminars

"What Value? Of What? To Whom?" (with Gail L. Beron). International Association of Assessing Officers, Fourth Annual Legal Seminar, New Orleans, LA, March 1984.
"The Three Levels of Feasibility" (Joint Presentation with Gail L. Beron). Society of Real Estate Appraisers National Conference, Los Angeles, CA, August 1986.
"Paired Sales Analysis." Appraisal Institute of Canada National Conference, Vancouver, British Columbia, Canada, October 1986.
"Using Statistics to Test the Reasonableness of Appraisals." Society of Real Estate Appraisers Symposium, Indianapolis, IN, October 1987.
"Real Estate Valuation in an Environment of Increasing Regulation." University of Wisconsin Symposium, Baltimore, MD, November 1987.
"Measuring Economic Impacts Through Multiple Regression Analysis" (Joint Presentation with Gail L. Beron). Society of Real Estate Appraisers Symposium, Montreal, Quebec, Canada, August 1987.
"The Role of Appraisers Under Federal Legislation." University of Wisconsin Symposium, Atlanta, GA, March 1988.
"Measuring Toxic Materials Facility Impacts on Property Values." American Real Estate Society, San Francisco, CA, April 1988.
"Market Analysis for Real Estate Investment Decisions." Northwest Professional Seminars, Inc., Cambridge, MA, May 1988.
"Valuation of Leased Equipment." Institute of Property Taxation, National Conference, Dallas, TX, June 1988.
"Keynote Speech: Emerging Challenges to Appraisers and Assessors." International Association of Assessing Officers, Annual Conference, Nashville, TN, September 1988.
"The Business Value Component of Operating Properties: Shopping Centers; The Impact of Proximity to Radioactive Materials Handling Facilities on the Market Value of Surrounding Residential Properties." International Association of Assessing Officers, Annual Conference, Fort Worth, TX, 1989.

"The Impact of High-Voltage Overhead Transmission Lines on the Value of Real Property" (with Phillip S. Mitchell and James R. Webb). American Real Estate Society Annual Conference, Arlington, VA, April 1989.
"Research and Analysis for Valuation of Real Estate of Shopping Center and Mall Properties." SCAN Conference, Chicago, IL, August 1989.
"The Impact of High-Voltage Overhead Transmission Lines on the Value of Undeveloped Land." Edison Electric Institute Symposium, Portland, OR, October 1989.
"The Effect of High-Voltage Overhead Transmission Lines on Sales Prices and Market Values of Nearby Real Estate: An Annotated Bibliography and Evaluative Analysis." Edison Electric Institute Workshop, Portland, OR, October 1989.
"Valuing the Real Estate of Regional Shopping Centers Independently of Operating Business Value Components: A Summary Analysis." Institute of Property Taxation, 1989 IPT Property Tax Symposium, November 1989.
"The Business Enterprise Value Component of Operating Properties: The Example of Shopping Malls" (with Jeffrey D. Fisher). At Annual Conference of American Real Estate and Urban Economics Association, December 1989.
"Some Observations on Current Issues Confronting Real Estate Market Analysis and Analysts." Homer Hoyt Institute, Weimer School of Graduate Studies, Singer Island, FL, January 1990.
"Measuring the Business Value Component of Operating Regional Shopping Centers." American Real Estate Society, Lake Tahoe, NV, March 1990.
"An Econometric Analysis of the Impact of a Release of Radioactive Materials on a Local Housing Market" (with Phillip S. Mitchell). American Real Estate Society, Lake Tahoe, NV, March 1990.
"Valuing the Real Estate of Regional Shopping Centers Independently of Operating Business Value Components: A Review of Recent Research." White Paper Educational Session, American Institute of Real Estate Appraisers, Chicago, IL, May 1990.
"Current Techniques and Procedures for Dealing with the Effects of Property Contamination and of Business Enterprise Value: The State of the Art, Keynote Address." At Society of Real Estate Appraisers SREA Symposium, San Antonio, TX, September 1990.
"Measuring the Business Value Component of a Regional/Superregional Shopping Center: A Case Study." Society of Real Estate Appraisers SREA Symposium, San Antonio, TX, September 1990.
"Measuring Locational Obsolescence: Proximity to Hazardous Materials Sites." Silver Anniversary Professional Seminar on Appraisal of Distressed Properties, International Association of Assessing Offices, Montreal, Quebec, Canada, October 1990.
"Wealth Transfer Under Rent Control Affecting Mobile Home Parks in California and New Jersey." Homer Hoyt Institute, Weimer School of Advanced Studies, Singer Island, FL, 1991.
"Methodologies for Valuation of Real Property Impacted by Pollution from Hazardous and Toxic Materials." Real Estate Counseling Group of America, Inc., Orlando, FL, February 1991.
"The Effects of Proximity to Contaminated and Polluted Facilities on Sales Prices of Nearby Residential Properties: Locational Obsolescence and the Stigma Effect." The Appraisal Network/Real Estate Counseling Group of America, Joint Educational Conference, Orlando, FL, March 1991.
"The Transfer of Wealth from Landlord to Tenant in Rent-Controlled Mobile Home Parks, An Econometric Analysis of In-Place Mobile Home Sales." American Real Estate Society, Seventh Annual Meeting, Sarasota, FL, April 1991.
"Impact of Proximity to Superfund Sites on Residential Property Values in Three Northern New Jersey Towns: A Case Study." American Real Estate Society, Sarasota, FL, April 1991.
"Emerging Issues in Market Analysis of Regional and Superregional Shopping Centers." Homer Hoyt Institute, Weimer School of Advanced Studies, Singer Island, FL, May 1991.
"Identification and Measurement of Business Enterprise Value in Regional and Superregional Shopping Centers." Institute of Property Taxation, Annual Conference, Los Angeles, CA, June 1991.
"Measuring the Effects of Contamination and Pollution on Property Values: The Focus of the 1991 Symposium in the Context of the Current State of Knowledge." Keynote Speech, Appraisal Institute Symposium, Philadelphia, PA, October 1991.
"Tools and Techniques for Measuring the Effects of Proximity to Radioactive Contamination of Soil on Single-Family Residential Sales Prices: A Case Study of Three Superfund Sites." Appraisal Institute Symposium, Philadelphia, PA, October 1991.
"Standards for Measuring Business Enterprise Value in Regional and Superregional Shopping Centers: Operating Entrepreneurship, Economic Rent and Profit Residuals." International Association of Assessing Officers, 1991 Annual Conference, Phoenix, AZ, October 1991.
"Wealth Transfer Under Rent Control—Mobile Home Park Rent Control Price Effects in California and New Jersey." Weimer School of Advanced Studies, Homer Hoyt Institute, North Palm Beach, FL, January 1992.

"Business Enterprise Value: Papers and Proceedings." California Assessors' Association and International Association of Assessing Officers Joint Seminar, Burbank, CA, February 1992.
"The Effects of Proximity to Sources of Pollution and Contamination on Market Value of Nearby Residential Properties and Vacant Residential Land: An Overview." Appraisal Institute, 1992 Annual Conference, Seattle, WA, July 29, 1992.
"Patterns of Property Value Impacts from Proximity to High-Voltage Transmission Lines: Analytical Update." Edison Electric Institute Conference, Duluth, MN, August 1992.
"Sales Comparison Approach: The Role of Highest and Best Use; and The Uniform Standards of Professional Appraisal Practice: Their Impact on Clients, Attorneys and Appraisers." Institute of Property Taxation, Property Tax Symposium, Tempe, AZ, November 1992.
"The Industrial Real Estate Market in Connecticut." Center for Real Estate and Urban Economic Studies, University of Connecticut, Annual Economic Conference, Waterbury, CT, November 1992.
"Marketability Effects and Proximity Impacts from Contamination of Industrial Properties." Society of Industrial and Office Realtors, December 1992.
"Market Rentals of Canadian Department Stores Located in Regional Shopping Centers, 1975–90." Weimer School of Advanced Studies, Homer Hoyt Institute, Singer Island, FL, January 1993.
"What Appraisers Can Do and Must Do To Estimate Market Value of Contaminated Properties." New Jersey Institute for Continuing Legal Education, Contaminated Property Valuation Conference, New Brunswick, NJ, March 1993.
"The Impact of Proximity to High-Pressure Natural Gas Pipelines on Single-Family Residential Property Values." American Real Estate Society, 1993 Annual Conference, Key West, FL, April 1993.
"The Impact of Proximity to a Proposed Limited Access Highway Designated for Transportation of Radioactive Materials on the Market Value of Nearby Residential Land and Residences." Transportation Research Board, National Research Council, 32nd Annual Workshop on Transportation Law, Santa Fe, NM, July 1993.
"What Appraisers Can Do and Must Do to Estimate the Impact of Contamination on Property Value." American Bar Association, Annual Conference, New York, NY, August 8, 1993.
"Anchor Department Store Rentals: Market or 'Subsidized' (Too Low)?" International Association of Assessing Officers, Annual Conference, Washington, DC, September 1993.
"Size, Sales and Rents: Comparing Shopping Centers in Canada and the United States" (with John R. Knight, Mary Beth Geckler and Jeffrey B. Kinnard). 1993 International Real Estate Conference jointly sponsored by the University of Connecticut, the American Real Estate and Urban Economics Association and the Federal National Mortgage Association, Mystic, CT, October 1993.
"Property Valuation: A Primer on Proximity Impact Research." Paper presented at a Conference on Electric and Magnetic Fields, Executive Enterprises, Inc., Washington, DC, January 1994.
"Estimating Market Rentals for Anchor Department Stores and Mall Stores U.S. Regional and Superregional Shopping Centers, 1975–93" (with Jake W. DeLottie, Jeffrey B. Kinnard and Mary Beth Geckler). American Real Estate Society, 1994 Annual Conference, Santa Barbara, CA, April 1994.
"Fear (As a Measure of Damages) Strikes Out: Two Case Studies, Comparisons of Actual Market Behavior with Opinion Survey Research" (with Mary Beth Geckler and Sue Ann Dickey). American Real Estate Society, 1994 Annual Conference, Santa Barbara, CA, April 1994.
"Entrepreneurial Profit, Business Enterprise Value and Rentals: The Example of Regional and Superregional Shopping Centers." Maryland Association of Assessing Officers, Ocean City, MD, June 1994.
"Fear and Property Value: Opinion Survey Results vs. Market Sales Evidence" (with Sue Ann Dickey and Mary Beth Geckler). International Association of Assessing Offices, Annual Conference, Seattle, WA, October 1994.
"Current Issues in Valuation of Centrally Assessed Utility Properties." Institute of Property Taxation, Real Property Tax Symposium, San Antonio, TX, November 1994.
"Canadian Anchor Department Store Rentals: Are They Too Low, Subsidized or at Market?" (with Mary Beth Geckler). Canadian Property Tax Association Program, Montreal, Canada, July 1994.
"Capitalization Rates Are Not Discount Rates: A Handy Guide to Identifying Misleading Appraisals" (with Mary Beth Geckler). American Bar Association/Institute of Property Taxation, Advanced Property Tax Symposium, New Orleans, LA, March 1995.
"There is REIT Value and Pension Fund Value, But Neither is Market Value (Usually)" (with Mary Beth Geckler). American Bar Association/Institute of Property Taxation, Advanced Property Tax Symposium, New Orleans, LA, March 1995.
"The Impact of Widespread, Long-Term Soil Contamination on Residential Property Values: A Case Study" (with Jake W. Delottie, Mary Beth Geckler and Benjamin H. Noble). American Real Estate Society, Annual Meeting, Hilton Head, SC, April 1995.
"Entrepreneurial Profit as an Integral Part of Cost New: Empirical Fact or Nonsense?" (with Mary Beth Geckler and Sue Ann Dickey). American Real Estate Society, Annual Meeting, Hilton Head, SC, April 1995.

"Current Trends and Developments in the Valuation of Canadian Regional Shopping Centers" (with Mary Beth Geckler). The Appraisal Institute of Canada/Institut Canadien des Evaluateurs 1995 Annual Conference, Victoria, British Columbia, June 1995.

"Applications of Bundle of Rights Analysis to Ad Valorem Property Tax Valuation in the US." Bundle of Rights Seminar, Quebec Chapter, Canadian Property Tax Association, Montreal, Quebec, September 1995.

"The Effect of Varying Levels of Negative Publicity on Single-Family Property Values: A Case Study of Soil Contamination from a Nearby Smelter" (with Mary Beth Geckler and Jake W. DeLottie). International Association of Assessing Officers Sixty-First International Conference, Chicago, IL, September 1995.

"Retooling a Profession and Its Professionals." 1995 Appraisal Institute Symposium, New Orleans, LA, September 1995.

"The Impacts on Residential Property Values From Proximity to Selected Sources of Alleged or Perceived Hazards to Human Health and Safety" (with Mary Beth Geckler and John K. Geckler). Appraisal Institute Seminar, Spokane, WA, September 1995. (Also presented at Environmental Law Institute, Newark, NJ, September 1995.)

"Market Evidence of Business Value in Operating Properties: The Examples of Shopping Malls, Hotels and Congregate Care/Retirement Facilities." Insight and Globe and Mail Conference, Toronto, Ontario, Canada, February 1996.

"Attitudes and Policies of Institutional Lenders and Investors Toward On-Site and Nearby Property Contamination" (with Elaine Worzala). Homer Hoyt Advanced Studies Institute and Real Estate Counseling Group of America Joint Meeting, North Palm Beach, FL, March 1996.

"Identifying and Measuring Business Value for Shopping Centers and Retirement Centers." ABA/IPT Advanced Property Tax Seminar, New Orleans, Louisiana, LA, March 1996.

"EMF and the Eighth Deadly Sin: The Literature on Property Value Impacts from Proximity to High-Voltage Transmission Lines Since 1994." Business Development Associates, Inc. and Executive Enterprises Joint Conference, Washington, DC, April 1996.

"Shopping Centre Valuation and Analysis." New Brunswick Association of Real Estate Appraisers Conference, Fredericton, New Brunswick, Canada, April 1996.

"Applications of Bundle of Rights Analysis to Ad Valorem Property Tax Valuation in the US." 1996 International Real Estate Conference joint sponsored by the University of Connecticut and American Real Estate and Urban Economics Association, Orlando, FL, May 1996.

"Valuation of Shopping Centers and Their Components." Twentieth Annual Conference of the Institute of Property Taxation, Boca Raton, FL, June 1996.

"Evolving Attitudes and Policies of Institutional Investors and Lenders Toward On-Site and Nearby Property Contamination." The Cutting Edge Conference, The Royal Institution of Chartered Surveyors, Bristol, England, September 1996.

"Effects of Proximity to High-Voltage Transmission Lines on Nearby Residential Property Values: An International Perspective." Chartered Surveyors' Education Channel Television Education Network, Ltd., The Royal Institution of Chartered Surveyors, London, England, September 1996.

"Post-1992 Evidence of EMF Impacts on Nearby Residential Property Values" (with Mary Beth Geckler and Jake W. DeLottie). Paper presented at the 13th Annual Conference, American Real Estate Society, Sarasota, FL, April 1997.

"Effects of Team On-Field Performance and Stadium Characteristics on Major League Baseball Attendance, 1970–96" (with Mary Beth Geckler and Jake W. DeLottie). Paper presented at 13th Annual Conference, American Real Estate Society, Sarasota, FL, April 1997.

"The New 'Non-Economics:' Public Interest Value, Market Value and 'Economic Use'" (with Bill Mundy). Paper presented at the 13th Annual Conference, American Real Estate Society, Sarasota, FL, April 1997.

"Effects of Proximity to High-Voltage Transmission Lines on Nearby Residential Property Values: An International Perspective on Recent Research" (with Sandy Bond, Paul M. Syms and Jake W. DeLottie). Paper presented at the 1997 International Conference of the American Real Estate and Urban Economics Association, Berkeley, CA, May 1997.

"Stigma and Property Values: A Summary and Review of Research and Literature." Paper presented at the Appraisal Institute Symposium, Washington, DC, June 1997.

"'Non-Economic Use', 'Public Interest Value' and Other Lexicographic Innovations: A Counter-Revolutionary Response." Paper presented at the Appraisal Institute Debate on "Public Interest Value," Washington, DC, June 1997.

"HVTL Proximity, Fear of EMF and Residential Property Values: Research Results from the USA, Canada, and New Zealand" (with Mary Beth Geckler). Paper presented at the 1997 International Conference of the International Association of Assessing Officers, Toronto, Canada, September 1997.

"Uncomplicating Appraisal Problems by Unraveling Some Common Shibboleths" (with Gail L. Beron). Paper presented at 1997 IPT Property Tax Symposium, Austin, TX, November 1997.

"Isolating and Quantifying Business Value and Other Intangibles from the Value of Real Estate and Tangible Personal Property in the Going Concern Value of Operating Business Properties." Seminar presented at First Annual Property Valuation Symposium, Pullman & Comley, Hartford, CT, February 1998.

"Measuring the Impacts of Property Contamination and Stigma on Real Estate Values." Seminar presented at First Annual Property Valuation Symposium, Pullman & Comley, Hartford, CT, February 1998.

"The Persistence of Memory: A Study of Pre- and Post-Remediation Stigma" (with Gail L. Beron). Paper presented at American Real Estate Society National Conference, Monterey, CA, April 1998.

"Rents and Occupancy Costs for Tenants in US Regional and Superregional Shopping Centers, 1975–1997: An Update" (with Gail L. Beron). Paper presented at American Real Estate Society National Conference, Monterey, CA, April 1998.

"The Valuation of Contaminated Properties and Associated Stigma: A Comparative Review of Practice and Thought in the United States of America, The United Kingdom and New Zealand." Paper presented at The Cutting Edge Conference, Royal Institution of Chartered Surveyors, De Montfort University, Leicester, England, September 1998.

"Identification and Measurement of Intangible Asset Values Associated with Operating Properties." Paper presented at the 1997 Canadian Property Tax Association Workshop, Halifax, Nova Scotia, October 1998.

"Valuation Methodology for Electric Assets in a Deregulated Market Environment." Paper presented at the Electric Asset Valuation Conference, The Center for Business Intelligence, Orlando, FL, February 1999.

"Comparative Studies of United States, United Kingdom and New Zealand Appraisal Practice: Valuing Contaminated Property" (with Elaine M. Worzala, Sandy Bond and Paul J. Kennedy). Paper presented at the American Real Estate Society Conference, Tampa, FL, April 1999.

"Valuation and Feasibility Analysis of Major League Stadiums: NFL and MLB." Paper presented at Stadium Development Seminar, Metro New Jersey Chapter, The Appraisal Institute, Montclair, NJ, April 1999.

"Business Enterprise Value: A Separate and Separable Part of An Operating Property." Paper presented at 1999 Annual Summer Conference, Appraisal Institute, Orlando, FL, June 1999.

"Nuclear Assets—Emerging Standards and Methodologies for Effective Valuation." Paper presented at Nuclear Power Conference, Center for Business Intelligence, Chicago, IL, November 1999.

"Commercial Real Estate Practice in the 21st Century: A Sneak Peek into the Clouded Crystal Ball." Paper presented at 1999 Connecticut Commercial Real Estate Conference, Center for Real Estate, University of Connecticut, Radisson Conference Center, Cromwell, CT, November 1999.

"Measuring Locational Obsolescence from Nearby Sources of Contamination or Fear." Paper presented at the Connecticut Chapter of The Appraisal Institute, Appraisers Conference 2000, Farmington, CT, March 2000.

"Intangible Assets in an Operating First-Class Downtown Hotel: A Comparison of Sources of Information in a Profit Center Approach to Valuation" (with Elaine M. Worzala and Dan L. Swango). Paper presented at the 16th Annual Meeting, American Real Estate Society, Santa Barbara, CA, April 2000.

"Impact of Electricity Price Competition on Assessment of Nuclear-Fueled Generating Plants" (with Gail L. Beron). Paper presented at the 16th Annual Meeting, American Real Estate Society, Santa Barbara, CA, April 2000.

"High Voltage Transmission Lines and Residential Property Values: New Findings About Unobstructed Views and Tower Construction" (with Sue Ann Dickey). Paper presented at the 16th Annual Meeting, American Real Estate Society, Santa Barbara, CA, April 2000.

"Illustrative Case Examples of Business Enterprise Value (or Not)." Paper presented at Valuation 2000 Conference, Las Vegas, NV, July 2000.

PREVIOUS AND CURRENT PROFESSIONAL POSITIONS

Director of Urban Redevelopment, Middletown, CT, 1954–55

The University of Connecticut (1955–82):

- Professor, Finance and Real Estate (1955–81)
- Head, Department of Finance (1957–67); Acting Head (1975, 1979)
- Director, Institute of Urban Research (1963–65)
- Director, Center for Real Estate and Urban Economic Studies (1965–69, 1977–80)
- Associate Dean, School of Business Administration (1969–72)

Acting Dean, School of Business Administration (1973–74)
Professor Emeritus (1981–Present)
Principal, William N. Kinnard, Jr, 1952–Present
Consulting Partner, Guillermo Silva Lopez and Associates (Puerto Rico), 1973–80
Principal, Real Estate Counseling Group of America, Inc., 1977–Present; President, 1988
President, Real Estate Counseling Group of Connecticut, Inc., 1977–Present
Partner, Beron and Kinnard: Consulting Valuation Economists, 1986–91

Educational Consultant and Advisor to

Society of Real Estate Appraisers, 1965–86
Society of Industrial Realtors, 1965–79
American Right of Way Association (International Right of Way Association), 1964–65
National Institute of Real Estate Brokers (Realtors National Marketing Institute), 1966–68
International Association of Assessing Officers
Connecticut Real Estate Commission, 1965–81
National Association of Mutual Savings Banks, 1968–70
Westland/Utrecht Hypotheekbank, Amsterdam, The Netherlands, 1978–80
The Appraisal Foundation, 1992–93

Teaching Faculty and Lecturer for

Drexel Institute of Technology, School of Business, 1947–48
University of Pennsylvania, Wharton School, 1948–50
Wesleyan University, Connecticut, 1950–54
University of Florida, 1951 (Summer)
The University of Connecticut, 1955–82
Brown University, 1963 (Summer)
University of California—Los Angeles, 1964 (Summer)
American Arbitration Association
American Institute of Real Estate Appraisers, 1962–91
American Society of Appraisers
The Appraisal Institute, 1991–Present
Appraisal Institute of Canada, 1978, 1989
Educatie Onroerend Goed, b.v., Amsterdam, The Netherlands, 1978–80
General Electric Credit Corporation, 1980
Institute of Financial Education (US League of Savings Associations), 1968–75
Institute of Property Taxation, 1986–Present
International Association of Assessing Officers
Mortgage Bankers Association of America, 1972–78
National Association of Mutual Savings Banks, 1966–77
Ontario (Canada) Association of Assessors, 1983
Society of Real Estate Appraisers, 1963–91

Fields of Research and Teaching

Property Valuation (Real, Personal, Intangible, Leased Fee/Leasehold), Methodology, Reviews

Property Taxation (Real, Personal and Intangible): Entrepreneurial Profit, Business Enterprise Value, "Special Purpose" Properties, Shopping Centers (Anchor Department Stores, Mall Stores, Market Rentals, Tenant Sales/Mix Studies)

Business Valuation; Income Capitalization Analysis; Capital Market and Rate Analysis

Property Investment and Feasibility Analysis; Marketability and Market Absorption Studies

Market and Economic Impact Studies (Rent Control; Gas/Electricity Transmission Line Proximity; Hazardous Material Handling or Waste Facility Proximity; Highway Proximity)

Instructor Training Consultant for

Appraisal Standards Board (The Appraisal Foundation)
Connecticut Association of Realtors
Connecticut Real Estate Commission
Educatie Onroerend Goed, Amsterdam, The Netherlands
New York State Board of Equalization
Society of Industrial Realtors
Society of Real Estate Appraisers
The University of Connecticut, Division of Non-Credit Extension

MAJOR PROGRAM APPEARANCES SINCE 1986

1986 Appraisal Institute of Canada National Conference (Vancouver, BC)
Society of Real Estate Appraisers National Conference (Los Angeles, CA)

1987 University of Wisconsin Symposium (Baltimore, MD)
SREA National Conference (Montreal, Canada)
SREA Symposium (Indianapolis, IN)

1988 University of Wisconsin Symposium (Atlanta, GA)
American Real Estate Society (San Francisco, CA)
Institute of Property Taxation, National Conference (Dallas, TX)
International Association of Assessing Officers, Annual Conference (Nashville, TN): Keynote Speech
Northwest Professional Seminars, Inc. (Cambridge, MA)

1989 International Association of Assessing Officers, Annual Conference (Fort Worth, TX)
Institute of Property Taxation, Real Property Symposium (Tulsa, OK)
Edison Electric Institute, Northwestern Regional Conference (Portland, OR)
American Real Estate and Urban Economics Association, Annual Conference (Atlanta, GA)

1990 American Real Estate Society (Lake Tahoe, NV)
International Association of Assessing Officers, Technical Seminar (Montreal, Canada)
Society of Real Estate Appraisers, Symposium (San Antonio, TX): Keynote Address

1991 American Real Estate Society (Sarasota, FL)
Homer Hoyt Institute, Weimer School of Advanced Studies (North Palm Beach, FL)
The Appraisal Network/Real Estate Counseling Group of America, Joint Educational Conference (Orlando, FL)
Institute of Property Taxation, Annual Conference (Los Angeles, CA)
Appraisal Institute National Symposium (Philadelphia, PA): Keynote Address
International Association of Assessing Officers, Annual Conference (Phoenix, AZ)

1992 Appraisal Institute, Annual Conference: (Seattle, WA)
Edison Electric Institute, National Land Management Workshop (Duluth, MN)
Institute of Property Taxation, Property Tax Symposium (Tempe, AZ)
Weimer School of Advanced Studies, Homer Hoyt Institute (North Palm Beach, FL)
Center for Real Estate and Urban Economic Studies, University of Connecticut, Annual Economic Conference (Waterbury, CT)

1993 Weimer School of Advanced Studies, Homer Hoyt Institute (North Palm Beach, FL)
American Real Estate Society, Annual Conference (Key West, FL)
New Jersey Institute for Continuing Legal Education, Contaminated Property Valuation Conference (New Brunswick, NJ)
American Bar Association, Annual Conference (New York, NY)
International Association of Assessing Officers, Annual Conference (Washington, DC)
University of Connecticut and American Real Estate and Urban Economics Association, 1993 International Conference (Mystic, CT)

1994 Executive Enterprises, Inc. (Washington, DC)
American Real Estate Society, Annual Conference (Santa Barbara, CA)
Maryland Association of Assessing Officers (Ocean City, MD)
International Association of Assessing Officers, Annual Conference (Seattle, WA)
Institute of Property Taxation, Real Property Tax Symposium (San Antonio, TX)
Canadian Property Tax Association Program, (Montreal, Quebec)

1995 American Bar Association/Institute of Property Taxation, Advanced Property Tax Symposium (New Orleans, LA)
American Real Estate Society, Annual Meeting (Hilton Head, SC)
The Appraisal Institute of Canada/Institut Canadien des Evaluateurs, 1995 Annual Conference (Victoria, British Columbia)

Canadian Property Tax Association, Quebec Chapter, Bundle of Rights Seminar (Montreal, Quebec)
International Association of Assessing Officers, Sixty-First International Conference (Chicago, IL) Appraisal Institute, 1995 Symposium (New Orleans, LA): Keynote Address
Appraisal Institute Seminar (Spokane, WA)

1996 American Real Estate Society, Twelfth Annual Meeting (South Lake Tahoe, CA)
International Real Estate Conference, American Real Estate and Urban Economics Association and Center for Real Estate and Urban Economic Studies, University of Connecticut, (Orlando, FL)
American Bar Association/Institute of Property Taxation, Advanced Property Tax Seminar (New Orleans, LA)
Insight and The Globe and Mail Conference (Toronto, Ontario)
Homer Hoyt Advanced Studies Institute and Real Estate Counseling Group of America Joint Meeting (North Palm Beach, FL)
EMF Regulation and Litigation Institute (Washington, DC)
Institute of Property Taxation, Twentieth Annual Conference (Boca Raton, FL)
The Cutting Edge Conference, The Royal Institution of Chartered Surveyors (Bristol, England)
Chartered Surveyors' Education Channel Television Education Network, Ltd., The Royal Institution of Chartered Surveyors (London, England)

1997 American Real Estate Society, Thirteenth Annual Meeting (Sarasota, FL)
American Real Estate and Urban Economics Association, International Conference (Berkeley, CA)
Appraisal Institute Symposium (Washington, DC)
Appraisal Institute Debate on "Public Interest Value" (Washington, DC)
International Association of Assessing Officers, 1997 International Conference (Toronto, Ontario) Institute of Professionals in Taxation Symposium (Austin, TX)

1998 First Annual Property Valuation Symposium (Hartford, CT)
American Real Estate Society, Fourteenth Annual Meeting (Monterey, CA)
The Cutting Edge Conference, Royal Institution of Chartered Surveyors (Leicester, England)
Canadian Property Tax Association Workshop (Halifax, Nova Scotia)

1999 Electric Asset Valuation Conference, The Center for Business Intelligence (Orlando, FL)
American Real Estate Society, Fifteenth Annual Meeting (Tampa, FL)
Appraisal Institute, Stadium Development Seminar, Metro New Jersey Chapter (Montclair, NJ)
Appraisal Institute Debate on "Business Enterprise Value: A Separate and Separable Part of An Operating Property" (Orlando, FL)
Nuclear Power Conference, Center for Business Intelligence (Chicago, IL)
Connecticut Commercial Real Estate Conference, Center for Real Estate, University of Connecticut, Radisson Conference Center (Cromwell, CT)

2000 Appraisal Institute, CT Chapter of the Appraisal Institute, Conference 2000 (Farmington, CT)
American Real Estate Society, Sixteenth Annual Meeting (Santa Barbara, CA)
Valuation 2000 Conference (Las Vegas, NV)

REPRESENTATIVE VALUATION AND CONSULTING CLIENTS

Business Corporations

Affiliated Food Stores, Inc. (Dallas)
Allis-Chalmers Corporation
Aluminum Company of America
ARAWANA Mills Co.
ARCO, Inc.
Arizona Public Service Company
Ash Grove Cement Company
ASARCO, Inc.
Atlantic City Electric Company
Azul Pacifico Mobilehome Park (Los Angeles)
Bank of America
Beneficial Finance Company
Big V Supermarkets, Inc.
Boeing
Caterpillar Tractor Company
Carolina Panthers
Central Maine Power Company
CMS, Inc. (Cogeneration Facility)
Coastal Javalina
Commonwealth Edison Company
Connecticut Hazardous Waste Management Service
Consumers Power Company (Michigan)
Crown Zellerbach Corporation
Dana Point Resort, Inc.
Diamond-Star, Inc.
Disney
Dow Chemical, USA
DuPont
Equitable Life Insurance Co.
Federated Department Stores, Inc.
Florida Gas Transmission Co.
Franklin Mushroom Farm (Connecticut)
General Electric Corporation
Granite Gas Transmission Co.
Hahn Company
Hallmark, Inc.
Harrah's
Harsch Corporation
Homart Development Company
Hughes Aerospace
Inn Group Associates, Inc. (Newport, Rhode Island)
Iroquois Gas Transmission System
Jensen's Mobile Home Parks, Inc.
Kern River Gas Transmission Company
Kimberly-Clark Corporation
Lake Ridge Development Company (Dallas)
L.A. Rams
Lockheed Martin
Lone Star Industries, Inc.
Long Beach World Trade Center
Los Amigos Mobilehome Park (Santa Barbara)
LTV Aerospace, Inc.
LTV Steel Company, Inc.
Marriott Corporation (Great America, Inc.; Host International, Inc.)
May Company
Merrill Lynch
Miller Brewing Company, Inc.
Mobil
Montgomery Ward, Inc.
New United Motors Manufacturing, Inc. (NUMMI)
NLO, Inc.
Northeast Utilities
Nun's Island (Montreal)
Oakland Tribune, Inc.
Orchard Supply Hardware Company
Penn Mutual Life Insurance Company

Penney, J.C. Company
Pier 39
Prudential Life Insurance Co.
Pullman Car Leasing Company
Rouse Company
San Diego Gas and Electric Company
San Francisco Giants
Sears, Roebuck & Company
Shippers Car Leasing Division, ACF
SkyDome Enterprises (Toronto)
Southern California Edison
Star Enterprises, Inc.
Stop & Shop, Inc.
Sunlaw Corporation
T. Eaton Co., Ltd. (Toronto)
Tenet (Healthcare), Inc.
Texaco, Inc.
Tosco Corporation
Trailer Train Company
Union Carbide Company
Union Electric Company
United Refining Company
US Radium Company
Wells Fargo Credit Corporation
Westinghouse Mohave Co-Generation Corp.
Wisconsin Electric Company
Woodward & Lothrop Department Stores, Inc.
Xerox Corporation

Governmental and Public Agencies

ADA (Michigan)
Appraisal Standards Board (Appraisal Foundation)
Arizona Attorney General's Office
Brookhaven, New York (Town)
Community Housing Ltd. (New Zealand)
Connecticut Department of Agriculture and Natural Resources
Connecticut Historical Society
Connecticut Resources Recovery Authority
Dearborn (Michigan) Assessor's Office
Easton, Connecticut (Town)
Federal Savings and Loan Insurance Corporation
Flint (Michigan) Assessor's Office
Illinois Task Force
Marion County (Florida) Property Appraiser's Office
Middletown (Connecticut) Redevelopment Agency
New Mexico Highway and Transportation Department
New York Power Authority
Palm Beach County (Florida) Solid Waste Authority
Puerto Rico Conservation Trust
Puerto Rico Telephone Company
Texas Nuclear Research Laboratory Commission
Texas State Property Tax Board
US Department of Energy
Volusia County (Florida) Property Appraiser's Office

Qualified as Expert Witness Before

Assessment Appeals Boards, California (Alemeda, Contra Costa, Kern, Los Angeles, Marin, Orange, San Francisco, San Mateo, Santa Clara, Santa Cruz, Counties)
Assessment Review Board, Cuyahoga County, Ohio
Assessment Review Board, Edmonton, Alberta, Canada
Commonwealth Superior Court, Puerto Rico
Court of Claims, New York State
Federal District Court, California
Federal District Court, Indiana

Federal District Court, Nevada
Federal District Court, New Jersey
Federal District Court, New York
Federal District Court, Ohio
Federal District Court, South Carolina
Provincial Court, Montreal, Quebec, Canada
State Board of Equalization, California
State Board of Tax Review, Illinois
State Commissioner of Revenue, Oregon
State Tax Commission, Louisiana
State Tax Commission, Missouri
State Tax Review Board, North Carolina
State Tax Tribunal, Michigan
Superior Court, State of Arizona
Superior Court, State of California (Los Angeles, Orange, San Mateo, Stanislaus Counties)
Superior Court, State of Connecticut
Superior Court, State of Florida (Collier, Dade, Marion and Palm Beach Counties)
Superior Court, State of Iowa
Superior Court, State of Louisiana
Superior Court, State of Minnesota
Supreme Court, State of New York (Suffolk County)
Tax Court, New Jersey
US Armed Forces Contract Review Board
US Bankruptcy Court, New York
US Bankruptcy Court, Texas
US Federal Power Commission Hearing Examiner
US Senate, Select Subcommittee on Small Business

EDITORIAL CONSULTANT, EDITORIAL BOARD MEMBER AND MANUSCRIPT REVIEWER FOR

American Heritage Dictionary of the English Language (Consultant, Social Sciences)
American Society of Real Estate Counselors (Editorial Board, Reviewer)
The Appraisal Journal (Editorial Board, Reviewer)
Encyclopedia Americana (Consulting Editor, 1957–68)
International Association of Assessing Officers (Reviewer)
Journal of the American Real Estate and Urban Economics Association (Reviewer)
Journal of Real Estate Research (Reviewer)
Lexington Books, D.C. Heath (Editor, Real Estate Series, 1975–85)
The Real Estate Appraiser and Analyst (Reviewer)

OTHER ACTIVITIES

Justice of the Peace, Mansfield, Connecticut, 1975–Present
Chairman, Mansfield (Connecticut) Zoning Board of Appeals, 1958
Planning and Zoning Commission, Mansfield, Connecticut, 1958–64; Vice-Chairman, 1960–62
Vice President, Connecticut Federation of Planning and Zoning Agencies, 1959–60
Chairman, Committee on Research and Statistics, National Association of Housing and Redevelopment Officials, 1956–1958
President, American Real Estate and Urban Economics Association, 1968
President, Connecticut Chapter, Society of Real Estate Appraisers, 1968–69
Member, Commercial Panel, American Arbitration Association, 1980–Present
Member, National Real Estate Valuation Council, American Arbitration Association, 1982–Present

Member, National Board of Directors, American Arbitration Association, 1984–85
Arbitrator, Real Estate Project and Lease Disputes, Connecticut, 1985–91
Outside Evaluator, University of Kentucky Real Estate Center, 1983
Independent Fiduciary, Aetna Life Insurance Company, Union Separate Account, 1989–Present
Independent Fiduciary, Aetna Life Insurance Company, Real Estate Separate Account, 1998–Present
External Examiner, University of Reading (United Kingdom), 1997

TIME

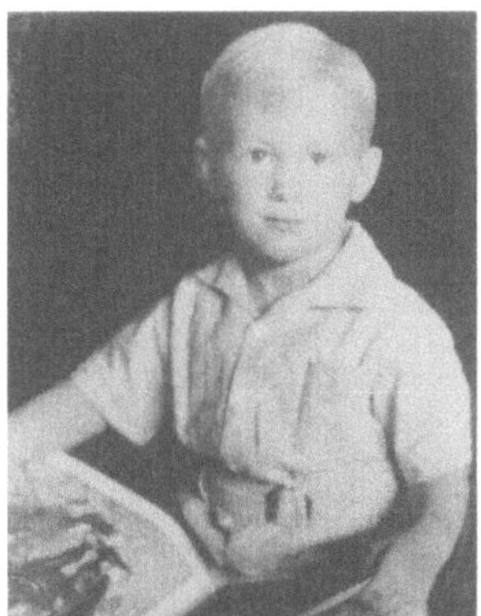

9. Ten Reasons Why Kinnard's *Income Property Valuation* (1971) is a Modern Classic

AUSTIN J. JAFFE AND KENNETH M. LUSHT

In February 1971, a serious textbook "directed toward the student of appraisal, with or without experience in the residential property field, who has little or no background in income property valuation,"[1] made its appearance on the Lexington Books list of new books. The author's stated objective was to build upon "prior exposure to the principles and techniques of real estate appraisal" using existing tools and ideas new to the appraisal literature but not new to others.[2] What was different, the author argued, was a "framework that is somewhat innovative."[3] Given the competition at the time (and for years to come), this book proved to be years ahead of its time.

This chapter identifies *ten* concepts, ideas, or contributions which advance the case that *Income Property Valuation* represents a major contribution to the academic and professional literature in real estate analysis. It is not our intention to claim that income property analysis begins with this text; indeed, the author is explicit in the Preface of the book that his work builds upon many others before him including Babcock, Rowlands, Ring, Ratcliff, Graaskamp, Harvey, Boyce, Dasso, and many others.[4] The authors' thanks are extended to numerous professional appraisers as well, especially to those associated with the Society of Real Estate Appraisers, with whom Bill Kinnard had been affiliated since at least 1962.[5] Our claim is that *Income*

[1] William N. Kinnard, Jr, *Income Property Valuation*. D.C. Heath and Company, Lexington, MA. 1971, p. xiii.
[2] *Ibid.*
[3] *Ibid.*
[4] *Ibid.*, p. xiv.
[5] *Ibid.*

Property Valuation is a modern classic due to the observation that it symbolizes a highpoint in valuation thinking and implementation during this era. Over time, it has impressively held up well some 30 years later. Our evidence is presented below as 10 major ideas.

IDEA #1: INCOME CAPITALIZATION IS A FINANCIAL VALUATION PROBLEM

Prior to the development of Bill's text, income analysis of property, especially for market valuation purposes, tended to be rather ad hoc and often disjointed. Although there were real estate valuation textbooks at the time, few treatments presented the "analytical tools and skills" needed in the field as did *Income Property Valuation*. In the Preface, the author noted:

> [As of 1971], appraising income-producing real estate [was] a challenging, stimulating, and intellectually rewarding occupation." [However, post-1971, income property analysis was] presented in a framework that is somewhat innovative... as a systematic effort in problem-solving.... It incorporates much of the modern approach to financial investment decision-making.[6]

It is interesting to note that the movement toward the financial analysis of real estate was also underway in other circles (e.g., Wendt and Cerf's 1969 real estate investment textbook[7]), but based upon a different paradigm (i.e., financial management) than Kinnard's valuation tradition. Here was a major manuscript that sought to modernize real estate valuation of income property *from within* the field. Furthermore, Bill sought to change professional practice rather than simply provide additional, theoretical fodder for academic debate.

> [This book] seeks to equip the reader or student with the necessary skills and mastery of technique to begin appraising income property interests in a professionally acceptable and meaningful way.[8]

IDEA #2: MARKET VALUE VERSUS INVESTMENT VALUE: NO PROBLEM!

In some circles, it was popular to draw clear distinctions between market valuation (appraising) and investment valuation (investment analysis). Appraisers could estimate market values and analysts (later called "counselors") could provide investment studies but never should either group tread on the others turf. The methods and terminology were said to differ between these groups and each kept their distance. This tradition was known to be somewhat arbitrary but had largely been maintained since the 1930s.

[6] *Ibid.*, p. xiii.

[7] Paul F. Wendt and Alan R. Cerf, *Real Estate Investment Analysis and Taxation.* McGraw-Hill, Inc., New York. 1969.

[8] See Kinnard, *Income Property Valuation, op. cit.*, p. 5.

To Kinnard, these distinctions made little sense.

When income property is appraised, whether to estimate Market Value or Investment Value, the appraiser must also forecast the amount and character of the income statement most likely to be received by the owner of the rights being appraised.[9]

... the mechanical techniques and tools of analysis used in estimating Investment Value are precisely the same as those employed to estimate Market Value.[10]

This was rather daring and nonconformist in real estate valuation circles at the end of the 1960s. But the author was convinced that real estate valuation should not limit its arsenal of techniques to those developed only within the appraisal field. In effect, investment analysis methods were fair game for appraisers even if the purpose was to estimate the market value of income-producing assets.

... it can be seen that the type of value to be estimated in an appraisal problem, and hence the purpose of the appraisal, depends precisely on whose viewpoint is to be taken in making the value or present worth estimate. Both Market Value and Investment Value (as well as Most Probable Selling Price) are expressed in terms of the standards and behavior of a potential buyer.[11]

Following Ratcliff in 1965,[12] Kinnard argued that there was no fundamental difference between the valuation of income-producing property and the appraisal of any real property.

The basic principles of real estate valuation are universally applicable to all appraisal problems. They therefore apply with equal force to the valuation of income-producing properties.[13]

The same basic principles of valuation and the same appraisal framework apply to every type of property, for every type of potential purchaser, and for every type of value estimate.[14]

Kinnard taught us that the fundamental valuation principles encompassed many types of studies, including investment analysis. The key was to employ the proper methods and to ensure that the correct data was used when making valuation estimates.

IDEA #3: AND YET, *INCOME PROPERTY VALUATION* IS AN INVESTMENT BOOK

Bill Kinnard sensed that his manuscript would precede the growing interest in investment analysis in the years to come.[15]

[9] *Ibid.*, p. 11.
[10] *Ibid.*, p. 14.
[11] *Ibid.*, p. 15.
[12] See Richard U. Ratcliff, *Modern Real Estate Valuation: Theory and Application*. Democrat Press, Madison, WI. 1965.
[13] See Kinnard, *Income Property Valuation*, *op. cit.*, p. 38.
[14] *Ibid.*, p. 33.
[15] These ideas were also hinted at in William N. Kinnard, Jr, The Financial Logic of Income-Producing Appraising. *The Real Estate Appraiser*, 1969, 35 (May–June): 13–21.

Indeed, much of Investment Value analysis focuses on estimating the value of the equity position. Each interest can also have a Market Value.[16]

[Income capitalization] is the present worth of the income stream, and may represent either Market Value or Investment Value.[17]

In addition, Kinnard's use of "financial terminology" brought real estate valuation closer to the rest of the financial community. He adopted the term "Net Operating Income" instead of the more traditional "Net Income Before Recapture" or "Net Income." He was comfortable moving to "cash flows" (anticipating the DCF Revolution to come) by advocating "Before-Tax Cash Flow" over "Cash Throw-off" and "After-Tax Cash Flow" over "Net Spendable Income." In this respect alone, his work was ahead of its time. Further, he anticipated the unbundling of property rights by making clear that the various interests may each have market values.

IDEA #4: *INCOME PROPERTY VALUATION* IS A "SYSTEMATIC PROCESS OF ANALYSIS"

Despite the new terminology and extensive calculations, Bill wanted to emphasize that there was a system of valuation underlying his approach; it was not just a randomized collection of financial calculations.

The Appraisal Framework is a systematic process of analysis. So, too, is the logical, rational investment judgment model which the appraiser of rights in income-producing real estate seeks to stimulate involving his value estimate.[18]

Readers familiar with the Appraisal Framework will note a striking similarity between [The Appraisal Process and the "Investment Decision Model" of *Income Property Valuation*]. Both represent a systematic process of problem-solving: [one is] used by the appraiser in reaching his value conclusion; [the other is] applied by the investor-client in reaching a decision based in part on the estimate of value provided by the appraiser.[19]

So for his readers, Kinnard was providing an "Application of the Appraisal Framework to Income Properties"[20] and with it, investment decision-making could be included within the world of real estate valuation.

IDEA #5: ARE THERE THREE APPROACHES? MUCH ADO ABOUT NOTHING

When it came to the 1930s tradition of three separate approaches to value, the author dismissed the matter as relatively unimportant.

There is considerable controversy current in appraisal thinking and writing over whether there are or are not "three approaches" to value estimation. Traditionally, it has been argued and

[16]See Kinnard, *Income Property Valuation, op. cit.*, p. 38.
[17]*Ibid.*, p. 62.
[18]*Ibid.*, p. 45.
[19]*Ibid.*
[20]*Ibid.*, pp. 46–63.

> generally accepted that there are. More recently, some leading writers have maintained there is only one "approach"—the market approach—and that the several alternative techniques and methods employed by appraisers are only different manifestations of market analysis and a single Market Approach.
>
> This argument is essentially one of semantics or terminology. Debate over labels is sterile, provided the tools of analysis are responsive to the needs of appraisers and the decision-makers they serve. What is really required is for neither side to be doctrinaire. If the labels are helpful in identifying tools and techniques that the appraiser should *consider* as potentially applicable in solving an appraisal problem, calling them "approaches" to value estimation may be appropriate. Certainly, all data used in appraisal analysis must be derived from the market identified as applicable to the problem. To this extent, every tool of analysis employed in an appraisal is part of a "market approach."[21]

Furthermore, Chapters 16 and 17 in *Income Property Valuation* treat the "Direct Sales Comparison" and "Improvements Analysis and Cost Analysis" approaches, respectively.[22] The author was quite traditional as a real estate academic and professional real estate appraiser. However, at the same time, he was pushing for modernization, which in retrospect, was long overdue.

> Whether there are or are not three "Approaches" (or more) to real property value estimation, or whether different techniques of measurement are all part of one general "Approach," is really irrelevant. The important point is that the different techniques that reflect alternative potential courses of action for the purchaser-investor are responsive to the needs and data available to approach problems confronting different types of investors in different types of properties.[23]

Kinnard's advice that the appraiser could consider the applicability of each approach, while heretical in 1971, is now a standard appraisal practice.

IDEA #6: *INCOME PROPERTY VALUATION* SORTS OUT THE CONFUSION OVER VALUATION TERMS

One of the very nice contributions is Bill's detailed attempts to be careful about valuation terms. For example, differences between nominal and effective interest rates, the mortgage interest rate and the mortgage constant, the interest rate and the discount rate, the capitalization rate and the overall rate, and the equity dividend rate and the equity yield rate are all explained.[24] Even the difference between capitalization in perpetuity and capitalization over a finite period is explicitly treated.[25] So, too, is the difference between (Net) Income and Cash Flows.[26] Although Kinnard cites Ellwood for his

[21] *Ibid.*, p. 53.

[22] *Ibid.*, see pp. 329–345 and pp. 347–381, respectively.

[23] *Ibid.*, p. 347.

[24] *Ibid.*, pp. 64–67. Of course, it is not certain that the explanations have been sufficient, given the confusion sometimes found in the literature even today.

[25] *Ibid.*, p. 68.

[26] *Ibid.*, p. 70.

contribution,[27] it appears that *Income Property Valuation* moved the field past single-period valuation measures into multiple-period calculations using their respective concepts.

IDEA #7: EXPLOITING THE BENEFITS OF "DISCOUNTING AND COMPOUND INTEREST"

Following the spread of the "Ellwood Tables" to real estate valuation practice (actually, Ellwood also advanced the use of six factors to perform present and future value calculations), Kinnard tried somewhat successfully to synthesize and organize the range of financial calculations and mathematical manipulations inherent in the Ellwood approach. Chapter 5 is devoted to the mathematical manipulations and the field has been changed ever since its appearance.[28] In addition, several extensions are presented such as techniques for valuing various payment patterns, for "payments in advance" (now called "annuities-due"), for periodic payments of less than a year (now referred to as "the rate of compounding"), for "non-level" annuities, and for deferred factors ("deferred annuities"). No doubt, Bill's "hands-on" calculations taught an entire generation of readers more about the "mathematics of finance" than probably any other book in this field.[29]

IDEA #8: AND YET, "APPRAISING IS NOT MATHEMATICS"

Despite Kinnard's interest and attention to mathematical detail, it is quite clear and important to note that mathematical calculations were not to replace appraisal judgment and careful data analysis.

> Discounting is the mechanical, mathematical process by which forecast future income receipts are capitalized to present-worth estimates. Once the future income forecasts have been made and the appropriate rate(s) at which those income receipts are to be discounted is established, the results are produced by inexorable mathematical logic .... But discounting is only a mathematical process; it is not appraising. It merely provides the *how* of capitalization.[30]

Mastering mathematical models is viewed as a critical skill for the appraiser but not at the expense of the valuation task at hand.

> The important point is that an income forecast is neither a mechanical projection of past performance nor a precise prediction of what will in fact occur. The income forecast represents the amount, timing, duration, and stability of cash flows most likely to be received by the holder of the property rights being appraised. The appraiser must therefore estimate *how much* is likely to be received, *when*, over *how many periods of what length*. He must finally evaluate the degree of certainty in these estimates.[31]

[27]See L.W. Ellwood, *Ellwood Tables for Real Estate and Financing; Part I: Explanatory Text*, Third Edition. American Institute of Real Estate Appraisers, Chicago. 1970.

[28]See Kinnard, *Income Property Valuation*, *op. cit.*, pp. 81–109.

[29]Also, the text differentiates between alternative "capitalization rates" including the "cap" rate as the sum of the discount rate and the capital recovery rate, the differences between capitalization rates and residual rates, the mortgage constant as a capitalization rate, and several "factors" including the Ring Factor, the Hoskold Factor, and the Inwood Factor. See *ibid.*, p. 182.

[30]*Ibid.*, p. 111.

[31]*Ibid.*, p. 112.

This passage above speaks to the freshness and modern air found in much of *Income Property Valuation*. Indeed, it is as if it were lifted from a textbook today.

IDEA #9: DEBT MATTERS

Given the impact of financial theory on capital structure and the interest in Ellwood capitalization of debt and equity components, it is not surprising that *Income Property Valuation* devoted an entire portion (Chapter 7) to the relationship between debt financing and valuation.[32] Anticipating the debate about the impact of nonmarket financing arrangements on market values to come in the years ahead, Kinnard's treatment of debt is ambitious, insightful, and easily ahead of its time.

For example, consider this general approach to the topic:

It has long been taught and accepted that Market Value estimation requires the valuation of the fee simple interest "free and clear of all encumbrances." These "encumbrances" include mortgages... [However,] [i]f the buyer seeks and obtains available financing, the appraiser as a recorder of market behavior cannot ignore it just to remain loyal to a "free and clear" concept of Market Value. Typically available mortgage financing and its terms can and do influence *value*, not just the price a specific purchaser-investor is willing or believes he can afford to pay. The "free and clear" argument fails to depict what the *market* is doing .... Thus, the terms and conditions of debt financing typically available to the most probable type of investor in the current local market represent a significant part of the market environment that surrounds and influences the income-producing property sales transaction.[33]

Although the financial impact of debt was yet to come in valuation theory, Kinnard's instincts seem remarkably good for 1971. Though our understanding today is that the free and clear assumption is functionally equivalent to the typical financing assumption, we also understand that typical financing impacts market values, just as Kinnard concluded. Further, he remained active in the field to see his early ideas bear fruit in the later years.

IDEA #10: MORTGAGE–EQUITY ANALYSIS IS A SPECIAL TYPE OF RESIDUAL METHOD

In the post-Ellwood era, mortgage–equity models became the rage in the valuation of income-producing property. Property no longer was viewed as the sum of "land and buildings"; now it was "debt and equity capital." This idea had its precedents elsewhere as well but it is interesting to note that Kinnard's approach was to view the class of models known as "mortgage–equity analysis" as special versions of residual models which were developed in the 1930s. As such, they were viewed as extensions of existing models rather than as a new, analytical revolution.

Mortgage–equity analysis is another form of residual analysis, with the property divided into its financial-investment components of mortgage and equity investment position. The principal

[32] *Ibid.*, pp. 145–171.
[33] *Ibid.*, pp. 145–146.

amount of the mortgage is known, while the present worth of the equity is the unknown residual.[34]

Mortgage–equity analysis does not differ from any other form of capitalization technique in the basic valuation formula. It is still V/R.[35]

Kinnard's understanding is comprehensive in this area: mortgage–equity models are treated as variants of the general valuation approach. For example, Ellwood's capitalization formula is a special case of more general valuation methods. In the text, alterative specifications are presented within the general family of models. As a nice touch, Kinnard presents models with and without Equity Buildup with the same ease as any of the other models.[36]

So, based upon these claims, we argue that Bill Kinnard's sometimes forgotten-textbook is a modern classic. This case is based further on the impact that these ideas have had on theory and practice, both of which were of special interest to Bill. The impact of his thinking and technique can still be felt years after the book appeared; modern books sometimes replicate what was shown in 1971 in essentially the same form, (including our books!). We believe *Income Property Valuation* is one of the modern classics in the field of real estate analysis and we are all indebted to Bill Kinnard for its many contributions.

[34] *Ibid.*, p. 257.
[35] *Ibid.*, p. 262.
[36] *Ibid.*, pp. 265–273.

10. New Thinking in Appraisal Theory

WILLIAM N. KINNARD, JR

REAL ESTATE APPRAISING is still appropriately described as an art rather than a science. The contention of this chapter is that it will remain so as long as the fundamental theoretical structure on which practice is based is outmoded, excessively abstracted reality, and not generally descriptive of market behavior.

UNCERTAINTY CREATES NEED

Appraising exists as a field because there is uncertainty on the part of potential buyers, investors, sellers, and others. This stems in part from the complex nature of the product (the real estate itself); and in part from the uninformed, imperfect, complex nature of the real estate market. Despite these difficulties, however, estimates of value must be made and appraisal conclusions reached, often in the absence of good data or even very much data at all. Indeed, it has been demonstrated that much of the present cumbersome, complex, and unrealistic framework of appraisal mechanics has developed in an attempt to compensate for a lack of adequate or appropriate market information in many instances.

Critical expressions of dissatisfaction with the current analytical methods available to real estate appraisers has come increasingly from both academicians and practitioners in the appraisal field. Moreover, there is growing dissatisfaction with the Neo-Classical, perfectly competitive, profit-maximizing, ruggedly individualistic economic-man approach of the economic structure that underlies most of current appraisal theory.

NEW TOOLS DEVELOPED

Within the past decade, a whole range of new tools (and new ideas) has developed in related areas of economics, business, and finance.

Reprinted with permission. *The Real Estate Appraiser*, 1966, Vol. 32, No. 8, pp. 2–13.

Two basic threads of development can be observed. On the one hand, a quantitative (mathematical–statistical) approach, based in large part on the availability of high-speed electronic data processing equipment, has made analysis of increasingly more complex problems feasible, where it was simply impractical before. On the other hand, from the social sciences and the behavioral sciences in particular (psychology, sociology, cultural anthropology), an expanding pattern of insights into human behavior in the decision-making process has emerged.

These insights have been applied successfully to business problems. Recent arguments by the author that these offer an outstanding opportunity of transferability to real estate valuation indicate the direction in which many writers in appraisal theory are moving. This is especially true of, but not restricted to, the field of financial capital theory.

It may be redundant to repeat the proposition here, but it is easy to overlook the fact that an appraisal is sought because a decision must be made. A problem exists, and the decision-maker (be he buyer or seller, landlord or tenant, condemnor or condemnee, borrower or lender) seeks expert advice. While there is still an important distinction between appraising and counseling, an appraisal also provides the basis for the client (and others) to make a more nearly rational business decision.

Therefore, good analysis is required which is descriptive of market behavior. A rigid, inflexible presentation of a nonexistant economic structure is hardly a sound theoretical foundation for appraisal investigation. Moreover, the analysis and its presentation must be comprehensible and meaningful to the layman, the client, the user. This is the challenge that confronts real estate appraisal theory at the present time.

PRODUCT OF '20s AND '30s

The current framework of appraisal theory is essentially the product of the economic theory and the state of the arts in appraising during the late 1920s and the early 1930s. Most appraisal "classics" were published during the period 1926–37. There have been substantial numbers of new theoretical developments in economics and related disciplines since then (e.g., the entire structure of Keynesian analysis, and the development of mathematical economics). Moreover, there are many more effective tools of inquiry available (linear programming, small sample statistics, and computer simulation, to cite just a few).

The "three approaches" evolved primarily because there were, and still are, several concepts of value. The same word was employed, but with quite distinct meanings, because basically different ideas underlay them.

Moreover, as has already been noted, the data required for a direct sales comparison estimate often simply were not available. As a result, complex and elaborate structures evolved to compensate for the lack of really defensible information. Among other things, both mathematical and social science disciplines have learned in the interim how to deal with the problem of uncertainty. We cannot now and never will be able to overcome uncertainty. We are, however, in a much better position today to be able to compensate for it appropriately when making market value estimates.

COURTS INFLUENTIAL

A further problem in the evolution of appraisal theory, which has been accentuated since the end of World War II, is that the courts have been most influential in setting definitions with which practitioners have had to live. Whatever their qualifications, judges and referees are rarely trained economic or financial market analysts. As a result, their definitions are usually oriented toward legalistic and/or "common sense" concepts of economic matters.

Beyond all this, much of the framework of current appraisal theory was established on an ad hoc basis, under considerable pressure to "get the job done." This is certainly true of the bases for appraisal concepts that were used in the early operations of the Federal Housing Administration, the Home Owners' Loan Corporation, and the Reconstruction Finance Corporation. There was no real body of appraisal theory. Rather, much of it was lifted in toto from the then-existing framework of economic theory.

Lest anyone contend that this argument is inconsistent here (since it has already been maintained that much of what has happened in recent years in both quantitative analysis and behavioral science is transferable and applicable to appraisal theory), a careful distinction must be drawn. There is an important difference between uncritical, total transfer of a body of theory from one discipline to another, and the selective application of new devices when logic and experience indicate that they represent appropriate materials for the field in question.

Over the last decade, there has been a considerable amount of mechanical tinkering with the basic framework, but little overall review of appraisal theory. There is substantial evidence and increasingly loud arguments that there is serious need for a thorough-going, sweeping review of appraisal theory. Meanwhile, appraisals must be made and practitioners must continue to function. This is where academicians interested in this field have such an important role to play.

INCREASED INTEREST

In the past 3–5 years, there has been significantly broadened interest in the field of real estate evaluation on the part of academic students of economics, and particularly of finance. The stimulating and outspoken writings of Dr Richard Ratcliff of the University of Wisconsin have been particularly noteworthy. Dr Ratcliff is only one of many throughout the United States, however, who are currently adding to thought and writing in this field; although he certainly is one of the most outstanding spokesman for the academic viewpoint.

Dr Ratcliff is particularly associated with the view that every appraisal is, in fact, a research project. It represents an application of a combination of urban land economics, market analysis, and investment analysis. In this context, it offers an interesting and stimulating challenge to academic students of value and capital theory.

Although there has been a considerable amount of theoretical work published in professional, trade, and academic journals in very recent years much of what is being written is not particularly new. Indeed, a substantial portion of these works involve the revival of old ideas that have long been ignored or forgotten: for example, the view that every income stream is an annuity, and that variations in its character can be adjusted for within the framework of annuity analysis. Much of the remainder of these writings represents an application of ideas and tools from other areas of analysis specifically to real estate and to real estate valuation.

FINANCIAL BACKGROUNDS

Most of the university personnel working in the area of real estate valuation have formal backgrounds in finance and financial analysis. This is no accident. There is a substantial community of interest between investment analysis and capital theory on the one hand, and real estate valuation on the other. Indeed, many of these academicians regard real estate valuation as simply one application of investment analysis and capital theory.

There is a major underlying theme that *the* appropriate approach to the valuation of income real estate is to regard it as an investment decision and to apply the concepts and tools of investment analysis to it. This is particularly stimulating to university personnel at present, because great strides have been made in modern capital theory in the past few years.

The most recent expression of the various efforts of academic researchers, whether operating in one of the several real estate research centers that have emerged in universities throughout the United States or in isolation, is Dr Ratcliff's *Modern Real Estate Valuation: Theory and Application*. In a sense, it represents in microcosm much of the current state of the arts in appraisal theory, much of the current dissatisfaction with that current state of the arts, and much of the new direction that the thinking of academicians is taking.

THREE EMPHASES

The journal articles and recent books have shown three major emphases in the thinking of academic real estate valuation theorists:

1. Mathematics and decision-making tools, aimed primarily at reducing uncertainty in business and investment decision-making.
2. Market analyses based on more and better data which are more effectively interrelated through the use of mathematical models and electronic data processing equipment.
3. Investments and capital valuation, with particular emphasis on capital budgeting, which to its proponents represents *the* real estate decision.

A pattern of underlying theory is emerging that promises to be more descriptive of the realities of the market place, more manageable, and more understandable to non-appraisers. The remainder of this chapter is concerned with a progress report on these developments and their implications for the foreseeable future.

In real estate activity, business decisions must be made continually. These are purchase-or-sale decisions, lease-or-buy decisions, buy-or-build decisions, among others. Uncertainty surrounds each of these decisions, because each must be based upon estimates of the future, as well as upon conclusions about the present state of the real estate and investment markets. Essentially, it is the appraiser's task to reduce the range of uncertainty through the application of economic analysis and his knowledge. Moreover, it is important to identify those areas in which uncertainty remains, and how great that uncertainty is.

MAJOR FIELD

Decision-making has arrived as a major field of study in the last several years, particularly in its applications to business administration. Although they are interrelated, there are two major patterns of development that offer prospects for meaningful application to the field of real estate appraisal. These are the widened range of analytical tools (mostly mathematical) that are now being applied to business decision-making; and the re-evaluation of appropriate goals or criteria for standards of performance.

The range of analytical tools available to the business decision-maker, who often is a decision-maker with respect to real estate (especially real estate investment), is discussed in considerable detail in a recent book of readings. It is edited by Professors Bursk and Chapman of Harvard University and titled *New Decision-Making Tools for Managers*. The book contains 25 articles on the application of these tools to actual business problems. These are case studies rather than abstract illustrations.

Without going into detail, it is possible to identify the major groups of these tools and to indicate their probable applicability to real estate appraisal.

1. *Systems analysis*, particularly as applied in benefit–cost analysis. This provides an important standard by which alternative courses of action can be judged. The benefit–cost ratio can be translated into a net rate of return on an investment.

2. *Critical path analysis* (Program Evaluation Review Technique). This is a method of systematic planning of work which identifies the tasks to be performed and the sequence in which they should be performed, in order to provide the most efficient utilization of time and resources. This is a particularly significant tool for practicing appraisers in the application of the appraisal process in their own work.

Error Range

3. *Probability analysis*. Through the development of Bayesian statistics and the application of finite mathematics, analysis of the probabilities of error and the range of error inherent in small samples (which most appraisal studies almost necessarily are) offers for the first time the prospect of an evaluation of the conclusions reached in appraisal analysis. This is precisely the type of representation that Ratcliff calls for in his discussion of most probable selling price. In many ways, this is the most exciting

of all recent developments, although at the moment it offers the least immediate applicability. For one thing, appraisers must first be trained in this type of analysis.

4. *Electronic data processing.* The most important single prospect of the application of electronic data processing to the appraisal field at the moment is that it permits rapid and systematic analysis of large volumes of data. Once a bank of reliable market data (sales, rents, or whatever) is available, then it is possible to talk with increasing degrees of accuracy about what difference a deficiency or excess actually does make on the market. The critical factor, then, is that EDP equipment permits large volumes of data to be manipulated quickly and consistently so as to produce appropriate results.

Use Models

5. *Model building.* Both maximizing and optimizing models are now utilized to assist in the allocation of resources, and in the choice of alternative courses of action. These models are mathematical representations of market situations, developed either on paper or in a computer. This is what is meant by *simulation.* The significant difference between simulation and model-building in general is that a closer approximation to reality is attempted in a simulation model. This means that many more factors are considered and the model is much more complex. In part, this is the result of the development and appreciation of mathematical techniques that were known for many years but did not appear to be applicable to real market situations. The other development, once again, that has made this knowledge meaningful is the high-speed electronic computer. Computer technology makes it possible to consider more complex sets of interrelationships with many more variables. The real market is indeed a complex phenomenon, and much closer approximations to it are possible as a result of these new tools.

RUTHLESS "ECONOMIC MAN"

In Neo-Classical economics, the central figure is the Economic Man. He is a ruthless maximizer. He is characterized in most writings as at least amoral, which has led economics to be called "the dismal science" in the past. This individual is omniscient (remember that he is the "typical" buyer in the most widely utilized definition of market value), and he always acts in what is termed a rational fashion. That is to say, he maximizes his own well-being, which is measured in most instances by maximization of net income.

As a result, the concept of highest and best use has been regarded as central to both urban land economics analysis and to real estate valuation theory. It is only through highest and best use that maximum net return can be achieved. Among the outgrowths of this concept is the fact that there are endless arguments over whether highest and best use refers to the land, the property, or is two concepts referring to both. One need only to look in the April 1966 issues of *The Appraisal Journal* and *The Real Estate Appraiser* for an illustration of this dichotomy.

The current position of increasing numbers of writers in the field of business decision-making, investment decision-making, and real estate valuation is that the typical purchaser of or investor in capital goods is *not* a maximizer. At least, maximum profits are not the only criterion. As a result, highest and best use has come to be regarded as an impossible standard for the measurement of market behavior or of individual decision-making, and it has been questioned as even a tendency.

If the decision-maker or investor seeks to maximize anything, it is a combination of measurable monetary rewards and related but nonmeasurable satisfactions, which provide for optimization rather than maximization. It has become possible to talk of seeking an optimum rather than a maximum solution, once again because of the volume of work that can be handled by electronic computers.

BEST UNDER CIRCUMSTANCES

An optimum solution is the most efficient solution under a given set of constraints. This most efficient solution can be a maximum (for such things as profit or present worth) or a minimum (for such things as cost.) It differs from a maximizing solution because it is the best combination of many factors, all of which can interact with one another as well as bearing on the objective. To this extent, it can be more realistic, even though it appears to be more abstractly mathematical in the procedure by which the optimum solution is reached.

Simultaneously with these developments, however, behavioral sciences in particular have brought out the notion that in their decision-making behavior businessmen and investors do not necessarily seek either a maximum or an optimum solution. When confronted with a purchase–no purchase decision, an investor may select an "acceptable" solution, rather than the "best" solution. This idea is especially useful in real estate investment analysis, when the decision-maker is held to select the first alternative that meets his minimum standards (e.g., a cash throw-off of at least 10%, or a mortgage constant no greater than 8.25%).

In this configuration, the decision-maker or investor sets a limit below which or above which he will not accept a proposal. At any given point in time, there may be no other alternatives to choose. Even if there were, it may not be worth the effort or the trouble to seek them out. Therefore, the investor does not look for the most profitable use or alternative, or the best possible alternative. He simply selects one that meets the standards or criteria that he has previously established.

CALLED "SATISFICING"

This procedure is called "satisficing." Since we know that in the real estate market the typical buyer is not informed about everything possible, no matter how sophisticated he may be, a notion that permits him to act on the basis of the best information available and to meet his own standards appears more realistic and more descriptive than one which presumes that he is omniscient and acts always to maximize one variable only: net rate of return. Indeed, there is strong empirical evidence that sophisticated institutional investors do not always seek to maximize net rate of return, and that other considerations do enter into the decision that constitute the "comparables" that appraisers must utilize.

It is, therefore the author's proposition that on the basis of this evidence a new concept for the selection among alternative uses must be developed. This is Most Probable Use, which would be that use to which the *realty* (both land and improvements) is most likely to be put by the type of purchaser or investor to whom it is attractive in the market at the time of the appraisal. This postulates typical buyers drawn from the experience of the market, rather than from an abstracted set of conditions unlikely and probably impossible to be achieved.

It cannot escape notice that Most Probable Use is also a necessary conclusion if Most Probable Selling Price is to be estimated, even though Dr Ratcliff has not made this point explicit.

The analytical framework of urban economics and urban land economics, within which real estate valuation theory must evolve, is no longer rigidly neoclassical, nor is it couched in terms of the maximizing economic man. It is much more flexible, more realistic, *and* more complex. Multidimensional problems can be solved, and it is recognized that they must be solved.

In particular, it is recognized that there are many interrelated goals, both public and private, of an urban community. Moreover, some of these goals are often mutually exclusive. As a result, more complex analytical frameworks are required, and policy conclusions in the field of urban economics are now characterized as "interrelated opportunity costs at the policy level."

MAKE WIDE UTILIZATION

The ability to cope with increasingly complex conditions requires that market simulation via computers be widely utilized in urban economic analysis now. Simulation permits the testing of alternative policies, as well as efforts at measuring their impact on the community. It helps to identify meaningful relationships among different factors, and hence provides guides to future actions. More important, from the point of view of the appraiser, simulation helps in the identification of those factors which are particularly critical or pertinent in community growth and development. In other words, it helps to identify the major indicators that the appraiser definitely should seek out, follow, and analyze.

Finally, simulation helps to indicate the costs of increasing precision in solutions. There comes a point of decreasing returns, when inputs of effort and time and money simply do not result in a desirable payoff.

As a result of simulation, models of community development are emerging that are considerably more helpful in estimating future patterns and trends of growth than are the concentric circles, spokes, wedges, and multiple nuclei of the simpler, more generalized and more abstracted models that are found in most current texts on real estate. It means that the forecast of community development can be considerably more specific, and (hopefully) more accurate as well.

SUBJECT TO ANALYSIS

Academic students of real estate valuation and practicing appraisers alike have historically emphasized the critical importance of an appropriate background for market analysis in setting the proper framework for appraisal work. The most important new development is that simulation once again provides an opportunity for more effective, more meaningful, and more realistic analyses than have been possible heretofore. Market analysis is simply good appraisal practice, but a more systematic approach such as can be provided through market simulation forces the appraiser consciously to consider potentially pertinent factors every time.

The analysis of the market environment is what Dr Ratcliff calls MacroMarket Analysis. Not only is this important in estimating the determinants of supply and demand in the real estate market, but it is also subject to independent analysis for predictive purposes. Through understanding of the interrelationships of major market factors, it is possible to appreciate the probable impact on real estate values of such phenomena as a change in the Federal Reserve discount rate or a shift in accelerated depreciation rules in the Federal internal revenue code.

An increasing number of market factors has been identified as influencing real estate value. In particular, the institutional, legal, political, and social framework of the community has been subjected to analysis and evaluation as it impinges on private real estate decisions. So, too, has public policy, such as planning and zoning.

Finally, the most important single addition to environmental or MacroMarket analysis is the recognition that the *tax system* has a tremendous influence on decision-making in the real estate field. The fact of a graduated income tax system with special treatment of long-term capital gains and of depreciation is the basis for the so-called "tax shelter" afforded many investors by real estate. Wide-spread recognition of the impact of the Federal income tax system on real estate values, and inclusion of this impact in market analysis, is a major development that is long overdue in real estate appraisal analysis.

COMPETE WITH SUBJECT

Dr Ratcliff discusses the selection of alternative investment opportunities on the part of investors in terms of those properties which are *competing* with the "subject" property in the mind of the potential purchaser at the time the decision is being made. This idea of competitive area rather than comparable properties is gaining increasing acceptance among academic students of appraisal. It recognizes that buy–lease and buy–build decisions are competitive with purchase–no purchase decisions. It also helps to delineate the market area that is significant for the type of property under consideration. It eliminates parochial thinking in geographic terms only, and forces substitution of economic or financial competition for physical comparisons.

In addition, the competitive area concept emphasizes terms of sale, particularly financing, at least as much as it emphasizes physical characteristics.

There is mounting dissatisfaction with the one-value concept in real estate appraisal. Moreover, there is strong feeling that the "three approaches framework" may do harm rather than good. The argument is that each type of property and each problem has one best or proper approach. The underlying philosophy of each of the three approaches is different enough so that the value which emerges from each of the methods is also different in concept. Therefore, the argument emerges that there is no necessity that the three be close to one another, because they represent quite different ways of looking at the same property depending on the *purpose* of the analysis. This view also holds that the process of correlation is more one of forcing than of reconciliation.

NOT FULLY INFORMED

It is also increasingly evident that the market is not fully informed, nor is the typical buyer fully informed. Moreover, the typical buyer is not necessarily a maximizer. It is necessary, therefore, to identify just who this typical buyer is in each problem. It is necessary to ascertain his motives and thought processes in order to reach a conclusion as to value through his eyes.

The appraisal process has already been noted as highly amenable to application of critical path analysis. This will offer outstanding prospects for more efficient utilization of time and other scarce resources on the part of practicing appraisers.

There is virtual unanimity among academic students of real estate appraisal (many of them experienced professional practitioners as well) that the cost approach is an inappropriate and inadequate method of estimating market value, market price, or, indeed, of any other meaningful value. Cost of production certainly does not represent value, nor is it a *direct* determinant of market price. It is an influence, admittedly, but it operates primarily on the supply side. Estimates of cost now represent reasonable checks against alternative courses of action, particularly in terms of the feasibility of proposed projects. In addition, buy–build choices involve consideration of probable cost.

In addition to its questionable validity, the cost approach is also excessively mechanical and subject to more guesswork in the estimation of accrued depreciation than is associated with any other alternative method of value estimation.

BASED ON ASSUMPTION

One of the major difficulties with the application of this approach to value estimation is that it is based on the assumption that which has occurred in the recent past is most likely to prevail in the near future, or at least is the best available guide to the near-term future. Moreover, there is dissatisfaction with the extent and quality of both macro- and micro-market analysis. This is not a conceptual problem so much as one of application. Nevertheless, it is a serious criticism of current practice.

Increasing emphasis is placed on the terms of sale, and particularly the terms of lending, as more data become susceptible to analysis in models through electronic data processing. It has already been observed that macro-market analysis has identified more factors operating as influences on real estate value, which means that more analysis is potentially necessary when "comparables" are being considered. The competitive market approach to comparable sales analysis also emphasizes economic rather than physical factors.

There are strong recommendations that the Direct Sales Comparison Approach (and this term is preferred over the more insipid, less precise "Market Data Approach") should have primary applicability for residential properties.

If there is unanimity of opinion on any point in the field of real estate appraisal, it is found in the view that the income approach to value estimation is a simulation or an attempted replication of the investment analysis process applied to real estate. It has already been noted that academic students of real estate valuation theory tend to be most interested in this particular area, in large part because their formal training is more likely to have occurred in the field of finance.

OFFER APPLICATIONS

Current financial and capital theory offers substantial opportunities for application to real estate valuation analysis. As a result, there is increasing emphasis on financing, terms of lending, market alternatives, investor expectations, and the like in appraisal literature.

One of the major contributions from financial analysis is the emphasis on cash flow rather than on net operating income as the basis for the capitalization process, from the point of view of the investor–purchaser. As a result, equity–mortgage analysis has gained increasing acceptance, both in practice and in theory.

Appraisal theorists argue widely that capitalization of income is *the* approach to the valuation of nonresidential properties, including special purpose properties. In the latter instance, the estimation of value in use via income capitalization for a special purpose property is less subjective, and hence more descriptive of a market decision-making process than is the guesswork inherent in assessing accrued depreciation in the cost approach. This is one area in which considerably more work needs to be done, but it is a most intriguing prospect.

There is a marked trend toward emphasis of the position that it does make a considerable difference in investment analysis just who (or what) the typical investor is. In fact, this process of identification represents the first step in Dr Ratcliff's micro-market analysis.

INVESTOR CHARACTERIZED

The investor is characterized by his tax status, his goals, the type of property he can reasonably be expected to be interested in, the amount he can invest as equity funds, and the amount and terms of financing available to him. Since these factors influence the evaluation of the anticipated income flow from the property, and the rate at which that income is to be capitalized, it follows that the identity of the typical investor and his characteristics is an important step prior to property valuation.

In effect, the typical (or most probable) investor identifies the market for the property in question by setting the range of competing possibilities that confront the property. Who or what is *most likely* to invest in this type of property? Moreover, what form of organization will this investor most probably have? This also makes a difference in how much is likely to be bid for the property, especially when the tax status of the investor is considered.

This is not the hypothetical informed buyer of more traditional appraisal theory; it is the most probable investor, most likely to be attracted to this type of property in this market at this time. The process of identification requires detailed and careful market analysis on the part of the appraiser.

The productivity of a property is its capacity to generate net income. This is the anticipated cash flow, rather than an accounting net return, in most current writings. This is at the root of expanded interest in the equity–mortgage approach to income capitalization.

The productivity of a property consists of *all* expected income or benefits from it, which means that both cash flow and the anticipated reversion must be included in capitalization analysis. The Ellwood approach in particular emphasizes this point, although other writers have noted it as well.

ARGUE AGAINST SEPARATION

Moreover, there is widespread argument from current writers that the income from land cannot be logically separated from the income from improvements, except in isolated land—lease cases. As a result, income productivity should normally be attributed to the total property, and therefore the property residual technique is the only appropriate residual technique to apply in capitalization analysis. This, too, is particularly associated with Ellwood's writings, as is the corollary argument that overall rates can and should be developed for income capitalization.

Finally, there is growing insistence that the net income to be capitalized—the net income that the typical investor is seeking—is not only cash flow (which considers financing charges and depreciation allowances), but net cash flow after provision for income taxes.

Investment decision-making or allocation is held to be an application of the capital budgeting process. In particular, this involves a comparison of cost of capital with net income to calculate the benefit–cost ratio. The result is a guide to investment selection in terms of comparative benefit–cost ratios. This can be helpful in making rent-or-buy and buy-or-build decisions, as well as simple buy–no–buy decisions.

Capital allocation may occur in terms of the best or most profitable alternative in an open system. However, when investment funds are limited and capital rationing or priorities are to be established, investment decisions can be made on the basis of "acceptable" return. This, once again, is "satisficing."

MOST PROBABLE SELLING PRICE

Perhaps the most stimulating and challenging new development in appraisal theory is Dr Ratcliff's contention that the objective of appraisal analysis should be the estimation—or prediction—of most probable selling price, rather than market value. Dr Ratcliff argues that this is more nearly descriptive of what the market does. The concept is more oriented to economic and market factors, rather than being based on legalistic notions of an abstract, "economic man" environment.

This idea is consistent with Dr Ratcliff's view that every appraisal is a forecast in terms of given market conditions, based on systematic research. In passing, it should be noted that Paul F. Wendt has pointed out that the Italian appraisal theorist Medici used the term "most probable price" as synonymous with his notion of market value. Moreover, most probable selling price appears to require acceptance of the criterion of most probable use, which has been discussed earlier in this chapter.

EVERY ESTIMATE A FORECAST

Most probable selling price brings out the point that every value estimate is a forecast—even a backward one—under given market conditions. It permits analysis in terms of something other than the perfectly competitive market of neoclassical economics that is assumed in traditional appraisal theory. To this extent, it can bring appraisal estimates closer to reality.

Finally, when modern methods of statistical probability analysis are applied to appraising which is aimed at estimating most probable selling price, both the reliability of the single value estimate and the odds on the range around it can be estimated with a high (and predictable and measurable) degree of confidence. This will become more meaningful as more and better data on market sales, rentals, and incomes are generated through the use of models and high-speed data-processing equipment.

These developments and new directions in thinking about appraisal theory offer both opportunities and challenges for appraisers. In order to take advantage of the one and to meet the other, however, appraisers must be prepared. Otherwise, the job may well be performed by other groups.

First, the skills to perform the functions and activities noted throughout this chapter—and in earlier presentations—must be developed formally and systematically by professional appraisal organizations. At the same time, they must learn and teach the appropriate technical terminology that accompanies the disciplines in which these skills are founded.

CAN BE INCORPORATED

Next, many of these concepts can be more widely incorporated into appraisal practice immediately without controversy: general annuity capitalization, discounted cash flow analysis, property residuals with shorter term projections, analysis in terms of tax structures and investor characteristics, applications of electronic data processing to market data analysis, critical path programming.

Finally, several of the foregoing concepts require further testing, through research and case studies, before they can be added to the operational tools of the practicing appraiser. These include market simulation, probability analysis, cost-benefit analysis, cost of capital studies, satisficing, most probable use—and most probable selling price. This testing is largely the province of academic students of appraisal.

These tests and this research will result in appraisal theory that is more realistic, more descriptive of real estate market activity, and more defensible.

11. The Ellwood Analysis in Valuation: A Return to Fundamentals

WILLIAM N. KINNARD, JR

In 1959, an innocuous-appearing red book was published which was destined to cause more excitement, commotion and misunderstanding in the appraisal field than any single publication since Frederick Babcock's *Valuation of Real Estate*, published in 1932. The book was L.W. "Pete" Ellwood's *Ellwood Tables for Real Estate Appraising and Financing*.

ACCEPTANCE TOOK TIME

As with all innovations and new directions of thinking, it took some years to gain understanding and acceptance by many leaders in the appraisal field. In the process of it being analyzed and utilized by appraisers and real estate economists throughout the United States, many misconceptions and abuses of both the tables and the thinking that underlies them have emerged.

The major purpose of this chapter is to attempt to strip away the complicated superstructure of the approach; and to indicate that it represents merely a practical application of good, sound, basic land economic, and investment theory.

Perhaps it is improper to use the word "merely" when referring to such an application. In the present state of the arts in appraisal theory, when complexity and sophistication of technique often substitute for sound application of basic principles, it is both refreshing and important to have what is a basically simple and direct approach.

MARKET ORIENTATION

Market orientation is the essence of the so-called Ellwood Analysis: the appraiser should approach the valuation of income-producing property from the same point of

Reprinted with permission. *The Real Estate Appraiser*, 1966, Vol. 32, No. 5, pp. 18–24.

view as does the prospective equity investor and/or the prospective mortgage lender. In a field in which much is made of viewing the property to be appraised through the eyes of the prospective, typical, informed purchaser/investor, the Ellwood Analysis most nearly approximates that significant goal.

There is a strong tendency to confuse the tables and the mathematical formulas contained in Mr Ellwood's book (and in his other writings) with the financial and appraisal theory that they represent. Certainly it is true that in order to apply the theory properly, a practicing appraiser must have a good working knowledge of the mathematics of finance. If he cannot work with compound interest tables, he cannot understand the basic principles of investment. Nevertheless, the mathematics and the appraisal principles *are* different!

This chapter will primarily ignore the mathematical manipulations that are involved in applying the formulas and tables found in Mr Ellwood's book, so that the basic theme can be given serious consideration. That theme is that good theory is the most practical of all. The real difficulty is that there is relatively little *good* theory evident in the appraisal field at the present time.

MUST PERFORM TWO FUNCTIONS

There are two basic functions that good theory must perform, and therefore there are two sets of criteria for the development of good theory.

First, good theory should provide an accurate description or representation of the market place. Second, good theory must serve as a basis for reliable forecasting or prediction, as Dr Ratcliff has so forcefully demonstrated. In the literature of real estate valuation, lip service has been given for years to the significance, and even the necessity, of going to the market and of looking at the appraisal problem through the eyes of a prudent investor, often referred to as "a typical, informed purchaser." The analysis is then supposed to assist the appraiser in reaching a value estimate which depicts what this typical, informed purchaser is most likely to be willing and able to pay for the property. This is, in essence, what we purport to do in estimating Market Value.

The difficulty is that in most instances, appraisal analysis has actually proceeded to construct an abstracted, hypothetical framework of analysis, that negates and denies most of what has previously been argued. Both the *mechanics* and the *theory* that underlie much of current appraisal analysis are at variance with the *realities* of the real estate investment market place.

A corollary, which has been brought to the fore, particularly through Mr Ellwood's analysis, is that these mechanical processes are also based on mathematical formulas whose basic premises are at odds with the facts of the market place. Without laboring this point any further, one need to only consider the implications of straight-line capital recapture in presuming a net income that declines constantly and predictably over the economic life of the improvements.

The Ellwood Analysis eliminates most of the pitfalls inherent in such thinking, although it is still possible to become so enamored of the tables and mathematics that the basic, underlying valuation principles are lost. Now, what *is* the underlying premise on which the entire Ellwood Analysis is based?

AUTHOR BEST SOURCE

No better source of information for understanding the theory of the Ellwood Analysis exists than Mr Ellwood himself. In his writing, he has indicated that his approach evolved from many years of experience in reviewing appraisals for an institutional mortgage lender. The starting point, therefore, was the viewpoint of a prospective mortgage investor. It followed that "the most helpful appraisal for the prospective mortgage investor is one which makes provisions for given mortgage requirements, and then concentrates on finding a price at which the equity could be sold to a well-informed and prudent buyer."[1]

The first important fact of the market place is that mortgage financing is typically required and/or sought by a purchaser. Beyond this, mortgage loan terms available to the typical investor in the particular type of property involved are ascertainable from the market. What remains, then, is to estimate the value of the equity portion of the investment.

This emphasizes the fact that, in the view shared with Mr Ellwood by most academic students of investment and real estate analysis, the investor is seeking to maximize the return on *his* commitment. He is only incidentally interested in maximum value of the entire property. As Mr Ellwood himself has put it, "The prudent buyer of investment real estate is motivated only by the prospect of profit on the cash outlay he must make to acquire the property under consideration."[2]

Therefore, the capitalization process is the only approach which, from the buyer's viewpoint, makes any sense in estimating the present worth of the investment in the real estate. The Ellwood Analysis is an effort to simplify and improve upon traditional capitalization processes, largely by substituting common sense and the facts of "well-remembered experience" for unrealistic and abstracted assumptions, which are often encountered in appraisal procedures.

THREE MAJOR STEPS

Paraphrasing Mr Ellwood, the development of his approach consisted of three major steps:

1. The margin of security for mortgage investment is the actual cash market value of equity above the mortgage.
2. When an appraisal of property offered as security for a mortgage loan is submitted in support of the application, the obvious and best way to test it is to analyze the imputed equity for market attractiveness.
3. The common-sense way to make the appraisal is to concentrate on estimating the price at which a prudent investor would buy the equity position, *after* provision has been made for mortgage requirements according to the loan-to-value ratio, mortgage interest rate, and recapture term available to a "typical" buyer.[3]

[1]Ellwood, L.W., Wherry Condemnation Spotlights Problem of Equity Valuation. *The Appraisal Journal*, April 1960, XXVIII: 165.

[2]*Ibid.*, p. 166.

[3]Excerpted from a letter from Mr L.W. Ellwood to the author, dated October 20, 1965.

TERMS ARE IMPORTANT

Since the application of the capitalization process is designed to estimate the value of the equity, it follows that mortgage loan terms are extremely important in establishing *both* the proportion of the investment that is represented by mortgage (borrowed) funds, *and* the amount of net return that is necessary to cover both interest and principle amortization on the mortgage. Amortization is a complication that is readily accounted for through the use of the Ellwood Tables. It is built in to the "Mortgage Coefficient" that Ellwood develops and has made available to the practicing appraiser.

The Shibboleth of valuation "as if free and clear" is laid to rest on the basis of market experience and activity.

The basic formula employed by Ellwood is simply a variation of the traditional $V = I/R$ (Value equals income divided by rate). The only difference is that he has developed a means for estimating the appropriate overall rate to apply to the annual income flow and to be anticipated.

Without going into the details of the formula for the derivation of the overall rate, it should be noted that it consists of several important ingredients. These include: (1) the yield currently being demanded by prudent investment capital on equity investments; (2) the ratio of mortgage loan amount to total investment that is currently available; (3) mortgage loan terms that are available, including the interest rate and amortization term; *and* (4) the investor's expectation of either capital appreciation or capital depreciation between the date of the investment and the anticipated date of disposition.

SIX ANALYSIS AREAS

Through the Ellwood Analysis, there are six major areas in which appraisers have greater potential for more effective application of both the facts of the market place and the thinking of the prudent or typical, informed investor, when attempting to appraise investment properties.

1. The capitalization rate is a compound of seven different ingredients, five of which are readily "knowable" from the market:
   a. The available loan-to-value ratio for the type of property or investment in question;
   b. The going mortgage interest rate on such loans;
   c. The maximum effective amortization period available for such loans;
   d. The average or "going" income projection periods for such investments in the present market (as opposed to the "economic life");
   e. The proportion of the purchase capital that will be recovered through mortgage amortization during the income projection term.

   There are also two ingredients which must be estimated but which can be derived through careful analysis and investigation of the activities of investors:
   f. The anticipated increase or decrease in market value of the total property during the income projection term (an alternative way of saying "the value of the reversion"); and
   g. The prospective yield that will attract equity investment.

2. The Analysis makes it possible to emphasize the importance of the various terms of mortgage lending:
   a. Rate of interest;
   b. Amortization period or term of the loan;
   c. Loan-to-value ratio;
   d. Amortization provisions (various combinations including balloon loans).

Yield to Maturity

3. The Analysis makes it possible to consider yield or return on investment in the same manner in which the investor thinks of it: as a *yield to maturity*. This is much more nearly consistent with actual practice in the market, and it is consistent with investment theory as well. There are two components of the yield: the annual net return based on income flow, and the gain or loss at the end of the income projection period when the property is disposed of. This can be either an addition to or a subtraction from the equity yield, but it *is* an ingredient in estimating the overall rate. The "maturity" involved here represents the duration of the investor's commitment that is anticipated, and not the maturity of the mortgage loan.

4. The Analysis makes it possible for the appraiser to understand and apply the importance of incometax considerations, without resorting to analysis of the specific tax liability of the particular investor. It takes into consideration both the fact that the prudent investor will seek to convert income flow from ordinary income into long-term capital gain to the extent that this is possible; and that he will seek to defer his tax-liability as far into the future as possible. On the basis of these two considerations, a pattern of tax minimization (as contrasted with tax evasion) can emerge.

5. The Approach offers adaptability and flexibility in terms of a variety of alternative problems. It is much more general than is true of other capitalization techniques even if they had the same basic theoretical foundations.

6. It is possible, utilizing the Ellwood Analysis, to explain different "markets," or situations, in which the typical, informed investor has different objectives or viewpoints. It is a serious mistake, for example, to assume that all prudent investors have the same goals in terms of profits, that all think in terms of the same income projection periods, or that all have the same tax status. The Ellwood Approach does make it possible to *adapt* to these different types of market situations.

POINTS AT VARIANCE

Within the framework of the Ellwood Analysis, there are at least 10 major points that are at variance with much of widely utilized appraisal practice. While these are not necessarily innovations, in the sense that they are new ideas put forth by Mr Ellwood, their presentation in combination *is* an important innovation that requires a new pattern of thinking on the part of practitioners unused to investment theory and analysis:

1. Mortgage financing *does make a difference* to the net income flow from the property that will be anticipated by the typical, prudent investor. *All* terms of lending,

and not simply the mortgage rate of interest, must be considered in evaluating the impact of mortgage financing on this net income flow.

2. The Ellwood Analysis makes it possible to develop an overall rate for capitalization of net income or yield to a present worth estimate.
3. The availability of an overall rate makes it possible to utilize the mechanically simpler and conceptually more defensible "Property Residual Technique" in capitalizing income to a present worth estimate.

Emphasizes Equity Value

4. The Analysis emphasizes estimating the value of the equity portion of the investment, since the typical purchaser is an equity investor who will utilize financing (trading on equity) to maximize the return on his investment.
5. The Analysis emphasizes the derivation of an equity yield or rate of return.
6. The equity yield is expressed in the form of a *cash* return, net of mortgage financing requirements, rather than an accounting return. This is much more nearly in keeping with the thinking of the typical informed investor.
7. The yield is expressed as an annual rate, but it is a *yield to maturity*, (as defined above). This means that it is calculated either after the fact or in terms of a specific income projection period.
8. The yield is a composite of an annual flow of net cash dollars *plus* an average annual adjustment for anticipated gain or loss on the sale of the property at the end of the income projection period.
9. The Analysis makes short-term projection feasible. In these terms, the Property Residual Technique is quite appropriate.
10. All of this concern with money and financing emphasizes the necessity to analyze the market competition for money and for investment outlets, as well as the market for real estate of the type being appraised.

ANALYSIS CONTRIBUTIONS

In addition to all of the considerations that have already been enumerated in this presentation, the Ellwood Analysis makes five major contributions to the craft of the appraiser of investment real estate which cannot go unacknowledged. They have made it increasingly imperative that any practicing appraiser become familiar with the thinking and the technique of the Ellwood Approach, because it is an increasingly useful tool in the hands of a knowledgable practitioner:

1. The Ellwood Analysis makes it possible for the appraiser to test the *reasonableness* of the capitalization rate (especially the equity rate), of the income projection period, of the reversion rate, and of the market value estimate itself. The Analysis also makes it possible for the appraiser to offer commentary on the *reasonableness* of a mortgage request or application. It can, in brief, be used effectively for management or investor decision-making. The Analysis underscores the fact that no appraisal is made without the need for some decision, particularly in terms of investment property.

Moreover, the Ellwood Analysis makes it possible for the estimation of present worth figures *other than* market value within a consistent analytical framework. Yet, it still provides a reasonable structure within which market value can appropriately be estimated.

2. The Analysis reduces the area of uncertainty, or of the intrusion of the views of the *appraiser*, in valuation analysis. It tends to maximize the reliance on those market data that are available and verifiable, as well as bring into sharper focus the areas about which doubt and conjecture still exist. This makes it possible at least to consider ranges within which an appropriate answer is most likely to be found.

Market Still Emphasized

3. Ellwood continues to emphasize the significance of the actions of the "individuals that make up the market." He still goes to the market for data, rates, *and* for the thinking of the participants in investment decision-making about the type of property under consideration.

4. The Analysis is really quite simple as a concept. Value is simply average annual income divided by overall rate. The important addition to this simplification is the fact that the same approach can legitimately be utilized every time, without an artificial division of the property into its *physical* components. Rather, it is divided into *economic* components, precisely as investors and other market participants divide it.

5. The Ellwood Analysis offers the first real possibility of an all purpose flexible tool for income capitalization and hence value estimation. It is an approximation to a general model for appraisers. Even though it does not meet all the requirements of such a general model, it is in the interest of every practicing professional appraiser to familiarize himself with this important technique.

A final note of caution is in order at this point. The Ellwood Analysis as yet does not solve every problem, and claims of universal applicability can be overdone. In fact, there is a tendency at the present time on the part of many proponents of the Approach to do just this. The real danger is in an unthinking application of the Approach, without care being taken. As with all powerful tools, it can be dangerous in the hands of an unskilled, improper user.

The Ellwood Analysis *is* a powerful tool, which is available to all appraisers of investment real estate. The appraiser must come to understand its basic premises, however, and to develop facility with its mechanics as well. This is the respect that a powerful analytical tool deserves, and that a professional analyst must provide.

12. Reducing Uncertainty in Real Estate Decisions

DR WILLIAM N. KINNARD, JR

The study of real estate is essentially an attempt to understand how and why decisions affecting the use of real estate resources can be improved.[1] Better decisions lead to greater profit levels, through greater efficiency in allocating and using real estate resources, and through less risk of loss or unexpected results.

It follows that the *practice* of real estate in whatever form—sales brokerage, rental brokerage, mortgage brokerage, development, financing, management, appraising, or counseling—should be the application of known principles and techniques to assist decision-makers achieve better decisions. In this way, action programs based on these decisions should come closer to realizing desired objectives.

Considered in its broadest aspect, the real estate business is concerned with economizing on limited resources (especially urban space) to achieve maximum or optimum satisfaction of human needs, wants, and desires.

These needs, wants, and desires include: shelter for people and businesses; satisfactory locations for homes and businesses; convenient access to supporting facilities, such as schools, shopping, recreation, cultural facilities, places of employment, sources of supply, and markets for goods; aesthetic and social appeal; availability of service facilities, such

This article was originally presented at the third annual Beyer-Nelson Distinguished Lecture in Real Estate at the Ohio State University, in cooperation with the Ohio Association of Real Estate Boards. The Lecture is sponsored by Ben B. Beyer, SREA, Cleveland and John Galbreath, MAI, Columbus in honor of Herbert U. Nelson, former Executive Vice President of the National Association of Real Estate Boards.

[1]This argument is developed effectively and at length in Arthur M. Weimer and Homer Hoyt, *Real Estate*, Fifth edition. New York, Ronald Press, 1966; Chapter 1.

Reprinted with permission. *The Real Estate Appraiser*, 1968, Vol. 34, No. 7, pp. 10–16.

as water, sewer, protection, streets, and refuse disposal; and income and profit. Both public and private market structures are organized to facilitate the efficient achievement of these ends.

Too often, the work of the real estate practitioner (and the broker in particular) is thought of as merely bringing two or more parties together to fulfill the terms of a transaction. The parties may be buyer and seller, landlord and tenant, or borrower and lender. This is only a superficial view, however, involving merely the tip of the iceberg of real estate activity. In every transaction, there is a whole series of important, usually difficult, and always risky (or uncertain) decisions to be made. Risk and uncertainty are treated as synonymous in this discussion, although there *are* technical differences between the two concepts. In helping to reduce uncertainty on the part of decision-makers—it can never be eliminated entirely—the broker, appraiser, manager, or counselor is performing the real service of the real estate profession.

Unfortunately, indifferent quality and success characterize these efforts at the present time. This is true despite significant developments in recent years that have made powerful and effective tools of analysis available to the real estate industry.

DECISION-MAKING PROCESS

In much of business and management analysis, the decision-making process has been developed into a systematic, logical procedure which goes far toward identifying the areas of risk and uncertainty involved in a particular decision. This in turn makes possible a program of action to reduce uncertainty, where possible, and to adjust plans to account for uncertainty which cannot be influenced or controlled by the decision-maker.

Any business decision has basic elements of risk in it. First, the future can never be known with certainty. Thus, there is always risk that future market conditions or responses (technology, tastes, political affairs, employment, and income) will be different from those anticipated when the decision is made. Moreover, elements of the market environment confronting the decision-maker may be unexpectedly beyond his control or influence and force a revision of plans or action to adjust to this altered current market situation. If adjustment is not possible, then anticipations or expectations must be amended.

The process of rational business decision-making involves six steps:[2]

1. Identification and understanding of the problem.
2. Definition and clarification of the goals or objectives sought.
3. Development of alternative programs for the attainment of the goals.
4. Analysis of the anticipated consequences of each major alternative program.
5. Appraisal of the alternatives in terms of the objectives sought.
6. Selection of the action program appearing most conducive to attainment of the goals.

[2]For a detailed discussion of these steps, see Calkins, R.D. The Decision-Making Process in Administration. *Business Horizons*, Fall 1959.

Within this framework, flexibility must be provided. Decisions are commitments of resources against an uncertain future. Allowance must be made for a margin of error in making estimates or forecasts. Perhaps the greatest contribution of *systematic* decision analysis is that it forces the decision-maker to identify and evaluate (within the limits of available data and his abilities) all of the factors which logic and experience indicate are likely to have an influence on the outcome of the decision. This is vividly illustrated in Dr Paul Wendt's discussion of the Land Use Forecast Model developed by the Bay Area Simulation Study:[3]

> The principal value of the research technique as outlined lies not so much in the quality of any particular forecast based upon this technique, but rather in the fact that the technique requires the careful specification of the many judgmental factors entering into forecasts. Further, the model makes it possible with almost ridiculous ease to measure the impact of alterations in assumptions with respect to . . . elements influencing any forecast.

This last point is most important. Decisions must be recognized as part of a continuum. Once made, they must be, and the system must make them capable of being, continually reappraised and reviwed in the light of subsequent events.

Decision-making basically involves making choices among available and known alternatives. It includes information problems (intelligence activity); prediction problems (design activity); and selection problems (choice activity).[4] At each level in each type of problem, the greater the quantity and the better the quality of information available, and the more comprehensive and systematic the analysis employed, the less uncertainty there is likely to be about the probable outcome of the decision.

NATURE AND INGREDIENTS

Real estate decisions are notoriously risky. Yet, more orderly and active markets plus greater return on total commitments of resources are possible through systematic efforts to reduce the risk of real estate decisions.

In applying the several steps in the rational decision-making process, every real estate decision involves answering five basic questions:

1. What are the goals to be achieved? This is the issue of *objectives*.
2. What is to be done? Is any action called for at all? This is the issue of *whether*. "No action" is always one reasonable alternative.
3. Which alternative for action is to be selected, assuming there is to be any action at all? This is the issue of *choice*.
4. In what manner is action to be taken? What specific arrangements (e.g., financing) are called for? This is the issue of *how much*.
5. When shall any action be taken? This is the issue of *timing*.

[3]Wendt, Paul F., Forecasting Land Uses, *Urban Land*, July–August 1967: 13–14.
[4]Weimer and Hoyt, *op. cit.*, p. 43.

In each instance, the decision-maker must also answer the question: "Why?" What market or property information dictates a particular conclusion or course of action? How does the selected alternative fit in with the objectives of the decision program?

Real estate decisions involve a wide variety of choices. Indeed, within any single decision program, a number of sub-decisions must also be made. For example, the seemingly simple decision whether to purchase a particular property involves a whole series of choices about use, location, financing, ownership, and timing. Only then can the decision-maker decide what price he can afford to pay, as well as what his bargaining strategy with the current owner should be.

Throughtout this decision process, he must also determine what outside professional assistance he requires to help him; and from whom to obtain it. This outside help could include legal advice, market analysis, financial advice, architectural and cost analysis, investment feasibility analysis, rental advice, general counseling, and of course marketing or brokerage advice. In each instance, informed professional opinion and methodology should be mobilized to help the decision-maker, although the ultimate responsibility for the decision is his alone.

Real estate decisions may involve the decision whether to buy or not; whether to sell or not; whether to rent (as either landlord or tenant) or not; whether to borrow or not; whether to lend or not. They include buy-lease decisions, or sale-lease decisions. There are financing decisions (such as the extent to which leverage is to be utilized) and investment decisions (including organization for investment). Location choices must be made; these are especially critical for investment real estate and involve a quite distinct body of analysis.

Land owners must decide whether to develop their property or hold it for speculative gain, provided they decide not to sell immediately. The type of use for new developments must be decided, as well as for conversions. The owner-investor must decide whether to retain or replace existing improvements. In deciding to dispose of property, timing decisions can be extremely important. Owners, users, and purchasers alike must decide what elements in the political or economic environment they should try to change. The market, as well as individual units operating in it, must decide whether private or public action is to be taken.

Most importantly, however, the decision-maker must select his objectives and goals. These set the standards in terms of which other choices and judgments are to be made. They also set the priorities for selecting action programs. For investment or income-producing real estate in particular, it is important to keep user objectives and investor-objectives separate, and to keep priorities straight between the two.[5] This is especially the case when a commercial or industrial firm owns and occupies its own real estate. Then extreme care must be exercised in differentiating between the gains from and objectives of *use* and the objective of investment *profit*, so that each can be evaluated in its proper perspective.

Finally, the operators of real estate firms have management decisions to make which are similar to those in any business enterprise. In order to free technical experts to do

[5]Messner, Stephen D., Corporate Real Estate Decisions, *Connecticut Industry*, July 1967, pp. 17–18.

their job of advising clients most effectively, the firms must be efficiently managed. This requires good working knowledge of the techniques of management decision-making, which follow essentially the same precepts as those presented for real estate decisions.

REAL ESTATE DECISION-MAKERS

Potential buyers and sellers are obvious decision-makers in real estate. So are would-be investors. Tenants and landlords are decision-makers. Borrowers and lenders are decision-makers. Land and property owners are confronted with decisions of whether to develop, hold for speculation, or sell. Potential users must decide whether to rent or own, and whether to buy or build. Users and developers alike are confronted with the selection of location.

Governmental bodies and public agencies are also decision-makers whose actions influence use patterns and values in many ways. Finally real estate practitioners themselves must make decisions about what information their clients need, and how best to serve the needs of their clients.

PECULIARITIES OF REAL ESTATE DECISIONS

While they are based on the same principles and involve the same systematic techniques as other business decisions, real estate decisions *are* different.[6] The most important points of distinction stem from the characteristics of real estate itself. It is fixed in location, which means that use and development decisions are limited to a specific site or sites. Moreover, real estate is a highly differentiated product. Every parcel or property is unique; no two are alike. This makes comparison for purposes of selection among alternatives particularly complex and difficult. It typically requires more judgment on the part of decision-makers than is true of most other types of business decisions; which normally involve products or services considerably less differentiated than real estate.

Real estate is also a very durable, long-term asset. As a result, real estate decisions frequently require longer-term commitments (more distant time horizons) than are involved in other types of business or consumer decisions. In such cases, committing resources into an uncertain future compels the decision-maker to rely heavily on long-term forecasts of dynamic changes in the market.[7]

Because of its fixed location, real estate is very much a creature of its environment; physical, economic, legal-governmental, and social. This means that particular emphasis must be placed on market analysis and market forecasts in making decisions about the purchase, use, or development of real estate.

That market environment is itself peculiar. It is relatively uninformed, and appropriate data are often difficult to come by. Especially in the residential sector of the

[6]The differentiating features of real estate decisions are expounded in a particularly lucid discussion by Arthur M. Weimer in Real Estate Decisions are Different, *Harvard Business Review*, November–December 1966.

[7]See Messner, *op. cit.*, p. 18.

market, participants are active only infrequently and sporadically. As a result, they are frequently uninformed about alternatives available to them and unsophisticated in their decision behavior. Moreover, real estate markets tend to be both localized and stratified; they are made up of many sub-markets with only slight overlapping. This means that very specific information about the past behavior and trends, current status, and future prospects of a particular market segment is required in any given decision process.

Finally, the relatively large amount of funds required to finance a single real estate transaction (stemming in part from the long payout period for income or benefits from real estate ownership) makes real estate financing decisions (especially about the equity-debt mix) particularly significant. Recent research has shown that financing is an area in which buyers (whether users or investors) are particularly aware of their need and desire for help from brokers and counselors, in making purchase decisions.[8]

RISKS IN REAL ESTATE DECISIONS

The basic risk in any investment is the risk of loss, whether in the form of negative income or of less income than was anticipated at the time of the investment decision. Real estate is no exception. In addition, however, there are four major types of decision risk that result directly from the peculiarities of real estate as an asset, and of real estate markets:

1. *Time risk.* Because real estate is a long-term asset, resources must be committed by the decision-maker over an extended uncertain future. The longer into the future a commitment is made, the greater the risk that changed or unexpected market conditions (changes in taste, standards, technology, competition) will produce results which are different from or less attractive than those anticipated at the time the decision and commitment were made.
2. *Location risk.* Because of its fixed location, the use and income productivity of real estate are especially sensitive to changes in its immediate environment, and to changes in the competitiveness of its location. This goes beyond market projections or forecasts. It requires very specific analysis of the future prospects for the particular site. Demand and profit may continue as expected for a given type of use in the market; they can simultaneously decline or disappear for the particular *location* in question.
3. *Information risk.* Because necessary market data may be unobtainable (either by intent or through ineffective channels of communication), real estate decisions must be made frequently on a judgmental or even an "informed guess" basis. With inadequate information on which to base a rational decision, risks are correspondingly increased. This type of uncertainty is particularly hazardous when it underlies long-term projections.

[8]This finding emerged from the research conducted in the preparation of *Industrial Real Estate* by William N. Kinnard, Jr, published by the Society of Industrial Realtors, Washington, DC in October 1967. For residential purchasers, the finding was confirmed in as yet unpublished research conducted by Donald E. Hempel for the Center for Real Estate and Urban Economic Studies at the Univesity of Connecticut.

4. *Goals risk.* The mixed character of real estate as an investment can easily lead to confusion in goals or objectives among user-owners in particular. This creates a risk that the apparent attractiveness of a particular parcel of real estate as an investment can overshadow or subordinate more significant questions about its effectiveness in use.

EFFECTIVE DECISION-MAKING

For real estate decisions to be effective and appropriate, there must first be a clear-cut and unequivocal enunciation of the goals and objectives of the particular decision. They must be realistic and obtainable in the light of known market conditions. They set the standards in terms of which choices can and should be made and the criteria for establishing priorities of choice. They must be rigid enough to allow for the alternative conclusion that *no* action is the best course of action.

Next, facts are required for the application of the selected decision standards to the problem at hand. There must be adequate data available about the market, the particular location, and the alternatives confronting the decision-maker. "Adequacy" of data includes both a sufficient quantity to make them representative of the market (or submarket) in question, and sufficient reliability to warrant basing forecasts on them.

Particular care must be taken in establishing alternative courses of action, from which the final choice is to be made. They must be feasible and warranted in terms of the data collected, and appropriate means of achieving the stated objectives of the decision-maker. Each alternative must be examined painstakingly to discover its implications—the probable results that can be expected from following that course of action.

In order for these results to be achieved, there must be an effective body of systematic techniques for the gathering, analysis, and evaluation of necessary data.

Moreover, appropriate methods must be utilized for the evaluation of alternative courses of action, and for the choice of the best alternative. The standards of what is "best" must be carefully developed and applied. Traditionally, these have been expressed in terms of maximum net income or benefits, according to the criteria of economic man.[9]

More recently, however, two more realistic standards have emerged for selecting the best course of action.[10] One is the "optimum" criterion, by which the decision-maker maximizes in terms of a specified, detailed set of constraints. The optimum solution is best in relation to market and institutional constraints; the maximum solution is an absolute level without constraints.

The second alternative criterion for selection is termed "satisficing." It represents a course of action which is satisfactory (or "good enough") in terms of standards of acceptability established by the decision-maker. Once the standards are established, any course of action which meets them may be selected, up to the limits of available resources. As of the time of the decision, the most attractive of known alternatives is still selected, but the search for alternatives is not as comprehensive or

[9]Kinnard, William N., Jr, New Thinking in Appraisal Theory. *The Real Estate Appraiser*, August 1966.

[10]For a detailed discussion, see the pioneering effort of Herbert A. Simon, *The New Science of Management Decision*. Harper and Row, New York. 1960.

time-consuming as in the quest for maximization or optimization. This most nearly describes the behavior of home buyers, investors, and mortgage lenders (among others) in the real estate market. It is a powerful device for testing the rationality of real estate decisions.

TECHNIQUES FOR REDUCING UNCERTAINTY AND RISK

Uncertainty and risk cannot be *eliminated* from real estate decisions. The future can never be known and data are never fully complete. Uncertainty and risk can be reduced, however, through the application of existing systematic techniques of decision-making, especially with the assistance of skilled and knowledgeable real estate specialists. The result can be greater levels of profits, fewer losses, and more efficient allocation of real estate resources among competing uses. The techniques are applicable to both private and public real estate decisions.

At present, these techniques are not widely utilized. Some are expensive for the small office; others require skills not frequently found in small offices. They can be, and are being, utilized effectively by investors and commercial or industrial users, however. They can and must be applied by real estate advisers and counselors if they are to serve their clients properly.

Probably the most dramatic and potentially exciting possibilities lie in the applications of computer technology to data gathering, storage, retrieval, and analysis.[11] Computer statistics and Bayesian statistics provide opportunities to apply quantitative methods and qualitative standards of judgment (quantitatively developed) to real estate decisions, freeing them from reliance on essentially intuitive judgments. These statistical techniques make it possible to deal with small numbers of observations meaningfully; this is a common situation in real estate decision-making. The meaning of both association and observed differences among real estate factors can be explained by these methods. They also permit the assignment of priorities for action.

Criteria and standards of choice can be made explicit through more conscious application of the basic economic concept of opportunity cost: The evaluation of alternatives in terms of what used to be given up (in income or benefits foregone as well as costs incurred) in order to realize each.

Opportunity cost analysis can be applied equally effectively to problems of optimizing, satisficing, or maximizing—each under conditions when they are most appropriate and descriptive of market behavior. In specific project evaluation through satisficing analysis, the use of the concepts of Most Probable Use and Most Probable Selling Price[12] (rather than the maximizing standards of Highest and Best Use, and Market Value) as meaningful standards of judgment becomes more realistic and appropriate.

In the case of public agency decision-making, which affects such matters as zoning, urban renewal, and public improvements, the relatively new technique of

[11]One such application is discussed in detail in Jack Lessenger, Towards a New Method and Theory of Appraisal. *The Real Estate Appraiser*, March 1968.

[12]See the discussion of these concepts in Kinnard, *op. cit.*; and Richard U. Ratcliff, *Modern Real Estate Valuation: Theory and Application*. Madison, Democrat Press. 1965, especially Chapter 3.

Benefit–Cost analysis is available for identifying and evaluating the factors which enter into the decision, even though they may not be subject to quantification. This approach offers promise of increased applications to public decision-making on a broad front.[13]

Both private and public real estate decisions, especially those involving large-scale projects such as New Town developments, can be aided by the use of computers and mathematical models through a technique known as simulation. This has already been mentioned in the discussion of the Bay Area Simulation Survey. The technique is quite expensive, demanding, and time-consuming, but it offers a community or a large developer the opportunity of testing results under a wide variety of differing assumptions. At least as important is the fact that it forces the analyst to consider every factor influencing the decision.

Recent developments in financial investment analysis, especially in the capitalization of cash flow and in capital budgeting, have particular applicability to the evaluation of real estate investment alternatives. Value in use is especially important to newer techniques of real estate investment analysis, whether in terms of maximizing, optimizing, or satisficing.

Finally, critical path analysis is an important device for planning real estate development and investment programs. It provides an effective means for scheduling the timing of interrelated stages in the process and indicates the sequence in which the several steps of a development or investment program can most efficiently and profitably be undertaken.

Every real estate decision is essentially a research problem.

Approached systematically and objectively, it can be solved with a significant reduction of risk to the decision-maker. Better and more nearly complete data (whose identity is provided by the decision-making process), more systematic quantitative techniques of analysis and application, and more conscious awareness of the probable consequences of alternative programs of action (through such analytical methods as simulation and model building) all can go far toward reducing the uncertainties inherent in real estate decisions.

Some sophisticated clients, especially those in the commercial and industrial fields, are already employing these techniques in their own decision-making programs. In order to serve the needs and requirements of such clients, and of others equally in need of such help, the real estate industry must embrace these analytical techniques to provide advice and counsel in decision-making. As a corollary, real estate practitioners will become more effective and more efficient, as well as more profitable, businessmen through the use of these tools, because they can economize on their own skills and time while simultaneously providing better counseling service to their clients.

[13]One significant application of this analytical tool to decision-making in urban renewal is found in Stephen D. Messner, *A Benefit–Cost Analysis of Urban Redevelopment*, Indiana Business Report No. 43; Indiana University, Bloomington. 1967.

SOURCES AND APPLICATIONS OF TECHNICAL SKILLS

The great bulk of the theoretical constructs and analytical devices which have applicability to the improvement of real estate decision-making have emanated, not suprisingly, from colleges and universities. It is here that greater emphasis is placed on the development of explanations of market behavior, and on techniques for analyzing and forecasting that behavior.

What is not so obvious, however, is the fact that many of the analytical methods have developed in fields not directly related to real estate. It has remained for a few interested academics sensitive to the problems of real estate analysis and decision-making to transfer these techniques and methods to real estate problems.

A growing number of examples of applications of data gathering and retrieval techniques to real estate decisions has appeared quite recently.[14] These show convincingly that they can be adapted to the real estate field, provided sufficient resources are made available for the effort.

Both market simulation and benefit–cost analysis have been applied successfully to real estate problems, especially those concerned with selecting from among alternative land use and development programs.[15] Investment analysis and feasibility analysis have come to enjoy much wider applicability to real estate problems, as evidenced by recent publication of significant findings.[16] Forecast models which both identify and analyze relevant factors in individual real estate decisions have actually been employed successfully in planning real estate developments.[17] Columbia, MD is an outstanding example. Others such as those presented at the annual meetings of AREUEA last December promise significant contributions to the solution of real estate decision problems concerning individual locations, as opposed to market-wide decisions.[18]

Perhaps most important, academic researchers investigating real estate decision problems are concentrating more and more on the effective application of the entire rigorous framework of the formal decision process. Widespread computer availability

[14]See, for example, Lessenger, *op. cit.*

[15]Simulation is best exemplified by the model described in Wendt, *op. cit.* See Messner, *A Benefit–Cost Analysis of Urban Redevelopment, loc. cit.* for an excellent presentation of the application of benefit–cost analysis.

[16]See, for example, Kinnard, *op. cit.*, and Richard U. Ratcliff, *A Restatement of Appraisal Theory*. University of Wisconsin, Madison. 1963.

[17]Significant examples may be found in the *1967 Proceedings* of the American Real Estate and Urban Economics Association; Storrs Center for Real Estate and Urban Economic Studies, University of Connecticut, 1968. They include:

Alfred N. Page, Towards a Theory of Residential Construction." R. Bruce Ricks, "New Town Development and the Theory of Location.

Columbia, MD is also being developed with the assistance of a growth and market forecast model.

[18]See, for example, Ronald Graybeal, A Model of Retail Development, *1967 Proceedings*, American Real Estate and Urban Economics Association, *loc. cit.*; and William N. Kinnard, Jr. and Stephen D. Messner, *A Housing Strategy for Southeastern Connecticut*, Real Estate Report No. 3; Storrs, Center for Real Estate and Urban Economic Studies, University of Connecticut, 1968.

has made the gathering, storage, and processing of required data feasible; it has also made possible the utilization of meaningful statistical techniques which have hitherto been impracticable.

It is to the universities and colleges, therefore, and especially to their urban economics and real estate research centers, that the real estate industry—decision-makers and adviser-practitioners alike—must turn for guidance and assistance.

The emphasis must shift from concentration on "how to" courses and studies of real estate practice, and focus instead on the translation of these new and powerful analytical and forecasting techniques to the use of real estate decision-makers and decision-influencers. This means courses and seminars on the techniques of data gathering and retrieval, market analysis, forecasting (especially with relatively simple forecast models), and financial and investment analysis. It also requires concentrated training in the process of rational decision-making, with particular emphasis on the development and application of meaningful standards of performance and criteria for choice.

At least as important is the stimulation of further research, essentially long-run and not specifically problem-oriented, into the development and further refinement of analytical techniques of real estate decision-making. This encouragement must take the form of making more resources available to work on the problem. Money helps, of course, but even more critical is the need to attract bright young technicians and theorists to work in the area of real estate decision-making. They need help and advice from the practitioners to identify what the *real* problems confronting the real estate field are; not just how to obtain listings more effectively, or what advertising media are most productive of sales. These latter are not entirely insignificant issues, but they are less basic and less susceptible to academic investigation than is the problem of bringing real estate decision-makers into a condition of lessened risk and uncertainty.

There are real economies and gains in bringing real estate students and researchers together in centers at selected universities. This has already been done with telling effect at the University of Connecticut, at Berkeley, at UCLA, at Pittsburgh, and at the University of Connecticut, among others. In California and Connecticut, a portion of real estate brokers' license fees is allocated to support teaching and research programs in real estate and urban economics at the state university. The result has been the assembly of a critical mass of brain-power that is producing meaningful studies with broad applicability to real estate decision problems of various types. The opportunity exists in Ohio to establish a similar center, building on the strong nucleus that already exists at Ohio State. This opportunity should be seized at the earliest possible moment, for the benefit of both the real estate field in general and Ohio Realtors in particular.

CONCLUSION

Real estate decisions are inherently risky and uncertain. They involve long-term commitments of resources into an uncertain and unknowable future. They are concerned with an asset whose fixed location renders it particularly vulnerable to external environmental changes. Despite these constraints, real estate decisions can be made more effective and less uncertain through the application of a systematic process of decision-making, and the application of relatively new techniques of forecasting and analysis.

By reducing the uncertainties associated with insufficient and improper data, inappropriate or ambiguous standards of judgment, and inadequate analytical techniques, the overall profitability of real estate investment and the general efficiency of resource allocation and use can be improved markedly.

Ample profit opportunities would remain for entrepreneurship, for pioneering, for assuming the basic risks of long-term commitments, and for waiting. Moreover, more time and resources would be available for redirecting those market environmental conditions which need to be altered and are in fact subject to change. Less time and energy would be directed toward impossible or unprofitable efforts at redirection.

Through the conscious and intelligent application of this approach and these tools, which are already at hand, to real estate decisions, brokers, appraisers, managers, and counselors will be much better equipped to perform their basic function of helping to improve real estate decisions. Many decision-makers already employ at least some of these techniques in their non-real estate decisions; others can use them most profitably if they only become aware of their potential and how to utilize.

The first requirement, then, is for professional real estate practitioners to familiarize themselves with the rational decision approach and techniques of analysis, so that they can best serve the needs and decision interests of their clients.

The opportunity exists for real estate practitioners to develop this familiarity with the approach and techniques through cooperative action with real estate research and study centers at colleges and universities. By setting aside the preoccupation with the mechanics of the trade which has characterized most real estate education to this point, and concentrating instead on the basic principles of systematic decision-making, the real estate industry (and its individual members) can serve best both their own interests and those of their clients. They will then be in a position to emulate the missionaries to Hawaii of another era, and "Do well while doing good."

13. The Financial Logic of Investment Property Appraising

WILLIAM N. KINNARD, JR

The development of the Society's new courses on income property appraisal and on special topics relating to real estate appraisal will involve the application of income capitalization analysis in some form or other. It is therefore appropriate to review carefully and seriously some of the basic precepts on which income property analysis (or investment property analysis) is based. Income capitalization can be most useful and very proper as a technique for estimating value, especially Market Value. The technique must be fully understood and properly handled, however. Its application must reflect the market behavior and the thinking of participants on the investment or income property market.

Appraisers who read appraisal periodicals regularly will have noticed the increasing appearance in recent years of expressions of criticism and dissatisfaction with the Income Approach (capitalization analysis), as we know it, as a basis for estimating market value. This criticism has been aimed particularly, but not exclusively, at many of the traditional methods of analysis that we have historically employed. I am referring especially to the land residual and building residual techniques, and to straight-line capital recapture.

EMPHASIS ON MECHANICS

It is argued that current teaching in the field of income capitalization has tended to concentrate on technique and mechanics. This includes even courses in

This paper was presented at the Great Lakes Appraisal Conference, Society of Real Estate Appraisers, in Detroit, Michigan in October, 1968.

Reprinted with permission. *The Real Estate Appraiser*, 1969, Vol. 35, No. 4, pp. 13–21.

mortgage–equity analysis and its variant, the Ellwood analysis. This emphasis on mechanics and the manipulation of figures has resulted in widespread discontent with the quality of the final answer derived.

It is further maintained that stressing the mechanics of income capitalization has led to a tendency to overlook the financial, the economic, and the market fundamentals that underlie many of these mechanical processes. The emphasis to a very large extent has been on "how" and "what" rather than on "why." If any of the techniques and methods currently being taught are to be applied appropriately in the market, there is a real need to understand the basic foundation on which they are built.

In my judgment, much of this criticism is justified. From personal experience in reviewing demonstration appraisal reports for several years, and from frequent discussions with highly qualified appraisers about the propriety of some of these techniques, I must conclude that much of the approach currently employed in income property appraising is highly mechanistic.

Moreover, the analysis frequently tends to become too abstract, and insufficiently oriented to the facts and operations of the market in terms of which the value estimate is being made.

In other words, much of the income capitalization analysis currently employed is not particularly descriptive of either the market or the behavior of informed investors and buyers on that market. In effect, preoccupation with mechanical devices has tended to put appraising, and some appraisers, into what approaches a mental strait jacket.

MARKET VALUE AND INCOME CAPITALIZATION

Yet in noting and sometimes decrying the current defects or shortcomings in our capitalization techniques and our teaching, we do run the risk of throwing the baby out with the bath water. In particular, the argument that market value cannot be estimated through income capitalization analysis seems entirely inappropriate to me.

In this discussion, my basic objective is to delineate and explain the basis for my disagreement with this extreme position. In doing so, I intend to concentrate on words rather than on arithmetic formulae or mechanical formulations. I have a fundamental belief that nothing which can be expressed numerically cannot also be expressed in words. One of the most important functions of an appraiser is to communicate his findings convincingly and well to a client, a reader, or a court. The ability to express his ideas and findings verbally is therefore extremely vital.

One of the pet expressions of my colleagues in the computer field at the University is: "When all else fails, read the instructions." In this presentation, my theme might well be stated as a paraphrase: "When all else fails, return to fundamentals."

What are some of these fundamentals of income capitalization and market value appraisal of income-producing properties that are frequently overlooked in the welter of figures and the detail? Perhaps most fundamental of all is our working definition of market value. The appraiser must live with this, even though it may vary widely from one jurisdiction to another. By and large, there is agreement on the basic components of "Market Value." They lead to the important point that the appraiser is in essence attempting to describe and predict the behavior of informed buyers on the market. In the analysis of income-producing, investment properties, there is a further consideration which I believe is too frequently overlooked in both appraisal literature, and in practice.

That is: just what is meant by the market?

IDENTIFYING "THE MARKET"

One of the basic problems confronting any appraiser with an assignment to estimate the market value of an investment property is the definition and delineation of precisely what market he is talking about. It is impossible simply to talk about "the market," and blithely assume that everyone understands and agrees what that phrase means. Rather, the market must first be defined through the kinds of properties that are truly competitive with the one being appraised.

Second, and to my mind even more important, the market must be defined in terms of *who* constitutes that market. This is necessary because the definition of market value effectively requires appraisers to examine the reactions and the behavior of a typically informed buyer-investor, through whose eyes the appraiser views the valuation problem.

Focusing on "who" in defining the market does *not* mean identifying it from the viewpoint of one specific purchaser or investor. This is what Dr Richard U. Ratcliff and others have characterized as investment analysis, and indeed it is. In market value appraisal, the approach should emphasize the characteristics of the most probable buyer or investor under given market circumstances for the type of property being appraised.

The issue then becomes: What *kind* of investor or what *kind* of purchaser is most likely to be interested in this type of property in this market environment at this time? What *kind* of investor or purchaser will probably actually purchase the property? There is evidence from studies that have come to my attention, as well as a few that have been undertaken in our Center at the University of Connecticut, that this identification is both possible and practicable.

In the process of identifying the typically informed investor and his characteristics, the appraiser is led inevitably into the realm of financial and/or investment analysis. This is because of the objectives, presumed as well as identified, of this informed investor. One of the recognized shortcomings of current appraisal analysis, which is reflected in recent appraisal literature (with the outstanding exception of mortgage–equity analysis) is the assumption that "an investor is an investor is an investor."

It requires little analysis of market structures and market behavior to recognize that this assumption is fundamentally invalid. Appraisers must be highly discriminating and selective in their evaluation of what the market is, who comprises that market, and the financial-investment objectives of the typical purchasers that make up that market.

INVESTOR OBJECTIVES

What are some of the objectives or classes of objectives that must be considered? The first and most fundamental is that, as investors, purchasers of income-producing property are seeking to maximize income. This is hardly a startling pronouncement. However, when market behavior is studied carefully, the interesting finding emerges that what has been called "income" for many years is an accounting device which is rather different from what a purchaser or investor is seeking. In particular, it differs in both content and characteristics from the kind of cash flow (case receipts, cash returns) over time that the investor typically is seeking. As a corollary objective, the investor-purchaser is usually looking to minimize his expenses, and thereby to maximize his net receipts. Some classes of investors are particularly anxious to minimize their income tax liability, among their expenses.

In recent years, there has been a great deal of discussion in appraisal journals and at appraisal meetings over the issue of considering or including income tax liability in income capitalization analysis. By and large, however, the basic text materials available to appraisers and newcomers to the field not only do not discuss income tax liability in any detail, but specifically and particularly ignore the subject. Much of the theory that currently serves as a foundation for the techniques and methods employed in income capitalization was developed during the 1920s and early 1930s. There have been changes in the superstructure, in some of the terminology, and in some of the mechanical manipulations.

Nevertheless, the fundamental precepts of that theory have not really undergone any major change in at least 35 years. That earlier era had its own economic and financial problems, many of which are still with us today. However, arranging a real estate investment and the financial package underlying it so as to minimize income tax liability was *not* one of the preoccupations of investors during that period. While income tax liability has always been something to be avoided if possible, tax considerations were not a controlling motivating force as they have become for many groups of investors today.

At this point, I must emphasize the word "many," because it is just as inappropriate today to utilize an analytical framework which assumes that *all* investors seek as a major objective to take maximum advantage of accelerated depreciation, or maximum advantage of long-term capital gains treatment of income. There is a notable countertrend in the real estate investment field toward investors of considerable magnitude—both individually and as a group—who either are tax exempt or have special tax status. As a result, their income tax liability is not a major motivating consideration in patterning their real estate investment decisions.

It is, therefore, possible to overstate the significance of income tax considerations in real estate investment decisions, just as current orthodoxy in appraisal analysis seriously understates that significance.

The important point is that the analytical framework employed by appraisers should include recognition of the fundamental fact that there is such a thing as a graduated income tax in the United States; there is favorable treatment (from the point of view of the taxpayer) of long-term capital gains; and there is an opportunity to take accelerated depreciation in improvements. Taken together, these considerations definitely influence the character of *who* (or *what,* in the case of corporate or institutional investors) is most likely to be a purchaser of the kind of property being appraised. The identification of this "typical investor" defines *the market* in the appraisal problem at hand.

Therefore, although appraisers must necessarily avoid inclusion of the individual tax liability, tax status, or tax bracket of a specific investor in estimating market value, it is equally necessary for appraisal analysis of income-producing properties to include consideration of the tax status of the most probable *type* of investor in the case in question. This is required to establish a definition of the market. It is essential to describe and predict the behavior that this most probable investor is going to exhibit when he (or it) actually purchases or makes a bid for an investment property.

In addition, the purchaser or investor is seeking to minimize uncertainty about the returns that he can reasonably anticipate receiving from the investment. Further, he wishes to minimize uncertainty about the risks that are involved in making the investment. He tries to account for them somehow through a rate of discount that represents adequate compensation for assuming these risks. There is considerable variation among different groups and types of investors with respect to their concern with tax avoidance, as I have already indicated.

Beyond this, some investors emphasize current income as opposed to long-term capital gains. Some are more interested in current cash flow than in gains at some time in the future. Investors can also be differentiated on the basis of their concern with long-term as opposed to short-term return on their investment. Another point of distinction among groups or types of investors is on the basis of their desire for stability and safety or return and/or principal, on the one hand; and their willingness to assume the risk of loss (of income and/or principal) in exchange for the chance of higher rates of return and higher capital gains, on the other.

SHORTCOMINGS OF PRESENT ANALYTICAL FRAMEWORK

These considerations all enter into the behavior of investors toward investment property. They are reflected in the way investors behave with respect to financial or capital markets. What is needed, therefore, is a system of appraisal analysis that takes these considerations into account.

The difficulty is that the current, orthodox, traditional approaches toward income capitalization tend to characterize the typical investor as: (1) bound to a long-term commitment of funds in the investment; (2) primarily interested in annual income flow; (3) convinced that depreciation in the value of improvements will occur, and therefore anxious to receive capital recapture over the remaining economic life of the improvements; and (4) willing to wait until the end of the remaining economic life of the improvements to receive capital recapture in full. In only one variant of the entire range of alternative techniques and methods currently available to the appraiser, is it even suggested that there might possibly be capital *appreciation*. That, of course, is the mortgage–equity analysis (including Ellwood analysis).

Current income capitalization practice in the appraisal field constantly refers to capital recapture or capital recovery in relation to the reversion that the investor is supposed to anticipate. Built into the structure is the assumption that remaining economic life is a meaningful concept to the investor, and that his anticipation of a reversion involves site only. Yet the experience of at least the last 20 years suggests that capital appreciation may actually occur, even though in terms of purchasing power this may simply offset increased replacement costs. There is also evidence that some types of investors turn over income-producing properties *before* the end of the remaining economic life of the improvements.

One of the great shibboleths of appraisal theory, teaching, and practice is that the appraiser must turn to the market for the data on investor behavior that is purportedly built into the framework of income capitalization analysis. This is constantly repeated in the face of mounting evidence that what the typical purchaser of income-producing property (who is, I repeat, most frequently an investor) does is quite different. Most importantly, the "typical" investor varies from one type of property to another, and from one market environment to another. Perhaps the greatest need within the framework of income capitalization analysis is a set of flexible tools which are adaptable to a variety of situations in which the character and objectives of this "typical" investor may be substantially different.

INVESTMENT ALTERNATIVES

As an investor, the purchaser of income property is very frequently an absentee owner. He is not interested in occupancy or use of the real estate himself. Rather, he seeks a maximum income flow or return from his investment. One important consideration frequently overlooked in current analysis of income capitalization is that the investor in real estate is typically not restricted to committing his funds to real estate in order to earn an attractive or competitive return on his money investment. There are other outlets competing for these investment funds. This point is rarely recognized in appraisal literature, or in the work of appraisers. Nevertheless, it is a fact of the investment market.

It is important for the appraiser to identify and evaluate the alternatives currently available to a potential investor in the type of real estate being appraised. He is interested in a money flow that provides him an appropriate, competitivé rate of return on his investment. The alternatives that confront him include, at the least, taking a lender's position as opposed to an equity position in real estate, and investing in securities.

Without going into any other alternatives, appraisers must recognize that these represent a considerable amount of competition for equity investment in income-producing real estate. The question is not simply, "Am I going to buy this particular apartment building rather than any other apartment building?"; or "Am I going to invest in an apartment building as opposed to an office building?" Certainly since 1966, the attractiveness of alternative financial and investment outlets has been dramatized for investors—particularly those not committed by law or policy to real estate as an outlet for their funds.

These considerations have great impact on the behavior of the appraiser because he must be concerned with and informed about competition from other segments of the money and capital markets. It is hardly startling news that 1968 mortgage interest rates were rather different from those of 5 years ago. This change has itself stemmed to a very large extent from considerably increased competition from alternative uses of long-term funds. Regardless of the source of pressures on the pattern of interest rates, the impact of these pressures on the money market exerts considerable influence on real estate investment decisions and real estate investor behavior.

First, it influences the price of money that investors must pay in order to borrow mortgage funds. Second, it requires re-evaluation of the rate of return necessary to cover the risk of taking an equity position. An equity investor paying 8.25%, 8.50%, or higher for mortgage money will not necessarily consider a before-tax equity return of 11% or even 13% particularly attractive. The effective spread between mortgage interest rates and equity rates must usually be maintained (either in absolute percentage point differentials or as a ratio) for the risks of equity investment to be compensated adequately.

Therefore, changing interest rate patterns influence the equity rate required to attract investors into a particular line of activity. What historically has been regarded as attractive and adequate is no longer so regarded. Even if equity rates necessary to attract investors had not changed, however, changing mortgage interest rates have had a considerable impact in and of themselves on the overall rate required by informed investors. The important point, then, is that appraisers must maintain currency with the facts and realities of the money market (especially the mortage money market) in order to keep abreast of appropriate rates of capitalization to use in converting annual money flows to a present worth estimate.

The appraiser of income-producing or investment property must therefore be familiar with the operation of at least the long-term money market. He must be current with what is happening in that market in terms of the alternatives available and the requirements of individual types of investors. Taken as a group, these investors make up what we choose to call a market.

MONEY AT INTEREST

Another major point for appraisers to recognize is that the mechanical techniques and devices currently employed in income capitalization are not totally inappropriate or wrong. This is true whether we are considering some of the more traditional methods of income capitalization, or whether the discussion centers on mortgage-equity (or Ellwood) analysis. Admittedly, it is easy to become lost in a welter of detail in trying to describe buyer-behavior through mathematical formulae. Moreover, it is frequently injudicious to attempt to explain to a client the derivation of compound interest tables. Nevertheless, in his work with income-producing properties, the appraiser must himself understand the fundamentals of the nature of money at interest.

In the first place, it is extremely important to have a sound working appreciation of the basis of this payment called interest. Why must it be paid? Why and how can it be paid? The answers to these questions are fundamental to the whole idea of investment. They represent together one of the truly basic ingredients in investment analysis. This understanding is also essential to an appreciation of the use of leverage, which underlies the development of both "interest rates" and overall rates for capitalization of income in market value appraising.

This thinking and terminology are much more prevalent at the moment in financial investment analysis than in real estate appraisal literature. However, an interesting trend is developing among many writers in the field of financial investment analysis. They have suddenly discovered that there is such a thing as real estate, and that it offers opportunities for their analytical framework just as much as securities do. It is through this avenue that I personally anticipate the most fruitful application of computer utilization to occur in the appraisal field.

Returning to the basic elements of interest theory, appraisers must become familiar with two concepts (or terms) that are fundamental to an appreciation of the operation of interest rates.

These are Liquidity Preference and Time Preference. While it is possible to utilize complex arithmetic formulae to describe how these two forces operate in the establishment and derivation of interest rates, they can be expressed relatively simply in words.

In essence, Time Preference means that people would rather have money or cash now than later. This is the basis for all capitalization or discounting of future income to present worth. An investor would prefer $1000 cash in his hands right now to an absolute guarantee of that same $1000 1 year from today. The process of applying the concept of time preference to valuation analysis simply involves ascertaining the appropriate *rate* at which the future should be discounted, to compensate for what is given up in order to wait, and for any risks that may be involved. These risks include the risk of non-payment in particular, but they also include such components as loss of purchasing power through inflation and lost opportunities for profit because the funds are not currently available.

Liquidity Preference refers to the fact that, all things being equal, one generally prefers cash to any other asset. Thus liquid assets have preferential status over non-liquid assets. Liquidity is the ability to convert an asset readily into cash without loss in capital value. Generally speaking, the less liquid the asset, the higher the risk of loss through non-liquidity, and therefore the greater the return necessary to compensate the investor for assuming that risk.

These two concepts indicate why interest must be paid: to overcome the time preference and the liquidity preference of lenders and/or investors. Interest *can* be paid, of course, because the use of the funds will—or is expected to—produce a higher rate of return in the investment than the cost to the investor of the money invested.

Another very fundamental concept is compounding. All discounting and capitalization procedures are predicated on the presumption that compound interest is to be earned. When money is left in an investment over a period of time to earn interest, the periodic interest receipts are added to the principal to accumulate and to earn interest themselves in subsequent periods. The result is a cumulative effect (compounding) which represents what lenders and/or investors are seeking in a long-term commitment of investment funds.

It should be noted that in making a long-term investment commitment, the investor is giving up, at least in part, his ability to take advantage of alternative investment outlets that may materialize. Compounding, therefore, is supposed to represent the way an investor thinks and behaves to compensate himself for this loss of freedom. It is the process by which the investor realizes a given principal sum at some future date, based on specified present and/or future payments.

If this idea is now reversed, the notion of discounting emerges. This is the process by which a future sum or a future flow of income is converted into an estimate of present worth. It defines the amount that must be invested today either to produce a given total at a specified future date, if the current investment earns compound interest at a given rate; or the amount that must be invested today in order to realize a specified flow of income over a given period in the future, provided the remaining investment earns compound interest at a stipulated rate. This is useful to the appraiser only to the extent that it is descriptive of the way in which investors, lenders, and savers behave on the money market.

There is, therefore, fundamental financial logic in the formulae, the tables, and the methodology employed by appraisers in the discounting process itself. We apply it by estimating the present worth either of a flow of income over time (the present worth of one per annum) or of a fixed sum to be paid at a future point in time (the present worth of one). However, in current analysis of income and investment real estate, several important analytical ingredients are either largely ignored or glossed over to an excessive extent.

This criticism is directed more at the framework of analysis available for the use of appraisers than at appraisers themselves. My purpose here is to suggest some directions in which appraisers and appraising should be moving. By doing so, I hope to encourage appraisers to think about these issues and react positively to them.

INCOME ESTIMATION AND PROJECTION

Perhaps the most significant single problem relating to income capitalization analysis today lies in the fact that nearly all the attention in both theory and practice is directed toward the "R" in the basic equation:

$$V = \frac{I}{R}$$

Net income, the "I" in the equation, is generally taken as given. It is supposedly derived from evidence and observations in the market, but beyond that there is little real analysis or evaluation of this figure or its components. Variations in rates of capitalization are supposed to account for differences in risk or uncertainty about the income flow, as well as possible (or even probable) variations in that flow.

Our traditional residual techniques in particular rely on a figure that is called "net income." Over the years, modifications such as "net income before recapture," "net income before capital recapture," "net income before capital recovery," and the like have emerged. Unfortunately for appraisers and for their communications with others, this particular "net income" figure bears little resemblance to other net income concepts used in financial or investment analysis.

There have, of course, been some moves toward recognition of the inappropriateness and non-descriptiveness of this concept in appraisal literature. In particular, L. W. Ellwood in much of his writing refers to "annual net cash flow income." Even this is a before-tax figure, however. The important point is that in the current market, and for some years, investors have been paying more and more attention to cash flow and less to accounting income. They are interested in cash returns *after* income taxes. Yet the framework of appraisal analysis involving income capitalization, again with the outstanding exception of mortgage–equity analysis, does not even offer an opportunity to develop cash flow estimates readily. Admittedly, the "net income before recapture" (NIBR) used in the traditional framework of income capitalization is a form of cash flow, but *before* deduction of any debt service or income tax liability. In my personal work, I choose to refer to this as Net Operating Income of the real estate, as opposed to the net income or cash flow of the investment to the owner-investor.

Using NIBR as the figure to be capitalized into a present worth estimate often ignores two important realities of the real estate investment market. First, investors (as well as user-purchasers) do tend to seek maximum advantage from debt financing and the use of leverage. Second, they also do take into consideration their tax liabilities, at least as a group. Their income tax status does influence the character and timing of the income flow they are seeking. This income flow is ultimately a *cash* figure. In order for it to be a meaningful description of what is going on in the real estate investment market, it must account for coverage of debt service during the investment holding period.

IMPORTANCE OF DEBT FINANCING

This is where we encounter serious problems of financial logic in our present framework. Ignoring financing (as obtainable by the most probable type of purchaser for the type of property in question) in the derivation of an income figure to be capitalized results in two fundamental logical inconsistencies. First, it ignores the realities of investor thinking and behavior, and does not provide an appropriate opportunity to develop and examine income estimates in terms of cash flow. Second, financing terms and conditions do influence the composition and structure of rates of capitalization used by appraisers. It appears totally inconsistent to build financing considerations into one part of the equation, and to ignore them totally by convention in another equally important part of the equation.

Development of rates of capitalization either through Band of Investment analysis or through Overall Rate analysis necessarily involves an inclusion of "typical" or most probable financing terms available on the current market to the most probable purchaser. This is tacit recognition of the importance of leverage or trading on equity to investors. Maximum or optimum use of leverage involves a quest for maximization of cash return. One route—although not the only one—for achieving maximum cash returns on an investment is to take optimum advantage of available debt financing. The principle is quite simple. The investor gives up control over some of his income by contracting for the payment of a fixed periodic amount (debt service) in anticipation of being able to earn or to generate a return which is higher, by taking an equity position. He expects, therefore, to be able to put borrowed funds to more productive use, in terms of rate of return, than the rate he must pay as mortgage interest.

Acknowledging the importance of annual debt service (or the Annual Constant, if we express annual debt service as a percentage of mortgage principal) brings to light another illogical position in much of current income capitalization analysis.

Only in mortgage–equity analysis (including Ellwood analysis) is the fact of constant-payment, systematically amortized mortgage loans truly incorporated. The basic form of Band of Investment derivation of "interest rates" presented in nearly all texts and courses treats the interest portion as a constant percentage of the annual net income that must be covered. With periodic amortization of principal, this is simply not the case. While it may be possible to develop estimates of market value (or present worth estimates) through the use of rates of capitalization that essentially ignore the fact of mortgage amortization, it is hardly descriptive of the thinking or behavior of equity investors in the income property field.

Moreover, at the present time only mortgage–equity analysis recognizes that terms of financing represent a package or pattern which together influence the ability of investor-borrowers to take advantage of leverage. Historically, too much emphasis has been placed on the mortgage rate of interest and on the loan-to-value ratio, and too little on the amortization provisions and payout period (term) of the loan. Unless appraisal analysis considers all of these ingredients as one package, it is not describing what goes on in the income-property financing and investment markets.

Taken together, those terms of lending influence annual debt service on a mortage loan. The amount of annual debt service, in turn, directly influences the before-tax cash flow of the investment to the investor. Further, recognition of *timing* is important in considering the influence of mortgage loan terms on cash flow and ultimately on the present worth of an investment. Here again, time preference comes into play. Generally speaking, investors would prefer to have cash income today (provided it is *after* taxes) rather than the promise or expectation of income in the future. This has led to the development of partially amortized loans with "balloon" payments at the expiration of the loan term. Such loans generally result in lower annual debt service requirements and higher before-tax cash flow over the term of the loan. Particularly when this is coupled with investor expectations of capital *appreciation* on resale, the necessity to pay off the remaining amount of the mortgage at the end of the loan term becomes a less significant consideration to the investor.

Only within the framework of the Ellwood analysis is even the *possibility* of this pattern of behavior and expectations covered. The difficulty with our other, more traditional methods and techniques is that recognition of these alternatives is not possible through the development of income flow projections. Rather, it must be compensated for and somehow accounted for in the *rate* of capitalization that is applied to the income flow. This places an inappropriate responsibility on the appraiser, calling for his judgment in making an adjustment in what is essentially the wrong part of the capitalization equation.

Even if the issue of tax liability is ignored for the moment, cash throw-off (NIBR *less* annual debt service) is a more meaningful figure both for clients (investors and lenders alike) to understand, and for appraisers to justify and explain. It is simply more descriptive of what is going on in the income property investment market.

DEVELOPMENT OF CASH THROW-OFF

The analysis of cash throw-off either as a dollar amount or as a rate of return permits rate development in non-dollar terms as well. The mortgage constant and loan-to-value ratio provide the basis for expressing the percentage rate of return on the total investment that is necessary to cover annual debt service. This requires adjustment of the mortgage constant for the loan-to-value ratio. It is precisely what is done in the Ellwood analysis through the "mortgage coefficient," with the additional feature that the impact of debt amortization is also taken into account. With periodic amortization, the proportion of the total investment represented by equity is constantly increasing.

These funds are committed to the investment until they are realized either through subsequent sale or refinancing at a later date. During the holding period, the equity investor is seeking to earn income at the *equity* rate on his entire equity commitment, and not simply on the initial equity payment or down payment. Expressing the idea in these terms brings out, in my judgment, the essential financial logic of the mortgage-equity or Ellwood framework.

It *is* possible, therefore, to start from what is essentially an NIBR estimate and work through to cash throw-off, even when the dollar amount of annual debt service is not and cannot be known. The difference in treating the matter this way is that the rates developed now specifically include recognition of the fact that a definable proportion of NIBR must be allocated to annual debt service before an appropriate cash throw-off estimate to be capitalized into present worth of the equity investment can be obtained.

This approach to income capitalization is surprisingly consistent with some of the traditional or orthodox thinking, to the extent that it also recognizes that there is a "residual" portion of the present worth estimate to be developed independently through appraisal analysis. The essential difference is that the breakdown of the investment into its component parts is along *financial* lines, rather than physical (land residual, building residual) or legal (leased fee, leasehold estate) lines.

This, I submit, is more realistically descriptive of the approach and behavior of investors than the artificial and uncomfortable division of investment real estate into physical components of site and improvement, "for purposes of analysis only." By taking the more descriptive and realistic financial investment approach, the appraiser thereby avoids the illogical strait jacket incorporated in the more traditional residual approaches, which has led appraisers to so much mental discomfort and verbal fencing, on the witness stand in particular.

IMPORTANCE OF MORTGAGE–EQUITY ANALYSIS

This discussion leads, in my judgment, inevitably to the argument that the most appropriate route for appraisal research and appraisal practice to take is to embrace and to advance mortgage–equity analysis when income-producing properties are to be appraised. Aside from its lack of general acceptance, the current formulation of mortgage–equity analysis is essentially in its infancy. The Ellwood approach is extremely useful and highly appropriate under certain specified conditions. However, these particular conditions, while reasonably widespread, are not always met in the market.

Another important limitation of the Ellwood analysis, as it is taught and applied at the present time, is that it is unnecessarily complex. The basic ideas are quite simple and direct, but they are couched in unnecessarily complex mathematical forms. In attempting to apply Ellwood analysis, the appraiser must first understand it fully himself. Then, even more importantly, he must somehow communicate its basic ingredients and applicability to clients and/or the courts.

Despite these limitations, the underlying thinking in Ellwood analysis (and mortgage–equity analysis in general) represents the direction in which appraisers and appraising should be moving. First, it specifically embodies consideration of the investor's objective of maximizing cash income. Moreover, it recognizes both annual income flow and receipts through resale or refinancing as necessarily interrelated components of that cash flow. Secondly, it specifically acknowledges the use of leverage as one means toward maximizing this cash income to the investor, by taking optimum advantage of debt financing. Thirdly, it recognizes that cash income to the investor comes to him in two forms: (1) annual cash flow over a specified period of time; and (2) the reversion or realization of a cash lump sum through either resale or refinancing.

Currently, appraisers frequently overlook the fact that one of the major attractions of mortgage-equity analysis lies in the possibility of reversion through refinancing. This is another feature of the real estate investment market which must be included more specifically in the framework of analysis utilized by appraisers.

Yet another major contribution of this line of thinking is its recognition that the investor will not necessarily maintain a commitment in the property throughout the remaining economic life of the improvements. At the same time, the possibility still exists for treating income flow over this remaining economic life, if this alternative actually represents the thinking and probable behavior pattern of the most probable type of investor-purchaser of the property in question. Economic life of improvements is still important in the analysis, but it does not necessarily represent the most important or relevant period to provide for either recapture of invested funds or the most probable timing of the reversion. An important and necessary element of flexibility and adaptability to different sets of investor behavior is therefore introduced through more realistic financial and investment approaches to income property valuation. This represents one step toward a more general tool for income capitalization and value estimation.

NEEDED ELEMENTS IN INCOME CAPITALIZATION ANALYSIS

If the capitalization of income is to be applied in a way which brings the appraiser and the appraisal framework to an appropriate estimate of market value, appraisers, and the body of appraisal analysis that they do utilize must therefore recognize three fundamental needs. First, there must be re-examination and more conscious awareness of the component elements and conditions of what is termed Market Value. Second, more precise delineation and identification of *the market* is necessary. Third, the framework of analysis must provide appraisers with an adequate and appropriate description of what investors and buyers are doing (and are most likely to continue to do) in the kind of investment environment that has been identified as most representative of the market for the type of property being appraised.

Within the framework of the present discussion, this means that appraisers must be significantly more sensitive to the state and behavior of relevant financial markets. Appraisers must be sensitive to the determinants and components of interest, and of compound interest in particular. They must recognize the basic applicability of compounding and discounting to financial investment analysis. They must have much greater awareness of and sensitivity to the variability of mortgage financing terms, and be current with the patterns of mortgage lending terms available in the pertinent market. They must be attuned to the impact of these terms of financing on the cash flows that are available to investors in income-producing real estate.

Finally, and perhaps most important, appraisers must recognize the impact of terms of financing on the rates of return that are necessary to make equity investments in income-producing real estate attractive, in competition with lending rates and with rates of return available on alternative types of investments that are realistic outlets for these investment funds.

In essence, what is needed is what has been needed all along: A system of analysis which is truly descriptive of the market behavior of investors, and which can be comprehended by both clients and the courts.

In point of fact, at least the basic beginnings of such a system exist right now. Because it is not entirely understood, accepted, or applied at the present time, much of what is done under the label of income capitalization results in an estimate of value whose relationship to the Market Value concept so assiduously sought by appraisers is questionable at best. Appraisers and the appraisal framework should concentrate on basic principles and avoid unnecesary complications in analysis or techniques. If this is done, there will necessarily be more understanding and use of basic financial analysis than has heretofore been applied, or even been capable of application given the analytical framework and the methodology available to appraisers.

If these basic principles, including a necessarily heavy dose of financial analysis, are applied to verified market data (the basic building blocks of appraisal analysis) appraisers of income-producing property will develop more meaningful, reliable, and useful estimates of Market Value. The essence of the problem, then, is that the wrong theoretical framework has been used, and has resulted in less than appropriate methods and techniques. The required theoretical framework exists right now. The challenge confronting appraising and appraisers is to embrace that framework, and to develop techniques for the analysis of market data that are less complex, less mechanistic, and more nearly descriptive of the market behavior of investor-purchasers of income-producing real estate.

14. The First Twenty Years of AREUEA

WILLIAM N. KINNARD, HERMAN G. BERKMAN, HUGH O. NOURSE, AND JOHN C. WEICHER*

Editors' Note. At American Real Estate and Urban Economics Association's (AREUEA) 1985 annual meeting, a special session was held to celebrate the 20th anniversary of AREUEA. The session was proposed by George Gau, the 1985 program chairman, and chaired by Patric H. Hendershott, the 1985 president. George and Pat selected four past presidents to discuss the first four 5-year periods of AREUEA's history. The presentations were so informative that the Board of Directors proposed publication in some form to preserve the historical record of AREUEA. With the financial assistance of the Homer Hoyt Institute and the efforts of Marc A. Weiss, we are pleased to publish a slightly edited version of the four presentations.

An appendix to this chapter lists the officers and members of AREUEA's Board of Directors since 1965 (any corrections should be drawn to the editors' attention). We note that four individuals have served on AREUEA's Board for a decade or longer: William B. Brueggeman, Hugh O. Nourse, Maury Seldin, and Halbert C. Smith. All were president and either editor or secretary-treasurer.

WILLIAM N. KINNARD, JR, 1968 PRESIDENT

I went back through my collection of notes and documents, and for once in my life I was glad that I am a pack rat. I have all manner of old items, many of which I would not bore you with, but some of which I think you will find most interesting.

*The authors are past presidents of the American Real Estate and Urban Economics Association.

Reprinted with permission from the American Real Estate and Urban Economics Association, 1988, *AREUEA Journal*, Vol. 16, No. 2, pp. 189–205.

A little bit of background first: back in the olden days, about the only gathering place for people who taught Real Estate in colleges and universities was an annual meeting and conference sponsored by the Education Committee of what was then the National Association of Real Estate Boards (NAREB). In 1964, on November 7th, at the Los Angeles meeting of the Education Committee, a group of somewhat dissatisfied and concerned academics got together and muttered among themselves about essentially being kept in a kind of academic ghetto, as far as the NAREB was concerned. They were allowed to speak but were not necessarily listened to and certainty were not allowed to participate in NAREB educational programming. Interestingly, however, many of those involved were designated members of some of the professional organizations within NAREB.

A formal organization was proposed and the first meeting of what was still an unnamed group was held at the Conrad Hilton Hotel in Chicago on December 29, 1964, during the Allied Social Science Association's (ASSA) annual meetings. President George Bloom, Vice-President Raymond Emery, and Secretary-Treasurer Halbert C. Smith were the founding officers and leaders on that fateful day in 1964. The directors were Richard U. Ratcliff, Arthur M. Weimer, James E. Chace, David T. Rowlands (my dissertation advisor), Fred E. Case, and Alfred A. Ring. The most critical piece of business handled at that meeting was, "What do we name this rascal anyway?" (Editors' note: Hal Smith was the first recipient of the George Bloom award which has been given annually since 1985 to someone giving extraordinary service to AREUEA. Bill Kinnard and Fred Case were the second and third recipients.)

Considerable controversy was experienced in selecting a name for the organization. Several people felt that the term "Real Estate" did not convey sufficient academic stature. Those present remembered the disdain from the era immediately following the Ford and Carnegie Reports which said that collegiate schools of business have to stop teaching all of these Mickey Mouse subjects like basket weaving, real estate, etc. Professor Bill Tsagris, from Sacramento State, also mentioned real estate's particularly unfavorable image in California and the possibility of the organization being confused with NAREB or state associations affiliated with NAREB. Dean Robert O. Harvey of Connecticut suggested Academy of Applied Urban Economics (AAUE). Others suggested that the term Science or Research be included in the name.

However, Professors Weimer and Edwards, both of Indiana, and Professor Ketchum of Chicago urged that the term Real Estate be included as the one most direct and meaningful label, and as one that would help attract outside funds. Professor Pickett of Kentucky moved that the name "American Real Estate Association" be adopted. After all the earlier fuss and commotion, the motion passed unanimously. Thus, the organization was named. Certain objectives were set out, resulting in a formal written Statement of Objectives in January 1966. The group also decided where to meet the next year, if they were allowed to meet at all.

This was a rump group that just decided to come together and form an organization. They all happened to be attending the ASSA meetings at that time. During 1965, significant tasks were setting dues and creating a membership list. After acquiring a number of members, "AREA" was allowed to meet with ASSA again. The American

Real Estate Association on Tuesday, December 28, 1965 had a full-day program, including a 5–6 p.m. reception and cocktail party for members, sponsored by the New York Real Estate Board. By that time AREA was already into the important things. As Jim Klopfenstein mentioned, starting in 1966 the Society of Real Estate Appraisers began to cosponsor the reception.

During 1965, NAREB got wind of the fact that this organization had organized and chosen the name American Real Estate Association with the initials AREA. At the December 1965 meeting, George Bloom was reelected president, Dave Rowlands was elected vice-president, and Hal Smith was reelected secretary-treasurer. AREA was approved for membership in the Council of Professional Education for Business. Following considerable discussion, it was suggested that AREA affiliate with that organization rather than with the ASSA.

The secretary-treasurer reported, "AREA has been incorporated in Ohio as a not-for-profit corporation. We have a hundred members and a cash balance of $613.21. We can start from that point to measure some of our progress on the fiscal front." Once again, at the December 1965 business meeting one of the critical points discussed was the change of the organization's name. This was prompted by a report by the president that NAREB had attempted to bring pressure for such a change. NAREB felt that the AREA name would be confusing to the public who might think that a rival trade association had been established in competition with NAREB or its constituent associates, such as the Arkansas Real Estate Association, the Alabama Real Estate Association, the Alaska Real Estate Association, and the Arizona Real Estate Association (among which there was apparently no confusion by the public).

The majority of members present agreed that the association should be identified with the field of Urban Economics. Bob Harvey made an impassioned plea on that point in which he alluded to the fact that the real estate research program at California was known as the Center for Real Estate and Urban Economics. The existence of the newly formed Center for Real Estate and Urban Economic Studies at Connecticut was also mentioned. This identification was the major action during the December 1965 meeting, which was actually our (the AREA's) anniversary meeting. In a sense, therefore, we are celebrating the 21st, not 20th, anniversary of the AREUEA.

The purposes of the organization, as stated in the first constitution, were:

- To promote education and encourage research in the field of Real Estate, Urban Land Economics, and allied fields.
- To improve communication and exchange of information in Real Estate and allied fields among college and university faculty members who are teaching and engaging in research in fields that are of interest to the Association.
- To facilitate mutual associations of academic and research persons in the field of Real Estate, Urban Land Economics, and allied fields.

Bylaws were also created by the constitutional committee, which was chaired by Marcus Whitman at the University of Alabama. He, by the way, was not upset that AREA could be confused with the Alabama Real Estate Association. Also, NAREB changed its name to the National Association of Realtors. Confusion was thereby reduced.

You might be interested to know that in 1966, dues for active members were $5.00 ($15.00 in 1986 dollars), for associate members (non-academic) $10.00, and for institutional members, $100.00. AREA actively sought institutional members. In February 1966, Hal Smith received a letter from Don Snyder, staff vice-president in charge of Education for the Society of Real Estate Appraisers, stating, "I am happy to enclose our $100.00 check and application for institutional membership. . . ." This was the beginning of a very long, fruitful, and mutually beneficial relationship. Recognizing our early joint work with the Society of Real Estate Appraisers, our objectives in the early years could be characterized as a quest for Survival, Respectability, Expansion, and Acceptance—SREA. These represent what we (the AREUEA members) were trying to do.

- We wanted to survive.
- We regarded survival as being at least partly a function of expansion.
- We actively sought membership, not only among academics, but among professional practitioners and researchers as well.
- We expanded the notion of researchers rather broadly to mean, in effect, any interested individual in real estate with $10.00.
- We were seeking respectability, both within the academic community and in the outside world. Much of that effort was focused on becoming, if not a part of ASSA, at least a regular participant in the ASSA meetings. After considerable correspondence and bickering back and forth, ASSA finally allowed us to participate in the program, as we do today, but not in the net proceeds and benefits thereof.
- We were looking for acceptance for our academic colleagues within the Real Estate and Urban Economics fields and also beyond.

Starting in 1966, we published Proceedings of the 1965 meeting. The records show that Carl Tschappat of Ohio State, the editor of that first set of Proceedings and of those for several years thereafter, managed to produce them in an increasingly less amateur format, until we reached the point where we wanted a journal. The Proceedings then evolved into the *AREUEA Journal.*

In the early years we tended to focus on real estate and the issues that were "academically respectable." This meant that we focused early on real estate finance (as we still do to this day), plus some emphasis on investments and a considerable amount on valuation or appraisal.

It was not until Herman Berkman became a member of the officer team that a major thrust toward coverage of the area of urban economics occurred. In the first 5 or 6 years, we tended to concentrate on real estate issues. Our programs reflect that tendency. This was done largely to convince others (and possibly even ourselves) that indeed the field of real estate had academic respectability and should have acceptability as well.

As a quick reminder, you should be aware that George Bloom was president for the first 2 years. Dave Rowlands was the second president, but in the third year (1967). I was elected vice-president that year and we immediately instituted the tradition that the vice-president-elect was automatically program chairman. Then I was elected president, and we decided we would have two vice-presidents. We also formally arranged to hold our annual meeting concurrently with ASSA. Fred Case was first vice-president, and Hal Smith, having served 3 years as secretary-treasurer, was elected second vice-president. Maury Seldin of American University became secretary-treasurer.

After my term as president, Fred Case was elected president. Following him, Hal Smith served as our fifth president, during our sixth year. During those 2 years, we consolidated, solidified, gained status within ASSA and reached real acceptance by NAREB/NAR. Under Hal's leadership we also established the midyear meetings (in cooperation with the FHLBB) and appointed a task force to study the feasibility of publishing an association journal. From that base, we began to evolve into the kind of organization we are today.

HERMAN G. BERKMAN, 1971 PRESIDENT

As I recall the beginning of AREUEA, it rests on foundations developed by Richard T. Ely. Ely, professor at Northwestern University, had written a book with George Wehrwein, *Outlines of Land Economics*. In that major work, land as a public trust was first postulated in the 20th century.

I think of AREUEA in terms of my own intellectual history and the people with whom I worked. I think also that my presidency marked the beginnings of introducing "urban economics" into the Association's credo. The most important early role of AREUEA was the attempt to legitimate the profession of real estate, real estate finance, and appraisal practice. In general, the field of real estate has been, and still is, viewed in some university circles as similar to the "art" of selling used cars. AREUEA was intended to replace such slanderous attitudes and to provide a forum for discussions and publication of research.

My work in Urban Economics began with public planning. My tutor was Homer Hoyt, who was working on the economic base of New York. He had written *One Hundred Years of Land Values in Chicago* and had quenched his thirst at the University of Chicago where he had obtained a doctorate. He worked on applying his theories to real estate. On Homer's recommendation, I went to work later with Dick Ratcliff who had just moved from Michigan, where he had worked with Ernest Fisher, to Wisconsin. Dick also was interested in developing and applying principles. The traditions of land economics at Madison were strong, but in the Graduate School of Agriculture, as in so many state universities, not in the School of Commerce. There was no Department of Real Estate. I got my doctorate with Dick Ratcliff, as did Richard Andrews and Scott Keyes, in the Department of Economics, which offered the first major in urban land economics. I took several courses in agricultural economics, however, with Ken Parsons, who had worked with John Black from Harvard and Ted Schultz of the University of Chicago.

My stay in Madison was interrupted by work at the University of Chicago with Frank Knight, Milton Friedman, and Friedrich von Hayek. They taught me the great classical theories of value and especially the ideas of David Ricardo, Thomas Malthus, and later inheritors of classical thought related to price, value, and rent. I also worked with the great geographers Charles Colby, Ed Ullman, and Chauncy Harris and sociologists of the University of Chicago (ecologists working on city structure and growth) such as Louis Wirth, for whom I was a research assistant.

I began writing on "rent" and problems of valuation, or what gives value to property. And I guess that still is the fundamental question. Location theory was developed by David Ricardo, von Thunen, Loesch, and the "Gravity/Central Place" people; contributions followed from regional scientists (geographers "competing" with urban economists). As president, I welcomed all into AREUEA. The whole question of appraisal valuation and creation of value is still most important, however. Ratcliff was concerned with the subjects included in the text, *Urban Land Economics*, which he acknowledges I helped write. These subjects related to market analysis in real estate, population change, family formation, the life cycle of families, fluctuations in construction and in real estate markets, financial instruments and institutions, and the nature of land and building products and processes. Ratcliff's book still is a classic, and perhaps *the* classic, in urban land economics, backstopping Weiner and Hoyt. I return to these histories to show that these subjects are part of the heritage of this Association and the field of real estate.

There are intellectual roots to the practice of real estate; there is theory and a set of principles that are expressed in practice, institutions, and in the real estate product. These principles are nested in economics, finance, geography, and studies of human organizational and administrative behavior. Art Weimer, Homer Hoyt, and Dick Ratcliff were seeking to explain real estate practices in terms of real estate principles. Homer was an early participant in the formation of economic base theory and took up the cause of eliminating substandard, blighted areas and slums. Later on he engaged in the "real estate process" itself. But for a long time, his major concern, as I recall, was to study long-term phenomena such as "long waves" and to develop, along with Art Weimer, sound intellectual principles of real estate development. His contributions to city structure growth were monumental. The Fellows of the Homer Hoyt Institute, the many real estate research bureaus in universities, and the industry itself benefit from Hoyt's application of principles to the practice of real estate.

The actors in the real estate industry are energetic and imaginative at real estate development, packaging, financing, and marketing. Intellectuals interested in this process sought a place to go. Creative real estate obviously had to find a home where teachers could reflect with each other on the meaning of their work and where respectability could be found. This led to our Association. Its intent was to afford some isolation from the day-to-day pressures of the real estate world, to find a home away from the acts of the sometimes unscrupulous actors, and to help further professionalism in the field. In my view, AREUEA was founded deliberately and intentionally to keep out those who only wanted to make big bucks fast or to manipulate the organization for their own ideological or financial gain. AREUEA was intentionally meant to be a place for those interested in thinking about the problems of real estate and development. It would also eventually provide a vehicle for publishing.

HUGH O. NOURSE, 1975 PRESIDENT

The AREUEA is for the first time challenged by an alternative group for representing the main organization of real estate faculty. This year a new organization called the American Real Estate Society (ARES) formed, organized a journal and had its first meeting. The second meeting will be next spring. Are we going to go the way of SREA and AIREA or of the American Finance Association and the Financial Management Association? If we are, I fear for the survival of a group identified with real estate academics because we are too small to support several organizations.

The issue about this representation has been with us for the entire 20 years of our organization. It has been at the center of AREUEA annual organizational controversies. The original name of our organization was AREA, as Bill pointed out. Something I did not know was the fact that the National Association of Realtors had something to do with our name change. I remembered part of the change being caused by wanting to broaden the organization and attract researchers beyond those in the real estate area: urban land economics, planning, and finance. These are associated areas from which researchers interested in talking about the issues of housing, location, real estate finance, and markets would come.

In 1981, Garrigan's survey of (AACSB) accredited business schools found 384 full-time faculty and about 200 part-time faculty. In 1984, a survey of the National Association of Realtors turned up 407 full-time faculty in real estate. These were not necessarily associated with an AACSB school, so there may not have been any growth. But, somewhere between 380–400 people is the base that this organization really has. There were fewer still in 1965, when we first organized. At that time there was a new and growing interest in urban economics and urban planning. I thought the leaders of the new organization had decided to open up membership to anyone interested in real estate, land economics, and associated areas, and so changed to the name American Real Estate and Urban Economics Association with its terrible acronym, AREUEA, that has haunted us ever since.

An agreement was arranged with the Federal Home Loan Bank Board to hold an annual spring meeting in Washington, DC. That meeting was not a regular thing; it was an experiment. The Board was sponsoring us so it specified the theme of the program to be a topic on housing and residential finance that the Federal Home Loan Bank Board wanted discussed. Every year we would ask whether the Board was willing to sponsor us again. I do not know whether it is still an uncertain thing, but in the beginning it was an open question every December whether we would have a spring meeting. That meeting was and is usually attended mostly by government economists and others in the Washington area. (Editors' note: Since 1987, the midyear meeting has been sponsored by a variety of Washington-based trade associations and/or sponsored agencies; the 1988 sponsors were FHLMC, FNMA, MBA, NAHB, NAR, and the US S&L League.)

The idea of broadening the group did work. We thought that we needed a certain size membership in order to reach a scale that would support a good journal. Membership grew from only a few hundred to around seven hundred when I was president in 1975. Somewhere in the late 1970s we broke 1000. Although it was a struggle, sufficient good papers were brought together to publish. At first, as Bill suggested, we only published papers that were from the annual meeting; those were the papers and proceedings for a number of years. Then in 1973 we began the *AREUEA Journal*. At first we only had two issues each year. I remember fighting to keep the number to two in order to improve the quality of papers being published. In 1977 we finally went to four issues a year. I was fighting and resisting this at the time, but we still got four issues out, and we managed it fairly well. By encouraging planners, economists, finance professors, and real estate faculty to think of our journal and by placing them on our editorial board and on the governing board of the Association, the *Journal* prospered. It is a respectable place to submit papers for review by our peers. Thereby, business schools will respect the real estate faculty for their research, promote them, and raise their salaries.

There were several debates that I can remember during my presidency. Someone wrote me a letter and wanted me to have a class at Arizona State draw up a logo for the organization. But when I went to the Board, it did not want to do that. Another organizational problem when Norbert Stefaniak was president and our meetings were in New Orleans was that we were stuck in a motel about 4 miles north of the central meeting place for the ASSA. We were not close enough that we could draw on the economists who would come and might be interested in the topics that we were presenting. After that we always made sure that the secretary went to the ASSA secretaries' meeting. The second key thing was that we always had to have a good local arrangements chairman. We were always trying to get someone who was there and could be at any of the local meetings to insure us a place in-house. When I was second vice-president and arranged the program, it was here in New York. I got Jim Heilbrun to be our local arrangements chairman. He was to go to meetings and make sure that we did not get kicked out of the Hilton or the Sheraton Center.

There have been three complaints about the organization in spite of its progress:

- The organization is closed; it is hard to participate in the organization's functions and operation.
- The *Journal* publishes articles that are too planning and aggregative-market oriented, and not enough management oriented.
- The organization has not responded to professional issues of interest to real estate faculty.

Let me address each of these.

The organization is not closed. We have always requested nominations for the board of directors and officers from members of the Association. Usually, as I remember, there was a scarcity of such submissions. The officers and board would then make recommendations that were submitted to a vote. Voters also had the opportunity for write-in votes. These elections have not been noted for their popularity. If I recall, the total vote at the end of my term, both for and against Robert Moore Fisher, was less than 100 votes. This year, the number of people who voted was more than ever before: 200 participated out of our total membership of over 700 individuals. Association meetings have been completely open with votes on almost all issues. These sessions often have been attended by 30 or 40 people. Participation in presenting papers and submitting papers to the *Journal* has always been open. At first we tried to set up some general themes, and sometimes a paper might have been excluded because it did not seem to fit a theme we were trying to promote. But rejection was never personal, and often there was a problem finding papers for the meeting or for the *Journal*. If more papers or articles are desired on subjects different from those currently being published or being presented at the Association meetings, then write a few on your favorite. My response is, *please participate*. In fact, I resigned my term on the board this year in order to make room for new faces at this election.

As for the *Journal*'s content, it is simply a result of the composition of high-quality submissions to the *Journal*. Researchers who think some areas are underrepresented should strive to ensure that high-quality manuscripts in these areas are submitted.

The complaint that the organization is not responsive to professional issues of interest to real estate faculty is difficult to address in the abstract, so consider two recent specific issues.

- Byrl Boyce and Bill Kinnard tried to create an appraisal standards board much like the standards board used by accountants to settle controversial methodological issues. The thought was that university professors of real estate could join others to set standards.
- Some of us tried to set up a conference to study the role of real estate education in the business school in anticipation of the forthcoming AACSB report on business education.

As an aside, Bill referred to the Carnegie and Ford reports as putting real estate in with basket weaving. It was not quite that bad, but close. What they did say was that real estate should not be a major, but they did not believe that marketing, finance, or anything else should be a major either. What they said was that there was room for one good analytical course in real estate in the business school curriculum.

In any case the AREUEA board was lukewarm to both the appraisal standards board and the conference. Nonetheless, we were given the opportunity to discuss the issues, organized a committee to give reports, and presented them for a vote. Both were defeated. For one reason or another, not everyone agreed to undertake these moves. The non-appraisers felt uncomfortable, perhaps, with the appraisal issue, and some felt that the proposed conference on the role of real estate in the business school would be unpersuasive coming from this special interest group. So, we moved on to other issues, new ones.

Thus, AREUEA has become a loose confederation of scholars and practitioners interested in exchanging views on real estate, urban economics, and related issues through twice-a-year meetings and the *Journal*.

The only group in AREUEA that uses the Association as its main professional identity is the real estate faculty. All of the other groups belong to other identifying organizations and belong to AREUEA to take advantage of the intellectual exchange provided. Let me demonstrate this point from the survey of AREUEA members conducted by Rabianski and Harris and published in the Winter 1979 issue of the *Journal*. In 1978 there were 761 individual and 255 library subscriptions to the *Journal*. Almost 500 individuals responded to their survey; the practitioners were underrepresented by the responses. In that survey there were 200 business faculty, 40% of the total membership, including both real estate or finance faculty. The authors assumed that they were primarily real estate faculty. There were 24 from Economics Departments, representing about 4% of the membership; 37 from Planning Departments, about 7% of the membership; and others were about 1%. The total academic membership was 267 out of the entire 497-person sample, about 53%. There were 57 from government that represented 12% of the 497 sampled, and 173 from industry that represented 35% of the sample. Of the 200 business school faculty only 46 belonged to the American Economics Association, and 58 to the American Finance Association (and many of those were duplicate memberships). Forty belonged to the National Association of Realtors, 38 to the Society of Real Estate Appraisers, and 35 were members of the Urban Land Institute. You could belong to two or three of these organizations, so they were smaller numbers compared to the 200 business school faculty. On the other hand, if you looked at the economists, 20 out of the 24 economists belonged to the American Economics Association. Twenty-four out of the thirty seven planners belonged to the AIP. They were really coming to us for the intellectual exchange. Our industrial members most often belonged to the National Association of Realtors (68 of them), 58 belonged to the Society of Real Estate Appraisers, and 49 to the American Institute of Real Estate Appraisers. If we were to look at the whole sample of 497, the other organizations that members belonged to in order of importance were the American Economics Association, the National Association of Realtors and the Society of Real Estate Appraisers.

The real estate academics are the sustaining core of this organization. If you review the board of editors for the *Journal* and the board of directors of the Association in the mid-1970s, and even today, you will find that real estate faculty are more dominant than ever. Approximately 50% were real estate faculty in 1976, 1977, 1978, and today the percentage is higher. We should be proud of what we have achieved.

To meet the challenge of the American Real Estate Society, we need to maintain the quality of our meetings and our journal. Our experience has been that only a limited number of people are writing and not all of the writing that we do is worth publishing. If we can continue to capture the quality papers, we will prevail. Researchers will want to place their papers in a more prestigious journal and that will work in our favor. The danger is that the scale will be so reduced in both organizations that the necessary support for publishing will be denied to both groups.

There is one particular area in which we could improve as an organization. It is a shame that almost all of the openings for real estate faculty are announced in the job book for the Financial Management Association. We rarely show more than five or six in our own news-letter, while nineteen or more will show up in the FMA announcement.

We have had a student look for a real estate faculty job in March; he decided late to pursue this field. He made a couple of telephone calls and found a job within 30 days. There were still openings as late as March because the market is not as efficient as perhaps it should be. We need to circulate among finance department faculty and deans of business schools the fact of our existence and of our job announcements. It seems to me one suggestion for solidifying the group as a professional organization of real estate faculty would be to do a better job of publicizing our real estate openings, vacancies, and positions sought.

JOHN C. WEICHER, 1982 PRESIDENT

I came to AREUEA relatively late. In 1964, when the other members of this panel were founding AREUEA, I was a callow graduate student running around the Hilton hotel trying to find interviews for my first job. I was in the field of urban economics, which was barely 5 years old. The field was hot because the cities were burning down and universities thought they should have an urban economist to discover what was happening around them. I was doing a dissertation on local government expenditures—police and fire protection, etc.—in relation to urban renewal. I continued to do research on state and local finance until the mid-1970s. Even though I was at Ohio State with a real estate economist on the floor above me and another on the floor below me, I never saw them except in the elevator.

With this as my background, when George Gau asked me to participate in this session as an elder of the Association, my first reaction was, "I ain't that old." I was no more at ease when he told me that Hugh Nourse would also be on the session, even though Hugh is just a few years older than I am and wrote under the same people at the same place. My second reaction was that I could not imagine what I could say about the last 5 years that everyone in this room—everyone active in the Association—does not already know. But on further reflection, I think there may be some aspects of the last 5 years worth discussing.

It occurs to me that the history of AREUEA coincides exactly with the modern era of inflation. The United States began to expand its money supply in 1965 to finance both the Vietnam War and the War on Poverty. My three predecessors on this panel have each been talking about 5-year periods during which the price level rose at an accelerating rate. I get to talk about the last 5 years of deflation.

This has some obvious implications for our field. The range of research topics has changed as the external economy has changed. For example, we see many more papers on the changes in the mortgage market. But there are also some less obvious implications for our professional association. We benefited professionally from inflation because it dramatically increased the value of most of the real assets that we know about. It also dramatically decreased the value of the corresponding financial assets, but we benefited from that because our knowledge was valuable in such an environment. In the last 5 years, we've faced a different market. Indeed, I know several very good housing economists, including Hugh Nourse, who have gone into other fields. Edgar Olsen has broadened his interest from housing policy and programs to growth areas such as health economics and gerontology.

AREUEA has done remarkably well in this market. To show you how well, let me go back just a few years to when it seemed that we might not do so well. In the recession of 1981–82, we lost a lot of members. The scope of the loss didn't become clear until late in 1982 because we didn't ask members to renew until the beginning of the calendar year, and renewals would trickle in all year. But late in the year, we knew we had a membership problem, and it was turning into a financial problem.

We solved these problems. To meet the immediate financial need, we raised our dues. This action was taken amidst concern that we might lose still more members. As a group of individuals and officers concerned with AREUEA, we went a step further. We employed a professional magazine business manager, Susan Laden, who took over our subscription and membership billing, and instituted much more efficient and effective financial management procedures. As important a step as this was in itself, it was still more important because of the coordinated effort and the time it required. As president in 1982, I first investigated the possibility of employing Sue at the end of the year. Dick Marcis, president for 1983, took up right where I left off and established the formal business relationship. Mike Goldberg, the next in line, encourage us both to follow through, and kept himself aware of the situation. We had a continuity of effort and concern. That made it possible to do something new and different to the benefit of the Association.

In addition, other members of AREUEA pitched in. Austin Jaffe was membership chairman; he organized a network of state membership chairmen, revitalizing an old structure that had fallen into disuse. Even if none of them recruited a single member, there were so many state membership chairmen by themselves that they must have alone increased the membership of the Association! As incoming co-editor of the *AREUEA Journal*, Jim Kau interested himself in the business side of the *Journal* and looked for ways to increase our membership. To my knowledge, he was the first editor to do so.

The result of all this was that we increased our membership about 48% while raising our dues 50%. That's a remarkable demand curve. We have held that membership and increased it by about 10% above the 1983 level. We have also generally been able to maintain and slightly increase our net worth from year to year. Realistically, we can now project a further increase in 1986 that will come close to our all time high, if not exceed it.

There is other evidence of our viability. In my term as president and as past president, I have had to chair search committees to fill each of the appointed positions in our Association: journal editor, newsletter editor, and secretary-treasurer. This has been difficult, and at times I have wondered what I ever did to deserve such a job. But the main reason that it's been difficult is that a good number of highly qualified individuals have been willing to volunteer their time and energy to fill these positions. This is a credit to them; it's also an indication of the stature of AREUEA. Serious scholars do not devote scarce resources to trivial organizations. Having so many outstanding candidates has been good for the Association, even if it was tough on me and the other members of the search committees.

There are numerous other measures of progress. In the early 1970s, AREUEA generally organized three or four sessions at these meetings. In 1978, when Bill

Brueggeman was program chairman, he had a dozen sessions. In 1979, I organized 15. I thought that might be an upper bound; two sessions in each time slot. But the next year, Hal Smith had more. And it has continued to grow gradually. This year, George Gau has organized 20. Somewhere there is a limit in terms of the time and effort the program chairman can devote to these sessions, but we have not found it yet. (Editors' note: In 1987 the limit was apparently hit with 25 sessions: the board voted to cap the 1988 sessions at 22.)

Moreover, we have expanded our meetings without reducing the quality of papers presented, at least based on my own nonrandom, nonsystematic sampling over these years. We have maintained our established tradition of sponsoring sessions jointly with AEA and AFA; we have done the AEA sessions for so long that we were grandfathered in when AEA decided to limit joint sponsorship. We have also organized joint sessions with many other associations in recent years.

Our journal is good and is getting better. It has established itself as the premier scholarly journal in real estate. It's way ahead of whatever's in second place. It's so far ahead that I hear occasional suggestions that we establish *another* journal, to serve one or another of the narrower segments of our field, providing an outlet for research of less general interest in real estate. The other available outlets just are not prestigious enough.

There are also some fundamental problems. We are basically an academic association. That means that there is probably an upper limit to our membership (if not to our meetings). About 10 years ago George Gau, then membership chairman, commented that it was difficult to hold nonacademic members, for our journal is scholarly rather than applied. While a number of individuals outside the scholarly community have contributed importantly to AREUEA—for example, Dick Marcis in recent years and Don Snyder a few years ago—George's experience is probably still true. This poses some organizational problems. We are a little small to take full advantage of professional business management; we are a little big for any one individual to handle subscriptions and membership "on the side" while he or she is simultaneously a professor and researcher. Our secretary-treasurers have had a difficult job, one that is underappreciated. I am glad to hear Jeff Fisher get recognition today. Most of the time, our secretary-treasurers only get recognized when something goes wrong. But time and technology are on our side; thanks to personal computers, the business side of AREUEA gets a little easier every year, even as our membership gradually expands.

Our second chronic problem relates to the topic that Hugh Nourse discussed. We are scholars in various disciplines who share a common interest in a particular subject. While we are all interested in real estate, we are not all housed in that academic field. We are an association of scholars in real estate, but also in urban economics and in housing finance; and a few of our members have interests or back-grounds that overlap with other disciplines. This has been a great net benefit to AREUEA and to us as scholars, but it also creates some tensions within the organization because we approach the same subject area from different perspectives. I think all scholars believe, deep down in their hearts, that what they are doing is more important than what their colleagues are doing, both within their own discipline and across related areas. It's easy to believe that your contribution is undervalued as a general proposition; it's easier if the journal editor or the program chairman comes from a different discipline. Over the years, I have heard AREUEA members from all three of our major disciplines complain about this. But we still stick together, and we profit from it.

There is one cost to our breadth. Our name is unwieldy and unpronounceable. There's only one language on earth where words with five vowels and one consonant are common—that's Hawaiian. I have heard five different versions of AREUEA from the members of this panel this afternoon.

Moreover, it presents quite a problem if you try to cite the *Journal* to someone else. I have written about housing policy in our journal and every so often scholars in other fields—political science, sociology, city planning—have called with a question. When I have referred them to a paper in the *AREUEA Journal*, I have been greeted with a dead silence on the other end of the line, followed by a more or less polite version of the question, "What's that?" I would then spell it out and they would say, in a dubious tone of voice, "Maybe we have that in our library system somewhere—in planning, maybe?"

Almost every AREUEA president I have known has wanted to change the name of the *Journal*. Some of us have changed it unilaterally. One of my fondest memories of this organization is a board meeting where Ken Rosen mentioned that he always cited the *AREUEA Journal* as "the Journal of Housing and Real Estate Economics," on his vita, because people would find that more informative. Where upon Larry Smith sitting next to him said, "Oh, is that what that is! I always wondered what that journal was doing on your vita, and why I never heard of it."

I think at this point we are stuck with the name; it's a trademark that is increasingly recognized among our peers, thanks to the work of the scholars who founded the organization and the scholars who have given generously of themselves to build it. I hope that 20 years from now, we can have a similar session, with a further record of accomplishment to look back on.

APPENDIX: AREUEA OFFICERS AND MEMBERS OF BOARD OF DIRECTORS

William R. Beaton, 1973–75
Herman G. Berkman, 1967–74 (1971*)
George F. Bloom, 1965–69, 1980–82 (1965–66*)
Max R. Bloom, 1968–70, 1974
Byrl Boyce, 1974–82 (1973–76***, 1979*)
Jan K. Brueckner, 1988
William B. Brueggeman, 1978–87 (1981*, 1980–82***)
Frederick E. Case, 1965–72 (1969*)
James Chace, 1965
Karel Clettenberg, 1974–75
George H. Lentz, 1988**
Kenneth M. Lusht, 1981–88 (1987*)
Richard G. Marcis, 1979–86 (1983*)
Stephen D. Messner, 1971–77 (1973***, 1974*)
Mike Miles, 1983–85
Norm Miller, 1985–86, 1988
Donald Nielsen, 1980–83
Hugh O. Nourse, 1971–78, 1981–85 (1975*)
Henry O. Pollakowski, 1988
John M. Quigley, 1987–88

APPENDIX (*Continued*)

Peter F. Colwell, 1982–87
James R. Cooper, 1976–77
John B. Corgel, 1987–88
Jerome Dasso, 1969–71, 1980–82
Douglas B. Diamond, 1986–88
Robert Edelstein, 1983–85
Roy Emery, 1965
Jeffrey D. Fisher, 1984–88 (1984–1987**)
Robert M. Fisher, 1973–79 (1976*)
James Follain, 1987–88
Harris C. Friedman, 1971–74**
James P. Gaines, 1981–83**
George W. Gau, 1981–88 (1986*)
James Gillies, 1967–70
Michael A. Goldberg, 1979–87 (1984*)
James A. Graaskamp, 1973–75
William G. Grigsby, 1971–73, 1976–80 (1977*)
Jack Guttentag, 1979–81
Jack Harris, 1984–88
David J. Hartzell, 1988
Robert O. Harvey, 1977–79
Donald Haurin, 1988***
Patrick H. Hendershott, 1982–88 (1985*, 1988***)
Austin J. Jaffe, 1984–86
Donald M. Kaplan, 1978–83 (1980*)
James B. Kau, 1982–87 (1983–87***)
A. Thomas King, 1986–88
William N. Kinnard, Jr, 1966–71, 1980–82 (1968*)
Daniel B. Kohlhepp, 1978–80
Sylvia Lane, 1973–75
Joseph Rabianski, 1978–80**, 1983–85
Ronald L. Racster, 1974–81 (1978*)
Chester Rapkin, 1969–71
Richard U. Ratcliff, 1965–68
Alfred Ring, 1965–69
Kenneth T. Rosen, 1982–84
David T. Rowlands, 1965–70 (1967*)
Maury Seldin, 1968–78 (1968–70**, 1972*)
C.F. Sirmans, 1981–87 (1983–87***)
Halbert C. Smith, 1965–73, 1979–81 (1965–67**, 1970*)
Larry B. Smith, 1980–82
Donald E. Snyder, 1972–77
Norbert J. Stefaniak, 1970–76 (1973*)
George Sternlieb, 1977–79***
Kenneth J. Thygerson, 1977–79
John A. Tuccillo, 1986–88
Kerry D. Vandell, 1983–88
Robert A. Van Order, 1987–88
Kevin E. Villani, 1982–85
Gregory H. Wassall, 1975–80 (1978–80**)
Susan Wachter, 1984–88 (1988*)
John C. Weicher, 1979–85 (1982*)
Arthur M. Weimer, 1967–69
Shirely F. Weiss, 1978–80
Paul F. Wendt, 1971–73, 1976–78
Marcus Whitman, 1967–68
Larry E. Wofford, 1983–85
Anthony Yezer, 1987–88
Robert H. Zerbst, 1985–87

*President
**Secretary-Treasurer
***AREUEA Editor

15. The Business Enterprise Value Component of Operating Properties

JEFFREY D. FISHER AND WILLIAM N. KINNARD, JR

Real property taxes are levied against real estate only, or at least they should be. In virtually all taxing jurisdictions, real property (real estate) and tangible personal property (fixtures, equipment, machinery, furniture, and the like) are separated for valuation purposes. In some areas, tangible personal property of businesses is exempt from property taxation; in others, it is subject to different property tax rates or different valuation procedures, or both.

The appraisal profession itself has also established standards that specify that real estate must be separated from non-real estate interests for valuation purposes.

Standards Rule 1–4, Subsection b, of the 1984 Standards of Professional Practice of the American Institute of Real Estate Appraisers (AIREA) stated that "an appraiser must identify any personal property or other items that are not real property but are included with or considered in connection with the real estate being appraised and contribute to the total value estimate or conclusion." This specification and requirement remains in effect today in the Uniform Standards of Professional Appraisal Practice (USPAP). Standard Rule 1–2, Subsection e, of the USPAP requires a real estate appraiser to observe specific guidelines, including a mandate to "identify and consider any personal property, fixtures, or intangible items that are not real property but are included in the appraisal."

The message is unequivocally clear. The tangible personal property and intangible components must be separated from the real property component of an operating property.

Reprinted/Adapted with permission from Aspen Publishers, 1990, *Journal of Property Management*, Vol. 2, No. 1, pp. 19–27.

In many instances the separation and measurement of the values of individual components of operating properties is admittedly difficult. Nevertheless, that difficulty does not constitute an excuse for ignoring the issue. It must be addressed directly and in a straightforward fashion. The business enterprise valuation approach is one way of doing so.

This chapter explains the method and uses the typical shopping mall as an example of its application.

THE BUSINESS VALUE COMPONENT IN OPERATING PROPERTIES—KEY TERMS AND CONCEPTS

Many types of properties have a business value component that extends beyond the real estate. For example, shopping centers constitute a business partnership involving the mall owner, mall tenants, and the department stores. The department stores may own their buildings and the land under them separately, but, through an operating agreement, they establish a business relationship with the mall owner. The lease agreements between the various tenants in the mall and the mall owner also help reinforce a business relationship. In an operating shopping center, the result is a symbiotic relationship that produces intangible value above and beyond that of the tangible property.[1]

The landlord is a manager whose efforts will ultimately make or break a center and, in essence, determine its value. Items like the tenant mix, association operations, the owner's promotional acumen, effect of covenants, and cross-easements all have an impact on value. One question is whether that value is real estate value or the value of the business enterprise of operating a shopping center.[2]

The Meaning of "Business Value"

The worth of a business enterprise is reflected in the going concern value or business value of the mall. Business value (sometimes called enterprise value or business enterprise value) is an intangible asset. The term refers to the measurable and transferable present worth of the business organization, management, assembled workforce, skills, working capital, and legal rights (trade names, business names, franchises, patents, trademarks, contracts, leases, and operating agreements) that have been assembled to make the business a viable and valuable entity on its competitive market. This business value is transferable independently of the real property (and of tangible personal property).

[1]This point was made in several papers presented at the IAAO Legal Seminar, San Francisco, California, October 13–14, 1988, especially Beebe, *The Assessor and the Shopping Center: Valuation Issues and Problems*, and A. Wood, *Assessment of Department Stores Associated with Regional Malls*. The symbiotic relationship among owner-operator and tenants of a regional shopping center is characterized as the working of "agglomeration economics" that produce the value of "business assets" in a paper presented at the IAAO Conference in Fort Worth, September 24–27, 1989 by McElveen and Diskin, *Valuation of Anchor Department Stores*.

[2]See Lafakis, *Valuation Concepts and Issues and the Taxpayer's Responsibilities Concerning Regional Shopping Centers*, paper presented at the IAAO Legal Seminar, San Francisco, California, October 13, 1988. Similar statements were made by other participants at the IAAO Legal Seminar. See for example, Beebe and Wood, supra note 1.

Business value or enterprise value is also sometimes called going concern value, which AIREA describes as

> the value created by a proven property operation; it is considered a separate entity to be valued with an established business. This value is distinct from the value of the real estate only. Going concern value includes an intangible enhancement of the value of an operating business enterprise which is associated with the process of assembling the land, building, labor, equipment, and marketing operation. This process leads to an economically viable business that is expected to continue.[3]

Similarly, the Society of Real Estate Appraisers (SREA) defines going concern value as "the value existing in a proven property operation considered as an entity with business established, as distinct from the value of real estate only, ready to operate but without a going business." SREA also says that going concern value "includes consideration of the efficiency of plant, the know-how of management, and the sufficiency of capital."[4]

Business Value vs. Goodwill

It is quite important to recognize that going concern value, as the indicator and measure of business value or enterprise value, is *not* synonymous with goodwill. Goodwill is widely defined in case law in every state. It is generally regarded as an economic surplus that stems from being in a monopolistic or advantageous position with little or no competition. Moreover, goodwill is also a specific concept in the context of US income tax laws. The Internal Revenue Code addresses the tax treatment of goodwill but is silent about business value, enterprise value, and going concern value.

USPAP, on the other hand, does address directly the issue of business value and business valuation under Standards 9 and 10. Those Standards also recognize the distinction between income attributable to tangible assets and that associated with enterpreneurial, managerial, and operational expertise.

Examples of Business Value in Operating Properties

The appraisal literature recognizes hotels as having a business or going concern value. Rushmore has explained that

> The business component of a hotel's income stream accounts for the fact that a lodging facility is a laborintensive, retail-type activity that depends upon customer acceptance and highly specialized management skills. In contrast to an apartment or office building where tenants sign leases for one or more years, a hotel experiences a complete turnover of patronage every two to four days.* * * Another facet of business value is the benefits that accrue from an association with a recognized hotel company through either a franchise or management contract affiliation. Chain hotels generally out-perform independents and the added value created by increased profits is exclusively business-related.[5]

[3]American Institute of Real Estate Appraisers, THE APPRAISAL OF REAL ESTATE 22, Ninth edition, 1984.

[4]Society of Real Estate Appraisers, Real Estate Appraisal Terminology 118 (Boyce ed. 1985).

[5]Rushmore and Ruben, The Valuation of Hotel and Motels for Assessment Purposes. The Appraisal Journal, April 1984. See also Rushmore, Hotel Business Value and Working Capital: A Clarification. *The Appraisal Journal*, January 1987.

When hotel properties are sold, the sales price typically includes payment for the land and building (real estate); furniture, fixtures, and equipment; the value of any franchise; the value of licenses and permits (assuming they are transferable); the value of any management or operating contracts; and the value of an established business operation in an established location with an established staff, which has an established reputation.

Similarly, when a shopping mall or major shopping center is sold, the purchaser acquires land and buildings, fixtures (including those that revert to the owner at the end of any leases), an established name and reputation, an established (but continually evolving) mix of tenants and character or theme, operating agreements with anchor tenants or with major stores on their own "pads" within the area of the shopping center site, leases with nonanchor tenants (so-called "B" tenants), and an operating management staff on site and in place.

The similarities of a shopping center to a hotel property are clear and obvious. The need to segregate the value of intangibles from the value of tangible property is identical. The methodology for measuring the value of the intangibles may differ, however, because of the differing arrangements (leases, operating agreements, and profit centers) that are peculiar to successful shopping center operations.

Economic Rent vs. Market Rental

Economists are careful to distinguish between the concepts of "rent" and "rental." Appraisers should be equally careful and precise.

Historically, the concept of *economic rent* has focused on the income and value *surplus* that ownership of land bestowed on all owners of supramarginal *land.*

More recently, a different source of surplus income and value has emerged: the entrepreneur. The entrepreneur is the ultimate risk-taker, who receives the *residual* income and the *residual* gains from development and sale after all the other factors of production have been accommodated through competitive market rates of return. The economist calls the return to the entrepreneur for the organizational, management, and risk-taking functions that an entrepreneur performs *profit.*[6]

Some profit is a competitive return for performing the function of the entrepreneur, whether as developer-creator, operator-manager, or both. Any return to a business enterprise or investment in excess of a competitive rate of return is the entrepreneur's surplus. The residual factor of production is *not* land (however defined) but entrepreneurship. The point is that *rental* includes a return to all factors of production. Factors of production include land, labor, capital, and entrepreneurship.[7]

[6]See, *for example*, Kahn, The Entrepreneur: The Missing Factor, *The Appraisal Journal*, October 1963.

[7]See ECONOMICS (Tenth edition 1976). Indeed, the noted Nobel Laureate Economist Paul A. Samuelson states that the term "rent" is used "to refer to the return to a factor whose supply is completely inelastic" and the word "rental" is used "to refer to money paid for the services over a period of time, *of any factor*" (italics added). Only land that had "*no other uses*" (italics are part of the quote from Samuelson), for example, land that could be used for only one agricultural product, has a completely inelastic supply curve and thus was said to earn a "pure economic rent" according to classical economists. Samuelson also points out that although the "total of land is inelastic in supply for *all* uses, to any *one* small firm or industry it is in completely elastic supply." According to Samuelson, "much of the land we use has been augmented by man: it has been drained, filled, and fertilized by investment effort quite like that which builds machines and plants."

Shopping Center/Shopping Mall Rentals

Value in a shopping center encompasses the trade names of department stores as well as the name of the mall itself. Nonanchor tenants indirectly pay a fee for the value of these trade names through their rentals. These rental payments are more than simply payment for real estate (land and building). Because a shopping center, especially a regional or superregional mall, is really a business that owns the trade name and is a going concern, a significant portion of the rental is payment for association with this business.[8]

Gelbtuch emphasizes that "successful shopping center appraisals depend on understanding the inner workings of the retail industry."[9] The reality of the marketplace is that rentals in shopping centers and shopping malls are established through negotiation between relatively small numbers of shopping center and shopping mall developer operators on the one hand, and relatively small numbers of department store and other store operators, together with relatively small numbers of regional or national chain "B" store tenants, on the other. Rentals that are favorable to the shopping center or shopping mall owner-operator are to a large extent the result of the entrepreneurial and operational management skills of the owner-operator. They properly belong in the category of business value or enterprise value, not real estate value.

The Developer as Customer. "One way of looking at the shopping center developer is as the customer of the suppliers of the various goods and services that the developer needs in order to create a shopping center."[10] This point is illustrated in the Exhibit. Retailers are also an important component that adds business enterprise value to the real estate (land and building materials). The shopping center developer requires all three components to be successful.

The Residual Factor—Entrepreneurship

Land is not the residual factor. "[T]enants typically view their contract rental payment as an operating cost, not as a residual economic surplus due to land owners because of the particular income-producing advantages associated with their properties."[11] In an *economic* (if not an accounting) sense, profit is the return to innovation and entreprenuership. According to Samuelson, "somebody must act as boss to decide how a business shall be run. Somebody must peer into the future to guess the demand for office space or what will be the price of money."[12]

[8]McElveen and Diskin, supra note 1, associate this rental premium or fee with the combined workings of managed or "planned agglomeration by mall developers" who then "orchestrate the development with the operating agreement." In their hotel example, Rushmore and Ruben, supra note 5, attribute 23% of the total property value to business value, another 7% to personal property, and the remaining 70% to real property.

[9]Gelbtuch, Shopping Centers Are a Business Too, *The Appraisal Journal*, January 1989. The article discusses the various factors that influence retail trade and the ways in which the business is changing.

[10]Schooler, As Retailing Becomes Vertically Integrated Will the Independent Retail Developer Carve Out a Niche or Be Carved Out? *Urban Land*, May 1989.

[11]Barlow, *Land Resource Economics* 177, Third Edition, 1977.

[12]Samuelson, supra note 7.

EXHIBIT

THE SHOPPING CENTER DEVELOPER AS CUSTOMER
The Creation of Real Estate and Business Value

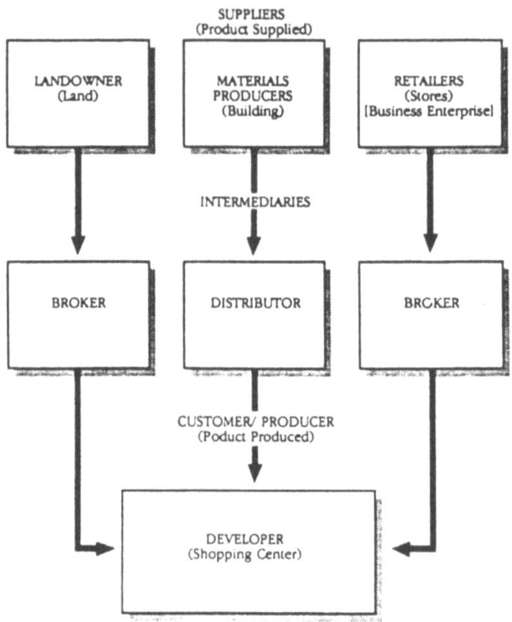

Based on article by Stuart D. Schooler, Urban Land, May 1987
Words in brackets [ ] added by the authors.

Profit is a return for bearing risk or uncertainty. The risk bearers receive what is left over after payment for land, labor, and capital. They may suffer losses. For example, a mall developer tries to maximize the returns to the development business, which are not necessarily in the form of increased capital value only. If space is vacant or expenses exceed expectations, the mall developer or owner suffers, not the landowner. Profits are, in turn, used for revenue enhancing activities like promotion, advertising, and product development so that the firm can maintain an edge. Clearly this is what mall developers and department stores (anchors) must do. To ignore the fact that developers must receive a return on their investment in a business beyond their due as passive investors overstates the return to the capital—that is, to land and improvements.

SOURCES OF BUSINESS VALUE

Various sources of business value show up in the market rental of nonanchor stores and in lease premiums (payments above the market rental because of overages or lease renewals at an above-market rate). Income from these sources represents additional return on the business value of the mall. Examples of these sources include:

- Management expertise;
- A controlled, balanced, and continually evolving tenant mix;
- A well-functioning owner's association;
- Advertising and promotion by the mall owner and department stores (both jointly and independently);
- Image and reputation of the shopping center;
- The trade names associated with the department stores;
- The trade names associated with national chains in the mall;
- Operating agreements with department stores;
- Contractual agreements with mall tenants;
- Income from license agreements (e.g., from pushcarts and concessions);
- Profit from provision of utilities to tenants; and
- Catalog sales by stores located in the mall.

One of the difficulties in identifying the business value or enterprise value component of a shopping center is that the developer and the operator-manager are frequently the same entity.

In the role of the developer, the entrepreneur realizes profit through the enhanced value of the shopping center facility itself, including the value of both real and personal tangible assets. To this extent, and to this extent only, real property value will be increased as the success of development entrepreneurship is capitalized into the asset that can be transferred to a new owner-operator. This value would have to be reflected in, and measured from, the open-market sale of a newly completed but not yet operating shopping mall.

On the other hand, profitable operations on a continuing basis are a direct function of the operational and management skills of the entrepreneur and are (and should be) capitalized into business value or enterprise value. These values tend to be reflected in the open-market sales prices of successful, operating shopping centers.

There is a genuine and significant difference between creating a location and *possibly* generating an attractive net operating income stream in excess of competitive levels and *actually* achieving supra-competitive levels of net income from operations. The former goes with the location; the latter stays with the operator-manager.

MEASURING BUSINESS VALUE

Separating business value from the real estate and other tangible property value is difficult, yet necessary "if a pure real estate tax is to be equitably maintained."[13]

One important point to remember is that real property tax laws focus on estimating market value. Moreover, the market value of the real property is what property tax legislation and case law (as well as thrift institution and bank regulations) require the appraiser to estimate. The standard is not use value or user value that reflect value in use,

[13]Lafakis, supra note 2.

although both AIREA and SREA regard the inclusion of going concern value (which is synonymous with business value and enterprise value) as reflecting value in use.

In particular, if a Marriott or Hyatt hotel commands a higher price because of its name or if a department store is more valuable because it is occupied by Walmart or K-Mart, the value indicated is investment value to the owner and use value or user value to both the tenant and the mall operator. All of these are reflections of value in use.

The Standard or Norm for Measuring Business Value

Because the degree of business enterprise value may vary considerably from property to property, the standard or norm for comparison purposes is critical to identification and measurement of intangible business value. Only after all of the factors of production have received a competitive rate of return on value does entrepreneurship receive any economic profit. Improper or inappropriate comparison standards can produce misleading results if one is attempting to measure the amount of business enterprise value.

In the case of operating shopping malls and shopping centers, it is inappropriate to compare only major, successful developer-operators with one another if the purpose is simply to measure the value of the real estate. Likewise, the standard or norm of comparison for shopping malls and shopping centers owned and operated by the Rouse Company, Melvin Simon & Company, or the Taubman Company, for example, should not be compared with only other malls with the same level of management expertise because all of these properties will have relatively similar business enterprise value components. Instead, the standard or norm should include, at a minimum, all anchor stores and all "B" stores in all operating shopping centers and shopping malls throughout the entire competitive metropolitan area. Indeed, because capital is essentially transportable within the United States (at least), the norm arguably should be the operating results of retail establishments in malls and centers throughout the entire region and possibly even the entire United States.[14]

It is even possible to argue that the use of all shopping malls and shopping centers as the norm is too restrictive. There are freestanding retail facilities as well as those in shopping districts or areas that are *not* subject to any centralized operational management of any kind.[15] Many argue that the operating results of all retail facilities, at least of similar types, should serve as the norm against which profitable operations are measured. This position implies that the difference between mall sales (or rentals) and those of freestanding non-mall facilities may represent a partial measure of business enterprise value.

Thus, one approach to measure business enterprise value would be to compare the rental paid by (or sales potential of) stores in malls to that paid by (or sales potential of) similar competitive freestanding stores. The higher rentals (sales potential) in the mall would be capitalized into an estimate of business enterprise value.

[14]One possibility for establishing the results of the "normal good management" assumed in estimating the market value of real estate, is to use the median figures in the Urban Land Institute's Dollars and Cents of Shopping Centers. These figures have some upward bias because of the self-selecting character of the response sample, but they still represent a reasonable standard of typical market results.

[15]See McElveen and Diskin, supra note 1 at 1–2, on this point.

Whichever supportable, reasonable norm or standard is accepted, the practical result is that intensive nonstratified market research is required into the operations of what is truly the competition for the consumer dollar. Only then can effective measurement of profitability and profit differentials occur.

Business Value Residual Valuation Technique

Business value is the residual (after returns to land and buildings and to tangible personal property). This view is consistent with financial theory, which suggests that corporations are in business to maximize the value of their shareholder's wealth—that is, the corporation seeks to maximize (or optimize) the value of the equity invested in the business owned by the stockholders. The theory applies equally to real estate developers. The developer selects a design, materials, and a site for development that maximizes the return to the business. The business receives the residual income after satisfying a return on investment in the land and building as compensation for management, risk bearing, innovation, entrepreneurship, and so forth. Thus business value can be measured by applying a *business value residual technique*.

It is interesting that the IRS requires use of the residual method in the allocation of purchase price of assets that constitute a trade or business. "Generally, under the residual method, the purchase price is allocated first to the assets to the extent of their fair market value, and any excess is allocated to goodwill and going concern value."[16]

Income Approach vs. Cost Approach

One implication of the business residual theory is that the value obtained by applying an income approach to mall income will exceed that derived by examining only the cost of the land and building *if the mall is the highest and best use of the site*. The mall income (based on the rental rate) includes business income. Capitalizing this amount results in value of the real estate and business.[17] Under the highest and best use of the land, the value of the real estate should not exceed the *cost new* of the real estate (including developer's profit), plus the value of the land under its highest and best use *as if vacant*.

Thus, the difference between the mall value (net of any tangible personal property) from an income approach (assuming business income is not subtracted) and value of the real estate from the cost approach represents the business value.[18] This approach is consistent with the old doctrine that cost sets the upper limit on value.[19]

Capitalizing Supra-Average Net Operating Income

One indicator of business value is profit to operating management (entrepreneurship) in excess of what is typical or normal for the type of space in its truly competitive market. Dollar amounts are inappropriate bases for comparison because different base

[16] CCH-STANDARD FED. TAX RPTS. §4656GB, discussing Reg. §1.1060-1T.

[17] The value of tangible personal property and of other intangibles is included as well.

[18] See Brown, Going-Concern Value in the Congregate Care Industry and R 41c. *The Appraisal Journal*, April 1987, for discussion of using this approach for congregate care facilities.

[19] See Wendt, *Real Estate Appraisal Review and Outlook 190*, 1974.

amounts and different levels of dollar flows are involved. Therefore, profit must be expressed as a rate of return on *something*.

Invested capital is a common and widely accepted base for measuring rates of return. For shopping centers and shopping malls, the only consistent, standard bases for measurement are original cost (including land and all fixtures and tenant improvements paid for either directly or indirectly by the developer-entrepreneur) and reproduction cost new of those same improvements plus land value. Above-average returns, especially if they are achieved regularly, represent strong indicators of return to entrepreneurial skill and ability.

Capitalizing that above-average income return on invested capital to a present worth figure produces a reasonable indicator of business value.

Alternatively, of course, one could go directly to the cost figures, on the presumption that informed, prudent, and rational developers-investors would not undertake that development and investment without a reasonable expectation of competitive rates of return on invested capital. The valuation model(s) can be as involved and as complicated as the analysis problem requires and the analyst deems necessary. The underlying concept, however, remains straightforward: an effective measure of the value of the real estate alone is its cost of production, suitably adjusted for changes in market conditions, locational impacts, and age-related diminution of normally expected total economic life.

Variance between Anchor Store and Mall Rentals—What is the Base Rental?

The issue of what constitutes market rental for either anchor store or shopping mall space requires careful consideration and analysis. Part of the fabric of any successful shopping center or shopping mail operation is a pattern of operating agreements between the mall operator and the anchor stores in the facility (especially, but not only, department stores). It has become common in some quarters to regard the rentals paid by department store tenants as below-market rentals. The argument runs that the department store is subsidized by the mall operator in exchange for signing an operating agreement that serves as a major basis for attracting shoppers to the mall and to the "B" store tenants.

However, there is strong market evidence (which needs to be refined and quantified) that shopping center locations are as attractive and beneficial to anchor store operators as the anchor stores are to the developers, owners, and operators of shopping centers. Moreover, there is a notable recent trend toward mall or center developments that are joint ventures of developer-operators and department store companies. Indeed, some large retailing organizations have become center and mall developers on their own.

All of this evidence suggests strongly that the benefits flow two ways. It also suggests strongly that the real base rental in a successfully operating shopping center or shopping mall is the rental the department store (or other) anchor is paying.

Therefore, the higher rentals that "B" store tenants pay represent a premium for being in the mall created by the developer and operated by the manager-entrepreneur. That differential is yet another indicator of likely enterprise income that creates business value or enterprise value.

As discussed, nonanchor tenants indirectly pay for the business value associated with the mall as part of their rental payment.[20] There may also be some business value in the rental paid by department stores, especially if a store is achieving above-average performance because of successful management and merchandizing and a percentage lease is pushing total rental above the market value. However, if department store rental is assumed to reflect the required return for space (land and building), a significant portion of the excess of mall rentals over department store rental may reflect a return to the business value in the mall.

Of course, some of the difference between the typical per-square-foot mall rental and the department store rental rates can be attributed to the fact that department stores rent significantly more space than most mall tenants do (135,000–150,000 square feet for department stores, compared to 2500–6000 square feet per mall tenant). Also, less risk is associated with typical department store leases than with that of the average mall tenant because of the department store's high credit rating, the guaranteed minimum rental in the lease, and the typical covenant in the lease requiring the department store to operate under that chain's trade name for a specified period of time (e.g., 15 years). Thus, the excess of mall rentals over department store rentals would have to be reduced by the effect of the economies of scale of larger space and the lower risk associated with the lease. The remainder would reflect a return to the business enterprise that could be capitalized into business enterprise value.

Excess Rentals as a Contribution to Business Value

Proper management and marketing of the mall results in a successful tenant mix and tenants with successful businesses. The mall owner participates in the success of the tenants through overages from percentage rents and from higher-than-market rentals on lease renewals. Upon lease renewal, a successful tenant on overages will often pay rent that exceeds what a new tenant would pay for the exact same space (size and location within the mall). Rather than relocate the business, the tenant pays the higher rent, thus allowing the mall owner to "get a piece of the action" that has resulted from successful entrepreneurial efforts developing and managing the mall. Furthermore, the tenant has an operating history in the mall and can better project the level of sales. Thus, the tenant has less risk associated with the rental payment than it would in a new location. Paying a higher renewal rental is justified relative to that which a new tenant could justify given the higher uncertainty about future sales.

Does this mean the "real estate" is worth more? Or, does it mean that the "mall business" is worth more? Economic theory supports the latter position. The residual value of excess rentals (supra-average rental income) from successful tenants should be attributed to business value—not real estate value. The market rental also includes some business value, but clearly excess rental should all be attributed to business value.[21]

[20]See McElveen and Diskin, supra note 1.

[21]Beebe supra note 1, states "we can now move on to the issue of when is income income." He continues "Can these 'percentage rent' arrangements be properly characterized as rental income? How much of such income is attributable to the business skill of either the tenant or the landlord, or both? (Remember, the

To help determine the actual amount, one could compare the lease payments for renewals of existing tenants to the market rentals paid by new tenants for otherwise comparable space. The difference represents at least a partial indication of business value that is extracted from the existing tenant who has a successful business (going concern). Of course, the new tenant's rental also includes a payment for business enterprise value. Thus, comparing the excess rental paid by existing tenants to that paid by new tenants only captures the *marginal* increase in business value attributable to lease renewals. For a successful mall this marginal increase in rental from year to year pulls up the average rental that all tenants (new and existing) must pay to be associated with the business enterprise.

One empirical test conducted by Fisher and Lentz for the Rouse organization (which used the data to develop a pricing model) compared the "excess rent" paid by tenants on a lease renewal to new tenants leasing otherwise comparable space during a 3-year period.[22] Data on all lease renewals over a 3-year time period for three different regional malls under the same operational management provided by the Rouse Company was used to develop a hedonic pricing (regression) model. The model included variables to control for other factors—like location within the mall, size of the space, the year that the lease was signed, and sales per square foot of the tenant—that would affect rent per square foot for a given space in the mall. A dummy variable, which was used to indicate whether the lease signed in a given year was for a new tenant or a lease renewal, was found to be statistically significant, suggesting that existing tenants do, in fact, pay higher rentals than new tenants for otherwise comparable space. This supports the theory that going concern value is being captured in mall rental rates.

CONCLUSIONS AND IMPLICATIONS

There is a substantial business value or enterprise value element in a successfully operating shopping center or shopping mall. That business value is an intangible asset over and above the market value of the real property and of any tangible personal property that is separately, and appropriately, valued.

The net operating income of a successfully operating shopping center or shopping mall includes elements of enterprise income (business value) as well as competitive market returns to invested capital (in both real property and tangible personal property). That enterprise income can be measured in a variety of ways. However,

(continued)
marketing skills of the landlord are a crucial factor in the success of the shopping center.)" Citing a landmark New Jersey Court decision, *Laurence Associates v. Laurence Township*, 5 N.J. Tax Court 481, 497, he further states, "The New Jersey Tax Court concluded that percentage rent should be included in the analysis which establishes economic rent. Moreover, since the percentage is based upon business performance, *its addition to income would tend to value the business rather than the property*" (emphasis added). Beebe states that, "The *Laurence* court concluded that if the owner could prove higher rents resulting from business skill, then the excess income above the economic rent could be discounted as an expense."

[22]Fisher and Lentz, *Measuring Business Value in Shopping Malls*, 1989.

more and better industry-wide and market-wide data are needed in order to do the job on a consistently effective and representative basis.

Because entrepreneurship is the residual factor of production, the return to that residual factor ("profit") is itself a residual after payments to invested capital in all tangible property are received. Capitalizing that residual income to entrepreneurship, and most especially the profit that represents an above-average market rate of return, produces an estimate of business value or enterprise value. This value must be eliminated from the value of the total "property" or facility before real property value can be estimated. An alternative avenue for estimating real property value directly is provided through appropriate use of the cost approach.

16. Graaskamp and Business Enterprise Value: It's in the Profit Centers

A Case Study of an Operating Downtown "Luxury" Hotel

WILLIAM N. KINNARD, JR. AND ELAINE M. WORZALA

Abstract

This chapter explores a major premise of the teachings and practices of James A. Graaskamp. It explores the concept of entrepreneurial profits and their impact on the value of an individual piece of real estate. He believed that the profit centers within a real estate enterprise often created a substantial part of the value of an asset and that the income must be attributed correctly to its different sources within a real estate venture. In this chapter, we use a case study approach and analyze the financial statements of an operating "luxury" hotel over the period 1991–96 to examine this fundamental concept of real estate value and explore the impact of separating the various income streams. Results indicate that, on average, non-realty assets (Furniture, Fixtures and Equipment; Intangible Assets; Profit Centers) account for 32% of the Going Concern Value of this operating downtown "luxury" hotel.

James Graaskamp[1] was himself an entrepreneur—both in business and intellectually. As specified in the economics literature over the past century and a half, he was an innovator, an adventurer (in the 19th century business sense), an undertaker (in the Marshallian sense) and most definitely a risk-taker.

GRAASKAMP AND PROFIT CENTERS

Moreover, Graaskamp espoused the entrepreneurial approach to economic analysis, feasibility analysis (Graaskamp 1991a)[2] and real estate analysis (Graaskamp 1976).[3] In this respect, (as in many others), he followed the Wisconsin tradition established by Ely et al. (1922)[4] and continued by Ratcliff (1949).[5] It is not by chance that he

[1]To his multitude of admiring and devoted students at Wisconsin (and elsewhere as well) he was simply "The Chief." To those of us fortunate enough to know him as a colleague and friend, he was "Jim" so this more informal title will be used throughout this paper.

[2]p. 130.

[3]"Real estate should be taught as a process of dynamic interactions rather than functional and historical facts. The result should be a real estate entrepreneur with the creativity of Leonardo da Vinci, the sensitivity for the natural world of John Muir, and the political humanity with cash management for profit of James Rouse." p. 24. Reprinted in Jarchow 1991, p. 44.

[4]Also see Haney (1936), p. 732.

[5]See especially p. 360.

Reprinted with permission. *Research Issues in Real Estate*, 2000, Vol. 6, pp. 231–258.

continually referred to real estate projects and properties as "enterprises."[6] In particular, he emphasized the opportunities for investors, developers, and especially operators of properties/projects to develop legal, temporal monopolies and exploit the opportunities offered by profit centers.[7]

Graaskamp regarded these profit centers as cashflow generators for the owner-operator who is often, but not always, the owner of the real estate "enterprise."[8] His primary emphasis in both feasibility analysis and its offspring, appraisal, was on the likelihood (and associated risks) of developing profit centers as cashflow generators, in as much profusion as the regulatory environment, market competition, and market demand (often "derivative" and therefore to some degree manipulable) would allow.

Jarchow (1991) summarizes this orientation of Graaskamp's analytical approach and underlying thinking[9] under the heading "Understanding Profit Centers" as follows:

> In the real estate process, unlike many businesses, a variety of profit centers may be part of the bottom line. Graaskamp excelled at understanding the various profit centers that could be tapped. On the basis of this perspective, he could untangle a participant's involvement and understand more fully the economic incentives of an investment. This understanding is critical to managing the gratification of the parties to ensure that a temporal commitment to a project matches that of the client. This profit center orientation is also necessary in arriving at an accurate estimate of value for a given investment.
>
> Profits for an investor in the deal are not necessarily found on the bottom line. An investor has the option of turning certain cost centers, i.e., operating expenses, into profit centers. For example, doing one's own management and maintenance and charging tenants for these services can turn costs into profits.
>
> An investor's real estate investment strategy should be to create a monopoly, if only for a moment in time, through differentiating the product. In establishing this monopoly, the investor does not have to own the land. The key is to control the land. Graaskamp defines effective equity ownership as the degree to which one controls or directs cashflows from a real estate project to compensate for contribution of land, materials, money or expertise.[10]

Entrepreneurial Skill: "Expertise"

Graaskamp pointedly refrains from limiting this factor or its definition to the physical process of real estate project development. Instead, he repeatedly emphasizes the role of the skilled *operator* of the real estate enterprise in identifying and evaluating profit centers.

The critical role of the entrepreneur's "expertise" is developed further in the notes for Jim Graaskamp's 1976 speech to the Chicago Lambda Alpha Chapter, titled "Feasibility Analysis—Father of Appraisal."

[6]See, for example, Jarchow, *op. cit.*, pp. xiii, Graaskamp (1991c), p. 34, Graaskamp (1991a), p. 130.
[7]See Jarchow, *op. cit.*, pp. xix and Graaskamp (1991b), p. 300, for example.
[8]Jarchow, *op. cit.*, p. xix.
[9]*Ibid.*
[10]"Expertise" is Graaskamp's term for "entrepreneurship." See also Kahn (1973).

1. Real Estate is artificially delineated units of space–time.
2. A real estate enterprise is any systematic convergence of space–time to money–time or vice versa by a cash-cycle enterprise that includes consumers of space–time, the public infrastructure on which real estate depends and the private sector of space production management.
3. A cash-cycle enterprise depends on a forecast of assumptions about future receipts and outlays.
4. All forecasts are subject to error and risk. Business and philanthropy are the variance between pro forma expectations and historical accounting realizations.
5. Enterprise management involves assumptions of a scenario and then control of variance and the execution of the program. The primary control of variance is expertise—entrepreneurial skill.
6. Therefore, the real estate business is essentially a service industry providing expertise in the management of cash-cycle enterprises in the conversion of space–time to money–time. In the private sector or the public sector, all profit centers lie in the delivery of services.[11]

To Jim Graaskamp, the value of a real estate "enterprise" is the result of the entrepreneur/skilled manager's "expertise" in the ability to create a legal monopoly. Profit centers can become monopolies; in turn they create additional value in a real estate investment (or "enterprise"). Since some of the value is generated from the monopolistic position of the business enterprise (or its components), value should not be allocated entirely to the real property. The business enterprise value component therefore needs to be identified and examined separately in numerous situations. These include valuation for *ad valorem* property tax purposes, which typically specifies that values are to be on the real property alone; and for federal income tax accounting purposes, since any depreciation deductions will vary according to how the Going Concern Value is allocated between personal, real and intangible property.

Application to Luxury Downtown Hotel Investment

This chapter applies some of the principles of Graaskamp's teaching, research and consulting practices to a luxury downtown hotel investment. In a similar vein to his primary method of teaching, a case study approach that uses an ongoing luxury hotel enterprise has been developed to illustrate the valuation of profit centers in a real estate investment.

An operating hotel is a business enterprise. According to Graaskamp (1991b), "the lodging industry is essentially a service industry using a large piece of real estate hardware."[12] It utilizes several different categories of assets to generate revenues (and, hopefully, business profits) to the owner-operators of the business. The asset groups necessary to produce revenues, operating income and expected profits include: (1) real estate (land, site improvements and buildings), (2) tangible personal property (most especially furniture, fixtures, and equipment (FF & E)), and (3) intangible assets.

[11]Graaskamp (1991a), p. 130.

[12]p. 296 ("Hotel/Motel Lecture: Class Notes").

The real estate may be owned separately from the hotel business by a passive investor. The hotel enterprise owns the attendant tangible personal property and intangible assets (including "expertise" in management and operation of that business).

Graaskamp (1991b) emphasizes that the cash flow format for hotels is somewhat different from other types of income properties because "revenues and costs both reflect a wide number of revenue or profit centers which form divisions of the total enterprise."[13] This point is developed and illustrated in the case study that follows.

The "property" of an operating hotel enterprise is a Going Concern that consists of real estate, tangible personal property, and intangible assets. When the hotel business is operated successfully, it produces competitive market returns on the investments in real estate, tangible personal property and those intangible assets that require commitment of investment funds. Any surplus of the net income to the hotel's Going Concern over and above the required competitive market rates of return on invested funds is *business profit.* That business profit goes to operating entrepreneurship. This is the fourth factor of production in any business enterprise. Graaskamp calls it "expertise" or "entrepreneurial skill." It is the *residual* factor of production for an operating business or project, receiving all income that is otherwise unaccounted for, and therefore "residual" or left over. The key issue is the difficulty in separating real estate from the enterprise as identified by Ratcliff (1949).[14]

Market-Derived Measures and Indicators vs. Property-Specific Data

In general, to estimate the Market Value of the real estate of an operating hotel (a Going Concern), an appraiser should use market-based and market-derived operating standards, sales data, rental data, and cost data. This information should be used to identify what an informed, prudent, and rational purchaser-investor should reasonably anticipate from the acquisition of an operating hotel property.

If the actual experience of the real property being appraised is similar to and reasonably comparable with market standards and averages, then that actual experience may be used to develop a figure that is labeled "Market Value." If there is a perceptible, measurable divergence from the market norms and standards, however, then an explanation for this divergence must be identified. This is particularly necessary when such divergence is based upon the existence and influence of intangible assets (e.g., copyright or trademark names,[15] licenses, reservation systems, supra-normal management and, of course, profit centers). In such circumstances, an appropriate allocation of total Going Concern Value to the source(s) of that value differential must be made.

[13] *Ibid.*, p. 300.

[14] See Ratcliff (1949), pp. 359–360 for a discussion of this key issue of separating real estate from the enterprise. Also, Babcock (1932) examines management and its impact on value (pp. 114–117). In this chapter Babcock specifically singles out hotel properties and indicates that the success of a hotel "may depend in large measure upon the ability of management." Finally, Dowell (1997); Fisher and Kinnard (1990); Graaskamp (1981) are additional sources that address this issue in some detail.

[15] In the hotel industry, a national or regional chain name affiliation, or a well-established, well-recognized individual property name, is commonly referred to as the property's "flag."

If property specific or investor-specific data are relied on solely, without any evidence that such data are representative of market standards and experience, then the result is either User Value or Investment Value. Both are based on Value in Use rather than Value in Exchange. Neither is indicative of Market Value, whether of the real property or of the Going Concern.[16]

Ultimately, the question(s) that must be answered by any appraiser or assessor who is estimating Market Value is:

> What would a typical informed, prudent, rational purchaser-investor pay for, or allocate to, the real estate of the total property or Going Concern being appraised, assuming continuation of the current use of the property, as of the Valuation Date(s)? Moreover, what would the buyer be buying? (Kinnard and Beron 1984)[17]

In the latter case, the most probable buyer needs to be identified (a concept established in the majority of Graaskamp's work) and a reasonable process determined to allocate value between the real property and the other components of the operating business or hotel.[18]

REQUIREMENT TO SEPARATE VALUE OF REAL PROPERTY FROM VALUE OF NON-REALTY

The *Uniform Standards of Professional Appraisal Practice (USPAP)*[19] govern the appraisal practices and procedures of nearly all state-licensed or certified appraisers in the United States, as well as the professional behavior of all designated members of the major appraisal societies in the United States and Canada (including the International Association of Assessing Officers). Standards Rule 1-2(e) of *USPAP*, included in every edition since 1990, requires an appraiser to consider separately items of realty and non-realty, most especially when the objective of the valuation assignment is to estimate the value of real property or realty. Moreover, when non-realty items constitute a measurable portion of the total "property" being valued, then *USPAP* requires that realty/real property, tangible personal property, and intangible assets all be valued separately.

It is quite clear that there are numerous measurable elements of non-realty at a hotel property which are separable from the real property/realty. These include:

1. Furniture, Fixtures and Equipment (tangible personal property).
2. Working capital for the hotel business (intangible asset).

[16]More information is presented in the appraisal textbooks published by the Appraisal Institute (1996) and the International Association of Assessing Officers (1996). Also see Boyce and Kinnard (1984); Eckert (1990); Kinnard (1970); and Weimer, Hoyt, and Bloom (1972) for discussions on market value.

[17]Basically, the appraiser is simulating the buyer and seller thought processes that leads to a sales price as discussed in Grissom and Diaz (1991).

[18]As indicated in Grissom (1985), this is equivalent to determining the value definition. Value definition is a combination of value theory which is concerned with the sources and bases of worth (value) of an asset and value premise which includes an emphasis on the appraisal logic being placed on the characteristics of value as they relate to an identified asset) with the value premise being constrained by policy and decision requirements.

[19]Appraisal Standards Board, 1990–99 editions.

3. Assembled, trained and skilled work force (intangible asset).
4. The name of the hotel and its reputation (intangible asset).
5. Affiliation with a chain or an association of independent hotels which provides a reservation system, a referral system for members or affiliates, group advertizing, both information for travel agents and publications aimed at travel agents, and an identifiable and recognized name/"flag" (intangible asset).
6. Licenses and permits that are specific to the business operator, as opposed to those "going with the property" (intangible asset). [Sometimes incorporated with name and reputation: Items 4 and 5 above.]
7. Profit centers (mostly guest services): Food and beverage, meetings/events, telephone service, valet/laundry service or concession, parking service or concession, health club/fitness center, business center (intangible assets).

TRADITIONAL APPROACH USED TO VALUE HOTELS: INCOME CAPITALIZATION

There is virtual unanimity among leading practitioners, theorists, and other authorities on hotel property valuation, that Income Capitalization is the preferred method for valuing an operating hotel property.[20] Indeed, many argue that Income Capitalization is the *only* appropriate approach to valuation. This is the case whether Direct Capitalization or a Discounted Cash Flow Analysis is utilized.

There is also nearly unanimous agreement among scholars, authors, and practitioners that there is a discernible, separate, and measurable Business Value component in an operating hotel. It is often termed "Business Enterprise Value" to distinguish this intangible asset from the total hotel operation, represented by Going Concern Value. One major element of the Going Concern consists of all the intangible assets. The other two are, of course, real estate/realty and tangible personal property (mostly, FF&E). Business Enterprise Value is only one part of the Intangible Asset Value. It is the residual which may or may not be positive depending on the profitability of the hotel "business" after all other claimants to income have been satisfied. The great majority of texts and articles by acknowledged authorities on the subject of hotel valuation do recognize and account for Business Enterprise Value (BEV) in one form or another.[21]

While there is some controversy or disagreement among authors concerning the extent, composition and amount of BEV in an operating hotel, there is no substantive or fundamental disagreement over the fact that the process of valuing the net operating income stream of an operating hotel produces an estimate of Going Concern Value. From that figure, the non-realty elements must be deducted in order to derive an estimate of the Market Value of the hotel real property/realty. (Rabianski 1996) The obligation to carry out this type of analysis and separation of realty and non-realty values appears as Standards Rule 1-2(e) in *USPAP*, which was cited

[20] See, for example, Rushmore, Ciraldo, and Tarras (1997); Lesser and Rubin (1993); Reynolds (1986); and Rushmore and Rubin (1984).

[21] Important examples are found in Berg (1994); Davidow (1996); Dowell (1997); Egan (1996); Love (1997); Matonis and DeRango (1993); Nelson, Messer, and Allen (1988); and Ramsland (1993).

previously. Those non-realty elements include tangible personal property (most especially FF&E in operating hotels) and intangible assets (most especially, but not only, BEV).[22]

THE CASE STUDY: VALUATION OF A HOTEL PROPERTY

In the Graaskamp tradition, an ongoing real estate enterprise is used to illustrate the incorporation of the various profit centers in a valuation assignment. The subject property is a 566-room, downtown luxury hotel property: the BaySide Towers (BS Towers) in the small-market, relatively isolated Pacific Coast city of BaySide. It is an operating business or "Going Concern," with five restaurants, a health club, a business center, several retail facilities, a ballroom, meeting rooms, and banquet facilities.

The property is owner-operated. BS Towers is also a member of a restricted-entry, international group of affiliated hotels and resorts: The Elite Associates ("TEA"). BS Towers must therefore meet and maintain the high standards of facility quality and service established by this organization. TEA advertises in selected target publications, maintains a centralized reservation and referral system, and regularly inspects member properties to ensure maintenance of standards adopted for all members of the group.

Guidebooks published for travel agents refer to BS Towers as the only "luxury" or a "4-Star" Hotel, in its market. Additionally, the property contains the only AAA 4-Diamond restaurant listed for BaySide. BS Towers is the most established, best-known and most widely cited hotel in the BaySide market. It has a national (indeed, international) reputation for the provision of high-quality service and amenities to its guests. Therefore, it commands premium prices for its rooms and its food services, in comparison with its local competition.

Because BaySide is a relatively small market area, little market sales activity among the seven major downtown hotels has occurred over the past 10 years. There are six competitors with BS Towers, all of which are newer, and five of which are somewhat smaller than BS Towers. They total 2154 rooms, which brings the total downtown market to 2710 full-service hotel rooms (including BS Towers).

Since any sale of an operating hotel includes both tangible personal property (especially FF&E) and intangible assets, the Comparative Sales Approach cannot be used effectively to value BS Towers. Graaskamp (1981) noted this difficulty more than two decades ago.[23] Similarly, the age of the building mitigates against reliable estimation of Market Value of the real property via the Cost Approach because "... after adjustment for wear and functional obsolescence [the cost approach] must fall back on the income approach to explain the economic obsolescence or premium that is due for a particular project."[24]

Therefore, "if the market approach and the cost approach are increasingly unreliable, then the income approach might be necessary, which brings the essay face

[22]How this may be accomplished is addressed in Benson (1999); P. Berg, *op. cit.*; Matonis, *op. cit.*; Nelson, *op. cit.*; Ramsland, *op. cit.*

[23]In particular see pp. 45–52. Reprinted in Jarchow 1991, pp. 138–142.

[24]*Ibid.*, p. 46.

to face with the problem of attributing income to real estate."[25] In what follows, we address the problem of attribution or allocation of the income to the Going Concern of BS Towers. In doing so, we follow the precepts, admonitions and examples provided by Jim Graaskamp to the extent that data availability (or lack thereof) permits.

To value the real property via the Income Capitalization Approach, it is necessary first to estimate the Going Concern Value of the entire hotel business operation. Then the value of the real property/realty must be estimated by subtracting the indicated value of FF&E, as well as the measurable values of the several profit centers and other intangible assets enumerated above.

Operating Revenues and Expenses

The operating revenues and expenses of BS Towers are presented by profit center category for the operating years 1992–96 in Table 16-1. The data were derived directly from the audited "Final Close" Financial Statement Reports for BS Towers. However, two changes on the operating expense side were made: in the Management Fee (for both management of the real estate and management of the hotel/business, separately), and Replacements (in lieu of "Reserve for Replacements").

Management Fee

A deduction for property management is standard procedure for any estimate of Net Operating Income (NOI) in applying the Income Capitalization Approach. This is the case whether the property owner is a passive investor or an active owner-manager.[26] Traditionally, the real estate management fee is expressed as a percentage of Effective Gross Income (Revenue Collections), based on market-derived standards or indicators. As with other components of operating expenses, however, actual expenditures can and should be used whenever they represent or approximate "market" levels. The typical market range for a hotel property is reported to be 1.0–2.0% of Total Revenues.[27] Similarly, the management fee for operating a hotel (independent of real estate/facility management) is typically expressed as a percentage of total operating revenues. The market percentage is usually in the range of 2.5–3.5% of Total Revenues.[28]

For BS Towers, it was not clear whether the line item titled "Management" included both Real Estate Management and Hotel (Business) Management. As a percentage of Total Revenues, however, it appears to include both types of fees. Therefore, we assumed and used 5.0% of total revenues as a charge for *all* "Management" fees: Real Property and the Hotel Business. This is indicated in Table 16-2.

[25] *Ibid.*, p. 46.

[26] See Appraisal Institute (1996) Chapter 21; and IAAO (1996) Chapter 10.

[27] For details, see Egan, *op. cit.*; Matonis and DeRango, *op. cit.*; Nelson et al., *op. cit.*; and Ramsland, *op. cit.*

[28] For further information, consult Johnson (1995) and Rushmore et al., *op. cit.*

Table 16-1 BaySide Towers Profit Center Operating Results 1992–96 ($000)

Profit center	1992	1993	1994	1995	1996
A. FOOD AND BEVERAGE					
Revenues	7,095	7,298	7,789	7,662	7,958
Less: Expenses[a]	6,465	6,768	7,264	7,098	6,878
Net operating income	630	530	522	564	1,080
B. TELEPHONE SERVICE					
Revenues	491	568	647	676	702
Less: Expenses[b]	337	347	430	409	425
Net operating income	154	221	217	267	277
C. ATHLETIC CLUB					
Revenues	751	785	776	923	897
Less: Expenses[c]	524	510	527	567	592
Net operating income	227	275	249	356	305
D. ROOMS DEPARTMENT					
Revenues	14,621	14,864	16,487	17,266	18,767
Less: Expenses[d]	9,353	9,452	9,897	10,691	11,253
Net operating income	5,268	5,412	6,590	6,575	7,514
E. TOTAL BS TOWERS GOING CONCERN					
Revenues[e]	22,958	23,515	25,696	26,527	28,324
Less: Expenses	16,679	17,077	18,118	18,765	19,148
Net operating income	6,279	6,438	7,578	7,762	9,176

Notes:
[a]Includes imputed rental@8% of total food and beverage revenues.
[b]Includes imputed rental/Fee@5% total telephone service revenues.
[c]Includes imputed rental@10% of Total athletic club revenues.
[d]Direct room department expenses; plus marketing and management expenses; plus pro rata allocation of all other overhead expenses.
[e]Sum of A–D.
Source: BS Towers annual "Final Close" financial statement reports.

Table 16-2 Actual vs. "Market-Derived" Management Fees 1992–96 ($000)

	1992	1993	1994	1995	1996
Annual total revenue of BS Towers (in $)	22,958	23,515	25,696	26,527	28,324
Actual fees charged (in $)	327	1,265	1,401	1,432	1,521
Percent of total revenues (%)	1.4	5.4	5.5	5.4	5.4
Market-derived fees					
1.5% Real estate management (in $)	344	353	385	398	425
3.5% Hotel management	804	823	900	928	991
Total management fee (5.0%)	1,148	1,176	1,285	1,326	1,416

Sources: BaySide Towers annual "Final Close" financial statement reports. Calculations computed by the authors.

Replacement Allowances

Elements of hotel structures wear out, break, malfunction or become inadequate by the standards of current users (e.g., guests, convention registrants or event attendees). These may include portions of HVAC systems; wall, ceiling and floor coverings;

plumbing fixtures and systems, electrical fixtures, equipment and systems; telephone wiring and systems; roof covering and structures; elevators. When any event listed above occurs, the worn out, broken, malfunctioning, or inadequate building component has to be replaced. Such expenditures are necessary to keep the building(s) functioning adequately.[29] In the case of the BS Towers facility, the level of performance and appearance must be consistent with that of a first-class, high-quality service operation (Rushmore and Rubin (1984)).

Similarly, FF&E must be replaced regularly, but over a shorter life cycle than that applicable to building and structural components. FF&E includes carpeting, room furnishings, public area furnishings, and equipment, front desk, and office furnishings and equipment, restaurant furnishings and equipment not included as structural components, plus any other items of non-realty fixtures or equipment being used as part of the hotel operations.

Traditional wisdom in the hotel industry has been that 3.0–5.0% of Total Revenues is sufficient to allow for replacement of both short-lived real estate components and FF&E. In 1995, however, the International Society of Hospitality Consultants (ISHC) published the results of a comprehensive survey of Capital Expenditures ("CapEx") by full-service, limited-service, and resort hotels in the United States. It covered the period 1983–93 (International Society of Hospitality Consultants 1995).

ISHC found that full-service hotels typically operate on a 25-year life cycle, at the end of which massive renovation and rehabilitation expenditures are necessary to maintain the facility's (and the operating hotel's) competitive status. During that life cycle, there are "spikes" of major replacement and renovation requirements centered around years 13, 16, 20, 21, and 25; lesser "spikes" occur in years 7–9.

On average, ISHC concluded that, over a 25-year life cycle, for a *new* hotel facility, average expenditures on CapEx at a downtown full-service hotel were 9.4% of Total Revenues per year. Similar but older hotel facilities averaged 9.6% of Total Revenues. The CapEx figures covered both building/structural component replacements and FF&E replacements. ISHC states unequivocally that "the 3 percent reserve is insufficient" after year 5 in the life cycle of a *new* facility. For existing "old" facilities, there are no "early years" of low capital expenditures for replacements.

The CapEx for Replacements found and reported by ISHC are exclusive and separate from "Repairs & Maintenance" (R&M), which in the ISHC study average 4.5% of Total Revenues for Downtown full-service hotels, and 4.4% for hotels built before 1981. Therefore, the market-derived charges for R&M at BS Towers should approximate 4.5% of Total Revenues.

Table 16-3 compares the actual expenditures for replacements at BS Towers with figures equal to 5% and 9% of each year's Total Revenues. Because expenditures for Replacements vary so widely from year to year, the actual reported expenditures were also averaged over the 5 years 1992–96. That average was $1,170,000 per year and is also included in Table 16-3.

[29]See Appraisal Institute, *op. cit.*; IAAO, *op. cit.*

Table 16-3 Annual Expenditures for Replacements

	1992	1993	1994	1995	1996
PANEL A: Actual vs. average, with and without add-on for FF&E ($000)					
Actual expenditures	729	1248	1712	1739	424
5% of total revenues (with FF&E)	1148	1176	1285	1326	1416
9% of total revenues (with FF&E)	2066	2116	2313	2387	2549
5-year average of actual expenditures	1170	1170	1170	1170	1170
PANEL B: Calculation of the recovery of the capital value of FF&E ($000s)					
Declared value	3268	3101	3760	3639	4348
Recovery of the capital value of FF&E	693	658	798	772	992

Note: If allowance for recovery of FF&E is not included in "Actual" or "5%" figures presented, then recovery over 7 years@11% is recommended. This produce a recovery allowance factor of 0.2122 or 21.22% per year. Using the FF&E declared values, this factor produces the capital value recovery in Part B of the table.
Source: BS Towers annual "Final Close" financial statement reports. Calculations by the authors.

While there is market support from the ISHC study to use a figure in excess of 9% of Total Revenues for "replacements," using a higher figure than actual expenditures would lower the indicated Going Concern Value of BS Towers unduly. The actual figures do, however, reflect a degree of below-market expenditures for replacements at BS Towers over the period 1992–96.

Since this analysis and the recommended valuation methodology based on it focuses on the Going Concern Value of BS Towers, it is clear that the reported "actual" replacements expenditures most likely reflect replacement of real property (building and structural) components only. They averaged only 4.8% over the 5 years 1992–96, so it was necessary to develop a procedure to account for recovery of the capital value of FF&E as well. This procedure is explained in detail in a "Note" to Table 16-3, Panel B.

Valuation of Going Concern

When Income Capitalization is used to arrive at the Going Concern Value, each year's Net Operating Income should be capitalized at that year's Effective Capitalization Rate, including the appropriate surcharge for that year's Effective Property Tax Rate.

To identify the base Capitalization Rate (R_o) for valuation of the Going Concern Value of BS Towers, information from three (3) widely available and widely recognized published sources was used: The American Council of Life Insurance (ACLI), the quarterly *Korpacz Real Estate Investor Survey* (Korpacz), and the quarterly *RERC Real Estate Report* published by Real Estate Research Corporation (RERC), as of January 1, 1992 through 1997.[30] Table 16-4 shows those findings.

The Korpacz and RERC figures are all *expected* (ex ante) or *required* ("hurdle") rates, derived from surveys of institutional investors and others looking for "investment

[30]See the References for complete citations of these data sources, as well as the Notes to Table 16-4. For further discussion on these different databases are Grissom and DeLisle (1998). Additionally, Liu, Grissom, and Hartzell (1990) contains a detailed discussion of the ACLI database.

Table 16-4 Estimated Base and Effective Capitalization Rates Applicable to BS Towers Hotel Valuation Dates: January 1, 1993–97

Year (as of January 1)[a]	Base capitalization rate (%)	Adjusted capitalization rate[b] (%)	Effective property tax rate[c] (%)	Effective capitalization rate[d] (%)
1993	12.0	13.5	1.4	14.9
1994	11.6	13.1	1.6	14.7
1995	11.2	12.7	1.8	14.5
1996	10.9	12.4	1.8	14.2
1997	10.7	12.2	1.8	14.0

Notes:
[a]Average of proceding fourth quarter and following first quarter rates.
[b]Base Capitalization rate risk premium (150 basis points)
[c]Assumed for each year; actual figures may vary.
[d]Adjusted capitalization rate plus effective property tax rate.
Source: *Quarterly Investor Surveys* published by Korpacz & Associates, and by Real Estate Research Corporation; plus Capitalization Rates for hotels published ni *Quarterly Investment Bulletin* of the American Council of Life Insurance. See also "Lodging Inustry Investment Criteria" published in *Real Estate Forum*, August 1997; and Bain, R., Hotel Capitalization Rate Study. *Assessment Journal*, 4: 4, July/August 1997.

grade" or "trophy" property. These generally represent the *lowest* rates necessary to attract institutional investment funds (e.g., pension funds, REITs) to hotels.

The ACLI rates, on the other hand, represent a composite of loan commitments by the 20 largest life insurance companies in the United States. Life insurance companies typically lend exclusively on new or proposed construction of major facilities in metropolitan market areas considered to be "growth" areas. Older properties are rarely, if ever, included in the ACLI study reports. As with the Korpacz and RERC survey results, the ACLI reports generally rank hotels as riskier investments than those in other property types.

Similar information from PKF Consulting was presented in the August 1997 issue of *Real Estate Forum* and is included in the data in Table 16-4. Biennial data from 1986 through 1994, with annual data for 1995 and 1996, show figures similar to those in the Korpacz reports, except that overall capitalization rates are slightly *higher*. Indeed, the entire pattern of market attitudes, reactions, and behavior toward hotel property investments that is reflected from these four widely recognized and accepted published data sources is one of above-average perceived investment risk.

In applying the Direct Capitalization method to establish the Going Concern Value of BS Towers, average capitalization rates were used with 150 basis points added to reflect the risk premium for the small size and relative isolation of the BaySide market. This premium was confirmed with hotel analysts and appraisers familiar with that market. Using the net operating income of the hotel operation from Table 16-1 and the effective capitalization rates established in Table 16-4, we derive each year's Going Concern Value for BS Towers as shown in Table 16-5. The figures range from $41,470,000 on January 1, 1993 to $65,543,000 on January 1, 1997.

Table 16-5 Estimated Value of Total Going Concern BS Towers Hotel as of January 1, 1993–97 ($000)

	1993	1994	1995	1996	1997
Net operation income[a] (in $)	6179	6438	7587	7198	9176
Capitalization rate[b]	0.149	0.147	0.145	0.142	0.140
Going concern value (in $)	41470	43796	52262	50690	65543

Notes:
[a]Includes proxy rents from profit centers: see Tables 16-1 and 16-11.
[b]Adjusted capitalization rate *plus* 140 basis points for effective property tax rate in 1993; 160 basis points in 1994; and 180 basis points in all other years. See Table 16-4.
Source: Authors' calculations.

Lump-Sum Deductions of Non-Realty Values from Going Concern Value

As noted previously, the indicated values of FF&E, and of measurable, quantifiable elements of Intangible Asset values (e.g., assembled workforce, working capital and hotel name, reputation and "flag" [or group affiliation]) must be deducted from Going Concern Value as part of the process of deriving an estimate of the Market Value of the real estate/realty of BS Towers. These lump-sum deductions must be derived as much as possible from market evidence.

Furniture, Fixtures, and Equipment (Tangible Personal Property)

In the BS Towers property, there is a substantial amount of FF&E: in the guest rooms; in the five restaurants, banquet/reception/meeting facilities and the pub and other bar areas; in the meeting rooms, the health club and the business center; and in the public areas, the front desk area, and the hotel offices. The values that were accepted by the assessor from the property tax reports of BS Towers ownership-management have been used to construct Table 16-3, Panel B. These figures are deducted from Going Concern Value to remove Tangible Personal Property Value.

Intangible Assets

Measurable elements of Intangible Assets include: (1) working capital, (2) an assembled trained and skilled work force, and (3) the value of the hotel's name, reputation and franchise or "flag" affiliation. The first two elements are calculated as the investments and/or expenditures necessary to achieve and maintain the level that is required for efficient and profitable operation of the hotel business. The third is calculated as the present worth of the supra-market room revenues (REVPAR) generated at BS Towers, which may reflect other elements of non-realty revenues that are not otherwise treated separately.

Working Capital. Working Capital is required for an operating hotel's continued operation/liquidity and success. Although some authorities have argued that Working Capital is derived from operations (Rushmore and Rubin 1984), a new purchaser would have to fund that amount until the hotel's revenues were at a level sufficient to provide that required liquidity and till cash for the new operation. Alternatively, the purchaser would pay the seller for the Working Capital on hand, as part of the purchase price for the

Table 16-6 Comparison of Estimates of Working Capital 1992–96 ($000)

	1992	1993	1994	1995	1996
3.84% of going concern total revenues (14 days) (in $)	882	903	987	1019	1088

Sources: BS towers going concern revenues from Table 16-1. Calculations computed by the authors.

Table16-7 Estimated Value of Assembled, Trained, Skilled Workforce 1992–96 ($000)

	1992	1993	1994	1995	1996
Payroll as percent of going concern revenues[a]	33.8	35.3	34.5	34.5	34.5
Total estimated BS towers annual payroll[b] (in $)	7760	8301	8865	9152	9772
6 weeks' training time (11.5% of payroll) (in $)	892	955	1019	1052	1124

Notes:
[a] *Trends in the Hotel Industry*, 1992–97, PKF consulting.
[b] BS towers going concern revenues are taken from Table 16-1.
Source: Authors' calculations.

hotel's Going Concern. Research suggests that somewhere between 10 and 15 days' revenues are necessary to maintain liquidity and sustain continued operations without undue borrowing. We have selected two weeks (14 days), which averages to roughly 3.84% of total revenues. This is indicated in Table 16-6, which shows the annual amount of Working Capital required for the BS Towers operations.

Assembled trained and skilled workforce. An assembled trained and skilled work force would have to be developed for a purchaser acquiring the real estate only. Therefore, a portion of any purchase price of an operating hotel is the opportunity cost of assembling and training the required work force. On average, a period of approximately six weeks of training (and hiring) are appropriate and reasonable for staff to be assembled and prepared for daily activities at an operating full-service hotel.

According to *Trends in the Hotel Industry*, payroll expenses at the Top 25% Full-Service Hotels, ranged between 33.8% and 35.3% of Total Revenues from 1992 through 1996, averaging 34.5%.[31] Based on these numbers, Table 16-7 contains the calculated payroll figures for BS Towers from 1992 through 1996. According to the CFO at BS Towers, the typical hotel employee can be trained in approximately 6 weeks. Therefore, a reasonable estimate of the value of an assembled, trained, and skilled work force would be 11.5% (6/52) of the annual payroll. The resulting calculations are shown in Table 16-7.

[31] PKF Consulting, 1992–97, Figure Number 10.

Business enterprise value: The value of the name and reputation, plus the value of group affiliation and related business intangible assets, for BS Towers. As previously noted, BS Towers is an operating business enterprise utilizing a combination of assets: (1) real estate (land and buildings/structures), (2) tangible personal property (FF&E), and (3) intangible assets (of which Working Capital and Assembled Workforce have already been quantified). What remains, therefore, is the quantification of the contribution to Going Concern Value from the hotel name, its reputation, and the effects of membership in The Elite Associates (its "flag" or "brand").

Advance reservations and past customer lists are also important Intangible Assets that help assure continued, uninterrupted operation of the hotel business following a change in ownership/management. Several recent studies have demonstrated quite clearly that name recognition, good reputation for high-quality service and "brand" or "flag" affiliation can add up to 20–25% to the Going Concern Value of a successfully operating hotel.[32] One measure of that enhanced BEV is the indicated increase in total annual room revenues per available room (REVPAR) that is identifiably associated with the name, reputation, and "flag" or "brand" affiliation of the hotel being appraised. That premium would include other Intangible Assets as advance reservations and past customer lists.

i. Competitive US and BS hotel markets vs. BS Towers. To establish the "competitive market," room department revenues at BS Towers were compared with the top 25% of full-service hotels in the United States, as reported in *Trends in the Hotel Industry*, published by PKF Consulting, for the Years 1992 through 1997. In addition, a study of larger, competitive hotels in the BS Towers market was commissioned. According to Smith Travel Research, there are six other hostelries that should legitimately be considered "competitive" with BS Towers. Each of the six comparable hotels contains at least 100 rooms, but only one is similar in size (590 rooms) to BS Towers.

The comparative Average Percent Occupancy (APO), Average Daily Rate (ADR) and REVPAR are shown for the sample as a whole and BS Towers in Table 16-8. APO rates for the six "comparative" hotels fluctuated within a relatively narrow range from 1991 through 1995; then it increased 3 percentage points in 1996. At the same time, ADR has increased each year, with a notable increase in 1996.

Operating figures for the "Top 25%" of US full-service hotels, measured by REVPAR, are also shown in Table 16-8. They indicate that APO increased moderately between 1992 and 1994, with a substantial increase in 1995–96. ADR was relatively flat in 1992–93, but increased markedly each year thereafter. This experience may be compared with that of BS Towers, which showed higher ADR, but a lower rate of increase, from 1992 through 1995. In 1996, however, ADR was flat (actually slightly lower) at BS Towers, in comparison with 1995, while it increased 6.6% among the submarket hotels, and a spectacular 13.0% for "Top 25%" full-service hotels in the United States. Nevertheless, ADR at BS Towers was still substantially above the average for the submarket hotels.

[32]See, for example, Berg, *op. cit.*; Dowell, *op. cit.*; Love, *op. cit.*; and Source Strategies (1996).

Table 16-8 Comparisons of Average Revenue per Available Room[a] Top 25% Full-Service Hotels in the United States, Six Local Hotels and BS towers 1992–96

	Average percent occupancy			Average daily rate			Revenue per available room[a]		
Year	Top 25% in US	The BS market	BS towers	Top 25% in US	The BS market	BS towers	Top 25% in US	The BS market	BS towers
1992	0.712	0.687	0.602	\$89.17	\$96.87	\$113.77	\$63.49	\$66.55	\$68.49
1993	0.717	0.667	0.610	91.48	98.99	115.98	65.59	66.02	70.75
1994	0.727	0.718	0.648	105.57	101.34	121.30	76.75	72.76	78.60
1995	0.761	0.715	0.640	119.44	105.58	125.51	90.89	75.49	80.33
1996	0.771	0.745	0.716	135.02	112.58	124.61	104.10	83.87	89.22
Growth rate[b](%)	1.6	1.6	3.5	8.7	3.1	1.8	10.4	4.6	5.4

Notes:
[a]Revenue per available room = average daily rate times average percent occupancy.
[b]Compound interest growth rate.
Source: Smith Travel Research; Authors' calculations.

Average Percent Occupancy also increased at BS Towers, but was at a perceptibly lower level than either the average for the six BaySide hotels in the Smith Travel Research sample, or (especially) the average for the Top 25% of US full-service hotels shown in Table 16-8. That spread with both the "Top 25%" and the "submarket hotels" decreased noticeably from 1992 to 1996.

ii. Average daily rate/average percent occupancy trade-offs. BS Towers exhibits the ADR characteristics of a "luxury" hotel, but because of the high degree of seasonality in its market, a lower APO than the Top 25% of full-service hotels in the United States This dichotomy of operating results suggests a higher level of investment and operator risk for the owner-operator of BS Towers than for typical ownership-management of otherwise similar, comparable or competitive hotels.

As a "luxury" full-service hotel, BS Towers offers a range of amenities and services not typically found in hotels outside the "Top 25%" category. These services and amenities are not directly dependent on, nor produced by, the real property. They stem primarily from the quality of FF&E; from personal services provided by a trained, skilled work force; and from profit centers such as restaurants, bars/pubs, valet/laundry service, and others available at BS Towers. This demonstrates the importance of separating the revenue and loss figures for each of the service areas when completing a valuation analysis. Expenses associated with the TEA affiliation are most properly assigned to the room sales department.

Using the ADR and the APO figures, we were able to derive daily REVPAR during the years 1992 through 1996, for the Top 25% full-service hotels in the United States, the submarket of six BaySide hotels, and BS Towers itself. These calculated figures are shown in the right-hand columns of Table 16-8. REVPAR is calculated simply by multiplying APO by ADR.

Table 16-8 also shows the comparative compound interest growth rates from 1992 through 1996, in APO, ADR, and REVPAR for the Top 25% full-service hotels in the United States, the BaySide submarket, and BS Towers. Both the Top 25% and local submarket hotels and higher growth rates in ADR than did BS Towers, from 1992 through 1996, but BS Tower's APO grew at over twice the rate of the others (3.5% vs. 1.6%) over that period.

BS Towers had the highest REVPAR of the three study groups of hotels until 1994. Then the United States Top 25% group soared ahead. Its growth rate from 1992 through 1996 was 10.4%, nearly twice that of BS Towers (5.4%). BS Towers REVPAR was consistently higher than that for the local submarket over the 5 years studied, and grew at a higher rate (5.4% vs. 4.6%). This is all clearly shown in Table 16-8.

While national or regional averages and trends in APO, ADR, and REVPAR are useful in identifying industry standards and norms, hotel property markets are and remain primarily local in character and operation. This stems from the obvious fact that hotels must necessarily provide their services at a fixed location. Therefore, the most important comparisons of BS Towers' operating results are with hotels operating and competing in BaySide, the *local* market environment. This is particularly true since Bayside is a mid-size but free standing city that is not influenced by a major financial center. Accordingly, the comparative analysis concentrates on the BaySide hotel market.

iii. Revenue per available room comparisons. One important comparison of hotel operations that can be made is the impact of REVPAR differences on operating revenues. Since REVPAR is the product of APO and ADR, it is an important reflection or measure of both management effectiveness and the appeal of a hotel's name, reputation, and "flag" (or group affiliation). These elements of the Going Concern (management quality, name recognition, and reputation) create separately identifiable components of BEV when they are favorable or positive in comparison with the hotel's local competition.

We concluded that the best method to analyze the income attributable to the management effectiveness, name recognition, and reputation of BS Towers is to "normalize" its room revenues by assuming that BS Towers experienced the APO and the ADR typical of the BaySide market. The "market" income that would be generated under these assumptions can then be compared to the "actual" room revenue reported by BS Towers. Table 16-9 reports the room sales revenue differentials achieved during 1992–96. It compares actual annual room sales revenues with what would have been realized if APO and ADR had been the same as the averages for the six competing local hotels.

The annual "premiums" or differentials are generally in the vicinity of $1,000,000 – $1,200,000, except in 1992, when the difference was only slightly over $400,000. These premiums, which are taken from BS Towers operating statements, are directly concerned with actual versus "market" room revenues. They also reflect differences in the lengths of individual years and in room nonavailability not otherwise reported (e.g., closings for repairs and maintenance). They provide important information necessary to calculate the BEV of BS Towers, which is attributable to its peculiar attractions to potential guests seeking high-quality, full-service hotel lodging amenities, and services.

Therefore, to establish the BEV, each year's revenue differential or the "brand name premium" was capitalized at an appropriate business Capitalization Rate (20%). This rate is higher than what is used for the real property as it reflects the greater risk

Table 16-9 Annual Room Sales Differential BS Towers vs. Local Submarket[a] Average based on Average Daily Rate/Occupancy Rate Trade-Off 1992–96

Factor/calculation	1992	1993	1994	1995	1996
BAYSIDE TOWERS[b]					
1. Room revenues ($000)[c]	14,621	14,864	16,488	17,26	18,767
2. Average daily rate ($)	113.77	115.98	121.30	125.51	124.61
3. Room revenue/average daily rate	128,514	128,160	135,927	137,567	150,606
4. Percent occupancy	0.602	0.610	0.648	0.640	0.716
5. Base figure room revenue/average daily rate/ percent occupancy	213,478	210,098	209,765	214,948	210,343
LOCAL SUBMARKET OF HOTELS[c]					
6. Percent occupancy	0.687	0.667	0.718	0.715	0.745
7. Percent occupancy × base figure ("5")	146,659	140,135	150,611	153,688	156,706
8. Average daily rate ($)					
9. Percent occupancy × base × average	96.87	98.99	101.34	105.58	112.58
daily rate (BS Towers revenues [$000] based on submarket percent occupancy and average daily rate)	14,207	13,872	15,263	16,226	17,642
Revenue differential ($000) ("1" minus "9") for BS towers	414	992	1225	1040	1125

Notes:
[a]Operating data from BS Towers.
[b]Averages for local submarket from Smith travel research; Table 16-8.
[c]Table 16-1.
Sources: Smith travel research; Authors' calculations.

Table 16-10 Calculation of Value of Name, Reputation, and Flag[a] BS Towers Hotel as of January 1, 1993–97 ($000)

	1993	1994	1995	1996	1997
Revenue differential[b] (in $)	414	992	1225	1040	1125
Capitalization rate[c] (%)	20.0	20.0	20.0	20.0	20.0
Capitalized value of revenue differential (in $)	2070	4960	6125	5200	5625

Notes:
[a] The Elite associates.
[b] From Table 16-9.
[c] Estimated rate for hotel business assets.
Source: Author's calculations.

associated with volatile intangible attitudes and perceptions of guests and customers of BS Towers. The resulting figures are presented in Table 16-10. They range from a low of $2,070,000 to a high of $6,125,000. Each year's figure represents the amount to be deducted from Going Concern Value to reflect the "brand name premium" in the BaySide hotel market, an intangible asset, unrelated to the real property. It is a reflection of the superior management, superior service, and resulting name recognition and reputation that attract guests to BS Towers rather than to other competing hostelries.

Table 16-11 Proxy Rents at Profit Centers BS Towers Hotel 1992–96 ($000)

	1992	1993	1994	1995	1996
A. FOOD AND BEVERAGE					
Revenues[a]	7,095	7,298	7,786	7,662	7,958
Proxy rent: 8%	567	584	623	613	637
B. TELEPHONE SERVICE					
Revenues[a]	491	568	647	676	702
Proxy rent: 5%	25	28	32	34	35
C. ATHLETIC CLUB					
Revenues[a]	751	785	776	923	897
Proxy rent: 10%	75	79	78	92	90
D. TOTAL PROXY RENTS					
To Hotel, from profit centers[b]	667	691	733	739	762

Notes:
[a]From Table 16-1.
[b]Included in room revenues, Table 16-1.
Source: Authors' calculations.

Table 16-12 Summary Calculations of Values of Profit Centers BS Towers Hotel January 1, 1993–1997 ($000)

	1993	1994	1995	1996	1997
A. FOOD AND BEVERAGE					
Revenues[a]	7095	7298	7786	7662	7958
Less: Expenses[b]	5898	6184	6642	6485	6241
Less: Proxy rent[c]	567	584	623	613	637
NOI	630	530	521	564	1080
Capitalized@20%	3150	2650	2605	2820	5400
B. TELEPHONE SERVICE					
Revenues[a]	491	568	647	676	702
Less: Expenses[b]	312	319	398	375	390
Less: Proxy rent[c]	25	28	32	34	35
NOI	154	221	217	267	277
Capitalized@20%	770	1105	1085	1335	1385
C. ATHLETIC CLUB					
Revenues[a]	751	785	776	923	897
Less: Expenses[b]	449	431	449	475	502
Less: Proxy rent[c]	75	79	78	92	90
NOI	227	275	249	356	305
Capitalized@20%	1135	1375	1245	1780	1525

Notes:
[a]From Table 16-1.
[b]From BS towers annual "final close" financial statement report.
[c]From Table 16-11.
Sources: BS Towers going concern revenues from Table 16-1. Calculations computed by the authors.

Establishing the value of profit centers The specifically identifiable profit centers at BS Towers are: (1) the food and beverage department (including banquets and event catering), (2) the telephone system, and (3) the health club owned and operated by BS Towers. Because the hotel has no garage or surface parking lot of its own, the usual parking service profit center is virtually nonexistent. Similarly, the essentially self-service business center (free use of equipment, which is plentiful, but no staff) and the modest valet/laundry concession have inconsequential impacts on both revenues and expenses for the hotel Going Concern.

Table 16-11 summarizes the operating results of the food and beverage department, the telephone service, and the athletic/health club, for the years 1992–96. Revenues have been both substantial and increasing. In order to reflect the opportunity cost of space occupied by these service activities, an allocation of proxy rent has been added to the reported operating expenses in each year: 8% of gross revenues for food and beverages; 5% of gross revenues for the telephone service; and 10% of gross revenues for the athletic/health club (which is entirely in the basement).

The value of the three profit centers can then be calculated by capitalizing the NOI attributable to them at 20%. Again, we are using a "pure" business capitalization rate, reflecting the additional risks of a business enterprise. There is no surcharge for an effective property tax rate, since profit center income (an intangible) is not subject to property taxation. The value estimates for the three individual profit centers are summarized in Table 16-12, which also presents their combined estimated value as of January 1, 1993 through 1997.

SUMMARY AND CONCLUDING OBSERVATIONS

Following the precepts and guidance of Jim Graaskamp, as provided in his writings, we conclude that a full service hotel is an operating business that utilizes real property (land and buildings), tangible personal property, and intangible assets to generate operating revenues and operating profits. When Income Capitalization is utilized to estimate the value of the real property of an operating hotel, it is necessary to value BS Towers Going Concern first, relying on actual operating revenues and expenses as much as possible. Management Fees and Replacement Allowances may need to be adjusted to conform to market standards and indicators. The result of deducting total Operating Expenses from total Operating Revenues is Net Income from hotel operations, which is capitalized to determine the Going Concern Value.

Then the value of the tangible personal property (FF&E) and of the intangible assets (especially BEV, as represented by the value of the hotel name and TEA; but also working capital and assembled/trained workforce) must be deducted from Going Concern. Additionally, the NOI of identifiable profit centers (adjusted to reflect proxy rent for the space they occupy) must be capitalized at an appropriate Business Capitalization Rate (20% in this example) to derive the value attributable to this part of the investment. The profit center values are also deducted from Going Concern Value and the remainder is the Market Value of the real property of the hotel.

In the case of BS Towers, this procedure was followed, as described in this chapter. The results of our analyses and calculations are summarized for the valuation dates

Table 16-13 Summary Calculations to Derive Value of Real Property BS Towers Hotel as of January 1, 1993–97 ($000)

	1993	1994	1995	1996	1997
Total value of BS Tower going concern	41,470	43,796	52,262	50,690	65,543
Less: FF&E	3,268	3,101	3,760	3,639	4,348
RE + Intangibles	38,202	40,695	48,502	47,051	61,195
Less: Assembled work force	892	955	1,019	1,052	1,124
Working capital	882	903	987	1,019	1,088
Value of name, reputation, TEA	2,070	4,960	6,125	5,200	5,625
Profit centers					
Food & beverage	3,150	2,650	2,605	2,820	5,400
Telephone	770	1,105	1,085	1,335	1,385
Athletic club	1,135	1,375	1,245	1,780	1,525
Total deduction for profit centers	5,055	5,130	4,935	5,935	8,310
Total deductions: FF&E intangibles, name and profit centers	12,167	15,049	16,826	16,845	20,495
Indicated value of real property	29,303	28,747	35,436	33,845	45,048
Real property value as a percent of going concern value	71	66	68	67	69

Source: Authors' calculations.

of January 1, 1993–97 in Table 16-13. These figures show that the indicated Market Value of the real property of BS Towers ranged between 66% of Going Concern Value to 71% and the mean was 68%. Thus, on average, non-realty assets (FF&E, Intangible Assets, Profit Centers) account for 32% of the Going Concern Value of BS Towers.

Graaskamp notes that "since Ricardo, a major premise and concern of urban land economists has been the proper attribution of net income [or] economic surplus to the instruments of production" (Graaskamp 1981). He defines the allocation of productivity for the purchase of the Going Concern of a business (e.g., an operating hotel) as "land, structure, personalty, and intangible assets and goodwill *plus* artifactual profit centers for management."[33] [Emphasis added.]

Applied to BS Towers, this means deducting the calculated value of FF&E, Intangible Assets, and Profit Centers from Going Concern Value. Graaskamp characterizes the hotel business as "a synergy of marketing, management and technical expertise which involves a specialized piece of real estate equipment [sic]. In valuing the real estate component of such a business, it is necessary to carefully allocate income [and value] among management, marketing and promotion skills, and real estate attributes" (Graaskamp 1980).[34] This is what has been done to value the real property of BS Towers and it works.

[33]p. 42. Reprinted in Jarchow (1991), p. 134.

[34]This is the position paper that Graaskamp as an expert witness for a tax appeal on a shopping center case. It has been published in a CD ROM, *The Graaskamp Collection* that has been put together by the Wisconsin Real Estate Alumni Association. This collection is a compilation of many of Graaskamp's business and personal files. The position paper can be found in Section IX: Projects and Correspondence with Industry. It is in Part C number 3 and the quote is on p. 3.

REFERENCES

American Council of Life Insurance, *Investment Bulletin: Commercial Mortgage Commitments*, Washington DC, First Quarter 1991 through Fourth Quarter 1996.

Appraisal Institute, *The Appraisal of Real Estate*, Eleventh Edition. Chicago, IL. 1996.

Appraisal Standards Board, *Uniform Standards of Professional Appraisal Practice*. Washington, DC: The Appraisal Foundation, 1990–99 Editions.

Babcock, F.M., *The Valuation of Real Estate*. McGraw-Hill Book Company, New York, NY. 1932.

Bain, R., Hotel Capitalization Rate Study. *Assessment Journal*, 1997, 4(4).

Benson, M.E., Real Estate and Business Value: A New Perspective. *Appraisal Journal*, 1999 (forthcoming).

Berg, P., Evaluating the Value of a Brand. *Lodging Hospitality*, 1994, 50(5): 13.

Boyce, B.N. and Kinnard, W.N. Jr, *Appraising Real Property*. Ballinger, Cambridge, MA. 1984.

Davidow, W., Why Profits Don't Matter: Until We Measure Intangible Assets Like Goodwill and Management Savvy, Bottom Lines Won't Mean Much. *Forbes*, 1996, 157(7): 24.

Dowell, B.T., Hotel Investment Analysis: In Search of Business Value. *Assesment Journal*, Fall 1997, 4(2): 46–53.

Eckert, J.K. (ed.), *Property Appraisal and Assessment Administration*. International Association of Assessing Officers, Chicago, IL. 1990.

Egan, P.J., Mixed Business and Real Estate Components in Hotel Valuation. *The Appraisal Journal*, 1996, 64(3): 246–51.

Ely, R.T., Shine, M.L. Arner, G.B.L. Rostovtzeff, M.I. and Whitbeck, R.H., *Urban Land Economics*. Ann Arbor, MI. Edwards Brothers, 1922.

Fisher, J.D. and Kinnard, W. N., Jr, The Business Enterprise Value Component of Operating Priorities. *Journal of Property Tax Management*, 1990, 2(1): 19–27.

Graaskamp, J.A., Feasibility Analysis—The Father of Appraisal, in *Graaskamp on Real Estate*, S.P. Jarchow (ed.). ULI—the Urban Land Institute, Washington, DC. 1991a, pp. 130–133.

——, Redefining the Role of University Education in Real Estate and Urban Land Economics. *The Real Estate Appraiser*, March/April 1976. Reprinted in *Graaskamp on Real Estate*, S.P. Jarchow, (ed.). Urban Land Institute, Washington, DC. 1991.

——, Guidelines for Attributing Project Income to Real Estate Components, *Concepts and Prospects for Policy Making in the 1980s*, A book of proceedings from the Richard B. Andrews Symposium on Institutional Land Economics, May 21, 1981, 42–59. Reprinted in *Graaskamp on Real Estate*, S.P. Jarchow (ed.). ULI—the Urban Land Institute, Washington, DC. 1991.

——, Hotel/Motel Lecture, in *Graaskamp on Real Estate*, S.P. Jarchow (ed.). ULI—the Urban Land Institute, Washington, DC. 1991b, pp. 296–300.

——, Wisconsin's Real Estate Program. Urban *Land*, 1978. Reprinted in *Graaskamp on Real Estate*, S.P. Jarchow (ed.). ULI—the Urban Land Institute, Washington, DC. 1991c, pp. 32–35.

——, Quaker Bridge Mall—Real Estate Tax Assessment Constraints. *Position Paper for Testimony in Property Tax Appeal*, ca 1980, *James A. Graaskamp Collection of Teaching Materials*, CD ROM of Graaskamp's papers published by the Wisconsin Real Estate Alumni Association, Section IX, c. 3, 1999.

Grissom, T.V., Value Definition: Its Place in the Appraisal Process. *The Appraisal Journal*, 1985, 53(2): 217–225.

Grissom, T.V. and DeLisle, J. R., Alternative Total Return Series for Direct Real Estate Investment. *Journal of Real Estate Portfolio Management*, 1998, 4(1): 17–33.

Haney, L.H., *History of Economic Thought*, Third Edition. Macmillan, New York, NY. 1936.

International Association of Assessing Officers, *Property Assessment Administration*, Second Edition. International Association of Assessing Officers, Chicago, IL. 1996.

International Society of Hospitality Consultants, *CapEx: A Study of Capital Expenditures in the US Hotel Industry*. ISHC, Memphis, TN. 1995.

Jarchow, S.P. (ed.), *Graaskamp on Real Estate*. ULI-the Urban Land Institute. Washington, DC. 1991.

Johnson, K., Management Companies vs. Owners: The Terms, They Area A-Changin'. *PKF Consulting—Hospitality Asset Watch*. San Francisco, CA. 1995.

Kahn, S. A., The Entrepreneur Revisited. *The Appraisal Journal*, 1973, 41(1): 113–118.

Kinnard, W.N., Jr, *Income Property Valuation*. D. C. Heath Company, Lexington, MA. 1970.

Kinnard, W.N., Jr and Beron, G. L., What Value? Of What? To Whom? *Paper presented at the Fourth Annual Seminar, International Association of Assessing Officers*. New Orleans, LA, March 1984.

Korpacz, *Korpacz Real Estate Investor Survey*, First Quarter 1991 through Fourth Quarter 1996.

Lesser, D.H. and Rubin, K.E., Understanding the Unique Aspects of Hotel Property Tax Valuation. *The Appraisal Journal*, 1993, 61(1): 9–27.

Liu, C.H., Grissom, T.V., and Hartzell, D.J., The Impact of Market Imperfections on Real Estate Returns and Optimal Investor Portfolios. *Journal of the American Real Estate and Urban Economics Association*, 1990, 18(4): 453–78.

Love, A.S., Allocation of Realty and Non-Realty Income and *Value in an Operating* "Brand Name" Hotel Property. *Paper presented at the IPT Symposium. Austin, T*, November 1997.

Matonis, S.J. and DeRango, D.R., The Determination of Hotel Value Components for Ad Valorem Tax Assessment. *The Appraisal Journal*, 1993, 61(3): 342–347.

Nelson, R.D., Messner, J.L., and Allen, L.G., Hotel Enterprise Valuation. *The Appraisal Journal*, 1988, 56(2): 163–171.

PKF Consulting, *Trends in the Hotel Industry: USA Edition*. PKF Consulting, San Francisco, CA. 1992–1997.

Rabianski, J.S., Going Concern Value, Market Value, and Intangible Value. *The Appraisal Journal*, 1996, 64(2): 183–194.

Ramsland, M.O., Jr., *Hotel Ad Valorem Tax Issues: The Separate Components of Value*. Duluth, Minnesota. October 13, 1993.

Ratcliff, R.U., *Urban Land Economics*. McGraw-Hill, New York, NY. 1949.

Real Estate Research Corporation, Quarterly Investment Survey, *RERC Real Estate Report*. Chicago, IL, First Quarter 1991 through Fourth Quarter 1996.

Reynolds, A., Attributing Hotel Income to Real Estate and to Personalty. *The Appraisal Journal*, 1986, 54(4): 615–617.

Rubin, K.E., Hotel Real Estate Tax Valuation: Current Issues. *The Real Estate Finance Journal*, Fall 1998, 14(2): 32–40.

Rushmore, S., Ciraldo, D.M., and Tarras, J., *Hotel Investment Handbook*. Warren, Gorham & Lamont, Boston, MA. 1997.

Rushmore, S. and Rubin, K.E., The Valuation of Hotels and Motels for Assessment Purposes, *The Appraisal Journal*, April 1984, 52(2): 270–288.

Source Strategies, Inc, *Business Value of the "Marriott Hotel" Name*. San Antonio, T. October 1, 1996.

Weimer, A., Hoyt H., and Bloom, G., Recent Trends in Real Estate Investment Valuation, Included as part of Chapter 12 in *Real Estate*, Sixth edition. Ronald Press Company. 1972, pp. 353–361.

Wisconsin Real Estate Alumni Association, *James A. Graaskamp Collection of Teaching Materials*. CD ROM of Graaskamp's papers, 1999.

17. Client Pressure in the Commercial Appraisal Industry: How Prevalent is it?

WILLIAM N. KINNARD JR, MARGARITA M. LENK, AND ELAINE M. WORZALA

INTRODUCTION

In the last few years, media stories, anecdotal comments, and litigation have fueled the perception that commercial appraisers have lost some of their independence. The related experiences of Prudential and Aetna, for example, illustrate the costs and perpetuate the perceptions associated with "captured" or "controlled" appraisers (Williams 1993, 1994a–c; Eichenwald 1994a,b). Evidence of this behavior has the potential to affect more than just the directly involved parties; ultimately, trust in the related capital markets and its individual investors may be reduced.

Graaskamp (1988) argued for federal regulation in the appraisal industry to eliminate controllable appraisers. One could argue that the Financial Institutions Reform, Recovery and Enforcement Act (FIRREA) and the resulting Uniform Standards of Professional Appraisal Practice (USPAP), as well as related ethical discussions in the industry, have been the direct result of failure within the financial marketplace. Fraser and Worzala (1994) also detail Graaskamp's views and argue the need for further appraisal reform. Fiedler (1996) refers to controllable appraisers as those from which clients order "appraisals of convenience."

Vinocur (1994, p. 50) states that institutional investors and consultants may "fear that the appraisal process is subject to manipulation by the real estate advisers who manage the properties and select the appraisers." Such a viewpoint may help explain why

The authors would like to acknowledge the support received from the Appraisal Institute for this project.

Reprinted with permission from *Journal of Property Valuation & Investment*, Vol. 15 No. 3, 1997, pp. 233–244.

Prudential recently publicized the creation of a valuation policy committee responsible for rotating appraisers and determining appraisal methodology (Connolly 1993, 1994) and why many courts have recently expanded appraiser liability to include the more liberal "foreseeable user" definition (Waller and Waller 1990; Maroney and Vickory 1991; Wheeler 1991).

These corporate, institutional and governmental reactions highlight questions as to how, why, and when client pressures compromise appraisers' independence. Therefore, the purpose of this study is to provide evidence as to whether commercial appraisers react to client pressure. An established behavioral methodology from the public auditing literature was utilized. The next section of this chapter discusses the existing related literature and states the specific research hypotheses. The following section discusses the behavioral research methodology. Finally, the results and conclusions are presented.

LITERATURE REVIEW

Client pressure may be a result of either the components of the contractual relationship between the commercial appraiser and the client of the market conditions in which this contract takes place. Currently, many asset managers (and loan officers) are compensated on the basis of the valuation of the real estate under management (or the portfolio of loans), making their livelihood a function of the independent appraisers' professional opinions. Consequently, these parties have an incentive to pressure the appraiser to maximize the property valuation. The competitiveness of the current appraisal market and the fear of losing large, institutional contracts may also motivate commercial appraisers to be influenced by their clients' needs.

Evidence and modeling of client pressure within the commercial appraisal industry is growing. Fletcher and Diskin (1994) discuss two agency relationship problems involving institutional asset managers. First, Commercial Real Estate Fiduciary asset managers receive a fee that is typically calculated as a percentage of the appraised value of the assets under management. Second, appraisers are financially dependent on the continuance of the appraisal contract with these managers. Horne and Rosenblatt (1996) compared appraised values with transaction prices and reported evidence of "tacit collusion" between appraisers and loan originators.

Rushmore (1993) discusses the need for ethics in the appraisal of hotels. He reports numerous experiences of both subtle indirect and hostile direct client pressure. While in most cases the threat involves loss of fees and future business, he also mentions threats of bodily harm. In addition, Rushmore also describes how appraisers can change data or assumptions to provide the client with a desired valuation. Rutledge (1994) includes client pressure in his list of ethical "conflicts of interest" found within the real estate industry. Most recently, Smolen and Hambleton (1997) report that almost 80% of their 292 respondents agreed with the statement "appraisers are sometimes pressured by clients to alter their values" (p. 12).

Client pressure effects have been repeatedly documented in the independent auditing literature where it is commonly termed "opinion shopping" (Knapp 1985; Farmer, Rittenberg, and Trompeter 1987; Emby and Gibbons 1988; Hendrickson and

Espahbodi 1991; Ponemon 1992; Goodwin and Trotman 1995; Lenk and Neumaier, 1996). Opinion shopping behavior is when a client seeks the views of successive auditors until one is located who will approve the desired financial statement procedures. Both the agency problems and empirical evidence of client pressure on independent auditors have been documented in auditing research (Emby and Gibbons 1988; Messier and Quilliam 1992; Salterio 1996).

The similarity of the structure of both the auditing market and its firms may assist in understanding these independence issues in the commercial appraisal industry. In both areas, the market is often characterized by increasing competition and bidding wars. Most firms are small with a few clients who represent a sizeable percentage of the firm's revenue. This structure, especially true for commercial appraisers of large insurance companies, pension funds, commingled real estate funds (CREFs), and lending institutions, creates financial incentives for the members of these firms to satisfy their clients. Clients have threatened auditors with the loss of contracts if they choose to disagree with the clients' positions (Hendrickson and Espahbodi 1991). In addition, management has paid a premium to the auditors who produce the desired outcome (Serlin 1985).

A second similarity involves the degree of judgment inherent in appraisal and audit reports. Because of the range of possible assumptions and/or the uncertainty of the particular real estate market, a range of acceptable value estimates may exist rather than a single point estimate. In these cases, a small value change requested by the client may seem to be more justifiable than a large value change. Auditing research has shown that client pressure is more likely to be successful when the values under dispute involve more discretionary judgments (Nichols and Price 1976).

Much of the auditing research on opinion shopping utilizes a behavioral methodology derived from experimental design. Typically, a case scenario is created that forces the auditor to make a decision on whether to accept or reject a client's treatment for a financial statement item. The scenarios, usually created with a factorial design, control for previously identified decision variables through manipulation. The results of that research have documented that auditors fear losing the client when disagreements on the financial statement balances are not resolved to the client's satisfaction (Serlin 1985; Church 1990; Messier and Quilliam 1992). The auditor's fear of client loss is referred to as a non-auditing factor that affects the auditor's opinion.

Lenk and Neumaier (1996) proxied the client pressure with the amount of the auditing firm's annual revenues provided by the client. Their results supported a direct relationship between client pressure and the choice to accept the client's preferred accounting procedures. Auditors are also concerned with another non-auditing issue—the risk of disciplinary action by the professional and regulatory agencies involved in the reliability of the audit opinion. Farmer, Rittenberg, and Trompeter (1987) documented that auditors consider the materiality of the requested accounting choice on the financial statement balances when making their opinion decisions. Disciplinary action for a commercial appraiser may originate with the Appraisal Institute or a State Appraisal Certification and Licensing Ethics Board. An appraiser may feel that the larger the value adjustment requested by the client, the more difficult it may be to defend the valuation.

Therefore, the goal of this research is to identify whether non-appraisal factors influence the valuation decisions of commercial appraisers. Specifically, the two non-appraisal variables of interest tested are the fear of client loss and the size of the valuation adjustment requested by the client. The effects of interaction between these two variables will also be tested, as Goodwin and Trotman (1995) found such a significant interaction effect on the opinion process of independent auditors.

Stated in the alternative format, the following hypotheses will be tested:

$H1_a$: Commercial appraisers' valuation decisions are affected by client pressure, as proxied by the percentage of annual revenues provided by the client.

$H2_a$: Commercial appraisers' valuation decisions are affected by the size of the value adjustment that is requested by the client.

$H3_a$: Commercial appraisers' valuation decisions are jointly affected by the size of the client and the amount of the value adjustment requested by the client.

RESEARCH METHODOLOGY

This research utilized a full 2 × 2 factorial, between-subjects experimental case design. One of the four commercial case scenarios is featured in the Appendix. The case places the commercial appraiser in a situation where the client is requesting a last minute increase in the valuation (owing to a purported new comparable sale). Verification of these new data was not possible in the time left for the report deadline. The appraisers are asked to decide whether they would accept or deny the clients' last minute request to increase the valuation.

Structured pretests were conducted on Hartford, Connecticut area appraisers to develop the case scenarios and to determine the levels of the variables of interest, client size, and adjustment size. The results of these pretests led to the manipulation of client size at two levels, low (5%) and high (30%) and the manipulation of the client-requested value adjustment size at two levels, low (5%) and high (15–20%). The between-subjects design allowed each commercial appraiser to receive only one cell of the factorial design, eliminating the possibility of identification of the manipulated variables. The four cells created by this design were as follows: a small client requesting a small adjustment, a small client requesting a large adjustment, a large client requesting a small adjustment, and a large client requesting a large adjustment.

The commercial appraisal case reported in this chapter is a piece of a larger study that investigated the responses of both residential and commercial appraisers associated with the Appraisal Institute in February 1996. The survey was mailed to 3028 appraisers who were asked to complete the case that best represented the bulk of their practice (commercial or residential). Each appraiser received two cover letters, one from the Institute and one from the researchers, two case scenarios, an exit questionnaire, and a return reply envelope. Table 17-1 provides a breakdown of the sampled appraisers who were randomly selected from the Institute's membership.

A total of 953 appraisers returned completed surveys resulting in an overall gross response rate of 32%. Twenty-six of the surveys were completely unusable responses (blank surveys) lowering the overall usable response rate to 31%. Of the usable

Table 17-1 Survey Mailants and Respondents

Certification\licence (total in category)	Number of surveys mailed (percentage of total)	Number of total responses (percentage)	Number of usable responses (percentage)
MAIs (5958)	809 (27)	231 (35)	176 (33)
SRAs (5086)	706 (23)	65 (10)	51 (9)
MAI and SRAs	—	91 (13)	67 (12)
MAI candidates (7099)	556 (18)	158 (24)	134 (25)
SRA candidates (4738)	454 (15)	41 (6)	36 (7)
SAAs (2940)	503 (17)	80 (12)	73 (14)
Total	3028 (100)	666 (100)	537 (100)

responses, 666 (72%) were commercial cases. Slightly over 50% of the commercial respondents also completed the residential case.

Table 17-1 also includes a breakdown of the respondents by certification type. Approximately 70% of the respondents were designated MAIs or were MAI candidates. In addition, other demographics were collected from the respondents. Two-thirds of the respondents were principals in a fee shop. The South region of the USA produced the most responses (32%), followed by the West region (24%). The remainder of the responses came equally from the North-east and Mid-west regions. Almost one-third of the respondents declared more than 10 years of commercial appraising experience. Over half of the respondents stated more than 6 years of experience. While over three-quarters of the respondents stated that they worked in firms with less than 10 appraisers, almost half of the respondents worked in small shops of one or two appraisers.

A logistic regression model was used to test whether client size, client-requested adjustment size, or the interaction of these two variables was associated with the appraisers' decision of whether or not to revise their valuation. The statistical model tested was as follows:

$$P_i = \beta_0 + \beta_1(X_1) + \beta_2(X_2) + \beta_3(X_1X_2) \quad (1)$$

where

P_i = appraisers' choice to revise or not revise the valuation opinion (0 = no revision);
X_1 = client size, as represented by percentage of appraisal revenues (0 = low);
X_2 = size of client-requested valuation adjustment (0 = low); and
X_1X_2 = interaction of the client size and the size of the adjustment.

An unexpected result was that over 70% of the respondents wrote comments on the surveys concerning client pressure. Codification procedures for the valuation decision variable therefore included a verification of whether the written comments agreed or conflicted with the appraiser's decision from the case. This verification procedure identified 129 respondents (19%) who had refused to make the valuation decision in the case and had returned the survey to share their written opinions on client pressure. A coding decision was made to eliminate these data points from the logistic regression model tests. Therefore, the remaining 537 responses, 666 minus 129, were utilized for the logistic regression model tests in this research.

RESULTS

The four case scenarios were mailed out in equal proportion (25%). The response rates for each of the cells of the research designs of returned, usable surveys were: small client/small adjustment, 120 (22%); small client/large adjustment, 150 (28%); large client/small adjustment, 128 (24%); and large client/large adjustment, 39 (26%). The test of the overall logistic regression model resulted significant ($\chi^2 = 6.67$ (3 df), $p > 0.083$). The results of the individual tests of the hypotheses are presented in Table 17-2.

A significant, direct relationship was documented between client size and the appraisers' likelihood of revising their valuation ($\chi^2 = 5.88$, $p > 0.015$). These results support the rejection of the null research hypotheses $H1_0$ of no effect, and provide evidence that the bigger a client is, the more likely it was for these appraisers to alter their valuation to accommodate client-requested valuation adjustments.

An insignificant relationship was the result between the client-requested adjustment size and the appraisers' valuation decision ($\chi^2 = 0.25$, $p > 0.614$). These results do not support the rejection of the null hypothesis $H2_0$ of no effect as the magnitude of a client-requested value adjustment did not cause a change in the appraisers' valuation behavior.

The interaction test also documents a nonsignificant relationship for the joint effects of client size and client-requested adjustment size variables on the appraisers' valuation decisions ($\chi^2 = 1.83$, $p > 0.176$). The cell frequencies, presented in Table 17-3, further illustrate that the only significant relationship in this model is the main effect of client size. A total of 218 appraisers (41%) chose to revise their original valuation to incorporate the client's unverifiable request. Of those who revised their valuations, 34%, or 73 appraisers, had received the large client/small adjustment scenario. A total of 319 appraisers (59%) chose not to revise their valuations to "satisfy" their client. Of this group, 24%, or 77 appraisers, had received the large client/small adjustment scenario.

The results reported in this section are from the 537 usable and codable responses of this survey. A multinomial logistic regression test was conducted to determine if the coding decision to eliminate the 129 "no-decision" responses affected the logistic

Table 17-2 Logistic Regression Model Results

Variable	Parameter estimae	Standard error	Probability > chi square	Support for alternative H_{1s}
Constant	−0.6397	0.178	0.0003	
Client size	0.5863	0.242	0.0154[a]	Yes
Adjustment size	0.1288	0.255	0.6138	No
Client-adjustment interaction	−0.4810	0.356	0.1764	No

[a]Statistically significant at the 95% confidence level.

Table 17-3 Experimental Design Cell Frequencies

	Small client (percentage)	Large client (percentage)
RESPONDENTS WHO DID REVISE THEIR VALUATION		
Small adjustment	49 (22)	73 (34)
Large adjustment	48 (22)	48 (22)
RESPONDENTS WHO DID NOT REVISE THEIR VALUATION		
Small adjustment	90 (28)	77 (24)
Large adjustment	80 (25)	72 (23)

regression results. To perform this test, the 129 responses were coded as a third dependent variable level. The results of this test were statistically identical to those reported above from the 537 data subset and indicate robustness concerning the related coding decision.

The exit questionnaire also contained several manipulation checks, designed to indicate whether the commercial appraisers were aware of the importance they placed on the manipulated variables within the case scenario. Their responses were measured on a Likert 5-point scale ranging from 1 (not important) to 5 (very important). Approximately two-thirds of the respondents indicated that client size was unimportant in their decision (67%), suggesting that the respondents were not aware that client size influenced their decision. Half of the respondents indicated that client-requested adjustment size was important to their decisions (51%). When asked how difficult the case decision had been for them to make, 65% of the respondents indicated that the decision had been easy. Finally, when asked if they had ever experienced client pressure, over 90% indicated that they had experienced such pressure.

Both the frequency and the nature of the respondents' written comments provide testimonial evidence that client pressure is a real and sensitive problem for commercial appraisers. Commercial appraisers stated that they felt significant pressure from common experiences of client pressure behavior, especially from mortgage brokers and bankers, a result that concurs with Smolen and Hambleton (1997). The respondents also wrote that their clients have threatened to "opinion shop" before hiring them, and that they have lost significant clients or payment when they stood by their values. These appraisers appeared tired of clients who behaved as if they know more than the appraiser and who blamed them for killing deals. Some appraisers stated that they are leaving the profession because of the client pressure situation.

The appraisers described their client pressure experiences as ranging from "one or two assignments a year" up to "almost every appraisal assignment" or "a daily occurrence" and were frustrated by their inability to compete against "adaptable" colleagues. Some appraisers indicated that they had cut back on appraisal work, or that they had decided to refuse to accept appraisal assignments from some of their more aggressive clients, specifically mentioning mortgage brokers.

The fact that the higher response rates occurred in the experimental cells with the small adjustment request (54%) may have tempered this measure of the amount of appraiser behavior related to client pressure. A small adjustment request may have been perceived as more ethical, motivating those appraisers to return the survey—especially given the assumption of a range of acceptable values rather than a point estimate. In addition, the most frequent return of a revise decision occurred in the case of a large client requesting a small adjustment (34%). This higher frequency may indicate that commercial appraisers feel that accommodating a small adjustment for a good client is an important aspect of customer service in their practices.

CONCLUSIONS

The purpose of this research was to measure the amount of client pressure on commercial real estate appraisers. A behavioral experimental design was utilized to test whether client size or value adjustment size affects the likelihood that commercial appraisers agree to client-requested valuation adjustments. Overall, 41% of the commercial appraisers revised their valuation estimates, without having supportive documentation, when requested to do so by their client. Client size was found significantly and directly to affect the valuation decisions of commercial appraisers. The appraisers' revising behavior was not significantly related to the size of the client-requested valuation adjustment, nor to the interaction between client size and valuation adjustment size. In addition, written comments indicated the presence of a significant amount of client pressure within the commercial appraisal industry.

This research contributes in several ways to the existing real estate appraisal literature. This has been the first use of an experimental, behavioral methodology to study client pressure in the commercial appraisal industry. Although these findings are not surprising, the results provide significant reliable evidence, rather than anecdotal hearsay, that client pressure exists in the US commercial appraisal industry.

Commercial appraisers value real estate portfolios worth billions of dollars and provide collateral values for loans worth millions of dollars. They are the party that serves as an independent check on the financial community. The results of this research indicate that commercial appraisers have lost some of their independence as an unrelated third party. Taken with the written comments, the results suggest the possibility that the certification and licensing requirements put forth by FIRREA, USPAP, and by the Appraisal Institute itself have not been effective to support refusal of assignments lacking independence. In fact, these measures may not have reduced the number of appraisers or increased the quality of appraisals as was expected when the legislation was first adopted (Lahey, Ott, and Lahey 1993). The written comments in this study suggest that increased competition, reduced fees, and no increase in product quality may be more indicative of the US commercial appraisal industry today.

When independent auditors succumb to client pressure, they have violated their professional code of ethics by compromising their integrity, their independence, their reputation, the reputation of their firm, and their profession. Further, they have harmed the reliability of their client's financial statements. Both of these outcomes are followed through with punitive actions through SEC regulation, required engagement change explanations, a working code violation grievance system, and litigation.

The results of this study recommend that the appraisal industry look to independent auditors for guidance in reducing client pressure. A simple solution may be for each individual appraiser to diversify their client portfolio, so that no one client is providing a significant proportion of their revenues. Perhaps rotating consortiums of commercial appraisers would be effective in reducing client pressure associated with appraisal work for large institutional clients (e.g., CREF managers). However, it is likely that practising appraisers dismiss this recommendation, as many of them enjoy a few large, reliable clients that provide stable income for their business.

This research is subject to the risks associated with a survey methodology and a behavioral design. It is not known with certainty who completed the survey and the survey requested the subjects to role-play. However, owing to the high response rate, the candid and detailed written comments, and the large number of respondents who signed their surveys, these risks are believed to be minimal. All the same, true commercial appraisal valuation behavior with respect to client pressure may be more complex than what this research design allowed. There is the possibility of omitted variables (internal validity). Moreover, only appraisers with relationships to the Appraisal Institute were included in the sample selected, possibly increasing the generalizability risks associated with the results (external validity). The results of this research, as well as the limitations, open further behavioral research avenues that test for other non-appraisal or market variables or utilize other samples of commercial appraisers. In addition, regulators and performance evaluators may be able to utilize these results to improve the appraisal environment for the future.

APPENDIX. A SAMPLE CASE SCENARIO: LARGE CLIENT SIZE AND SMALL ADJUSTMENT SIZE

Assume that you have been hired to estimate value for an income-producing investment property by a financial institution. Your firm has enjoyed a good working relationship with this client over the past 5 years and they represent about 30% of your total annual revenues.

You have chosen to rely on Direct Capitalization to estimate value for the property. The property is a large 2-year old, 60,000 square foot warehouse in a developing industrial park near the major airport of a large metropolitan area. The building is fully occupied by one high-credit ("blue-chip") company paying approximately market rate. The lease calls for annual CPI adjustments in the rent and the tenant is responsible for all operating expenses except insurance and exterior building maintenance and repairs.

You have identified three similar properties that you consider to be "very good comparables". All have occurred within the past year, have leases and tenants similar to the subjects and are located in the same industrial park. As a result, you are very comfortable with the Capitalization Rate that you have developed for use in a Direct Capitalization of the income.

On Friday of last week, the pension fund manager, David, telephoned to inquire how the appraisal was coming along, since it was due the following Monday at 5.00 p.m. He also asked what the value of the warehouse was likely to be. Since you had completed your final review and your office editor was just checking the report for grammar and consistency, you felt able to provide a preliminary estimate of value. In response, David expressed some concern and surprise at the value and asked what comparables you had used to develop your Capitalization Rate. You gave him a quick summary of the three sales and their terms, stressing how good and reliable you considered them to be, since they were quite recent sales and in the same basic location.

On Monday morning (today), as you are putting the finishing touches on the narrative appraisal report, you receive a fax from David which contains the details of two additional "comparable" sales that just closed in the last week. In the fax, David notes that the data came from a competing appraisal firm who also works closely with this bank. You know that this appraisal firm does quality work. Your preliminary analysis of this new data indicates a lower Capitalization Rate which would increase the value estimate by 5%. You have spent the day playing telephone "tag," but you are unsuccessful in your efforts to personally verify the new data. You are aware that a stiff late penalty will be applied towards your fee if the report is delivered after 5.00 p.m. You have discussed the situation with your colleagues and they have mixed opinions as to whether or not you should revise your report.

David calls at 4.00 p.m. and asks what you plan to do. You decide to (choose one of the choices below):

- Revise your report to incorporate the new data.
- Turn your original report in as it is.

REFERENCES

Church, B.K., "Auditors' Use of Confirmatory Process". *Journal of Accounting Literature*, 1990, 9: 81–112.

Connolly, J., "Pru's PRISA Portfolios will get an Independent Review". *National Underwriter*, 1993, 97(50): 27.

——, "Restitution on Overvaluations may Cost Prudential $50 Million". *National Underwriter*, 1994: 98(19): 4.

Eichenwald, K., "Prudential Said to Inflate Appraisals". *New York Times*, 8 February, 1994a, p. D5.

——, "In shift, Prudential Concedes a Whistle-blower was Right". *New York Times*, 20 April, 1994b, pp. A1, D2.

Emby, R. and Gibbons, M., "Good judgment in public Accounting: Quality and Justification". *Contemporary Accounting Research*, 1988, Spring: 287–313.

Farmer, T.A., Ritterberg, L.E., and Trompter G.M., "An Investigation of the Impact of Economic and Organizational Factors on Auditor Independence". *Auditing: A Journal of Practice & Theory*, 1987, 7(1): 1–14.

Fielder, L.E., "The problem with Commercial Property Appraisals Today". *Real Estate Review*, 1996, 25(4): 33–36.

Fletcher, S. and Diskin, B.A., "Agency Relationships in Appraising for Institutional Asset Managers". *The Appraisal Journal*, 1994, 62(1): 103–112.

Fraser R.R. and Worzala, E.M., "An insight into the ideas of Professor James A. Graaskamp on practice and reform in appraisal", in *Appraisal, Market Analysis, and Public Policy in Real Estate: Essays in Honor of James A. Graaskamp*, Delisle, J. and Sa-Aadu, J. (eds.). The American Real Estate Society/Kluwer Academic Publishers, Boston, MA, 1994, pp. 237–258.

Goodwin, J. and Trotman, K., "Audit Judgments of Revalued Non-current Assets: The Effect of Conflicting Risks". *Accounting and Business Research*, 1995, 25(99): 177–185.

Graaskamp, J.A., US 100th Congress, Transcription of Testimony in Support of HR 3675, with reference to The Real Estate Reform Act of 1987, Committee on Government Operations, 25 February. 1988.

Hendrickson, H. and Espahbodi, R., "Second Opinion, Opinion Shopping and Independence". *The CPA Journal*, 1991, 61(3): 26–29.

Horne, D.K. and Rosenblatt, E., "Property Appraisals and Moral Hazard". Paper presented at the American Real Estate Society meetings, Lake Tahoe, CA, 1996.

Knapp, M.C., "Audit Conflict: An Empirical Study of the Perceived Ability of Auditors to Resist Management Pressure". *Accounting Review*, 1985, 60(2): 202–211.

Lahey, K.E., Ott, D.M. and Lahey, V.M., "Survey of the Effects of State Certification on Appraisers". *The Appraisal Journal*, 1993, 61(3): 405–413.

Lenk M.M. and Neumaier, K.A., "An Investigation of the Effects of Non-accounting Variables on 'big six' versus non 'big six' Auditors". *Working Paper*, Colorado State University, CO. 1996.

Maroney, P.F. and Vickory, F.A., "Real Estate Appraiser Liability to Parties with Whom an Appraiser is not in Privity". *The Appraisal Journal*, 1991, 59(2): 173–178.

Messier, W.F., Jr and Quilliam, W.C., "The Effect of Accountability on Judgment Development of Hypothesis for Auditing". *Auditing: A Journal of Practice and Theory*, 1992, 11(supplement): 123–138.

Nichols, D.R. and Price, K.H., "The Auditor-firm Conflict: an Analysis using Concepts of Exchange Theory". *Accounting Review*, 1976, April: 335–346.

Poneman, L.A., "Ethical Reasoning and Selection-socialization in Accounting". *Accounting Organizations and Society*, 1992, 17(3,4): 239–258.

Rushmore, S., "Ethics in Hotel Appraising". *Appraisal Journal*, 1993, 61(3): 357–363.

Rutledge, J.K., "Conflicts of Interest or Thou Shalt not Steal' Revisited". *Real Estate Issues*, 1994, 19(3): 15–19.

Salterio, S., "The Effects of Precedents and Client Position on Auditors' Financial Accounting Policy Judgment". *Accounting Organization and Society*, 1996, 21(5): 467–486.

Serlin, J.E., "Shopping Around: A Closer Look at Opinion Shopping". *Journal of Accounting, Auditing and Finance*, 1985, 9(1): 120–125.

Smolen, G.E., "Do We Need a Statewide Appraisal Peer Review System?" *The Appraisal Journal*, 1994, 62(1): 86–93.

Smolen, G.E. and Hambleton, D.C., "Is the Real Estate Appraiser's Role too Much to Expect?" *The Appraisal Journal*, 1997, 65(1): 9–17.

Vinocur, B., "Pru's Appraisal Mess: Is it a Piece of the Rock or Tip of the Iceberg?". *Barron's*, 1994, 74(20): 50–51.

Waller, T.H. and Waller, N.G., "Real Estate Appraisal: The Legal Liability", *Real Estate Law Journal*, 1990, 18: 233–258.

Wheeler, A.L., III, "Real Estate Appraisal Malpractice Liability to Nonprivy Third Parties: Questioning the Applicability of Accountant Liability to Third Party Cases". *Real Property Probate and Trust Journal*, 1991, 26(1): 725–754.

Williams, T., "PRISA Suit Airs Appraisal Issue". *Pensions and Investments*, 1993, 21(24): 2, 43.

——, "Prudential Dismisses Jorgensen". *Pensions and Investments*, 1994a, 22(4): 2, 39.

——, "What Really Happened at PRISA". *Pensions and Investments*, 1994b, 22(10): 1, 101.

——, "Suit Says PRISA Fund Losing $750 Million". *Pension and Investments*, 1994c, 22(20): 12, 38.

18. The New Noneconomics: Public Interest Value, Market Value, and Economic Use

BILL MUNDY AND WILLIAM N. KINNARD, JR

Abstract

Some appraisers apply the term "public interest value" to what they call "noneconomic uses" of real estate. In particular, they have identified conservation use and preservation use (e.g., historical, geological, cultural, and open space) as "noneconomic uses," uses that do not produce money income. This article examines the history and development of the concept of highest and best use as it is presented in trade and academic publications, and addresses the traditional underlying meaning of "economic" and "economics" to evaluate the implications of "noneconomics" to real estate valuation.

A major debate has developed within the real property valuation profession over the appropriate definitions and applications of the concepts of highest and best use and market value. This debate has focused on the valuation of land, principally when it is undeveloped and might be used for preservation or conservation purposes. Also included are sites on which significant archaeology, paleontology, wildlife habitats, and vulnerable ecosystems are found.

The term "public interest value" derives from federal legislation written in the 1970s, relating to federal land acquisitions and federal income taxes. Although "public interest value" is not specifically defined in either *The Appraisal of Real Estate* or *The Dictionary of Real Estate Appraisal*, the textbook does note that "the issue of public interest value has come up in determining the just compensation required in land acquisitions by federal agencies."[1] This is its first mention in either of the principal publications of the Appraisal Institute. Woodward Hanson, the 1996 chair of the Appraisal Institute's Appraisal Standards Council, wrote:

As a result of considerable discussion and debate, the Appraisal Institute's position on PIV [public interest value] and the related family of concepts is summarized as follows:

- If the purpose of an appraisal assignment is to estimate market value, then highest and best use of the property to be appraised must be an economic use.
- Preservation and conservation are not recognized as economic alternatives to be considered in the highest and best use analysis.

[1]Appraisal Institute, *The Appraisal of Real Esate*, Eleventh edition. Appraisal Institute, Chicago, IL. 1996, p. 27.

Reprinted with permission. *The Appraisal Journal*, 1998, Vol. 66, No. 2, pp. 207–214.

- Transactions involving purchasers whose intent is to preserve/conserve privately owned natural land should not be considered as reliable evidence in support of the market value estimate.

Until such time as the definitions of market value and highest and best use are changed, and until new systems are introduced to replace the current legal and market systems of our country, the above policy will clearly govern the members of the Appraisal Institute. It should also serve as a guide to the profession, governments, and other users of appraisal services, and the public at large.[2]

These same points are made in *The Appraisal of Real Estate*, which states:

Huge amounts of public funds are at stake over what has become a highly controversial issue. Proponents of the public interest value concept recommend a redefinition of highest and best use and market value (*to recognize preservation or conservation as a highest and best use*), extension of the market concept to include public agencies and *conservation groups*, and adoption of alternative valuation methods (emphases added).[3]

NATURE OF THE DEBATE

The new nontraditional position is, therefore, that market value and highest and best use must reflect an economic use. Moreover, preservation/conservation is *not* an economic alternative to be used in a highest and best use analysis. However, "economic use" remains undefined and undelineated. Samuelson defines an *economic good* as "a good that is scarce relative to the total amount of it that is desired. It must therefore be rationed, usually by charging a positive price."[4] If such a good can have alternate uses, are any of these alternate uses noneconomic? Land uses, such as residential, grazing, religious, forestry, archaeological, and wildlife habitat, all represent goods that are scarce, rationed, and priced. However, because some of these uses have been identified as "noneconomic," some appraisers assert that their sale does not reflect market behavior or market values.

Real estate appraisal activity is governed, at least for those appraisers who are licensed (in most states) or are members of most professional appraisal associations, by The Appraisal Foundation in Washington, DC. Its *Uniform Standards of Professional Appraisal Practice* (USPAP) does not differentiate between economic and noneconomic uses, nor does it indicate how some types of property can be valued under the definition of market value, while others are valued under the definition of public interest value (which is not included in the USPAP glossary).

[2]Woodward S. Hanson, Public Interest Value and Noneconomic Highest and Best Use: The Appraisal Institute's Position. *Valuation Insights and Perspectives*, Spring 1996: 48.

[3]*The Appraisal of Real Estate*, Eleventh edition. p. 27.

[4]Paul A. Samuelson and William D. Nordhaus, *Economics*, McGraw-Hill, Inc., New York, NY. 1995, pp. 4–5, 750.

Land use for preservation/conservation has generated the greatest disagreement. It has attributes that allow it to be precisely defined. Some of those attributes are:

1. Presence or absence of cultural resources.
2. Forested nature of the tract.
3. Presence or absence of merchantable timber.
4. Whether the property is a desert, wetland, or coastal property.
5. Existence or diversity of geomorphic features.
6. Size of the property.
7. Size of proximate population centers.

These features can be used to differentiate nonurban lands from one another. Once differentiated, the categories exhibit unique patterns of prices within separate submarkets. Therefore, price becomes another differentiating variable.[5]

One part of the controversy revolves around whether sales of preservation/conservation property to various federal and state agencies represent arm's-length transactions. Sales of such property also occur between private entities, however. Other than *The Appraisal of Real Estate*, no authority has officially questioned the propriety of using private transactions, as have federal and state transactions. Therefore, a part of the "noneconomic" debate centers on whether sales public agencies represent legitimate evidence of market value.

Market value is inferred from market prices. Price is derived from transactional evidence. As long as a purchase or sale is an arm's-length transaction, regardless of who the buyer or seller is or the purpose for which the property is acquired, that transactional evidence is a legitimate market indicator of price and, hence, of value. Based on our research, there is no sound theoretical basis or justification for introducing the disruptive concepts of public interest value and noneconomic land use.[6]

ECONOMIC VERSUS NONECONOMIC HIGHEST AND BEST USE DILEMMA

It is unclear what is meant by the dictum that "highest and best use ... must be an economic use." If it refers to the use to which a particular site is being used, is the test whether the site generates monetary income (as opposed to amenity income)?

For example, assume a tract of nonurban land located in an area that is agricultural (alfalfa and pasture land that generates low income per acre) but can be used to grow nursery stock. Nursery stock generates greater cash flow per acre. Adjacent to it is a parcel of land that lies fallow. It is owned by an urban developer waiting for market support to change from agriculture to urban development. This land is held for

[5] See, for example, Victoria Adams and Bill Mundy, "The Valuation of High-Amenity Natural Land," *The Appraisal Journal* (January 1991): 48–53.

[6] According to Fred N. Kerlinger, *Foundation of Behavior Research*. Holt, Rinehart & Winston, New York, NY. 1986, p. 9: A theory is "a set of interrelated constructs (concepts), definition, and propositions that present a systematic view of phenomena by specifying relations among variables, with the purpose of explaining and predicting the phenomena."

investment purposes. An analysis of transactional evidence in the marketplace indicates that other land in the vicinity is selling at a price greater than that for agricultural land, the value of which must be supported by the income it generates. Is nursery use the only "economic use"? Is alfalfa–pasture use "economic"? Is the land held for investment currently in an "economic use"? Suppose nursery sites sell for $5000 per acre, agricultural land at $2500 per acre, and investment/speculative land at $7000 per acre. Can one estimate market value for only the nursery and agricultural uses? What kind of value does the investment land represent? If a property can be put to any of these three uses, what is its highest and best use? To complicate things further, assume that the parcel has a wetland area that is a popular waterfowl habitat and that a conservation entity (public or private) interested in preserving the whole site will pay $8000 per acre. What then?

Highest and best use as an economic use can be interpreted in another (and in a preferable) way. A use generates a certain level of utility, which allows property to command a certain price in the marketplace. Here, "economic use" is used in the context of a market transaction, market pricing, and relative utility. The level of economic benefit (price) derived from the sale of any particular property is a function of the utility that the property can generate. In other words, there is a relationship between the use intensity of a property and its utility, so that as the use intensity increases, so would its utility. As the utility increases, so would its value, or the price at which it would be transferred on the market.[7]

In the wetland and investment scenarios, economic use is based on the transaction/price/utility framework. In the nursery and agricultural transactions, economic use is derived from the monetary productivity of the property. Monetary productivity is viewed in a very short-term context. In the longer-term preservation context, real estate (or any commodity or service having utility and scarcity) that has a market has an economic use that can be measured by transaction prices, which in turn can be used to establish value.

In the marketplace, the process of bidding sets prices and values. Frequently, the bids come from prospective purchasers (users) who intend to use the real estate for different purposes. This is especially true with vacant, undeveloped land. In dealing with environmentally sensitive properties, two bidders might be (1) someone who wishes to mine fossils from a property and (2) an environment/conservation entity which intends to preserve the fossils. Both parties have equal knowledge regarding the nature and extent of the fossils on the property. Bidding will take place until one of them reaches a price threshold. For the fossil prospector, this would be a function of the rate and nature of the net income stream expected to be generated, as well as the prospector's rate of return expectations, from the mining operation. For the other bidder, the price threshold would be the resources available for this purchase.

Depending on the utility to be obtained and resources available, one of the bidders will prevail. The proposed nontraditional position suggests that the miner

[7]For an in-depth discussion of use intensity and price, see Harvey Barlowe, *Land Resource Economics*. Prentice Hall, Englewood Cliffs, NJ. 1986, p. 154.

proposes an economic use, while the conservationist proposes a noneconomic use. Moreover, the price paid by the miner would purportedly be used to estimate market value, while the price paid by the conservationist could be used to estimate market value.

Assume that the conservationist prevails and several other similar types of properties in this vicinity are also acquired by conservationists. In all cases, the conservationists outbid alternative users (miners) of the property. If the owner of a property with similar fossil resources located on it asks a real estate appraiser to identify what the market value of the property is, the stated new position is that the appraiser cannot estimate the *market value* of the prospective owner's property for conservation purposes. Rather, the appraiser must estimate the value based on miners' bids for the property or on some less intensive or productive use, such as grazing. The new position also indicates that estimating the value of the property, using as market evidence the conservation acquisitions, requires that some label other than market value (i.e., public interest value) be applied to the value estimate.

It is important to understand the distinction between market value and public interest value. In nearly all litigation contexts, the appraiser is *required* to estimate market value. When an appraiser is requested to provide a lender with an estimate of the property value for underwriting purposes, that value estimate must be market value. The essence of the new position of *The Appraisal of Real Estate* is that any transactional evidence of sales between government entities, conservation organizations, and private individuals cannot be used for market value estimates when the intended use is for preservation or conservation.

The Appraisal Institute's textbook makes it very clear that highest and best use is:

> An economic study of market forces ... Highest and best use is shaped by the competitive forces within the market where the property is located. Therefore, the analysis and interpretation of highest and best use is an *economic study* of market forces (emphasis added).[8]

This statement does not refer to *financial* use of the land, such as grazing, which might generate income. The text states that highest and best use is a market-driven concept in which transactional evidence is used to determine the most profitable use of the land being appraised:

> An understanding of market behavior is essential to the concept of highest and best use. Market forces create market value, so the interaction between market forces and highest and best use is of crucial importance. When the purpose of an appraisal is to estimate market value, highest and best use analysis identifies the most profitable competitive use to which the property can be put. Therefore, highest and best use is a market-driven concept.[9]

Most profitable use is necessarily based on transactional (price) evidence.

[8] *The Appraisal of Real Estate*, Eleventh edition, pp. 48, 50, 298.
[9] *Ibid.*, p. 298.

CLASSICAL ECONOMICS

The Appraisal of Real Estate establishes a summary theoretical basis for value. The chapter titled "The History of Value Theory" includes a discussion of the classical school of economics. It notes that Adam Smith, one of the original contributors, developed the notions of utility, scarcity, and value in exchange.

The Scottish economic thinker, Adam Smith (1721–1790), suggested that capital, in addition to land and labor or productivity, constituted a prime agent of production. Smith acknowledged the role of coordination in production, but did not study its function as a primary agent. He believed that value was created when the agents of production were brought together to produce a useful item.

In *The Wealth of Nations* (1776), the first systematic treatment of economics, Adam Smith considered value as an objective phenomenon. By virtue of its existence, an item was assumed to possess utility. Scarcity also imparted exchange value to goods.[10]

Smith's work was further developed by Thomas Robert Malthus and Jean Baptiste Say. Their thoughts and writings were parallel to Smith's in regard to utility and price as a measure of value in exchange:

Thomas Malthus (1776–1834) elaborated on Ricardo's theory of rent and, in the process, identified value in use, value in exchange (price), and intrinsic value ... John Baptiste Say (1767–1832) rejected the relationship between labor and value, concentrating instead on utility as the determinant of value.[11]

The Appraisal of Real Estate goes on to discuss various challenges to the classical theory. However, the concepts of utility, demand, and value were economic principles that remained steadfast in economists' thinking. For example:

The other challenge was presented by the marginal utility or Austrian school ... [V]alue is regarded as a function of demand, with utility as its fundamental precept ... Eugen von Boehm-Bawerk (1835–1882) [another member of the Austrian school] defined value as "the significance a good acquires in the contribution of utility toward the well-being of an individual."[12]

The textbook then states that "four interdependent factors create value: utility, scarcity, desire, and effective purchasing power."[13] Therefore, the Appraisal Institute seems to have adopted the theoretical principles formulated by classical (and neoclassical) microeconomics that there is a relationship between utility, scarcity, and value (price) expressed through a market exchange system.

A significant amount has been written about utility, scarcity, markets, and price in economics literature that is not included in *The Appraisal of Real Estate*, the Appraisal

[10] *Ibid.*, p. 30.

[11] Appraisal Institute, *The Appraisal of Real Estate*, Tenth edition. Appraisal Institute, Chicago, IL. 1992, p. 27.

[12] *The Appraisal of Real Estate*, Eleventh edition. pp. 30–31.

[13] *Ibid.*, p. 32.

Institute's educational curriculum, nor many other college-level real estate courses. Although Adam Smith is cited briefly, some of his more significant writings in the area of market price are not discussed. Smith reasoned, "At each level of economic development the price of commodities reflected the average cost of labor, the average level of profit, and the average rent of land."[14] He called this the "natural" price, the lowest price at which a given commodity could be produced without loss and, hence, the lowest price at which it could be made available over an extended period of time. According to Smith, the actual price at which a commodity or good is sold is market price. He stated, "That price is determined by the relationship between the quantity offered by producers and the amount desired by those with the ability to pay for it."[15]

Smith recognized the difference between natural price (what economists call price and appraisers call value based on the cost "new" to produce a commodity or spatial product) and market price (what a consumer is willing to pay for that product based on market sales comparisons). In the case of market price, Smith emphasizes the importance of transactions.

NEOCLASSICAL ECONOMICS

In a more contemporary environment, Nobel laureate Paul A. Samuelson still quotes Smith's *paradox of value:*

> Nothing is more useful than water, but it will scarce purchase anything. A diamond, on the contrary, has scarce any value in use, but a very great quantity of other goods may frequently be had in exchange for it ... Economics relies on the fundamental premise that people tend to choose those goods and services they value most highly.[16]

This choosing of goods and services is what establishes price. For the producer, to maximize price and, therefore, profit means that the benefit to the consumer must be maximized. Nothing in the literature of economics suggests that goods and services consumers demand are separated into "economic" or "noneconomic" categories, for *all* are "economic."

Applications to Land Use Analysis

Land use capacity is "the relative ability of a given unit of land resource to produce a surplus of returns and/or satisfactions above the cost of utilization, according to Harvey Barlowe,"[17] Use capacity has two major components: accessibility and resource quality.[18] Resource quality involves the "relative ability of land resources to produce desired products, returns, or satisfactions .... It also involves aesthetic considerations

[14]Jerry Z. Mueller, *Adam Smith in His Time and Ours: Designing the Decent Society*. Princeton University Press, Princeton, NJ. 1993, p. 74.

[15]*Ibid.*, p. 74.

[16]Samuelson, pp. 73, 82.

[17]Barlowe, p. 12.

[18]*Ibid.*, p. 15.

such as scenery, trees, water attractions, nearness to parks or open space, access to schools, and cultural opportunities."[19] Land uses reflect various resource qualities, one of the two components of use capacity. "The concept of use capacity is often used in land economics to distinguish between the comparative abilities of different units of land resources to provide their operators with net returns *and other satisfactions*" (emphasis added).[20] Therefore, different types of land have different types of use capacities. These various use capacities provide differential returns in owner/user satisfactions (utility). Because they have different returns, they have different price structures.

There is a relationship between the use capacity of land and its intensity of use. For example, land that has superior locational attributes (use capacity) is likely to be used more intensely. Zoning affects the use capacity of land. Land that is zoned for residential use usually has a lower intensity of use than land zoned for commercial use.

The highest and best use of land is a function of the use capacity of alternative land uses. It is correlated to resource (land), quality, and access. When used in the context of the rent-generating ability of land (e.g., commercial, residential, farm, and forestry), rent is used as an indicator of land use intensity. Land use intensity, in turn, is a function of the supply of and demand for a resource. The greater the demand and the less the supply, the greater the land use intensity. The greater the intensity, the greater the land rent or value.

Applications to Highest and Best Use

According to Barlowe, "The concepts of land rent and highest and best use can be used to explain both the competition between land uses and the resulting allocation of land resources between uses."[21] Therefore, economic highest and best use is directly related to the utility and scarcity of land and the intensity to which it is used. This intensity of use can be measured by price (capitalized land rent) and has nothing to do with whether land can actually generate rent in the form of a cash return. Intensity of use cannot be used to differentiate between economic and noneconomic uses.

Highest and best use can have both an economic and social context:

> In facing up to the conflicts that occasionally develop between private and social priorities in land resource development, it is important to note the reason for the differences. The succession that takes place in private land resource use often reflects the bidding and counter bidding that takes place in a relatively free, competitive market. No problems arise as long as the owner or top bidder puts the property to some socially acceptable use. Real conflicts may develop, however, if the operator decides to maximize profit or other ownership satisfactions by shifting to a use that damages or exploits the interests of neighbors or of the community at large.[22]

Barlowe means that an economic highest and best use may have a value (price) that includes certain social costs (externalities), such as view blockage or the destruction of an

[19] *Ibid.*
[20] *Ibid.*
[21] *Ibid.*, p. 187.
[22] *Ibid.*, p. 203.

endangered species habitat. Taking these social costs into account, therefore, decreases the margin of total utility associated with a particular property. This results in a lower use capacity, less use intensity, and therefore a lower price. Zoning, especially height restrictions, such as in Washington, DC, and the *National Environmental Policy Act of 1969*[23] are examples of societal limitations placed on untrammeled economic use of land.

For example, assume that an industrial site with a substantial part of the property affected by a wetland is deemed to be a significant wildlife habitat. For the industrial park developer, the value of this parcel, or the price that can be paid, may be $1 million. However, the value may be $1.25 million to a conservationist who can use the property for industrial purposes and still maintain the wildlife habitat, or use the entire property as a wildlife habitat. Conservation, therefore, represents both the economic and the social highest and best use. It represents a different use capacity and different intensity of use, plus a price premium of $250,000. This is the social component that the *market* is willing to pay. In summary, it represents a different use capacity, different intensity of use, and different market price. It has nothing to do with "economic" or "noneconomic" highest and best use.

ECONOMIC OR NONECONOMIC NATURE OF A GOOD OR SERVICE

According to *The Appraisal of Real Estate*, "Value is regarded as a function of demand, with utility as its fundamental precept—a concept borrowed from the theory of marginal utility.[24] If a good (art or real estate) or service (laborer or professional) has utility and is scarce (limited supply), then demand for that good or service will result in a certain price at which the good or service will trade (clear the market). Cumulative price levels are appropriate value indicators. A good or service does not have to be "economic" (i.e., generate money income) to have utility. It must satisfy human needs, desires, or wants. The level of usefulness and level of scarcity can be quantified and measured. The indicator of utility or scarcity is price. The price at which a good or service sells has nothing to do with whether it is "economic" or "noneconomic" (i.e., whether it produces monetary income).

Different goods and services sell at market-determined prices regardless of whether they produce money income. For example, a 15-unit apartment building in Seattle recently sold for $1 million. This is an income-producing good. On the other hand, the items that, in total, were sold for $1.282 million from the Jacqueline Kennedy Onassis estate (such as an oak rocking chair, portraits of the former first lady, and a 1992 BMW 3251, four-door sedan, among others) do not produce income. The possible exception is the BMW, which might be leased. These "noneconomic" goods were clearly more valuable on the market than the "economic" good, the 15-unit apartment building. Yet, the "economic use" advocates would have us believe that there is market value associated with one set of goods (the apartment building), but *no* market value associated with the others (the Kennedy Onassis memorabilia).

[23]PL 91-190. This law was the catalyst for much of the environmental legislation we have today, including the *Clean Air Act* (1970).

[24]*The Appraisal of Real Estate*, Eleventh edition, pp. 30–31, and Samuelson, pp. 74–76.

LEGAL FOUNDATION

The U.S. Internal Revenue Service recognizes conservation easements as a land use, recognizes the rights associated with that use, and accords them full market value. In fact, a conservation easement qualifies as "like kind property" for a Section 1031 exchange of other real estate. In this case, a waterfowl habitat could be exchanged for farmland, ranch land, or commercial property.[25]

In November 1996, voters in Colorado approved legislation to protect 300,000 acres of state land and establish preservation as a legitimate use of land.[26]

A position paper formulated by the Interagency Land Acquisition Conference, and adopted on April 14, 1995, on the issue provides significant insight into whether a noneconomic highest and best use can be a proper basis for the estimate of market value:

> Fair market value is to be determined with reference to the property's *"highest and best use"—that is, the highest and most profitable use for which the property is adaptable and needed or likely to be needed in the near future.*[27]

Appraisers use several methods to estimate value. Typically, these are the cost, income, and sales comparison approaches. The purpose of each approach is to estimate market value or the price a seller is willing to accept and a buyer is willing to pay for a particular good (e.g., real estate). According to James Eaton, "The courts appear to prefer the sales comparison approach to value overwhelmingly."[28] This is equivalent to saying that *transactions* are the best measure of value. In the suggested new lexicon, are some transactions "economic" and others "noneconomic," based on whether the properties involved are expected to produce money income?

CONCLUSION

Market sales transactions are based on the relative utility and scarcity of various goods and services. When goods and services are exchanged, typically for money, a transaction occurs, and the transaction price is easily quantifiable.

Real estate can be put to various uses. Because of the variable characteristics of real estate, it can be used at varying levels of intensity. These various use intensities are reflected in the marketplace through transaction prices. The maximum use intensity for different land use categories represents their highest and best use.

Therefore, whether real estate is put to an economic use has absolutely nothing to do with its utility, scarcity, exchange price, most productive use, or market value. Because market value is based on transactional evidence, preservation/conservation as a land use category is consistent with the definition of highest and best use, when it represents the highest price that a property will command in an arm's-length, open-market transaction. The prices for transactions that anticipate preservation/conservation as the highest and best use are therefore market-based indicators of market value.

[25]Department of Internal Revenue Service, letter ruling 9601046, Washington, DC, 1996.

[26]Conservation Fund, *Common Ground* (July/August 1996): 3.

[27]Interagency Land Acquisition Conference, position paper, Washington, DC, 1995, cites the following source for this definition: *Olson v. United States*, 292U.S.246, 266 (1934), A3, 8.

[28]J. D. Eaton, *Real Estate Valuation in Litigation*, Second edition, Appraisal Institute, Chicago, IL. 1995, p. 198.

19. The Effects on Residential Real Estate Prices from Proximity to Properties Contaminated with Radioactive Materials

WILLIAM N. KINNARD, JR AND MARY BETH GECKLER

On December 1, 1983, the US Environmental Protection Agency (USEPA) and the New Jersey Department of Environmental Protection (NJDEP) jointly announced that concentrations of radon gas and levels of onsite gamma radiation were well above regulatory standards in three residential neighborhoods in three adjacent towns in northern New Jersey. The elevated levels of radon and gamma radiation resulted from the presence of radium-contaminated fill material on many lots in the neighborhoods.

The three neighborhoods were placed on the National Priorities List and included in the Superfund program in October, 1984. These three Superfund Site Areas (SSAs) are referred to in this article as Towns A, B, and C.

Extensive remediation programs were initiated promptly in Towns A and C; these programs were completed during 1985. In Town B, on the other hand, a program to excavate contaminated fill material (and later to replace the material with clean fill) was only partially completed before it was abandoned in September, 1985. Because a disposal site was not available, NJDEP was forced to place the excavated fill material in sealed drums, which were stored openly on the lawns of vacated houses.

The initial announcement of the elevated radon and gamma radiation on the sites received widespread publicity in both print and electronic media. There also was continuous, daily publicity about the open storage of the contaminated fill material. Danger! Radiation signs and radiation warning symbols were displayed on a fence surrounding the sites on which the drums were stored. The drums of contaminated

A case study of three Superfund sites in New Jersey and how they were affected by single-family residential property sales prices.

Reprinted with permission. *Real Estate Issues*, 1991, Vol. 16, No. 2, pp. 25–36.

materials were removed in September, 1987, which also generated considerable publicity, and they eventually were shipped out of state. Not until June, 1990, was a USEPA remediation program approved.

Property owners seeking to sell or lease properties within the three SSAs were required by state law to reveal the most recent radon readings (if any) to any potential buyer or tenant.

THE RESEARCH ASSIGNMENT

In October, 1989, the Real Estate Counseling Group of Connecticut, Inc., (RECGC) was retained to conduct a market research study of all single-family residential property sales within the three SSAs. In addition, RECGC was asked to study all residential property sales within a larger study area that extended one mile beyond the outer limits of each SSA.

The study period extended from July 1, 1980, through June 30, 1989, and it included 67 months of post-announcement sales experience. The analysis identified, reported, and measured the actual market sales behavior of buyers and sellers. Both the impact on sales prices and the changes in the volume of sales transactions were analyzed.

Questions to be Addressed

Statistical tests were conducted on the assembled residential property sales transaction data to answer the following questions:

- What was the pattern of inflation-adjusted sales prices per square foot of single-family residences in each town, within each SSA and within selected distance zones up to one mile from the SSA? What was the pattern in the 41 months preceding the public announcement of the existence of radioactive contamination within the SSAs? What was the pattern in the 67 months that followed the announcement?
- What changes in levels of inflation-adjusted sales prices per square foot of living area were identifiable and measurable after the announcement? How did these prices compare with levels of inflation-adjusted unit sales prices before the announcement?
- What patterns of sales volumes of single-family residential properties were observed during the 41 months before the announcement and over the 67 months afterward? What changes in those patterns occurred before and after the announcement?
- How far distant from the outer boundary of an SSA did a residential sales property have to be before there was no measurable negative impact on the inflation-adjusted sales price per square foot of living area or on the volume of sales associated with proximity to the SSA?

RESEARCH PROJECT DESIGN

Analytical Models

Three categories of analytical, statistical models were utilized. They provided comparisons of inflation-adjusted price levels and of rates of change in those price levels for single-family properties at varying distances from the three SSAs before and after January 1, 1984. They also provided comparisons of sales volumes within the study areas.

- *Comparison of averages.* Arithmetic means of inflation-adjusted prices were calculated and compared by year for each distance zone.
- *Trends.* Percentage changes in levels of inflation-adjusted prices and in volume of sales were calculated and compared.
- *Multiple regression.* Sales data were assembled into four data sets: one for each of the three towns and one for the combined total. Dependent and independent variables were entered into regression models in the standard Hedonic Pricing Model format to test the influence and statistical significance of time, location (distance from an SSA) and property characteristics on the inflation-adjusted sales price per square foot of living area. Multiple Linear Regression Analysis (MRA) often is used to identify, measure, and evaluate the influence, relative importance and statistical significance of all property, transaction and location characteristics that influence sales prices. In this study, it was used to isolate, measure and test the significance of both distance from an SSA by zone *and* the likely effects of post-announcement awareness of radon gas and gamma radiation concentrations within the SSAs.

Data Requirements

Certain categories of information were required to apply the analytical models.

- *Sales price data.* Every transaction had to have a recorded sales price to be used in the study. Sales prices were deflated to December, 1983, dollars through the use of the All Urban House-holds Consumer Price Index. The result of this deflation was the adjusted sales price (ADJSP). Because *size* (square feet of living area) is one of the most important determinants of sales price, the ADJSP was refined to incorporate square footage. The adjusted sales price per square foot (ADJSPSF) was the dependent variable used in this study.
- *Time.* The date of sale was recorded for every sales transaction by year and month. Two measures of time and its possible influence on ADJSP or ADJSPSF were employed. The first was the date of the deed (DDATE), which indicated the year and month of the execution. The second measure of time indicated whether the deed was recorded *before* or *after* (BEFAFT) January 1, 1984. For the purposes of this study, any deed recorded during December, 1983, was excluded because it did not represent a sale that was affected by the announcement.
- *Property characteristics.* All properties in the study were single-family residences. Two of the most important influences on the sales prices of residential properties are size (square feet of living area) and age (in years) at the time of sale. Data on size and age therefore were gathered on all sales transactions. Any sales transaction for which either the size or the age of the residence could not be obtained from an official source was excluded from further analysis.

Because it was not possible to identify retroactively the condition of the property at the time of sale, age at the time of sale served as a proxy for the condition of the property. In addition, data on lot size, type of garage, number of parking stalls, number of stories of residence and exterior finish were obtained. Data were not available on the number of rooms, number of bedrooms or number of bathrooms.

- *Location: Distance from the SSA.* The focus of the research project was to ascertain any impact from or effect of proximity to the SSAs on sales prices (adjusted for inflation and size). Therefore, particular attention was paid to the location and distance from an SSA for each sales transaction property. The measure of distance was obtained by identifying the distance zone in which each sales property was located.

Data Collection and Data Recording

Data Sources

Listings of all property sales coded as residential were obtained for each fiscal year (July 1–June 30) from 1980–81 through 1988–89. These data came from SR1A forms on which local assessors report all bona fide, arm's length real estate sales transactions for the year.

Additional information came from Real Estate Data Incorporated (REDI). This subscription service summarizes sales transaction data within communities in northern New Jersey quarterly and monthly. REDI listings provided the street addresses of most sales properties, which were correlated with the block and lot number provided in the SR1A summaries.

The major source of information was assessor's property cards for each of the three townships. The property cards frequently provided corroboration of data obtained from other sources as well. If critical information was missing from the assessor's property cards and could not be obtained from other sources, the property was not included in the data base.

Finally, visual inspections of the exterior of all sales properties were conducted to check and verify (or correct, as necessary) the information obtained from REDI and the assessor's property cards.

Mapping and Distance Zone Identification

The distance of each sales transaction property from the pertinent Superfund site in its town had to be identified. Since the Town B Superfund site extends into Town C, some properties that are relatively distant from the Town C Superfund site are actually relatively close to the Town B Superfund site.

To identify distance from or proximity to each SSA, distance zones were established. (The zone definitions are summarized in Table 19-1.) Every sales transaction property was mapped, and its zone location was recorded.

Data Screening and Usable Data Sets

A total of 2317 sales were identified from the SR1A forms as likely candidates for analysis. It was necessary, however, to eliminate those sales transactions and properties that did not meet the eligibility standards of the research study.

Table 19-1 Identification of Distance Zones

Zone	Distance from SSA* (feet)
S	Inside SSA
A	1–250
B	251–500
C	501–1000
D	1001–1500
E	1501–2500
F	2501–3500
G (Control area)	3501–5280

* Distance from the SSA is the linear distance of the nearest portion of the sales transaction property to the outer boundary of the closest SSA.

Table 19-2 Summary of Sales Data Screening Process (by Town, by Reason)

	Town A	Town B	Town C	Total
Total unscreened sales	541	831	945	2317
Less: Outside limits of property characteristic parameters				
Located beyond 1 mile	15	13	70	98
Bought before 7/1/80	0	1	0	1
More than 5,500 square feet	4	28	5	37
Not a single-family dwelling	7	316	347	668
Subtotal: Outside limits	26	358	422	804
Balance	515	473	523	1513
Less: Record data missing				
Square foot of living area	21	23	27	71
Year built	7	0	8	15
Number of families	0	1	1	2
Subtotal: Data missing	28	24	36	88
Screened, usable sales	487	449	487	1425

First, a complete data file was necessary for the sales transaction to be included in the study. Any file without data on square feet of living area, date of construction of the dwelling (to provide age at the time of sale) or the number of families (only single-family residential property sales were usable) had to be eliminated. Table 19-2 shows that 88 sales transactions were eliminated because of unavailable record data.

Ninety-eight sales were eliminated because more precise measurement on large-scale maps revealed that they were located more than one mile from an SSA. One sale that occurred prior to July 1, 1980, also was eliminated.

The SR1A reports include both one-family and two-family properties in the "2" property coding for sales transactions. As Table 19-2 shows, 668 two-family (or other non-one-family) sales had to be removed.

DEPENDENT VARIABLES	
Inflation-adjusted sales price per square foot	(ADJSPSF)
INDEPENDENT VARIABLES	
Deed date (year, month)	(DDATE)
After January 1984 (Yes–No)	(BEFAFT)
Square feet of living area	(SFLIVARE)
Square feet of lot area	(LOTSIZE)
Age in years at time of sale	(AGE)
Number of stories of residence	(#Stories)
Shingle/wood siding (Yes–No)	(SHINGLES)
Brick exterior finish (Yes–No)	(BRICK)
Stucco exterior finish (Yes–No)	(STUCCO)
Stone exterior finish (Yes–No)	(STONE)
Number of garage/carport stalls	(GARSTALS)
Attached garage (Yes–No)	(ATTACHED)
Detached garage (Yes–No)	(DETACHED)
Carport (Yes-No)	(CARPORT)
Basement garage (Yes–No)	(BASE GAR)
Within Zone A (Yes–No)	(A ZONE)
Within Zone B (Yes–No)	(B ZONE)
Within Zone C (Yes–No)	(C ZONE)
Within Zone D (Yes–No)	(D ZONE)
Within Zone E (Yes–No)	(E ZONE)
Within Zone F (Yes–No)	(F ZONE)
Within Superfund site (Yes–No)	(S ZONE)

Figure 19-1. List of Variables for Multiple Regression Analysis

Finally, no property was included in the final data set if one of three major characteristics was outside the 99% confidence interval around the mean for that characteristic: square feet of living area, age at the time of sale, and lot size. This eliminated another 37 sales as nonrepresentative outliers.

Table 19-2 shows that the final total usable data set for all three towns contained 1425 sales. The sales were almost evenly divided among the three towns, with 487 usable sales in both Towns A and C and 449 sales in Town B.

Variables for Multiple Regression Analysis

MRA requires the identification of both a dependent variable and the independent variables that will be used in the analysis. The dependent variable used in this study was inflation-ADJSPSF of living area. In each MRA run, only one time variable was used: either the DDATE or BEFAFT January 1, 1984. Figure 19-1 identifies, explains and lists the dependent variable and independent variables that were used in the MRA models.

RESEARCH FINDINGS

Average Property Characteristics

Average of property and transaction characteristic values provided a basis for comparison as well as indications of what is typical or representative of the market.

Inflation-Adjusted Sales Price

The average ADJSP in each zone for each year was compared within the three-town usable sales data set and the data set for each town. A notably consistent pattern of findings emerged. First, during the years 1980–83 (before the announcement), the average ADJSP in Zones S (the SSAs), A and B was typically *lower* than the average ADJSP in more distant zones. Some exceptions were found in Zone B. Although there was no absolute decrease in average ADJSP, rates of increase in Zones S, A, and B were lower than those in the other zones after 1984. ADJSP in general was lower in 1989, regardless of zone.

Size of Dwelling (Square Feet of Living Area)

In the three-town total, the houses in Zones S, A, and B were typically smaller than those in other zones both before and after January 1, 1984. In Town A, the smallest houses were in Zones S, A, and B. In Town B, the houses in Zones S and A also averaged the smallest. In Town C as well, the houses in Zones S, A, and B were well below average in size. Part of the explanation for lower average ADJSP in Zones S, A, and B is the smaller (below-average) size of houses in those zones in each of the three towns. This was true both before and after the December, 1983, announcement.

Age of Dwelling at the Time of Sale

The study areas in the three towns tended to be concentrated in older neighborhoods. The average age of dwellings at the time of sale for the 1423 total usable sales was 64 years. The *lowest* average age of dwelling at time of sale was in Zones S and A.

The same general pattern of average age distributions appeared in each of the three towns. Generally, the houses in Zones S, A, and B averaged 60 years old or less. Average ages tended to increase for houses that were more distant from a Superfund site. The one exception was in Town C, where the lowest average ages at the time of sale were in Zones F and G. However, age of dwelling at the time sale did not help explain the generally lower average ADJSP in Zones S, A, and B.

Lot Size (Square Feet of Land Area)

The average lot size for the three-town data set was 10,700 square feet. Throughout each of the three towns and in the three-town total, lot sizes in Zones S, A, and B were consistently smaller on average; the smallest average sizes usually were in Zone S.

Therefore, in Zones S, A, and B (especially Zone S), average house sizes were smallest, and these smaller houses were located on smaller lots. The combination of smaller houses on smaller lots helped to explain in part the lower average ADJSP found in Zones S, A, and B both before and after the December, 1983, announcement.

These observable and measurable size and age differences suggested strongly that simple comparisons of averages by zone over time probably would fail to capture enough of the influence of proximity to an SSA on ADJSP. That is, why comparisons of averages and of trends were supplemented with multiple regression analysis.

Sales Volume (Number of Sales)

One indicator of changing market conditions is a change in the number of sales that occurs in a given area or zone over a specified time period. This reflects changing buyer attitudes toward owning and living in that location. One important way for potential buyers to react negatively to a given market situation is to withdraw from the market and refrain from purchasing.

The sales data in the study showed an overall decline in residential real estate market activity in all three towns (and in the county) after 1985. This is the context within which sales volumes in the three study areas were examined and analyzed.

There was an across-the-board decrease in residential property sales volume after 1985, but there was no perceptible or measurable decrease in sales volume in 1984 and 1985, the two years immediately following the December, 1983, announcement. This suggested that there was no negative reaction to residential property purchase in the three-town total. Moreover, sales volume actually increased in Zones A and B in 1984 and 1985. There was a very modest decline in sales in Zone S in 1984, but sales recovered again in 1985. In 1989, sales volumes in Zones S, A, and B declined more than in the more distant zones.

Buyer reactions to proximity to the three SSAs apparently varied considerably from one town (and SSA) to another. Proximity to the Town B SSA appeared to be more of a deterrent to would-be buyers than was proximity to the SSA in either Town A or Town C.

Inflation-adjusted Sales Prices per Square Foot of Living Area

Table 19-3 shows average inflation ADJSPSF by zone and by year for each town studied and for the three-town total data set.

For the three-town total, levels, and trends of average ADJSPSF in Zones A through D were roughly similar. Averages were higher in Zone E, especially in 1988 and 1989. The average for Zone S followed essentially the same pattern as that for every zone except E.

In the individual towns, there was considerably more variation in average ADJSPSF by zone from year to year. There also were gaps for those zones in which no sales occurred during the given years.

The total pattern of levels and variations in average ADJSPSF by zone suggested that some measurable negative impact probably occurred in Zones S, A, and B in Town B and possibly in Town C; no such negative impact occurred in Town A.

Before–After Changes

Comparisons of average ADJSPSF and of sales volume by zone and by town BEFAFT January 1, 1984, helped to clarify whether any discernible negative impact on average ADJSPSF or sales volume was evident after the announcement. (The results of these comparisons are presented in Tables 19-4, 19-5 and 19-6.)

Average ADJSPSF by Zone, Before and After January 1, 1984

Table 19-4 shows the percentage changes in average ADJSPSF by zone.

Table 19-3 Average Inflation-Adjusted Sales Price per Square Foot (by Year, by Zone)

Year	Zone (in $)								
	S	A	B	C	D	E	F	G	All
THREE-TOWN TOTAL									
1980	48.66	55.30	37.15	54.04	45.83	41.49	48.15	39.37	45.90
1981	52.78	57.58	48.59	49.68	45.47	45.19	40.36	39.99	46.38
1982	49.40	45.88	49.80	43.37	36.65	48.91	44.74	53.64	47.64
1983	50.27	54.56	47.81	53.39	43.74	57.31	47.18	42.46	48.94
1984	56.53	57.87	61.85	61.20	51.86	55.32	62.12	54.22	56.89
1985	71.25	66.75	72.02	66.75	68.60	64.86	68.97	63.40	67.31
1986	90.25	92.25	87.55	97.49	85.81	89.99	81.60	78.98	87.59
1987	102.50	103.87	103.29	94.97	97.93	101.43	94.06	104.57	100.37
1988	112.75	100.81	106.19	106.90	112.54	116.73	98.92	101.41	107.71
1989	97.50	92.42	90.49	103.25	100.32	129.34	101.77	98.12	104.39
All	74.34	76.43	74.38	76.29	74.77	72.92	68.00	66.99	72.24
TOWN A									
1980	52.31	63.79	48.01	65.80	51.75	39.68	43.57	46.78	51.42
1981	55.89	61.49	49.19		45.02	55.64	42.73	45.60	52.79
1982	53.97	57.35	64.17	38.25	45.08	53.38	47.87		53.42
1983	54.68	59.35	65.97	63.87	55.78	79.66	49.46	50.53	56.74
1984	61.89	76.74	62.89	132.60	55.29	63.78	61.00	52.44	62.88
1985	81.47	80.23	90.10	66.26	82.89	80.05	79.86	65.59	78.62
1986	103.65	109.48	123.57	102.00	104.47	97.28	102.05	83.83	101.37
1987	104.71	122.80	158.01	108.46	113.99	109.06	101.02	103.02	108.30
1988	116.49	110.61	115.97	114.13	117.50	126.36	99.69	95.72	112.06
1989	108.79		107.37	87.36		108.08	92.81	119.30	106.02
All	81.09	87.48	89.21	86.55	82.18	82.15	72.78	70.39	80.14
TOWN B									
1980	22.99	62.83		45.86	30.64	41.61	40.31	37.49	41.13
1981	35.36			23.58	47.81	39.70	43.70	30.21	38.87
1982	40.36	37.16	40.23	43.38	43.56	50.75	44.67	54.60	47.85
1983	37.05	39.21	50.46	48.14	38.00	46.16	45.51	39.85	42.17
1984	45.08	47.20	48.87	44.78	48.87	51.79	62.71	46.38	51.35
1985	55.09	46.57	62.07	75.97	47.61	54.79	61.18	65.44	59.64
1986	61.77	79.56	78.73	96.04	80.42	91.14	69.84	65.82	78.54
1987	87.42	82.32	126.54	83.41	70.49	97.67	82.79	89.91	88.17
1988	84.85	91.84			86.54	81.61	96.97	99.12	92.66
1989			59.06	124.95	58.19	136.38	108.23	100.74	106.46
All	52.68	62.77	63.63	68.84	58.66	64.89	64.23	59.71	62.18
TOWN C									
1980	46.28	35.05	35.34	50.46	47.69	45.99	60.56	32.09	44.74
1981	58.67	38.02	48.41	54.03	40.27	41.38	31.31	44.17	44.99
1982	48.59	47.86		44.64	33.58	40.57	44.20	50.76	44.22
1983	45.86	56.51	43.65	46.85	36.89	40.41	20.13	24.65	42.06
1984	51.48	46.37	67.64	50.21	50.32	47.78	63.29	62.61	55.29
1985	64.33	57.46	70.41	60.51	66.62	64.07	66.68	56.92	63.58
1986	76.12	83.17	82.22	95.00	84.07	79.81	74.94	88.92	83.39
1987	104.80	95.28	92.15	90.57	94.16	98.27	105.43	116.23	100.25
1988	98.67	93.85	100.60	104.19	115.19	122.50	104.80	108.89	109.36
1999	86.21	92.42	92.92	99.32	142.44	136.49	78.44	75.73	101.88
All	69.63	70.09	72.34	75.24	79.34	73.55	67.98	76.15	73.63

Table 19-4 Inflation-Adjusted Sales Prices per Square Foot (by Zone) before 1/84 and after 12/83

	Zone (in $)								
Time	S	A	B	C	D	E	F	G	All
THREE-TOWN TOTAL (1423 SALES)									
Before	50.41	53.53	45.75	50.21	43.25	48.87	45.48	44.10	47.45
After	86.91	82.91	84.79	89.49	85.57	83.32	79.35	77.66	83.09
Percent change	+72	+55	+85	+78	+98	+70	+74	+76	+75
TOWN A (487 SALES)									
Before	54.45	60.82	56.78	61.67	50.55	60.94	47.64	48.18	54.36
After	96.18	97.23	101.37	97.21	93.13	89.97	86.16	79.76	91.73
Percent change	+77	+60	+79	+58	+84	+48	+81	+66	+69
TOWN B (449 SALES)									
Before	36.28	46.40	42.79	44.14	41.64	46.04	44.09	42.74	43.41
After	64.26	68.54	69.58	89.43	68.28	76.21	74.13	71.33	73.19
Percent change	+77	+48	+63	+103	+64	+66	+68	+67	+69
TOWN C (487 SALES)									
Before	48.95	44.03	42.73	49.50	40.05	41.31	44.42	43.40	44.24
After	77.05	74.53	83.68	85.65	89.16	84.12	79.28	83.79	82.82
Percent change	+57	+69	+96	+73	+123	+104	+78	+93	+87

Table 19-5 Number of Usable Sales (by Zone) before 1/84 and after 12/83

	Zone								
Time	S	A	B	C	D	E	F	G	All
THREE-TOWN TOTAL									
Before	73	28	28	41	36	77	67	83	433
After	139	99	77	81	105	178	133	178	990
Percent change	+36	+253	+175	+98	+192	+131	+99	+155	+129
TOWN A									
Before	47	15	6	9	9	21	25	19	151
After	83	41	16	21	26	57	47	45	336
Percent change	+77	+173	+167	+133	+189	+171	+88	+137	+123
TOWN B									
Before	12	6	4	15	13	36	30	50	166
After	17	17	14	18	23	60	61	73	283
Percent change	+42	+183	+250	+20	+77	+67	+103	+46	+70
TOWN C									
Before	14	7	18	17	14	20	12	14	116
After	39	41	47	42	56	61	25	60	371
Percent change	+179	+486	+161	+147	+300	+205	+108	+328	+220

Table 19-6 Number of Sales as a Percentage of Each Year's Total (by Zone)

	Zone (%)								
Year	S	A	B	C	D	E	F	G	All
THREE-TOWN TOTAL									
1980	16.25	8.75	8.75	11.25	8.75	13.75	15.00	17.50	100.00
1981	17.31	5.77	8.65	6.73	9.62	23.08	11.54	17.31	100.00
1982	15.24	5.71	4.76	10.48	6.67	20.95	17.14	19.05	100.00
1983	18.06	6.25	4.86	9.72	8.33	13.89	17.36	21.53	100.00
1984	12.43	8.65	7.03	3.78	5.95	23.24	14.59	24.32	100.00
1985	12.39	11.50	7.08	7.52	11.50	19.03	14.60	16.37	100.00
1986	14.03	12.22	9.05	10.41	11.76	14.03	13.57	14.93	100.00
1987	19.14	8.02	5.56	8.02	11.73	16.05	15.43	16.05	100.00
1988	13.43	11.94	8.21	8.21	14.18	17.16	8.21	18.66	100.00
1989	12.90	1.61	12.90	16.13	6.45	19.35	11.29	19.35	100.00
All	14.90	8.92	7.38	8.57	9.91	17.92	14.05	18.34	100.00
TOWN A									
1980	32.14	10.71	3.57	10.71	3.57	10.71	14.29	14.29	100.00
1981	33.33	12.82	5.13	0.00	7.69	17.95	7.69	15.38	100.00
1982	41.18	5.88	11.76	5.88	5.88	23.53	5.88	0.00	100.00
1983	26.87	8.96	1.49	7.46	5.97	10.45	25.37	13.43	100.00
1984	19.70	9.09	6.06	1.52	6.06	25.76	16.67	15.15	100.00
1985	18.42	17.11	3.95	6.58	11.84	15.79	15.79	10.53	100.00
1986	25.35	14.08	4.23	9.86	5.63	12.68	14.08	14.08	100.00
1987	32.76	8.62	1.72	6.90	10.34	13.79	13.79	12.07	100.00
1988	27.78	12.96	7.41	5.56	5.56	14.81	9.26	16.67	100.00
1989	36.36	0.00	9.09	9.09	0.00	27.27	9.09	9.09	100.00
All	26.69	11.50	4.52	6.16	7.19	16.02	14.78	13.14	100.00
TOWN B									
1980	3.85	7.69	0.00	11.54	3.85	26.92	15.38	30.77	100.00
1981	11.54	0.00	0.00	3.85	19.23	19.23	23.08	23.08	100.00
1982	5.36	3.57	5.36	10.71	1.79	23.21	23.21	26.79	100.00
1983	8.62	3.45	1.72	8.62	10.34	18.97	12.07	36.21	100.00
1984	5.77	3.85	5.77	1.92	3.85	25.00	21.15	32.69	100.00
1985	6.58	6.58	5.26	6.58	6.58	22.37	19.74	26.32	100.00
1986	5.56	6.94	6.94	11.11	13.89	19.44	19.44	16.67	100.00
1987	10.81	5.41	2.70	5.41	5.41	18.92	29.73	21.62	100.00
1988	4.55	13.64	0.00	0.00	9.09	18.18	22.73	31.82	100.00
1989	0.00	0.00	4.17	8.33	8.33	20.83	20.83	37.50	100.00
All	6.46	5.12	4.01	7.35	8.02	21.38	20.27	27.39	100.00
TOWN C									
1980	11.54	7.69	23.08	11.54	19.23	3.85	15.38	7.69	100.00
1981	5.13	2.56	17.95	15.38	5.13	30.77	7.69	15.38	100.00
1982	18.75	9.38	0.00	12.50	15.63	15.63	12.50	15.63	100.00
1983	15.79	5.26	26.32	21.05	10.53	10.53	5.26	5.26	100.00
1984	10.45	11.94	8.96	7.46	7.46	19.40	7.46	26.87	100.00
1985	12.16	10.81	12.16	9.46	16.22	18.92	8.11	12.16	100.00
1986	11.54	15.38	15.38	10.26	15.38	10.26	7.69	14.10	100.00
1987	11.94	8.96	10.45	10.45	16.42	16.42	8.96	16.42	100.00
1988	3.45	10.34	12.07	13.79	24.14	18.97	1.72	15.52	100.00
1989	14.81	3.70	22.22	25.93	7.41	14.81	3.70	7.41	100.00
All	10.88	9.86	13.35	12.11	14.37	16.63	7.60	15.20	100.00

For the three-town total set of usable sales, Zone A exhibited the lowest percentage increase, suggesting some possible negative impact. The percentage increase in average ADJSPSF for Zone S was approximately equal to the average for all study areas.

Virtually the same pattern in average ADJSPSF by zone was exhibited in Towns A and B. In Town C, on the other hand, the percentage increase after January 1, 1984, was lowest in Zone S. This finding indicated a possible further negative impact.

Number of Sales by Zone, before and after January 1, 1984

A different pattern was shown for changes in sales volume (Table 19-5). For the three-town total, the smallest percentage increase was found in Zone S. The largest percentage increase in sale volume occurred in Zone A, and the third highest percentage increase occurred in Zone B.

A spotty pattern of percentage increase in sales volume by zone appeared when before and after sales volumes were compared from town to town. This pattern suggested that any negative market response was confined to the SSAs themselves.

Percentage Distribution of Number of Sales, by Zone and by Year

Table 19-6 expresses the number of sales in each zone as a percentage of total sales for that year.

For the three-town total, no consistent pattern of relative change emerged among the zones closest to the SSAs. That inconsistency became even more evident when data for the individual towns were considered. There was substantial variation over time by zone from town to town. Moreover, the evidence suggested a short-term (1984–85) avoidance of properties in Zone S. The small numbers of sales in individual zones in each town in each year made it both difficult and potentially misleading to draw further general conclusions.

Multiple Regression Analysis

The dependent variable used in all MRA models was inflation-adjusted sales price per square foot of living area (ADJSPSF). Two time variables were employed: DDATE (date of deed: year and month) and BEFAFT, which indicated whether the deed was recorded before January 1, 1984, or after December 31, 1983. If the recording occurred after December 31, 1983, BEFAFT was assigned a value of 1; if the sale occurred prior to January 1, 1984, the value of BEFAFT was 0.

The price influence of all reported distance zone locations was compared with that of Zone G, the most distant zone from each SSA. Therefore, the values or coefficients for each of the reported seven zone variables (S and A through F) represent dollar differences in comparison with the price effects of a Zone G location. A negative coefficient meant that the dollar level of price influence for the zone in question was *lower* than that for Zone G. A positive coefficient meant that it was *higher* than that for Zone G.

Adjusted Sales Price per Square Foot as the Dependent Variable

MRA was applied separately to the three-town total data set and to the Town A, Town B, and Town C data subsets.

The results were impressive statistically. The coefficient of multiple determination (R-squared), which indicated the percent of variance in ADJSPSF explained by the independent variables, was at acceptable to high levels. Moreover, the high F ratios in the models mean that it was almost totally unlikely that the results occurred by chance.

Both DDATE and BEFAFT were highly significant and *positive*, which indicated a continuing (implicitly linear) increase in ADJSPSF over the entire study period. Lot size and square feet of living area were next most significant, followed by number of garage stalls and age at the time of sale.

In Town A, *none* of the zone variables was statistically significant. Moreover, they all were positive. In Town B, on the other hand, *all* zone coefficients were negative. Coefficients for Zones S, B, and D were statistically significant. These results indicated a probable negative influence on ADJSPSF associated with Zones S, B, and D (and possibly Zone A) locations relative to Zone G.

In Town C, as in Town A, *none* of the zone variables was statistically significant. The Zone S coefficient was negative in both time models, but there was a high probability that this was a chance occurrence.

In summary, there was no evidence of negative price impacts from locations in Zones S, A, and B in Town A; there was a small but almost totally insignificant negative impact in Zone S in Town C. In Town B, on the other hand, the negative influences of proximity to the Superfund site (Zones S, A, and B as well as D) were both apparent and statistically significant.

Time–Distance Interactions

The MRA models discussed above took into consideration the separate price influences of both time and distance from the pertinent SSA in each town. Other property and transaction characteristics also were included in the analysis with ADJSPSF as the dependent variable.

RECGC made further tests in an attempt to identify and measure the *combined* or *joint* effects of time and distance zone location on ADJSPSF. Special emphasis was placed on "time" after January 1, 1984.

In MRA models, any existing joint or combined effect can be identified and measured through the use of an interactive variable. In this instance, the interactions of the time and location variables were calculated and tested.

(Table 19-7 shows the interactions of the deed date with each of the distance zone indicators to produce the seven time–distance interactive variables included in the models. Similarly, Table 19-8 shows the results of using before–after/distance zone interactive variables. Tables 19-7 and 19-8 identify the same highly significant variables: DDATE or BEFAFT, SFLIVARE and LOTSIZE. AGE and GARSTALS also are significant.)

All of the distance zone variables were not significant in the three-town total data set. Similarly, all the time–distance interactive variables were not significant except for D/BEFAFT (which was positive). Only the interactive variable for Zone B in Table 19-7 was negative; all the others in both models were positive. For the three-town total data set, therefore, no post-announcement negative effect of any consequence on ADJSPSF was associated with proximity to the SSAs.

Table 19-7 Comparison of MRA Coefficients and *t*-values Time–Distance Interactions[a]

Variable	Three-town total	Town A	Town B	Town C
SFLIVAREA	−0.01	−0.01	−0.01	−0.03
	(14.67)**	(−6.85)**	(−6.56)**	(−12.49)**
AGE	−0.16	−0.16	−0.25	−0.16
	(−4.47)**	(−2.49)*	(−4.40)**	(−2.56)*
DDATE	8.30	8.14	7.74	7.97
	(15.04)**	(9.21)**	(9.51)**	(7.39)**
LOTSIZE	0.0007	0.0008	0.0007	0.0011
	(16.01)**	(4.66)**	(7.68)**	(15.55)**
GARSTALS	6.64	2.60	5.66	9.99
	(5.56)**	(1.37)	(2.74)**	(5.07)**
Zone S	−60.55	−95.68	−113.72	−51.23
	(−0.88)	(−1.06)	(−0.66)	(−0.37)
Zone A	−29.59	−87.86	49.55	−51.03
	(−0.34)	(−0.76)	(0.26)	(−0.34)
Zone B	18.66	−111.46	−160.13	50.16
	(0.22)	(−0.78)	(−0.64)	(0.42)
Zone C	−0.05	15.78	−132.78	32.48
	(−0.0007)	(0.12)	(−0.90)	(0.26)
Zone D	−100.61	−215.06	151.70	−163.19
	(−1.27)	(−1.53)	(1.08)	(−1.30)
Zone E	−76.04	−162.86	−111.82	−74.62
	(−1.14)	(−1.57)	(−1.08)	(−0.61)
Zone F	−79.97	−234.42	−36.98	−5.23
	(−1.11)	(−2.11)*	(−0.35)	(−0.04)
S*DDATE	0.71	1.13	1.13	0.58
	(0.88)	(1.07)	(0.55)	(0.36)
A*DDATE	0.35	1.09	−0.60	0.59
	(0.35)	(0.81)	(−0.32)	(0.33)
B*DDATE	−0.23	1.36	1.68	−0.56
	(−0.23)	(0.81)	(0.58)	(−0.39)
C*DDATE	0.03	−0.12	1.54	−0.36
	(0.04)	(−0.08)	(0.88)	(−0.25)
D*DDATE	1.16	2.55	−1.91	1.94
	(1.25)	(1.55)	(−1.16)	(1.33)
E*DDATE	0.90	1.96	1.27	0.84
	(1.15)	(1.61)	(1.04)	(0.59)
F*DDATE	0.95	2.77	0.38	0.09
	(1.12)	(2.13)*	(0.31)	(0.05)
R-Squared	0.62	0.69	0.62	0.71
F Ratio	80.91	35.80	24.25	39.18
Standard error of estimate	20.75	17.29	21.14	20.19
Durbin–Watson	1.54	1.79	1.58	1.83
Number of Sales	1403	485	445	473

[Note: Numbers in parentheses are *t*-values.]
[a]Time is deed date; ADJSPSF is the dependent variable.
*Significant at the 0.05 level.
**Significant at the 0.01 level.

Table 19-8 Comparison of MRA Coefficients and *t*-values Time–Distance Interactions: BEFAFT January 1, 1984[a]

Variable	Three-town total	Town A	Town B	Town C
SFLIVAREA	−0.01	−0.01	−0.01	−0.03
	(13.78)**	(−5.30)**	(−7.01)**	(−11.41)**
Age	−0.10	−0.10	−0.23	−0.09
	(−2.36)*	(−1.24)	(−3.54)**	(−1.18)
BEFAFT	30.00	30.36	29.94	26.69
	(9.12)**	(5.06)**	(6.79)**	(3.63)**
GARSTALS	5.88	0.94	6.90	8.23
	(4.14)**	(0.38)	(2.93)**	(3.43)**
LOTSIZE	0.0008	0.0009	0.0008	0.0011
	(15.19)**	(4.40)**	(7.22)**	(14.58)**
Zone S	−4.94	−7.74	−19.78	−4.30
	(−1.19)	(−1.22)	(−2.51)*	(−0.44)
Zone A	−1.99	−2.94	−11.80	0.30
	(−0.36)	(−0.37)	(−1.13)	(0.03)
Zone B	−7.29	−3.11	−17.58	−4.01
	(−1.34)	(−0.30)	(−1.41)	(−0.45)
Zone C	−2.02	−1.87	−9.63	−0.15
	(−0.42)	(−0.21)	(−1.35)	(−0.02)
Zone D	−8.75	−5.98	−9.84	−5.41
	(−1.76)	(−0.67)	(−1.29)	(−0.57)
Zone E	−1.37	−0.02	−6.00	−7.35
	(−0.34)	(−0.00)	(−1.13)	(−0.81)
Zone F	−3.43	−3.29	−7.87	−6.65
	(−0.85)	(−1.22)	(−1.42)	(−0.68)
S*BEFAFT	7.12	13.58	−1.08	4.59
	(1.47)	(1.89)	(−0.11)	(0.43)
A*BEFAFT	2.25	7.69	−0.39	0.22
	(0.36)	(0.86)	(−0.03)	(0.02)
B*BEFAFT	9.33	8.96	−1.51	12.02
	(1.47)	(0.75)	(−0.11)	(1.21)
C*BEFAFT	10.35	11.21	10.51	8.43
	(1.81)	(1.06)	(1.13)	(0.84)
D*BEFAFT	11.62	8.74	−2.62	16.78
	(2.02)*	(0.84)	(−0.28)	(1.63)
E*BEFAFT	1.32	3.05	0.09	6.04
	(0.28)	(0.37)	(0.01)	(0.62)
F*BEFAFT	5.81	8.38	3.45	10.70
	(1.18)	(1.03)	(0.50)	(0.95)
R-Squared	0.47	0.49	0.51	0.58
F Ratio	43.37	15.34	15.22	21.47
Standard error of estimate	24.60	22.18	24.10	24.51
Durbin–Watson	1.70	1.96	1.66	1.95
Number of Sales	1403	485	445	473

Note: Numbers in parentheses are *t*-values.
[a]ADJSPSF is dependent variable.
*Significant at the 0.05 level.
**Significant at the 0.01 level.

Very similar results were found for Town A. Only the Zone C/DDATE interactive variable in Table 19-7 was negative. All others, especially for Zones S, A, and B, were *positive*. Moreover, only the positive interactive variable for Zone F in Table 19-7 was statistically significant. None of the BEFAFT interactions was statistically significant.

In Town B, on the other hand, the interactive variables for Zones A and D in Table 19-7 and for Zones S, A, B, and D in Table 19-8 were all *negative*. All others were positive. None of the interactive variables for Town B was statistically significant, however.

In Town C, only the interactive variables for Zones B and C in Table 19-7 were negative, but both zones were quite insignificant. *All* interactive variables were positive in Table 19-8. *No* interactive variable was statistically significant in either Table 19-7 or 19-8.

These interactive variable findings showed a clear and reasonably consistent pattern. Any negative effects that could be identified and measured in association with proximity to one of the SSAs *after* January 1, 1984, were confined to Town B. Even the negative effects in Town B were not statistically significant, however; they could easily have occurred by chance. In Towns A and C, no measurable or discernible negative effect from proximity to the SSA was indicated, especially after January 1, 1984. Moreover, the interactive model results indicated that the passage of time after the announcement did not enhance or exacerbate any negative effects that a location close to the SSA in Town B already had on ADJSPSF.

SUMMARY

A total data set of 1423 usable sales of single-family residential properties in three towns in northern New Jersey was studied over the period July 1, 1980, through June 30, 1989. Detailed property and sales transaction information was gathered from public records, published sources and field inspections. The location of each sales property was identified by distance zone from the boundaries of a SSA in each town. Sales within the SSAs themselves, both before and after January 1, 1984, also were included.

The data sets were subjected to a series of statistical tests to provide a basis for reaching judgments about: (1) whether proximity to a known SSA had a negative effect on residential property values in any of the three towns; (2) how far away from the SSA any negative price effect was felt; and (3) how persistently any such negative effect was felt over time. Three statistical procedures were employed:

- Simple comparisons of averages resulted in graphs depicting the movement of average ADJSPSF in different distance zones.
- Percentage changes were calculated by comparing averages of ADJSPSF before and after January 1, 1984. Trends in sales volume were similarly tested and compared. In addition, changes in the percentage mix of sales by zone for each year within each town were compared.
- Multiple regression analysis received major emphasis. ADJSPSF was the focal dependent variable.

Within MRA, the standard Hedonic Pricing Model was applied using two time measures: (1) deed date, a continuous variable; and (2) BEFAFT January 1, 1984, a binary variable. The coefficients for all reported distance zones represented incremental differences from the price of the most distant zone (G) which served as a control.

Finally, the Hedonic Pricing Model was modified to incorporate time–distance interactions of both deed date and BEFAFT time in combination with distance zone.

CONCLUSIONS

The results of the statistical tests and their findings led to the following conclusions.

Only in Town B was there any systematic, significant negative effect on ADJSPSF *and* on sales volume for properties close to the SSA. In Towns A and C, where remediation and cleanup were completed promptly, no systematic or significant negative effect was evident except in sales volume in 1989. The period of this decline in sales was too brief to provide a basis for generalization.

After January 1, 1984, patterns of negative effects on ADJSPSF were spotty, un-systematic and generally insignificant. The only consistent negative impacts appeared in Town B, in Zones S, A, B and D. Even there, negative interactive time–distance variables were not significant. Most consistent was a lower rate of increase in average ADJSPSF in Zone S generally and in Zones A and B in Town B.

Sales volumes in the distance zones closest to the SSAs did not decline perceptibly in the years immediately following the December, 1983, announcement. Any decreases that did occur were quite temporary. In 1988 and 1989, however, when the general level of residential sales volume decreased throughout the market area, the declines were much sharper in Zones S, A and B. No direct association with proximity to the SSAs was demonstrated, however.

No measurable negative impact beyond the SSA was evident in Towns A and B. Even there, the post-announcement effects were not significant. In Town B, on the other hand, negative price (and sales volume) effects were found with properties located at least 500 feet from the outer boundary of the SSA through Zone B. It is arguable that the negative impact extended through Zone D (1500 feet away from the SSA) in Town B, even though the measurable effects in intervening Zone C was *positive*.

Standard MRA using the Hedonic Pricing Model supported and clarified these conclusions based on comparisons of averages and comparisons of trends. Negative statistically significant coefficients associated with location were found in Town B only. There the coefficients for Zones S, A, and B were both negative and statistically significant. There was no such impact in Town A or Town C.

The foregoing conclusions also were reinforced when interactive time–distance variables were incorporated into the Hedonic Pricing Model. The negative impacts noted in Zones S, A and B in Town B were generally not significant; nevertheless, there was a continuing negative impact associated with property locations in Zones S, A, and B after January 1, 1984, in Town B only, through at least June, 1989.

Any continuing, significant negative price impacts associated with proximity to an SSA were limited to Town B. The SSA within Town B was the site within which barrels of radioactive soil were prominently stored in the open for more than two years with attendant continuing publicity. Several contaminated properties in this town were fenced off, and danger signs warning of radiation hazards were prominently displayed.

The Superfund sites in Towns A and C, on the other hand, were cleaned up expeditiously, and they had none of the adverse publicity that persisted in Town B. As a result, their potential negative impacts were effectively eliminated. Accordingly, no significant negative effects on ADJSPSF or sales volume emerged. Indeed, with the exception of properties within the Superfund site itself in 1988 and 1989, no negative price effect was identified in Towns A and C.

Therefore, the market response to proximity to a known SSA was a direct function of the speed and apparent effectiveness of any remediation or cleanup effort. These results were generally consistent with findings from other, similarly designed and executed statistical studies in other states.

20. The Counselor as Expert Witness: Hazards, Pitfalls, and Defenses

WILLIAM N. KINNARD, JR

There is a rich and varied literature on the topic of How To Be An Effective Expert Witness. In the real estate field, most of the material appears in professional journal articles, papers, or monographs which focus on real estate appraisers and the handling of valuation issues. There is an even richer and fuller literature in law journals and texts that deals with *How to Handle Expert Witnesses*, obviously addressed to attorneys specializing in litigation.

Real estate litigators regularly publish articles addressed to real estate professionals (again, mostly appraisers), with checklists of Dos and Don'ts for the real estate expert whose opinions will be given in court or before any hearing board or tribunal. These checklists tend to have two important features in common. First, they generally cover the same content, although organized differently and frequently using different words. Second, they are always presented from the point of view of the attorney, to ease the professional burden on the attorney. Few if any of these written statements by attorneys appear to be aimed at easing the burden or pain of the expert real estate witness.

Real estate counseling is different from appraisal, and The Counselors of Real Estate are different from professional real estate appraisers. Yet there admittedly is considerable overlap between the two disciplines and their practitioners. This might help explain why almost nothing has been published on the particular needs and requirements of real estate *counselors* when they are called upon to give expert testimony in their capacity as real estate *counselors*.

Reprinted from *Real Estate Issues* with the permission of the Counselors of Real Estate of the National Association of Realtors®, vol. 18, No. 2, 1993.

This chapter is specifically directed toward four issues that are likely to confront any Counselor of Real Estate (CRE) called upon to give expert testimony in his capacity as a counselor.

REVIEW OF GENERAL RULES AND ADMONITIONS FOR EXPERT WITNESSES

The published lists of Dos and Don'ts for expert witnesses generally, for real estate appraisers, for real estate academics, and for other real estate professionals can serve well as an appropriate starting point for any CRE about to give expert testimony. Participating in a deposition is every bit as important as providing formal court testimony. Indeed, a deposition is simply one type of formal testimony in a different format: It consists almost exclusively of questioning of the expert witness, in an adversarial mode, by the attorney(s) for the opposing side.

Whether involved in direct testimony, cross-examination, rebuttal testimony, deposition, or simply serving as an informed observer of the testimony of others (when permitted by the rules of the particular jurisdiction), the CRE serving as an expert witness needs to follow certain general rules and guidelines. The literature on expert testimony is full of long checklists for expert witnesses to follow. There are very few short lists.

A good rule for memorization of facts, including checklists, is: Don't do it. When one memorizes, one typically gets the materials *almost* right. In court proceedings, "almost right" is not good enough for the counselor serving as an expert witness.

Nevertheless, there are a few points that need to be emphasized as "rules to live by" for CREs serving as expert witnesses.

1. *Tell the truth.* Remember, a witness has sworn to "tell the truth, the whole truth, and nothing but the truth."
2. *Be prepared.* Indeed, be over-prepared (hyperprepared).
3. *Be skeptical.* Don't believe anything that is presented during deposition or trial proceedings as *fact*. Always treat the *facts* presented by anyone else as assumed conditions in a hypothetical case.
4. *Answer only the question asked.* Don't embellish. Above all, do not volunteer information beyond the direct answer to the question asked. (This can be particularly difficult, especially when it is manifestly clear to the CRE that he knows so much more about the topic than the examining attorney does.)
5. *When a question is asked, think first,* pause (take a deep breath), answer fully and honestly, then shut up.
6. To the extent possible, try to *keep answers straightforward and understandable* to the court: the judge(s) and/or the jury. It is not necessary for opposing counsel to understand your answers. (Indeed, he will feign confusion or lack of understanding on many occasions.) However, it *is* necessary for members of the jury or any tribunal to understand you.
7. To the extent possible, *address answers to the jury, the judge, or the tribunal.*
8. *Keep answers short.* Remember that the vast majority of questions can be answered "Yes," "No," "I don't know," "I don't remember," or "I don't understand; please rephrase the question." If a question can be answered that way, it should be.

9. *Keep to the point.* Try not to stray. Once again, do not volunteer information.
10. Difficult as it may be, work hard *never* to *become visibly upset.* Do not treat negative comments or implications about oneself as personal assaults or affronts. Always strive to be polite and courteous, no matter what the provocation.
11. *Avoid making assumptions or drawing inferences from questions asked.* Accept any assumptions provided in the statement of a question, and be sure to label them as "assumptions" in your response. Also, recognize that the answer to any question that begins "Isn't it true that..." is probably "No."
12. In the courtroom, the hearing room, the deposition room, and nearby, *maintain an outward appearance of independence, objectivity, even aloofness.*
13. *Be prepared* and *tell the truth.*

Within the framework of these general guidelines, four major concerns require particular attention by real estate counselors who serve as expert witnesses.

PROFESSIONAL AND ETHICAL STANDARDS

Real estate counseling is not as widely recognized or as carefully delineated a discipline as are, for example, real estate appraisal, real estate management, and real estate brokerage. Indeed, the necessarily broad, sometimes comprehensive, nature of counseling means that it is perceived and interpreted differently by clients, observers, and practitioners alike. It may appear somewhat as the elephant did to the blind men in the fable. For Counselors of Real Estate, both the CRE Code of Ethics and the Code of Ethics of the National Association of Realtors (NAR) are applicable to their behavior in the preparation and presentation of testimony as an expert witness.

Many attorneys are unfamiliar with the Codes of Ethics and Standards of Professional Practice applicable to the work of the CRE. It is the obligation and responsibility of CRE members to make attorneys with whom they are working aware of the contents and implications of applicable professional standards and ethical codes.

The situation of the individual CRE may be more involved if the individual is professionally designated in any other organization(s) that also has a Code of Ethics and Standards of Professional Practice. This is particularly true if the CRE is a professionally designated appraiser in an organization that subscribes to the *Uniform Standards of Professional Appraisal Practice (USPAP),* which are listed in the "Suggested Readings" at the end of this chapter.

The reason for this particular concern is that, within *USPAP,* Standards IV and V deal specifically with "Real Estate Consulting." *USPAP* establishes requirements and specifications for the conduct of a "Real Estate Consulting" assignment and for reporting the results of that assignment. Offering testimony in a trial, a hearing, or a deposition as an expert witness constitutes reporting the results of a real estate consulting assignment, within the framework of *USPAP.*

The situation is further complicated by the fact that real estate appraisers must be licensed or certified in every state, the District of Columbia and Puerto Rico as a result of Section XI of the federal Financial Institutions Reform, Recovery, and Enforcement Act of 1989. In many states, it is a misdemeanor (or worse) to practice real estate appraisal without a license or certification. Moreover, some states define "real estate appraisal" so broadly that it encompasses many activities that would ordinarily be regarded as real estate counseling. Examples include feasibility analysis, market analysis, marketability analysis, investment analysis, and highest and best use analysis, to cite a few. In those states, it is necessary to become licensed or certified as a real estate appraiser in order to carry out such counseling activities for a fee. That includes testifying about them in court or at hearings.

In addition, a handful of states include real estate counseling as an activity that requires a real estate broker's (or salesperson's) license.

It is therefore critically necessary for a CRE contemplating an assignment that is expected to require expert witness testimony in a state in which the CRE is not currently licensed or certified as a real estate broker or real estate appraiser, to investigate carefully the requirements of that state. Licensing and certification can be a time-consuming and expensive process. The client and the client's attorney should be aware of any time and expense required for licensing or certification, and, from the outset, that should be included in the counseling fee agreement.

One implication of having *USPAP* apply to the real estate counseling assignment is that CREs would be required to develop and maintain a written record of the data, notes, and analyses. That written file must be made available in any court proceedings (including depositions). The expert often cannot legally respond positively to an instruction not to put anything in writing. This is simply one example of the concerns that may confront a CRE serving as an expert witness, as well as the attorney(s) with whom he is working.

HYPERPREPARATION

It is axiomatic that expert witnesses should be thoroughly and fully prepared. For the real estate counselor, this means more than simply reviewing any factual information, notes of meetings, or field inspections and reports prepared by others. Particularly if no written report (as opposed to the *USPAP* required written file) is to be prepared, and therefore referred to during the course of deposition or trial testimony, the counselors and the attorneys with whom they are working must thoroughly understand not only the problem and its proposed solution, but each other's mindset and approach to that problem.

Depending on the experience and knowledge of the attorney with the particular topic at issue, it may be necessary for the CRE to instruct the attorney in the technical and analytical aspects of the problem, at least to the extent that the work and testimony of the CRE impinge on the resolution of that problem. This takes time which needs to be built into the original proposal and budget.

An important rule in dealing with clients and attorneys in litigation is: "No surprises." Therefore, the CRE has a responsibility to identify the apparent level of expertise and technical understanding that the attorney possesses. This needs to be done at an early meeting before the final work schedule and budget are completed.

Ample time must be budgeted to cover any necessary education of the attorney, review of the counselor's own deposition, review, and discussion of technical reports of others, and preparation for the counselor's testimony. When reports of others are to be reviewed, it is imperative to make sure that complete copies of the reports, including *all* appendix or addendum materials, are received for review. The text alone is rarely enough. Failure to review everything that is presented in the reports of others, as well as the complete transcript of any depositions of other experts or participants in the proceeding, can lead to embarrassment at least and impeachment of the counselor's position and testimony at worst.

If the counselor is to provide independent, objective, technical, professional opinion testimony, then he should not simultaneously serve as an advocate for the client and the client's attorney. The objectivity and credibility of excellent testimony can be undermined quickly if the counselor is seen passing notes to the client's attorney or conferring with the attorney while the trial is in progress. This is particularly true if it occurs while experts for the opposing side are being examined or cross-examined.

It is perfectly acceptable and appropriate under any standards to serve as an advocate for the client's interest. This should be done openly from the outset and not in conflict with an initial appearance of disinterested objectivity and independence.

Hyperpreparation in advance of testimony can pay substantial dividends when the counselor testifies, both on direct and cross-examination. If the CRE takes the witness stand with no notes or documents in his possession, the impression of thorough knowledge and understanding of both the counselor's field of expertise and the facts of the case is greatly enhanced. Any materials that need to be consulted can be provided by the attorney for the client, or even by the opposing counsel.

In the first instance, the importance of thorough advance preparation is underscored. If the attorney with whom the counselor is working has all the documents needed to support and sustain the counselor's direct testimony readily at hand and is thoroughly familiar with their use and application in the presentation, there is no need for the counselor to have any extra notes in his possession (especially since they are all discoverable). Everything required for reference will be available through the client's attorney.

On cross-examination, it is always permissible for the witness to request a document to which the cross-examining attorney is referring or from which that attorney is reading. That request will not always be granted, but the overall result is that a well-prepared expert witness need not have any document with him unless it is provided by one of the attorneys involved.

MAINTAIN FOCUS

No one individual is an expert in everything. Moreover, the scope of the problem which is the source of the litigation, coupled with the scope of the counselor's assignment, sets the limits of expertise and knowledge that a qualified professional counselor can and should claim in any proceeding. If unchallenged or allowed questions on cross-examination go beyond the scope of the assignment, especially if they go beyond the scope of the counselor's factual knowledge, then the best response is simply "I don't know." Assuming knowledge beyond one's level, stretching the limits of one's actual experiences or claiming expertise in areas where one is *not a bona fide* expert, almost inevitably leads to discomfort, lost credibility, and disaster.

There is a natural tendency to want to accommodate a questioner, and, of course, not to admit one's own limitations in public. Nevertheless, sharp and clear limits to the claimed expertise, knowledge, and opinions of the real estate counselor need to be set. This is part of the hyperpreparation already discussed. It is the responsibility of CREs alone, however, when they are on the witness stand being cross-examined.

This sharp and narrow focus is especially important when the cross-examining attorney presents hypothetical situations based on assumed facts and fails to identify them as hypothetical conditions or assumptions. Recognizing this potential hazard takes experience and continuous alertness on the part of the CRE being cross-examined. An important part of one's education to become an expert witness is to be a spectator at trials relating to problems in which the counselor is not personally or professionally involved. Also, participating in a deposition frequently gives important clues to the approach, technique, and mind set of the opposing counsel. This can be an important learning experience for the expert witness CRE, prior to cross-examination before a judge and possibly a jury as well.

MAINTAIN POISE AND OBJECTIVITY

The real purpose of cross-examination is to discredit the expert witnesses and their opinions. In addition to eliciting facts and information, the cross-examining attorney will frequently call into question the counselor's skill and training, experience, objectivity, and integrity. If CREs have given expert witness testimony previously in similar cases, excerpts from the transcript of that testimony, often read out of context, may be used in an attempt to impeach the counselors with their own words. Worse still, if the CRE has published articles in journals or books, similar excerpts out of context may well be read to try to demonstrate inconsistency and therefore untoward advocacy on the part of the counselor.

This tactic by opposing counsel requires the counselor to be particularly alert and to focus on the precise wording of every question. This is particularly the case when the question is a lengthy oral essay with a rising inflection or "Isn't that right?" at the end. The longer and more involved the question, the greater the probability that it makes sense for the counselor to ask that the question be reread, repeated, or rephrased.

Also, it is quite important to be aware that the attorney with whom the counselor is working may (and undoubtedly will) raise objections to questions, or statements disguised as questions, posed by the cross-examining attorney. This is yet another reason why it is important to develop the habit of pausing before answering *any* question and to do so regularly and consistently. Once an objection is raised, the counselor should remain silent until instructed to proceed. If the argument over any objection is prolonged and distracting, it is both proper and wise to ask to have the question reread or rephrased.

One particular hazard in cross-examination is to permit the cross-examining attorney to misuse or adapt technical terminology without challenge to suit the purposes of the question. The CRE as expert witness must be sensitive to this and, before responding to the substance of the question, correct any such misuse, or abuse of technical real estate terminology.

Similarly, opposing counsel may misstate facts on the record or mischaracterize previous testimony, both of the CRE expert witness or of others. To the extent that the counselor has knowledge that a misstatement or mischaracterization has been made, any such error should be corrected before the question is answered. If the counselor does not have such knowledge, or is not sure, then response to the question should be prefaced with "On the assumption that the assertions that you have made are correct ..."

Counselors should never take any attempts to impugn their testimony, opinions, skill, experience, objectivity, or integrity as personal attacks. This may well be difficult in some circumstances, but as expert witnesses on the stand, they should never show upset, annoyance, or aggravation. That is easier to say than to do, but it is important. The objective must always be to appear calm, in control, thoughtful, objective, courteous, and totally believable.

Knowledge, skill, and hyperpreparation can lead to this posture. One should try to emulate Tennyson's Sir Galahad: "My strength is as the strength of ten, because my heart is pure."

CONCLUSIONS

Whether for the first or fiftieth time, CREs called upon to serve as expert witnesses, to present their professional opinion, should first identify whether they are qualified to accept the assignment. In this instance, qualification includes identifying whether some form of license or certification is required in the state in which the testimony is to be given. If the CRE decide to go ahead with the assignment, then the necessity for hyperpreparation must be recognized from the outset in preliminary discussions and budgetary allocations with the client and the client's attorney. CREs should study their favorite list of Dos and Don'ts as a refresher.

As an objective, independent expert, the CRE must create and maintain an aura of impeccable integrity, skill, and expertise based on experience in order to develop and maintain credibility.

Continuing alertness and care in responding to *all* questions (especially under cross-examination) should be the unflagging approach to serving as an expert witness. Moreover, as an independent, objective expert, the counselor serving as an expert witness is literally alone. One may be employed by a party, but such employment does not mean that the counselor has been "bought." Rather, the counselor's knowledge, experience, and expertise have only been rented for the duration of the case. Consistency of thought, of oral presentation, and of conclusions in similar circumstances is an absolute necessity.

None of this is easy, but if it were, the demand for really capable counselor expert witnesses would not be as great, nor would the rewards and satisfactions. There is, in all probability, no better opportunity for the CRE to expand knowledge, sharpen analytical skills, and gain experience in such an intensive, concentrated fashion.

Throughout the entire process of preparation and participation in litigation requiring expert witness testimony by a CRE, the words of Polonius to Laertes in *Hamlet* can serve the counselor well: "This above all: To thine own self be true, and it must follow, as the night the day, thou canst not then be false to any man."

SUGGESTED READING

1. Appraisal Standards Board, *Uniform Standards of Professional Appraisal Practice.* The Appraisal Foundation, Washington, DC. January 1993 Revision.
2. Baen, John S., Waller, Theresa H., and Waller, Neil G., Real Estate Professionals as Expert Witnesses. *The Appraisal Journal,* January 1988.
3. Black, Roy T. and Carn, Neil G., The Real Estate Academic as Expert Witness. Presented at American Real Estate Society Annual Conference, Key West, Florida, April 1993.
4. Carn, Neil G., When the Academic Performs as an Expert Witness: Professional and Ethical Considerations. Presented at American Real Estate Society Annual Conference, Key West, Florida, April 1993.
5. Carn, Neil G. and Rabianski, Joseph, *The Appraiser as Expert Witness,* Revised Edition. Society of Real Estate Appraisers, Chicago, IL. 1988.
6. Carn, Neil G., Rabianski, Joseph, and Vernor, James D., Trial Techniques of Expert Witnesses. *Real Estate Review,* 1986, Spring.
7. Danner, Douglas, *Expert Witness Checklists.* The Lawyers Co-Operative Publishing Co., Rochester, NY. 1983. (Cumulative Supplement issued March 1992).
8. Dombroff, Mark A., *Expert Witnesses in Civil Trials, Effective Preparation and Presentation.* The Lawyers Co-Operative Publishing Co., Rochester, NY. 1987.
9. Feder, Harold A., *Succeeding as an Expert Witness: Increasing Your Impact and Income.* Van Nostrand Reinhold, New York, NY. 1991.
10. Grover, Michael R., *Expert Witness: The Forensic Appraiser.* Appraisal Institute of Canada, Winnipeg, MB. December 1991.
11. International Association of Assessing Officers, Use and Destruction of Expert Witnesses. *Papers and Proceedings: 12th Annual IAAO Legal Seminar.* International Association of Assessing Officers, Chicago, IL. 1993.
12. McCann, William A., The Real Estate Appraiser's Role as an Expert Witness in Zoning Matters. *The Appraisal Journal,* January 1991.
13. McCracken, Daniel D., *Public Policy and the Expert: Ethical Problems of the Witness.* The Council on Religion and International Affairs, New York, NY. 1971.
14. Poynter, Dan, *Expert Witness Handbook: Tips and Techniques for the Litigation Consultant.* Para Publishing, Santa Barbara, CA. 1987.
15. Rabianski, Joseph and Carn, Neil G., Cross-examination: How to Protect Yourself and the Appraisal Report. *The Appraisal Journal,* October 1992.
16. Ratcliff, Richard U., What is the Role of the Professional Appraiser as a Real Estate Analyst and Consultant? *The Real Estate Appraiser and Analyst,* September–October 1969.
17. Seymour, Charles F., More and More of My Reports Are Valueless. *The Appraisal Journal,* October 1967.
18. Shampton, John F., Waller, Theresa H., and Waller, Neil G., Appraisal Malpractice: Sources of Liability and Damages. *The Appraisal Journal,* July 1988.
19. Thomas, Deborah W. and Gregson, Terry, The Real Estate Appraiser in Tax Court. *The Appraisal Journal,* July 1988.

Part III. Testimonials

21. List of Testimonial Letters

William A. Blake, Director, Acquisitions, UBS Realty Investors, LLC, former student
Dr Sandy Bond, Senior Lecturer, University of Auckland, New Zealand, co-author
Paul A. Champagne, CRE, MAI, Vice President, CIGNA Real Estate, former student and colleague
Dr John M. Clapp, Professor, University of Connecticut, colleague
Mary Beth Geckler, colleague at University of Connecticut and the Real Estate Counseling Group of CT
Mark H. Goldman, Goldman Realty Corporation, former student and colleague
Edward F. Heberger, Executive Vice President, CB Richard Ellis, former student and colleague
Dr Keith B. Johnson, Professor Emeritus, University of Connecticut, colleague
Jeffrey Kinnard, son and business partner
Dr John R. Knight, Associate Professor, University of the Pacific, colleague
Paul J. Lagassey, Eastern Investments, LLC, former student
Dr Stephen D. Messner, Professor Emeritus, University of Connecticut, colleague
Dr Mike E. Miles, Principal, Guggenheim Partners, colleague
Dr Bill Mundy, MAI, CRE, CEO, Mundy Associates LLC, co-author
Judith Bartell Paesani, former assistant director, Center for Real Estate, University of Connecticut, colleague
Elliott B. Pollack, Esq., Pullman & Comley, LLC, colleague
Frederick J. Richard, Vice President, CB Richard Ellis, former student
Gregory F. Richo, former student
Dr Dan Swango, MAI, CRE, Swango International, colleague

UBS Realty Investors, LLC, Hartford, CT, colleagues and friends
Bruce R. Weber, MAI, Director, Integra Realty Resources, colleague

Dr. Kinnard was my instructor for several classes at the University of Connecticut in 1980 and 1981. He also taught several of the weeklong Appraisal Institute courses I attended. I later hired him as an expert witness representing my employer, a bank, which was a defendant in a jury trial.

In the classroom, he had a strong presence with a superb command of the English language. He would pace about, gesturing with his hands, sometimes raising his index finger at a concluding point. Bill had a tremendous cadence in his speech, often enunciating the last consonant in a word (worDUH). The students he taught at the University of Connecticut were upperclassmen, mostly real estate majors, and they knew his stature and treated him with respect. This made for productive classes. His reputation preceded him.

Bill was a master at using a few short words to simplify a complex subject matter. With regard to investment analysis, he would often remind us, "who gets what when?" and its corollary, "who pays what when?" Another favorite of his was "which value, and to whom?"

Bill treated his students to his dry sense of humor with deadpan delivery. When talking about comparables, he would quote a joke that I think came from Henny Youngman:

"How is your wife?"

"Compared with what?"

Bill shared his wisdom with his students. When talking about forecasting, something appraisers have to do, he once remarked,

> … No one knows what will happen in the future and no one could, because if they did know they would change their actions and those changes would alter the future that they thought they know.

He made this comment very matter-of-factly, yet it is a concept that is philosophically deep, while undisputedly true.

William A. Blake
Director, Acquisitions
UBS Realty Investors, LLC
Hartford, CT

I first met Bill at the ARES conference at Lake Tahoe in 1996. He had asked Elaine Worzala to be introduced to me as he had heard that I was doing research on the impact of high power transmission lines on residential property values in New Zealand, a research area he was very familiar with. As a newcomer to the academic scene, I was humbled and impressed by this distinguished professor's interest in me and my research: a young, fresh "unknown" from the down-under country of New Zealand.

Subsequently, we fostered a strong collaborative relationship, together with Elaine Worzala, and became regular co-authors. I was particularly impressed with his gracious and friendly manner, and his efficiency and professionalism when we undertook joint research comparing perspectives of contaminated land in the US with those in NZ. We would catch up annually at the ARES conferences, often presenting joint papers.

Bill has provided tremendous support and encouragement to me and contributed a vast amount to my academic career since we met. He has worn many hats through his association with me. In addition to providing paternal friendship and co-authorship, he has acted as referee for me in my promotion, scholarship and job applications and more recently acted as an external examiner for my doctorate (completed 1999).

His death on 6 April 2001 came as an enormous shock, particularly as I was preparing to see him and his wife, Iris, at the AREUEA conference in Cancun just a few weeks later. He had invited me on to a special panel that he was chairing titled *The Challenges Confronting Property Valuation Practitioners Internationally.* I was providing the Australasian perspective. This was a particularly moving conference due to Bill's noticeable absence.

More personally, Bill has been a warm, generous and kind friend that, despite the distance between us, I felt I could always call on for support and encouragement when needed. I will always feel indebted to him for all that he has done for me. Bill will be sorely missed.

Sandy Bond, Ph.D., MBS, ANZIV
Department of Property
Faculty of Architecture, Property, Planning & Fine Arts
University of Auckland

Dr. Kinnard was the consummate teacher. In everything he did his desire to further our knowledge was paramount. I learned much from Dr. Kinnard and owe my start in real estate to him.

While a student at the University of Connecticut, I was fortunate to obtain an internship with The Real Estate Counseling Group of Connecticut in the summer of 1983. The offices were tucked in the back of a small commercial center behind 7–11, just down the road from the Storrs campus. I remember walking into the office and wondering whether the wall of boxes was the creation of a master or the result of a pack rat.

My first task was to sort through and organize one mountain of boxes resulting from ongoing litigation over the Shoreham nuclear power plant on Long Island. The next task, seemingly concurrent, was to organize sale data associated with a study of the effects of power lines on residential housing prices. Then on to tabulating statistical results using an obsolete HP 38-C calculator, one of about 10 behemoths stored safely in the interns' desk. Despite these myriad tasks, Dr. Kinnard was able to shift his attention and focus as if it were the only project consuming his time.

Dr. Kinnard also helped me launch my professional career in real estate as a commercial appraiser. Over the years, our paths had crossed many times. We served both together and apart on complicated valuation assignments. He taught seminars and courses that I attended. He served as fiduciary for a fund for which I managed the valuation. Through it all his teaching never changed, his dedication never wavered.

I have never met a man who worked so hard or enjoyed so much. He would bounce between teaching Appraisal Institute courses and researching timely real estate issues, between writing papers or books and testifying in court. He was always bridging the gap and linking the academic and professional worlds of real estate, advancing both at the same time. His dedication to the real estate profession is unheralded and his contributions will be eternal.

Although our paths crossed many times in the relatively small real estate universe, I was never able to call him anything other than Dr. Kinnard. His intelligence and accomplishments always warranted the formal name. I will miss his intellect, his dedication and his sense of humor. My real estate career exists because of his involvement. Real estate as a profession has advanced because of his contributions. We have lost a wonderful teacher and he will be greatly missed.

Paul A. Champagne, CRE, MAI
Vice President
CIGNA Realty Investors
May 2002

I first met Bill Kinnard in the spring of 1981. He was "retiring" and I was interviewing for his teaching position at the University of Connecticut. I was immediately impressed by his sharp questions during the seminar and by his attention to the details of my visit. He and his long time associate, Mary Beth Geckler, took me to lunch at a converted train station known as "The Depot." On the way to lunch he drove me through some spectacular farm country, explaining that life in Storrs would not be the same as in the big cities that I had known (Washington, DC, Los Angeles, New York and Boston).

I was immediately impressed with his honesty and his sense of humor. He carefully explained the negative aspects of working at UConn as well as the positive. I still remember his phrase for introducing this topic: "there is always a cloud behind every silver lining."

Filling Bill's shoes has been a daunting, and ultimately impossible, task. There is no way I could match his compelling lectures or his skill as an administrator. He had been the head of the Real Estate Center, Finance Department Head and Dean of the School of Business.

There is one part of the Bill Kinnard tradition that I have been able to carry forward. Bill had a deep and abiding understanding of the importance of real estate market analysis. There may be more money in finance, and finance departments rarely see the value of real estate economics. But, it is impossible to talk about real estate investment or financing decisions without understanding supply and demand in local markets.

Two examples illustrate Bill's understanding of this issue. The first involved expert testimony on alleged damages caused to a developer by the State of Connecticut. Bill and

I met and engaged in some banter before the deposition testimony. But, I was shaking inside. True to form, Bill made a strong case, in his elegant and humorous style, that delay had been costly because of changes in market demand. In the end, I was very fortunate to have been on the right side of the case in terms of the underlying issues.

Second, Bill strongly influenced me in the 1980s with his thinking about Federal regulations (e.g., R-41b) requiring lenders to do better real estate market analysis. He had an excellent case study showing the difference between the wholesale and retail value of a condominium complex. He showed that the dynamics of supply and demand in local markets govern this difference. His work on this issue has permanently improved lending practice.

John Clapp
May 2002

William N. Kinnard, Jr, PhD, SRA, SREA, MAI, CRE
AKA Dr. Kinnard, Bill, WNK and Doctor Freebee.
Theoretician, Teacher, Mentor and Friend

Many of you saw Bill wear his many "hats." Over the years, I was privileged to see most of them. The following describes those that I remember the best.

"*Theoretician*" A person who formulates, studies, or is expert in the theory of a science or art. (*The American Heritage Dictionary*)

Bill was one of the leaders, in the late sixties, who transformed real estate appraisal theory, practice and industry to the way it is accepted and applied today. His theories culminated in his first book, *Income Property Valuation*, published in 1970. His theories lead to development of evaluating income property by emphasizing the income approach. His book became the basic text used in colleges and the professional real estate appraisal courses for many years. While developing theory was important to Bill, what was more important to him was teaching thousands of students over the years.

"*Teach*" (1) To impart knowledge or skill; to give instruction to; (2) To provide knowledge of, and instruct in; and (3) to cause to learn by example or experience (*The American Heritage Dictionary*).

Bill was one of the few true teachers I have encountered. He really cared about those he taught, what he taught and how he taught it. My background, prior to meeting Bill, was in elementary education. Interestingly, at the time there were very few instructors with or without their PhDs who actually "taught"—most simply lectured. Anyone who ever took a class from Bill could sense how much he truly cared about his students. This caring and resultant quality of teaching meant a great deal to me, as I am certain it did to many others. Bill was one of the best teachers any student could hope to encounter.

Bill influenced so many individuals: undergraduates, graduate students at the University of Connecticut (UConn) and professionals in the real estate industry. Bill's life was dedicated to imparting knowledge and helping people to develop the thought processes, whether it was through the courses he taught or the books he wrote: *Income Property Valuation, Industrial Real Estate*, and *Appraising Real Property*. Further, Bill continued his teaching through the courses and seminars he developed and taught for real estate professionals through the Society of Real Estate Appraisers and the American Institute of Real Estate Appraisers (now merged to the Appraisal Institute), speeches he made and articles he wrote for the Society and Institute, as well as the American Society of Appraisers, The Institute of Property Taxation, *The Journal of Property Tax Management*, Property Tax Management and the Canadian Institute of Real Estate Appraisers and dozens more.

"*Mentor*" (1) Gk. Myth. Odysseus' trusted counselor under whose disguise Athena became the guardian and teacher of Telemachus, and (2) a wise and trusted counselor or teacher. (*The American Heritage Dictionary*)

While in some ways this term may seem to overlap with the teacher definition, I really do believe there is a difference. Bill took many under his wing. He would always be there for these individuals. He took the time to help them work through the situation. They included students, professionals and academics. He encouraged and assisted them in their careers. Obviously, I include myself in this category. He was one of those unique individuals who would always be there to help with answering a question or resolving a problem or difficulty one was experiencing.

There was many an occasion, during the period I worked with him at The Real Estate Counseling Group of CT, when we were under a very short deadline to finish a report or project when he would take a call from one of these special and important people. Frequently the time given to others required him to make an 80 mile round trip to the Federal Express depot at Bradley Airport to insure that the report was received on time.

"*Friend*" (1) A person whom one knows, likes and trusts; (2) An acquaintance; (3) A person with whom one is aligned in a struggle or cause: comrade; and (4) One who supports, sympathizes with or patronizes a group, cause or movement. (*The American Heritage Dictionary*)

The part of this definition I agree with is number (1). Bill was close to his family, a small group of personal friends and a very good friend to UConn's Real Estate Center (which, by the way, he and Robert O. Harvey established in the late 1960s).

Bill was essentially a shy person. That may seem incongruent with his teaching large groups of individuals and speeches that frequently numbered over 200 and the jokes he told. But he was more comfortable talking with a few friends. He would do anything he could for one of his friends, whether they were his family, personal friends, professional friends or clients that he developed closeness with.

I feel privileged to have known and worked with Bill. I know there are many of you who do as well.

God speed Bill/WNK.

Mary Beth Geckler

William N. Kinnard, Jr was the first real estate instructor that I had as a real estate major in 1975. He was my professor in Finance 230, *Practices and Principles of Real Estate*. I knew that he was a noteworthy person when his name was referenced in the textbook for that course. I was already a real estate developer in our family home building business. The class made a significant contribution to solidify my understanding of my business. I always looked forward to that class. It was informative and Dr. Kinnard taught it with a great depth of practical knowledge.

I fondly remember the day I came to school with a $50.00 check for "show and tell." Dr. Kinnard smiled as I exclaimed that I could actually use the information from class to make money. I had received the fee from an appraiser for doing a new fangled mortgage–equity analysis for an appraisal report he was doing on an income property. Dr. Kinnard had taught me to use the "peanut butter spreader" to make the investment yield curve needed by that appraiser. Little did I know that I was just starting to make a living with the skills I learned in the real estate program.

As I advanced in my real estate studies, I made a point to do extra work at the Center for Real Estate and Urban Economic Studies (CREUES). As a result, I had the opportunity to get to know Dr. Kinnard better. I was a couple of years older than most of my class mates, since I had taken a two-year hiatus from college after leaving UCLA. I worked in our family real estate development company. I think that my real life professional experience and a bit of extra age made it possible for me to get to know my instructors on a personal level. My enthusiastic interest in the subject matter also kept me close to my teachers. As a result, I came to respect Dr. Kinnard's wit and genius. He was a man with an incredible mind. He was well versed in a wide range of academic disciplines as well as the arts. When he wasn't writing books, he was reading them. He had an amazing vocabulary. For a while, he used to post his word of the day on the chalkboard in the CREUES office. I do not recall ever seeing one of his words that did not require a trip to a comprehensive dictionary for a definition. He could discuss politics, economics, music, theatre, literature (classic and contemporary), philosophy and art with the brilliance of a college professor in any of those fields.

After graduation from UConn in December 1977, I did odd consulting jobs with Dr. Kinnard, as well as Dr. Boyce and Dr. Messner. This gave me greater access to his intellect. During these assignments, Dr. Kinnard taught me to devise analytical models for a wide variety of real estate investment problems. That was invaluable. Not only did I master the use of standard methods for real estate analysis, Dr. Kinnard gave me the skills to do analysis on projects with unique conditions. He had the mind to devise defensible models to evaluate railroad rolling stock, timberland using an income approach for trees that are harvested every 25–50 years, value impact from proximity to power transmission lines and many other valuation problems. He possessed the ability to teach others to devise models for other applications.

Dr. Kinnard was a person who liked to spend social time on work assignments. It was simply fun to work with him. Shared meals were garnished with incredibly witty banter, (never get into a pun contest with him), enlightening reviews on the arts, well founded opinions on philosophy and many, many, many other subjects. There would also be challenging discussions on investment analysis and valuation problems. It was imperative to him that any model must be accurate and defensible in court. The longer discussions on a particular problem would usually conclude with a simple, yet bulletproof, solution. I view this as a tribute to his academic integrity. I once asked him why his *Income Property Valuation* book was so long. He replied that he did not have the time to write a shorter version. That was 25 years ago, and I feel that I am just starting to understand the wisdom of his response.

I have been retained as a real estate valuation consultant on several large cases during the past few years. When I meet colleagues and formidable opponents, I often ask about their credentials. In the case of those with the greatest level of skill, William N. Kinnard, Jr. is usually found in the lineage of their teachers. His fundamental work in valuation theory is the stock and trade in the real estate industry today.

Bill Kinnard was an innovative thinker with an amazing intellect. He was warm, witty and charming. He was proud of his family. He could teach others to think and reason with improved acuity. He was a pioneer in the professional field of real estate valuation. He was a lexicographer. He was an honest and honorable man. I am proud that he was my teacher and my friend.

Mark Goldman
Goldman Realty Corporation
May 2002

Bill Kinnard meant many things to me. The three most prominent were teacher, mentor and friend.

In 1956, I was attending the University of Connecticut and took Bill's course in *Principles and Practice of Real Estate*. (Bill started teaching at UConn in 1955.) In 1958, Bill decided to teach a postgraduate course in real estate appraisal and contacted people who had taken his real estate course. I had decided on a different career path, but took the course anyway. During this course, Bill inspired me to become a real estate appraiser and even assisted me in my first real estate appraisal job. After graduation, Bill and I stayed in close touch and I was even invited back to talk to his classes. Bill is largely responsible with my choice of a career and whatever success I have enjoyed as a result.

Bill's contributions to the profession are enormous. Arguably he may have contributed more than any other single individual. Bill's most outstanding contribution may have been his authorship of *Income Property Valuation*, which was significant in bringing the real estate appraisal profession out of the "Dark Ages" and into modern economic thought and theory. This was followed up by Bill, Steve Messner and Byrl Boyce preparing courses for the Society of Real Estate Appraisers and others that continued this trend. Bill also put together the symposiums for the SREA that led to some appraisers learning to become analysts and counselors.

Bill authored or co-authored two other major books, *Appraising Real Property* and *Industrial Real Estate* as well as many articles and monographs. Bill's accomplishments are too numerous to list in this testimonial, but he continued to contribute until the day he died.

Bill enjoyed life. He had a wonderful ingratiating personality together with a terrific sense of humor. He had a fertile mind and continually came up with new and original ideas. Anyone with a problem to solve could call Bill, who would take the time to help find a solution. He was modest and unassuming and never looked for recognition for himself. He was a mentor and helper to all who asked for his advice and assistance. There is no way that Bill's contribution to society, both personally and academically, can be adequately measured.

His was a life well lived.

Edward F. Heberger
Executive Vice President
CB Richard Ellis
April 2002

Bill Kinnard was truly a man for all seasons. My comments here address dimensions that are mainly peripheral to his career as an acknowledged leader in real estate appraisal and education. The real estate area, which was central to his highly productive career, is better addressed by others. My close personal friendship and academic association with Bill extended for nearly four decades, most of it when we were colleagues in UConn's Finance Department.

The very best professors in professional schools, like Bill, are great developers of talent. They open the eyes of young students to exciting ideas and opportunities upon which they can capitalize and grow. Bill also was an outstanding mentor of young faculty in the development and, ultimately, the publication of meaningful research. Names such as Boyce and Messner in the 1960s and 70s come to mind, as do Knight and Worzala in his post-"retirement" years, and continuing into the 21st century. Indeed, he had several collaborative works-in-progress when he died. Bill was recognized as a master of the English language and its usage and his editing and re-writing skills explain why he is acknowledged as a Contributor in the front of *The American Heritage Dictionary*.

A man of unflagging energy, Bill lived and worked each day to the fullest. He was a prolific user of his portable dictation unit, which was his constant companion. He often dictated in the elevator and in the hallway as he walked to his office, turning out tape upon tape of finished correspondence, reports and manuscripts for his typists. Another feat of multi-tasking that impressed me immensely was his ability to grade essay exam booklets and term papers at home while watching Giants football games on TV. After retiring from UConn, if Bill wasn't at home, chances were that he was racking up thousands of frequent-flier-miles enroute to another consulting assignment.

In conclusion, here are some random observations on the lighter and personal side of this remarkable man's life. Firstly, I cannot think of one acquaintance of Bill Kinnard's who ever had anything but the utmost respect and admiration for this thoughtful, modest, funny, articulate, generous and multi-talented man. He was generous to a fault with his time and assistance for everyone. If you could not recall the lyrics in a favorite Broadway musical, or something about a classic, a novel or a movie, you could rely on Bill. He enjoyed good food, fine wine and Macallan's, his favorite single-malt scotch. Last but not least, he was a proud and caring family man.

Bill, for countless reasons, you are sorely missed.

Keith B. Johnson
Emeritus Professor of Finance
University of Connecticut

Bill Kinnard wore many hats. He was a loving husband, father, father-in-law, grandfather, professor, "expert witness," Justice of the Peace, businessman, colleague and friend. He touched thousands of lives directly, and many more indirectly. He was a problem-solver and the more difficult the problem, the more he relished being involved in finding a solution. I can remember sitting in our office listening to him on a conference call in the other room, enjoying hearing his brainwork even as I understood scarcely a word of what he was saying. He had an unbelievable mind, an insatiable curiosity, and a desire to constantly find new ways to look at things.

The ability to look at large quantities of information and to notice only a few opens the door to a whole new set of opportunities—William N. Kinnard, Jr.

Although he was a master teacher, he was also a student ... a student of life. And I know he loved his life.

My father was raised in a time when children were supposed to be seen and not heard. This did not sit well with him. I get the distinct impression that he had plenty to say starting at a very early age and was not immediately allowed to do so. But this minor setback only fueled the outpouring of words that was to come later. He became a teacher, a speaker, a writer, an editor and, of course, a wonderful conversationalist. He knew how to speak in terms his listener could understand, be it the CEO of a major corporation or a young grandchild. He particularly enjoyed reading *The Night before Christmas* to his grandkids. And he deserves credit for adapting to a world where children are definitely *heard* as well as seen.

He was truly a man of letters. He was well read, interested not only in words but also in the origins of words and of languages. He enjoyed thought-provoking word problems and crossword puzzles. When I was around twelve years old, my dad sort of "disappeared" for a year or so. I later came to understand that he had been writing a book. Still later I realized that he had not simply written a book, but in many ways he had actually written "The Book." His contributions to the field of real estate appraisal are legendary. He helped to bring consistency, standards, and creativity to a field that lacked them before. His influence continued to grow throughout his life, right up until the day he died, and hopefully even after that. He wrote numerous papers, reports, articles, books and letters, aided by his trusty dictating machine. Of course, he had several of these because they weren't always so trusty, especially with the amount of use they got.

He was an educator and an author, traveling far and wide to educate others. On several occasions, my family would accompany him. We spent two summers in Berkeley and Malibu, CA, as well as several trips to Puerto Rico. He loved to travel, and I was fortunate enough to visit Denver, Hawaii, Maine, Mexico, Canada, the Caribbean, and many places in between with him. We even packed up the old Rambler and drove cross-country one summer. Of course, this was before we had air-conditioning in the car. If not for that cooler full of ice cubes I don't think we would have survived.

Anyone who knew Bill was surely touched by his sense of humor. He loved to hear and tell good jokes (as well as some wicked ones) and the sound of his laughter is one of the things I miss the most. I have actually seen him laughing so hard I thought he was going to keel over and die right in front of me. I will always remember watching Rowan and Martin's Laugh-In with him. At a time when communication between us was somewhat limited, to put it mildly, the universal language of laughter was something that brought us closer together and kept that tenuous bond between teenager and parent alive. We also enjoyed the Smothers Brothers, Stan Freberg, and Allan Sherman, among others.

What can I say about my dad? He was always there for me, my sister Susie, our mom Iris, our spouses, our grandparents and our kids. He would do anything for us. He chartered a boat and took me deep sea fishing in Malibu when I was ten years old because he knew I would love it. Can you picture this man, bobbing out at sea on a tiny boat with a fishing pole in his hand? He did it because he loved me. Many years later, on the occasion of my parents' 50th wedding anniversary, he treated us all to a wonderful Caribbean cruise. I must say he looked more comfortable in the Admiral's Club atop the Royal Caribbean cruise ship with a drink in his hand than he did on that little boat in Malibu. But his motives were the same. He lived life to the fullest and took us all along for the ride. And I will never forget the ride.

His first heart attack in 1979 actually brought us closer together. One thing led to another and we did some work together for the Xerox Corporation. I was fortunate enough to be able to work with him at the Real Estate Counseling Group of Connecticut, Inc. for 14 years, during which time we became closer than we had ever been before. I was lucky and privileged to have worked with and for him, although the idea of following in his footsteps was something I knew I could never do. Although it was somewhat difficult at times, and we both realized I needed to try my own separate career in 1994, we still remained friends. He continued to support me unconditionally in everything I ever tried to do, and would you believe that on the day he died, the raw data for the 2001 Xerox study was sitting on the tables in his office, waiting for me? It's the truth. And I am so fortunate and proud to have maintained that relationship with him.

On April 6, 2002, one year after his death, I was home feeling low so I searched the Internet for William N. Kinnard, Jr. Among other things, I discovered a web page on the *Appraisal Today* site where six or eight people had written an email about him. I was overcome with emotion as I read each one. They were all personal, all different ... but put together they painted a wonderfully accurate picture of my father. It was exactly what I needed at that moment and I thank everyone involved with it from the bottom of my heart. My family and I would also like to thank everyone who has put this book together. It means a great deal to us.

Life will never be the same without my dad. We all knew him in our own special way. It still seems impossible to me that he is gone. But there is comfort knowing that although he definitely objected to the timing, he died the way he wanted to, doing what he loved to do. His work was his passion, and so were his family and friends.

Rest in peace, Dad.

Love, Jeff

I first met Bill Kinnard in the fall of 1990 when I arrived as a neophyte professor at the University of Connecticut to teach in the business school where Bill had made his academic mark. I was in awe. Here was one of the founders of the American Real Estate and Urban Economics Association, and the man I regarded as the father of modern appraisal. The more I got to know Bill, the more awed I became. It seemed that each time I spent with him I learned of a new talent or quality that characterized this giant in the real estate field.

The quality that impressed me first and foremost was Bill's unflagging intellectual energy and curiosity. He continued to contribute to the field at a time of his life when many would be satisfied to rest on laurels, particularly when the laurels were as numerous and significant as Bill's career had produced. His lifelong craving to expand his knowledge, and to contribute to the knowledge of others, continues to be an inspiration to me as an academic. I know he has inspired others in this same way.

The other qualities I remember most fondly are Bill's warmth, wit and generosity. After I left Connecticut in 1995, Bill and I managed to get together once or twice a year during my annual UConn sojourns and at the American Real Estate Society meetings. Dinners with Bill and Iris Kinnard were memorable occasions. You could depend on being entertained with funny stories, puns, quips, one-liners and the occasional magic trick. After each dinner, I always considered how lucky I was to know these wonderful people.

It's hard to accept that Bill is gone, but the impressions he made as a scholar and man of energy and fun remain indelibly etched. I remember one story Bill loved to tell about a man who was being ridden out of town on a rail. The man told his tormentors, "Were it not for the honor, I'd just as soon walk." Walk or ride, Bill, you choose. Either way, it is a great honor for me to be counted among your friends.

John R. Knight
August 19, 2002
University of the Pacific
Stockton, CA

I became involved in the real estate program at UConn shortly before Bill retired and got to know and respect him initially through his books. Over the years, I got to know him at reunions and functions and shortly before his passing, I had the opportunity to work with him on a professional level. His smile was contagious, his quick wit brilliant, and analysis always on the mark. It was always a pleasure to see him.

There are many things I could say about Bill Kinnard, but I can summarize my thoughts in a few short sentences. Bill was a wonderful man, devoted to his family, a brilliant academic and a true pioneer in the real estate appraisal field. He enriched the lives of those who knew him, and through his work touched the lives of many. I am glad I got the opportunity to know Bill and will always be fond of him in my memories.

Paul Lagassey
August 28, 2002

William N. Kinnard, Jr, Mentor, Friend and Colleague
Bill Kinnard was taken from us in April 2001, and this event has left a great void for many, many people. I can only guess what he meant to his many family members, other friends and colleagues, and the many persons in the field of real estate appraisal who have benefited from his teaching and writing. I need not guess, however, as to the impact he had on me and my career.

I met Bill for the first time at the 1965 Academic Meetings in December in New York. The School of Business was looking for a Professor of Finance and Real Estate and I was seeking my first full-time academic position. I met with the team of Bill Kinnard and Dean Robert O. Harvey and they told me of the newly created Real Estate Center. It was clear that Bill was the driving force in the creation of the Center and was the first Director and intellectual leader.

I can't help but remember this first meeting because it established the tenor of the close relationship that Bill and I enjoyed for many years after. Actually, we spent over 35 years learning to know one another. We co-authored three books and over a dozen articles. We took over 100 trips together and he corrected at least 1,000 of my grammatical errors. I came to realize that he had a profound impression on me and many others by:

1. Unselfishly helping others achieve their career goals by opening doors and paving the way.
2. Providing intelligent, thoughtful and valuable advice on research projects and on a whole range of important professional decisions.
3. Making time for friends and colleagues when they sought help, no matter how pressured he was with his own projects and activities.
4. Exerting firm but quiet leadership by example and not by proclamation.

I am so glad to have had the opportunity of knowing and working with (and for) Bill for so many years. I will always be grateful for his help, guidance and friendship.

His friend,
Steve Messner

The passing of William Kinnard, this long time real estate thought leader, offers us a time to pause and reflect on thought leaders of the last decade.

Real estate thought leadership has passed through numerous hands over the last century. Many observers believe the discipline began with Ely just after the turn of the century. Most would include in the leadership contingent, of their respective day, the creators of the FHA and VA, the originators of the master planned community, the builders of the first regional mall, etc. These important leaders and their contributions are now recorded history. The last decade still awaits a similar determination.

As we look back on the last decade, who were the true leaders, the movers and shakers of the industry? Despite the new-found reverence for John Adams in recent biographies, this process is usually more like baseball All Star balloting than careful research into private correspondence. The list below is based on a very non-random survey with considerable ability to stuff the ballot box. This is probably the way Kinnard would have wanted it. Hidden behind his erudition was a love of irreverence.

Here they are for your consideration, the people who take their places along side the Jim Graaskamps as the thought leaders of their time, in Letterman descending order:

10. Mort Zuckerman for convincing us that 24-hr CBDs were the winners.
9. The Japanese collectively for a new record in sustained real estate price deflation.
8. Alan Greenspan for taking away our beloved inflation.
7. Frank Gehry for giving us the Guggenheim Museum in Bilbao.
6. The "Platforms" (PPR, REIS, and Torto Wheaton) for taking over the research momentum from the investment manager research shops.
5. Mark Zandi for nearly running all the other regional forecasters out of business.
4. The tech quartet: Costar for an unparalleled combination of great technology with terrible PR; Teleres for coining the word vaporware; The REALM for most promises on a single website; and Peter Pike for telling us about the first three.
3. San Francisco collectively for giving us the first totally geek neighborhood-Multimedia Gulch.
2. The CMBS duo-Ethan Penner for putting a ton of gas in the CMBS tank while throwing some great parties; and Andy Stone for doing at two companies what Penner did so dramatically at one.
1. The REIT trio-Milton Cooper as the first one out of the new REIT box, the one who gave the industry respectability by showing the REITs were real companies; Bill Sanders for first seeing the arbitrage opportunity in REITs as the next thing in real estate finance; and of course, Sam Zell for convincing us that bigger is better in public real estate companies.

Mike Miles

Bill Kinnard was one of those unique individuals that walked the fine line between academics and professionalism perfectly. Not only did he make significant contributions to the real estate and urban economic body of knowledge from an academic sense, but he was a person that was able to distill that material into something very meaningful from a practical and applied sense. To me one of the best examples of that process was his phenomenal work for the Society of Real Estate Appraisers regarding the development, implementation and success of their real estate education program.

Interestingly, there was another body of knowledge and fine sensual line that Bill also possessed. That was his love of, interest and knowledge in fine Chardonnay wine. Now, while Bill and I had a mutual interest and enjoyment in the area of real estate and urban economics, we carried on a "love affair" with Chardonnay. There was the ongoing evaluation between several of California's fine Chard': Sonoma-Cutrer, Ferrari-Carano, Acacia and Kistler. Which had the best golden hue, the most subtle French oak and "buttery" character, the best acid-ph-sugar balance, the best mouth-feel, and what lingered longest in ones mind? To me, these are all attributes that distinguished these fine wines, but more amazingly they also characterized Bill. He was as subtle as French oak, a real character with wonderful balance, a person with a wonderful way with words and one that will linger in our minds in a beautiful hue for a long, long time.

Bill Mundy, Ph.D., MAI, CRE, CEO
Mundy Associates LLC

"How can anyone get work done when he talks so much?" I said to myself shortly after I joined the staff of the Center for Real Estate and Urban Economic Studies in 1974. From my next-door office, I could hear Bill Kinnard talking, talking, and talking. When I finally gathered enough courage to peek into his office, I realized he was not talking, but dictating, dictating, dictating. In fact, he was rewriting the Society of Real Estate Appraiser's 201 course.

I soon understood that Bill was a master at using the English language. He could dictate in final copy, including spelling, paragraphing and punctuation. A stickler for using THE precise word to convey meaning, he did not hesitate to criticize anyone who was sloppy in word usage.

We teased Bill about his constant use of the dictating equipment, saying the microphone unit was becoming a permanent extension of his arm and his pacing back and forth was wearing out the floor. He was unfazed by our barbs and continued his pacing and dictating in an almost rhythmic pattern.

One summer when he was away from Storrs for several weeks, I made a bright yellow burlap cover with fringe for the microphone. When he returned to the office, he never said one word about the cover, but he left it on the unit. Over time, the burlap became filthy and, because he put the microphone to his mouth, unsanitary. When I suggested we toss the cover, he said, "Don't you dare touch it."

Several years later, when Bill retired from the University of Connecticut, we sadly helped him pack his years of accumulation. When I arrived at the Center the morning after he left, I found the yellow burlap cover on the middle of my desk.

No one is indispensable; however, a few people are irreplaceable. Bill Kinnard heads the list of those who are irreplaceable.

Judith Bartell Paesani
University of Connecticut
Center for Real Estate and Urban Economic Studies
July 2002

I was not fortunate to know Bill until late last century when our paths first crossed professionally. However, his brilliant books, articles and monographs, some of which he co-authored with colleagues, were well known for years as singularly illuminating contributions to the world of property valuation and appraisal technique.

What always struck me about Bill's writing was its clarity, creativity and willingness to tackle what sometimes were incredibly complex subjects. In an era in which too many experts' judgments are divorced from or at least not solidly based on fact, Bill stood out as a candid, data-driving thinker. And when he had to jump a logical ravine to make an assumption that he could not clearly and cleanly support with facts and figures, he said so. Equally as important, Bill took what many thought to be dry subjects and infused them with wit and his warm personality.

Leaving aside the printed or e-mailed word, who can forget how delightful it was to sit at his feet when he delivered a talk at a professional gathering or a trade association meeting? Rumpled, and rumbling just a bit, Bill was not content to remain on the dais. Whenever possible, he would walk up and down aisles filled with his seated acolytes, discoursing, hypothesizing, probing and questioning. During the first of his talks which I attended, it seemed that I was back in law school, decades earlier, learning from a wonderful, friendly and empowering intellect.

Bill's personal qualities and his ability to share friendship with legions need little elaboration here. I never ceased being amazed at how many former students and colleagues from his pre-academic life, as well as his years on the University of Connecticut faculty, spoke of him so fondly and with such great warmth. Few of us can claim such a hold on the affections of our associates and peers.

The shock of Bill's passing, far, far too soon, can only be counterbalanced by the volumes of moving personal and professional recollections retained by all who knew him and responded to his grace and charm. We will not see the likes of Bill Kinnard soon again.

May his memory be for a blessing.

Elliott B. Pollack
Pullman & Comley, LLC
December 26, 2001

I first met Bill Kinnard in the summer of 1991 as a student with the Center for Real Estate and Urban Economic Studies at the University of Connecticut, an academic department Bill founded. Bill's consulting practice was located close to the UConn campus and given his close relationship with CREUES, he would typically hire at least one summer intern each year. Fortunately for me, the internship lasted beyond that summer and through my last year of school.

Bill's company, the Real Estate Counseling Group of Connecticut, would typically get involved in very unique and unusual consulting and valuation assignments. Many involved studies measuring the impact on value created by proximity to such environmental hazards as overhead power lines, gas pipelines and contaminated property. Bill was a pioneer in the use of multiple regression analysis and other statistical techniques in such valuation assignments, and regularly employed these tools in his practice.

One rather unique assignment with which I had the pleasure of assisting Bill was an appraisal of a cemetery. A utility company was taking a portion of the property for construction of a pipeline and Bill's company was hired to estimate the damages. As a college student with no appraisal experience, I was perplexed by such an appraisal problem. With his usual dry wit, Bill described a cemetery as "nothing more than a residential subdivision with very tiny lots" and sent me on my way.

Our relationship lasted beyond graduation on both a personal and professional level, and Bill continued to provide me guidance throughout my career. Bill was always a phone call away and he never hesitated to help a colleague in trouble. I frequently consulted Bill when confounded by an appraisal problem and in his selfless manner he always offered me guidance. Although he had retired from teaching years before, he still thrived on educating and mentoring real estate appraisers.

Bill was a generous, thoughtful individual who touched many lives throughout his career. In his modest and unassuming manner, he always gave more than he received. I am proud to say that Bill was my mentor and, more importantly, my friend. I am privileged to have worked closely with him, even if only for a short while. Looking back at the time I was with his company, I wish I could have more fully appreciated then, rather than later, what a great person he was.

Frederick J. Richard, MAI

In May of 1992 I was awarded the William N. Kinnard scholarship.

Shortly before the award ceremony, I was speaking to Professor Johnson, Finance Department Head. During our conversation, he described Bill as a "Prince."

Although I didn't know Bill well, it is easy to understand why he is held in such high esteem. I'm sure that Dr. Johnson's remarks still resonate with many of Bill's family, colleagues, students and friends.

We are fortunate that he served UConn for so long.

Greg Richo MBA, 1992
University of Connecticut
May 2002

William N. Kinnard, Jr

Always helping.
Always with a humorous wit.
Always thinking, always active.
Always with a smile.
Always with a positive attitude.
Always with a sound suggestion.
Always with time to talk and listen.
Always an effective communicator.
Never with an attitude of superiority.

Intellect. Common sense. Humor. Friendship.
He is missed.

Dan Swango
Appraisal Institute
July 2002

Lessons Learned from Uncle Bill -
My eternal gratitude for his friendship, kindness, thoughtfulness ... and his coaching by word and deed (and to think he called me coach!) during our 35+ year friendship.

As we worked together, taught together, learned together, shared a wonderful closeness, here are but a few lessons learned from mentor 'uncle Bill,' not in any particular order ... the first 21 to come to mind, anyway:

1. Don't be mechanical; think. Get a 'feel' for what you're doing. Get out of the mold. Make connections; use knowledge gained from other disciplines.
2. Try something new, try a new approach, be creative.
3. Detail IS important. Devils and Angels are both there.
4. When others are done; keep researching, thinking, writing.
5. Network, know people, make genuine and sincere, respectful contacts. You can do anything but no one is self made—but stands on the shoulders of others. In turn, be a resource for others. Being a knowledgeable servant is a great honor.
6. Generosity. You receive most when you give it all away—knowledge, time, material and money, even credit for work and ideas.
7. Write. Share your thoughts and ideas freely. Don't even try to either hog it or take it with you, whatever 'it' is.
8. Enjoy the classics and fine things and people, enjoy culture and cultures. Music, art, food, literature, fine arts—explore, ask questions, enjoy.
9. Words are powerful friends, precision tools, not to be used carelessly or lightly. They are precious—use sparingly.
10. Wit, humor, and your smile add immeasurably to life.
11. Examine everything. Question everything. Look and really see everything. Seek understanding, insight. Appreciate the examined life.
12. Don't waste time.
13. Don't take yourself too seriously. Don't fall into the trap of believing your own press releases.
14. Don't 'retire'; its unproductive, unsatisfying, pointless.
15. Dedication—to your profession, to students, friends, family.
16. Thoughtfulness—a call, a card, a gift; little things mean a lot.
17. Tolerance and patience.
18. Explanatory straightforward simplification eschewing obfuscation.
19. There is reward and power and unmatched satisfaction in long-term genuine friendships.
20. Develop your mind and memory; link; make associations.

21. Inspire others. Be there with encouraging enthusiasm, insights, whatever sort of help appropriate, time, and sincere friendship.

Dan Swango, PhD, MAI, CRE
Tucson, AZ, USA

William N. Kinnard, Jr

A genial gentleman with an impish grin
A man with a jolly countenance and an engaging sense of humor
A caring family man
A popular college professor
A world-renowned expert on real estate
Author of numerous textbooks and papers on the valuation process
Founding Director of UConn's Center for Real Estate and Urban Economic Studies
President of The Real Estate Counseling Group of Connecticut
Closer to home, the independent fiduciary to the investors
in several real estate accounts managed by UBS Realty
A good friend, mentor and teacher

These are descriptions that come to mind when remembering Dr. William N. Kinnard, Jr. A co-worker once said, "Oh, yes, Bill Kinnard—he wrote THE book on valuation." One assumed that he was generalizing—until he reached into his bookcase and produced a well-worn volume that had been one of his textbooks when studying *Income Property Valuation* with Professor Bill Kinnard at UConn. First published in 1971, this particular edition (1979) was the tenth printing and continues to be utilized as a reference.

We at UBS Realty Investors have many fond memories of Bill—as a teacher, consultant, real estate authority—and VSP (Very Special Person). At times, he'd arrive at our offices after just flying into Bradley Airport, returning from some distant part of the country where he had been summoned to testify as an expert witness on real estate matters. He came here to provide his unbiased expertise regarding matters that concerned the clients invested in the funds he represented.

People here recall his incredible command of—and love of—the English language, as well as some of the questions he asked—again and again in the classroom (Which value? To whom?—in the context of valuation and appraisal, of course). His students had tremendous respect for him. They say that Bill Kinnard "lived and breathed real estate."

As a world-renowned expert on real estate matters, Bill was asked to consult upon or testify regarding some very unique valuation topics. Some colleagues who interned for him recall his involvement in several "off-the-wall real estate situations." Included among them were: a cap rate study on an oil refinery, the value of leased railroad cars in California, the impact of power-line rights of way on residential real estate, the effect of nuclear plants on surrounding housing.

One former student, who today heads the UBS Realty Investors Valuation area, calls Bill Kinnard "a god in terms of real estate analysis, valuation and counseling—a captain within the real estate industry." All of us at UBS Realty who knew him were honored to have been associated with Bill—and to learn from him. We miss his wisdom and counsel, his kindly manner and good humor. He will not be forgotten.

His friends at UBS Realty Investors
Hartford, CT

Unfortunately, I didn't have the opportunity to know Bill Kinnard as well as I would like to have. I first met him at a class on leasehold interests that he was teaching in San Diego for the Appraisal Institute. Initially, I was impressed by his teaching style. He had a tendency to walk around the room and look people in the eye, talking slowly, very distinctly, and with great enunciation. He was a great communicator and seemed to enjoy teaching. He was very good at what he did.

Years later, I started going to ARES meetings with the same trepidation that I had when I first joined MENSA and started going to their meetings. I was sure that other MENSA Members would start to grill me on my understanding of relativity... or Newton, to say the least. I met Bill at one of my first ARES meetings when I was looking for someone to talk to about the valuation of contaminated land. It was hard to imagine someone that was such an icon being so unpretentious. He insisted that I call him Bill and suggested that we go have a drink and then began to freely provide his opinions on the topic.

Later on, we both found ourselves scheduled to present papers at one of the Cutting Edge conferences sponsored by the Royal Institute of Chartered Surveyors, at the University of West England, at Bristol. I had hoped to get to know Bill better then, and I left early to spend some time with associates in London and Edinburgh just prior to the conference. Unfortunately, I was unavoidably detained in York for over a week and was unable to attend the conference. Bill and Paul Syms went ahead and quickly studied my obscure paper and presented it for me in my absence.

Bill was the type of person that I had thought appraisers would be all about. Someone with an insatiable thirst for knowledge, best practices, and even better practices that could be used in the future. It soon became apparent that he was one of the few persons in the appraisal business that made use of hedonics in a search for truth and justice—what made markets work vs. a simple emulation and second-guessing of the workings of the "invisible hand of the marketplace." He seemed to want to know why things worked a certain way, rather than taking satisfaction with a simplistic application of dogma.

Fortunately, his hospitality was the reason why I kept attending meetings where I was an outsider that did not belong. His search for new ideas was representative of the American Real Estate Society and its siblings. It is a very interesting association of the brightest minds in real estate in a setting in which everyone tries to grow and share new experiences. This association enabled me to go places I had never dreamed of.

This openness was a welcome contrast to the real "dark side" of the world of real estate where information has typically been privileged and one needed a pedigree to have access to it.

Bill was, above all else, a gentleman that seemed to take a sincere interest in others – and not for personal gain. He was a great individual with a stature like that of Jim Graaskamp and possibly a few others. He will be sorely missed by those that admired him.

Bruce R. Weber, MAI
Integra Realty Resources

INDEX

MIX
Papier aus verantwortungsvollen Quellen
Paper from responsible sources
FSC® C105338

If you have any concerns about our products,
you can contact us on
ProductSafety@springernature.com

In case Publisher is established outside the EU,
the EU authorized representative is:
Springer Nature Customer Service Center GmbH
Europaplatz 3, 69115 Heidelberg, Germany

Printed by Libri Plureos GmbH
in Hamburg, Germany